RELIGION AND WOMEN IN INDIA

TANIKA SARKAR

Religion and Women in India

GENDER, FAITH, AND POLITICS
1780s–1980s

SUNY PRESS

First published by Permanent Black D-28 Oxford Apts, 11 IP Extension, Delhi 110092 INDIA, for the territory of SOUTH ASIA. First SUNY Press edition 2024. Not for sale in South Asia.

Front cover credit: "Rai Raja", 1800, black ink, color paint, and graphite underdrawing on paper, Cleveland Museum of Art, Gift of William E. Ward in memory of his wife, Evelyn Svec Ward.

Back cover credit: Kalighat pat from 1875, collection of Bodleian Library, University of Oxford.

Cover design by Anuradha Roy.

Published by State University of New York Press, Albany
© 2024 Tanika Sarkar
All rights reserved
Printed in the United States of America

No part of this book may be used or reproduced in any manner whatsoever without written permission. No part of this book may be stored in a retrieval system or transmitted in any form or by any means including electronic, electrostatic, magnetic tape, mechanical, photocopying, recording, or otherwise without the prior permission in writing of the publisher.

Links to third-party websites are provided as a convenience and for informational purposes only. They do not constitute an endorsement or an approval of any of the products, services, or opinions of the organization, companies, or individuals. SUNY Press bears no responsibility for the accuracy, legality, or content of a URL, the external website, or for that of subsequent websites.

Library of Congress Cataloging-in-Publication Data

Names: Sarkar, Tanika, author
Title: Religion and women in India
Description: Albany : State University of New York Press, [2024]
  Includes bibliographical references and index.
Identifiers: ISBN 9798855800289 (hardcover)
  ISBN 9798855800296 (ebook) | ISBN 9798855800272 (paperback)
Further information is available at the Library of Congress.

to

ADITYA, ANNA, and SUMIT

with all my love

Contents

Preface		xi
1	WOMEN'S HISTORIES, GENDER STUDIES: AN OVERVIEW	**1**
	Historiographical Shifts: A Very Brief Glance	3
	Pre-Modern Gender	9
	The British at Home: How Similar and How Different	18
	References and Suggested Readings for Chapter 1	21
2	REDESIGNING GENDER LAWS	**24**
	Colonial Lawmaking	24
	Personal Laws	25
	Parsis	29
	"Tribal" Custom	30
	Muslim Laws	35
	Christian Personal Laws	40
	Hindu Personal Laws: The War Over Widows	44
	War Over Widows: Remarriage	52
	Beyond Personal Laws: Female Infanticide	57
	Beyond Personal Laws: Civil Marriage	58
	War Over the Child Wife: The Age of Consent Act of 1891	61
	Matriliny	67
	Property Laws	68
	Back to Civil Marriages: The New Century	70

	Back to Child Marriages: The New Century	71
	References and Suggested Readings for Chapter 2	75
3	REDESIGNING GENDER: REFORMERS AND THE ORTHODOXY	**80**
	Changes in Tribal Culture	81
	Hindu Reformers and the Orthodoxy	84
	Widowhood	90
	Rebellious Women	96
	Educating Women	102
	Dalit Social Reforms	105
	Christian Reforms	107
	Muslim Reformers	109
	Sikh Reforms	121
	Births, Birth Control, and the Spectre of Female Sexuality	122
	References and Suggested Readings for Chapter 3	127
4	GENDERING WORK	**132**
	Work Within Households	132
	Slaves, Servants, Artistes	134
	Factory Work	135
	Labour Reformism	143
	New Professions	145
	References and Suggested Readings for Chapter 4	149
5	GENDERING POLITICS	**153**
	The Queen of Jhansi	153
	Associations and Movements	156
	Mass Movements	161
	Armed Revolutionaries	172
	Gender on the Left	178
	Gender on the Right	181
	War, Independence, and Partition	184
	References and Suggested Readings for Chapter 5	189

6	**HOLY AND UNHOLY GENDER**	**194**
	Holiness	194
	Unholy Gender – Beyond the Two Genders	203
	Courtesans, Concubines, Sex Workers	205
	Interracial Relationships	209
	Beyond Heteronormativity	211
	Prisons and Lunatic Asylums	215
	References and Suggested Readings for Chapter 6	217
7	**WRITING AND PERFORMING GENDER**	**220**
	The World of Printed Books	221
	Gender in the Modern Journals	234
	Gender on the Stage	235
	References and Suggested Readings for Chapter 7	239
8	**POST-COLONIAL INDIA**	**242**
	Gendering Births and Deaths	247
	Gendering Labour	250
	Gendering Property	258
	Gender in Households	259
	Social Work for Gender Reform	263
	Legal Reformism	269
	Women's Political Activism and Feminist Politics	283
	Gendering State Repression	292
	Gendering Pogroms	295
	Re-Presenting Literature: Gender	297
	Gender in the Cinema	301
	References and Suggested Readings for Chapter 8	306
9	**THE "OTHERS", PAKISTAN AND BANGLADESH**	**313**
	Early Political Vicissitudes	313
	Scripture, Custom, Norms	316
	The Gendering of Dress	318
	Women's Activism	319
	The Hudood Decade	324

Bangladesh: An Outline History	331
Gendering War	335
Culture vs Labour	337
Political Women	339
Gender and Faith	342
References and Suggested Readings for Chapter 9	347
Index	351

Preface

USING THE BROADEST of brushstrokes, I have assembled a brief overview of gender relations in colonial and postcolonial India. There is a very brief survey, too, of the politics of gender in Pakistan and Bangladesh – so as not to lose sight of adjacent processes in the three nation-states that once constituted undivided India.

However modest the scope of this book, it proved a difficult enterprise. Matters of gender are at the same time intensely private as well as glaringly public and visible. They straddle caste, politics, culture, and laws as well as religious beliefs and intimate relationships, the disposition of bodies along with the disposition of minds. The absences, therefore, unavoidably surpass the substance of the book.

Personal inclinations as well as the constraints of time and space dictated the pattern of omissions and inclusions. The few illustrious women in positions of power and influence in the anti-colonial movements and during the decolonising process did not interest me quite as much as did ordinary women in various kinds of movements and struggles. I bypassed serious engagement with poetry and art in the cultural field: without reproducing visual or poetic texts in their entirety it is somewhat reductive to reflect on their meanings. I have focused only on the British-ruled parts of India and avoided the princely states – just as I steered away from the work of Western women in Indian women's organisations.

Some regions have received a disproportionate amount of attention – Bengal, for obvious reasons – while Punjab is sadly neglected. I did draft some sections on social and cultural processes in

Pakistan and Bangladesh but constraints of space forced me to abandon them. All these are important themes that have been the subject of excellent studies, so I deeply regret not being able to make use of them.

I have also refrained from referring to canonical feminist concepts because they are far too complex to unpack adequately, and passing mention of them would not have added significantly to what was being said. Implicit borrowings and arguments with several of them, nonetheless, influenced my writing. I have provided a select list of further readings at the end of each chapter: the domain of religion, gender, and women's histories is too overcrowded for an exhaustive bibliography.

The book's title notwithstanding, much of its content exceeds the domain of faith. Gender practices were significantly reordered by new market relations and contractual labour regimes, by capitalist worksites and political vicissitudes, by vast cultural changes. Why, then, the emphasis on religion as a framing category, particularly when many scholars contend that its importance in modern South Asia is largely exaggerated? There is, moreover, a growing opinion that Hinduism, most specifically, cannot be called a religion, lacking as it does a central text and church, and being too multifarious and changeable. The imposition of the category on such an amorphous domain is surely a product of Western colonial misunderstanding and distortion.

As I look around me, however, I do not find a visible secularisation of social life, nor an erosion of spaces, themes, and practices connected with the sacred – rather, the reverse. Obviously, individual beliefs and ritual forms have changed, but they changed in pre-colonial times as well, even if at a slower pace. Modern caste relations, for instance, have acquired new functions and sites. But the ineluctable principles of hierarchy and inequality, of purity–pollution norms, have survived, as is evident from the frequent atrocities against Dalits when they transgress the spaces and bodies of the upper or dominant castes. The invocation of faith has certainly been repurposed these days to feed new political ideologies, but faith has always been invoked in the service of power. The staggeringly large numbers of religious places, new ritual practices and festivals, and of the sectarian leaders and preachers that feverishly proliferate around us should modify the Weberian understanding of modernity as a disenchanted world. Arguably, there is a thinning out of the specifically doctrinal, spiritual, and devotional content from worship, but religious activism continues to multiply.

Religious injunctions, prescriptions, customs, and rituals have always underpinned the arrangement of gender relations and they possess plural and contradictory possibilities for women. The dictates of faith have undoubtedly constrained women's worlds, and have commanded and justified their subordination. But women have, at the same time, drawn solace from religious messages; and pleasure from reading or listening to mythological verses, devotional songs, and sacred texts; and derived joy from ritual festivities. They have extracted peace from the promise of deliverance in another life far removed from the injustices of the present one. If this is particularly true of subaltern women, elite women justify their unearned privileges with notions of religious theodicy: they turn to conspicuous ritual investment in the hope of ever-larger slices of privilege. Post-colonial states and political parties in South Asia increasingly secure endorsement for their legal and penal powers in the name of faith. The relationship between faith and gender is, therefore, an exceptionally complicated one.

We refer to "patriarchy" in feminist analyses, and justifiably so. Yet the term suggests too absolute a condition – a sense of internal variations, modulations, shifts, or fractures largely eludes it, so that patriarchy can appear as unchanging through history. Such a seamless condition was never a reality, and it is particularly inapposite for our period. Modern times actually seethed with new activities, imaginations, articulations, and representations around gender –

multifarious and contentious, often without historical precedent and, increasingly, the creation of both men and women who could be orthodox, fundamentalist, reformist, or rebellious. Even if the older norms remained compelling and experiences did not change dramatically on the ground, there was a seismic shift in the structures of thought, in the radical emergence of a new episteme. A number of scholars – from the different stripes of political and cultural nationalists, to those belonging to the decoloniality persuasion – have described these discursive transformations as imperialist implantations of alien Western values masquerading as universal and universalisable ones: the Global North imposing its distortive perceptual categories on the Global South. I differ from such views; neither the Global South nor the Global North, as I see it, was a homogeneous category in the realm of gender, both were crisscrossed with multiple internal contradictions and relations of power. These, in some ways, proved more decisive than even the imperial encounter.

In part, changes in gender relations were powered by the introduction of new material resources – cheap print, mature prose, the spread of popular theatre, folk satire, and new literary as well as visual forms that travelled across social barriers and allowed many different voices to speak and be heard for the first time. Effective arguments for and against change, moreover, always came from Indian men – though also, increasingly, from women. Even when they refashioned conservative tradition in the name of preserving it, they tried to align their interpretations to the new values. A few sought to overthrow even sacred scripture and custom: Pandita Ramabai, Begum Rokeya Sakhawat Hossain, Jotirao Phule, B.R. Ambedkar, Periyar – the last three braiding caste and gender injustice together in an insurrection against entrenched social power. Modernity saw social upheavals the like of which had never been seen before.

What did the changes indicate? A deepening interlocution of social norms probably ruptured at least parts of the familiar comfort zone of doxa. Tentatively, a number of men and women began to see themselves as rights-bearing persons. Others proclaimed the virtues and beauties of embeddedness in tradition, of culture-bearing selfhood. Rights are, of course, part of an ambiguous terrain, deeply riddled with contradictions between individual and community – especially minority – rights, between the rights of colonised cultures and the rights of marginalised women who remain embedded in their communities. There can be no easy resolution for these contradictions. Yet, a sense of immutable entitlements for women – at first asserted as a legal right to life – gradually acquired the language of equal capabilities, challenging the foundational logic of sexual asymmetry and inequality. Even though I value Nancy Fraser's argument that formal rights in the public domain may mystify and intensify women's subordination in the private realm, I would suggest that the acquisition of even formal rights does not come easily. It indicates at least a cognitive shift, and even the smallest of shifts is always significant and pregnant with possibilities.

What enabled the break? Judith Butler thinks that change comes through a reiterated performance of prescribed gender roles – something slips through or is added during the course of repeated enactments. Michele Moody-Adams contends that all historical epochs contain plural moral norms, some remaining submerged at points of time but resurfacing in a new epoch. Seyla Benhabib argues that there cannot be a totally disembodied abstract sovereign self: there is a narrative continuity between the rights-bearing person and the social and moral matrix she emerges from. Their arguments are compelling. There is, moreover, Gramsci's important concept of contradictory consciousness, available in all ideological systems, and carrying the potential to challenge the hegemonic order. While obedient to the order by and large, it may offer, from time to time, fleeting glimpses of dissident solidarities and oppositions, of other possible worlds which cannot be fully controlled by any authority and which keep alive the spaces for counter-hegemonic activities. Why such spaces open up or close down at different points of time, why there are sudden ruptures and closures, remains something of a mystery.

I kept these problems in mind as I wrote. I also remained fully aware that gender is never a standalone category, it is entangled with, and co-constituted by, caste, class, and racial inequalities, by different political movements. It is caught up in many histories.

My acknowledgements will be brief. Covid stopped much needed visits to libraries but I am grateful that I could work, whenever I could afford it, at the British Library, the Cambridge South Asian Centre, the Nehru Memorial Museum and Library, the National Archives of India, and the West Bengal State Archives.

I am always embarrassed about inflicting my work-in-progress on other scholars, but I did impose on Samita Sen and asked her to review a chapter. I am very grateful for her warm encouragement and comments.

Above all, I am indebted beyond measure to my publisher, Rukun Advani. He has identified and corrected more mistakes in the text than I like to remember. He has also added much to the book. His friendship has sustained my erratic efforts at writing over the years.

These are bleak times for secular socialist feminists and peace activists, and I admire with all my heart those who continue to struggle against near-impossible odds all over the world. I thank my friends whose help and generosity see me through the pressures bearing down relentlessly upon my life. They are far too many to mention individually, but I would like to thank in particular Pamela Philipose and Achin Vanaik, Farida Khan, Satya Sagar, and my childhood friend Swapna Mukhopadhyay.

I wish my mother were here to see this book. I wish too that Sumit was well enough to provoke me with his incisive criticisms.

For a feminist scholar it is embarrassing to admit that the men in her life – father, husband, son – have been better feminists than she ever was. I am infinitely grateful for the rare privilege of being able to admit this. I thank Anna Sailer for joining our family and adding so much to it.

And, finally, I thank Aditya for everything.

1

Women's Histories, Gender Studies

An Overview

LET ME BEGIN WITH two elementary questions: first – when, why, and how do men and women begin to think and behave as if they belong to two entirely different species? And second – how have their ideas and practices about gender roles changed in different historical situations? Together these comprise a large question which, over time, has raised very many debates among scholars. I will try to put a few of their explanations into the smallest and simplest possible nutshell.

Studies of women's worlds – their problems as well as achievements – have had a long lineage in Western history. Interestingly, some of the earliest such work focused on the lives of labouring women. Important feminist studies began to appear from the 1980s which focused on the differences between white women and women of colour; between bourgeois women and working-class women; between women from Third World countries and those from the imperial metropolis. These made it clear that, for instance, the African-American woman slave may have had far more in common with her male counterpart than with the white mistress of the household. The broad argument was that, for too long, feminists had taken the First World metropolitan white bourgeois woman as the archetypal or paradigmatic Woman, and that this figure had obscured the experiences of women from other races, classes, and countries.

Sexual differences, therefore, are not self-sufficient explanatory units: they are entangled in diverse socio-political formations such as class, race, region, and historical contexts, all of which come together to co-constitute particular gender regimes. Neither men nor women inhabit a single identity; their gendered lives overlap with their identities as subjects of a particular race, a class, a caste, and regional affiliation.

The larger and complex domain of gender may be loosely defined as a bundle of religious prescriptions for men and women, as well as the social and cultural norms which regulate their mutual relationships. Different systems of socialisation have existed, and still exist, in all historical periods, and these enlarge the basic biological differences between men and women to institute two quite separate and distinctly gendered lifeworlds. This then sharply differentiates the status, functions, and forms of their relationships with one another. Feminists argue that, despite their historical and social differences, all or almost all gender systems institute the subordination of women to men as a general principle of social ordering. Some feminists object to a straightforward mapping of gender upon already-sexed bodies: they argue that bodies do not pre-exist gender.

Women's Studies as a separate sphere of knowledge found formal recognition in the Indian academic domain when Neera Desai set up the first women's university – the SNDT Women's University – in Mumbai in 1975. From the 1990s, several Indian universities began to institute Women's Studies departments where the worlds of these different categories of women, past and present, were recognised as a valid form of knowledge.

A parallel conviction in Women's as well as Gender Studies is that the conventional historical literature has, by and large, ignored or marginalised the existence of women and issues pertaining to gender, and that this massive omission has severely constricted the scope of the discipline of History. If we bring the ignored elements into the mainstream of Historical Studies and develop a "doubled vision" or optic which establishes the presence of women and the equal validity of their experiences, the past is bound to look very different and very much more complicated than it does now.

This said, it is also true that, with few exceptions, Gender Studies has focused rather strongly or exclusively on the experiences of women. Studies of gender with men and masculinity thrown in are relatively recent and still sparse, full of exciting possibilities though they are. Moreover, if Gender Studies scholars had hoped to mainstream their field – that is, to revise all histories in the light of their research – the hope has been largely belied by the practice of academic segregation. With few exceptions – social anthropology is an example – the mainstream academic disciplines have often ghettoised their work into the separate stream of Women's Studies – a consequence of which has been that the historical scholarship on gender has not really been able to inflect other histories, and vice versa.

Historiographical Shifts: A Very Brief Glance

Gender concerns suddenly erupted into the emergent Indian public sphere in the early nineteenth century to form a particularly busy and raucous arena. We need to refresh our sense of wonder at its sudden arrival and massive prominence. It had never acquired such a public life, nor such a contentious one, in our earlier histories. True, the older historical chronicles had recorded the names and lives of some particularly distinguished women of the Indian past, and the literary record had explored at length the romantic – especially the erotic – relationships between men and women. Moreover, normative religious texts had prescribed the rules and regulations for gender practices and women's duties in great detail. But all these older discourses – from the Dharmasutras, the Dharmashastras, and the Smriti literature of ancient

India – which began from the early centuries CE – to the Persian conduct manuals that advised kings and princes in late medieval royal courts had quietly buried the analysis of gender regimes under religious strictures regulating social morality and everyday relationships and practices. These practices had changed from time to time, but almost imperceptibly, at a glacial pace. So this burst of gender concerns in the nineteenth century requires some reflection on why and how they came to be so absorbing at this particular historical juncture.

It began with the work of early imperialist historians who deduced the state of Indian civilisation from the "status" of pre-modern women. Colonial history textbooks, exceedingly self-congratulatory about "England's work in India", often represented Indian women in a state of perpetual degradation – from which the British apparently rescued them via progressive laws and schools. James Mill's history of India in the Company period unabashedly characterised all of Hindu civilisation as "backward", this backwardness being seen in particular as exemplified in the Hindu ill treatment of women. (To be fair to Mill, he also mentions untouchability.) The ritual of widow immolations was emphasised and the historian urged the Company to civilise Indians by abolishing such evils. Mill's three-volume *History of British India* became paradigmatic for large sections of East India Company officials as well as for contemporary British scholars and public opinion, edging out the many contrary views that had also prevailed among many early Orientalist scholar-officials: William Jones, among many others, had shown deep respect for the Hindu classical literature and laws.

Reacting sharply against such imperial contempt, Hindu nationalist ideologues sought to retrieve textual references to the few women from ancient times famed for their spiritual knowledge. These exemplars were now displayed as irrefutable evidence of learning, freedom, and mobility among ancient Hindu women in general. Rammohun Roy used certain scriptural sources to recover ancient laws of inheritance and early ritual practices which, he argued, had ensured women's lives and property rights. Many others claimed that such freedom had been lost under centuries of Muslim rule when, supposedly, Hindu womanhood was pushed into secluded domesticity for shelter against Muslim attacks.

Late-nineteenth-century Indian Muslim opinion-makers developed a counterargument about the relatively superior rights of their women under pristine Islamic laws which, in their argument, had been compromised by centuries of unhealthy Hindu influence. Scholars like Maulana Ashraf Ali Thanawi declared that Islam expected Muslim women to be educated, pious, and efficient in order for them to be as proficient in Islamic theology as some men. But to attain that scholarly status they should avoid Hindu custom as well as British laws, recover the knowledge of authentic Islamic norms, and immerse themselves in the scriptures. Sayyid Mumtaz Ali, on the other hand, argued that Islam believed women's capabilities were equal to men's in every respect. Their education should, therefore, be non-gendered.

Hindu and Muslim versions of gender history, though mutually antagonistic, both claimed an ideal past for their community, which, interestingly, they extrapolated from the status of their women. This was a new compulsion which signified the emergence of new values. A particular image of the woman – educated, autonomous, honoured – had clearly found strong purchase among these communitarian civilisational claims.

A race began to discover more and more such individual women, and a "Great Women" brand of history-writing gained traction. On the other hand the broad contours of gender relationships, and of the everyday lives of ordinary women remained hidden in obscurity. The exemplary Hindu women selected as models of virtue were largely derived from the ancient chronicles of the Indo-Gangetic plains, and from the Tamil Sangam literature of the first three centuries CE.

An external event, among several other developments, jolted this broadly rosy scenario. To celebrate the International Women's Year in 1974, the Government of India commissioned a group of feminist scholars who, in the shape of a Committee on the Status of Indian Women, published *Towards Equality* (1974), a survey of contemporary Indian women. This disclosed a shocking state of affairs: though the Indian female population had increased by 163 million between 1901 and 1971, the male population had grown far more, leading to an imbalance in the sex ratio – which stood in stark contrast with the global trend. The reason for the demographic imbalance was an unusually strong son-preference among Indians which, in tandem with the country's undervaluation of women, had led to the neglect of daughters and caused higher morbidity and mortality rates among women.

The report – embarrassing for India's civilisational claims – stimulated a search for critical social, cultural, material, and ideological histories which now moved beyond the preoccupation with a few accomplished women to dominant gender norms in various historical periods. This entailed an examination of the normative order, differentiated processes of the socialisation of men and women, discriminatory rules for ascribing status and functions, and the nature of familial relationships. This shift from Women Studies to Gender Studies later broadened out into critical analyses of the entire structure that fell under the umbrella term "heteronormative patriarchy" – meaning the privileging of heterosexual and conjugal relationships, the subordination of women in general, and the stigmatisation of non-heterosexual bodies and desires in particular.

Marxist-feminist scholars now aligned their studies of modern gender regimes to the new material and political conditions that came with colonial rule, especially the introduction of capitalist relations of production and the consequent marginalisation of women in labour processes. Following Friedrich Engels' work, they believed that capitalism and bourgeois property relations constituted the real roots of modern patriarchy. They also argued that all the greatly valorised Indian social reformers who had tried to eradicate a few abuses in the lives of middle-class women had ignored the condition of women in the subaltern classes; and that their reforms had, moreover, been largely – and merely – inspired by contemporary Victorian ideals of domesticity.

From the late 1980s the writings of Edward Said and Ashis Nandy came to profoundly influence South Asian post-colonial historical scholarship. Said argued that the self-image of the Orient had been shaped by Western knowledge which had constructed the Orient as the inferior Other of the West. Nandy held that social identities used to be remarkably fluid in the pre-modern era, but modernity had instituted impenetrable divisions between masculinity and femininity. Post-colonial scholarship also sought more generally to trace the persistence of Western knowledge among modern Indian thinkers: specifically, Partha Chatterjee located the ways in which Indian nationalists had used and re-created aspects of Western knowledge in their own thinking and politics. These influential trajectories of thought introduced a serious analysis of discourses – literary, political, and polemical. Simultaneously, it started a trend that saw modern Indian histories largely through the lens of their relationship with Western intellectual traditions.

This approach spawned two important consequences. First, a generation of post-colonial feminist scholars began to assume that the British had, in order to prove their "civilising" intent, incorrigibly transformed and modernised Indian gender relations. And second, Marxist-feminists assumed that Western bourgeois domesticity had become the sovereign template for social change in India. Partha Chatterjee suggested that the notions of the appropriate realms of belonging for women and for men – to the home and to the world, respectively – were formulated in the nineteenth century, though in his account the separation happened more under the initiative of Indian nationalists than under colonial or capitalist direction. On a different register, Ruth Vanita claimed that gay–lesbian and transgender habits were widely practised and tolerated in the pre-colonial era, whereas the colonial government had indicted and repressed them.

The general run of scholarly assumptions therefore suggested that pre-modern gender had been relatively flexible and hospitable to women and to non-heterosexual practices; and that modernity, by contrast, had ushered in unbending classificatory systems, laws, and derogatory cultural stereotypes. These new perspectives led to a deep and critical engagement with colonial modernity and its impact on the lives of women – often ignoring, in the process, social forces and cultural practices within Indian society.

Such assumptions about an unequivocal and regressive break with the past can only be substantiated if we were able to compare the lives and relationships of modern men and women with the lives and relationships of their counterparts in pre-modern times. That is, of course, an impossibly large historical terrain and task. The pre-colonial was not a monolith, and, since it comprised many centuries of extremely variegated histories, generalisations about it would inevitably falter. Similarly, as we shall later see in more detail, the modern world too possessed immensely heterogeneous experiences of gender which pulled in contradictory directions. Moreover, to assert that women *became* domesticated subjects without rights implies that they had been free and rights-bearing in pre-colonial times – a dubious proposition for which we lack convincing evidence.

In recent years fresh horizons have opened up in South Asian gender histories. Not that colonialism is forgotten, but it is no longer considered the sole or dominant historical actor. Its work, and Indian responses to it, are now situated within far wider dense, complex, multidimensional and multidirectional histories of law, labour, caste, sexuality, intimate relationships, property arrangements, social and moral dissidence and deviance, religious norms, cultural and material change, and public-sphere resources. In what follows I will look at some of these; but first, a brief overview of pre-colonial gender.

Pre-Modern Gender

On the whole – and here I too am driven to generalise – gender stereotypes and a gendered distribution of spaces and functions are nothing really new as concepts. Manu, the eponymous ancient Hindu lawgiver of enormous authority on social conduct, had put it with admirable clarity: "The woman must be under her father's rule in her childhood, under her husband's in her youth and under her son's in old age: never should she be autonomous."[1] The *Bhagavad Gita*, a sacred text for Hindus, had equated women with "low" castes – creatures born of sin (*paapa yoni*).[2] As we shall see, upper-caste women were ordained to be uncompromisingly monogamous and dedicated to their husbands as *pativrata*s (devoted wives) while men could be profusely polygamous if they wished and enjoy an active public life denied to women. The ancient Puranic and Smriti texts, and subsequent regional legal traditions – Dayabhaga for East India and Mitakshara for the North, written between the eleventh and eighteenth centuries CE – had elaborated stringent caste and gender disciplinary norms and penalties for disobedience. Caste genealogies in seventeenth- and eighteenth-century Bengal demonstrate the absolute importance of caste-defined marriage rules in attributing honour and purity among lineages. If the veil was enjoined on women in Islamic scripture, Hindu texts defined a woman of virtue as *asuryampashya* – one unseen even by the sun. Such injunctions remained fairly constant across the centuries, ranging from the *Manusmriti* to the *Streedharmapaddhati* by Traimbakayavajivan in the eighteenth century, the latter even

---

[1] The *Manava Dharma Sastra* (The Laws of Manu), attributed to Manu, was composed approximately between the second century BCE and the third century CE. Cited in Bandyopadhyay, *Smritishastre Bangali*, p. 136; translation mine.

[2] Cited in Thapar, "Being a Woman in Earlier Times", p. 3.

asserting that the only form of religious life women needed to have was worship of their husbands.

Islam similarly prescribed domesticity and subordination for women on the grounds that women were essentially amoral and unreliable. Indian Muslim women, moreover, suffered from certain customary regulations relating to divorce which are rarely found among non-Indian Muslims. At the same time, Islam was the earliest major world religion to allow divorce, and also to allow divorced women to remarry. The Muslim woman's bundle of formal inheritance entitlements was somewhat larger than that of "respectable" caste-Hindu women.

Some Hindu literary and mythological imaginaries, in contrast with the *Manusmriti* and the *Streedharmapaddhati*, constructed quite libertarian images of powerful Hindu women. The epic heroine Draupadi of the *Mahabharata* had five husbands – it being often forgotten or conveniently elided that this aspect of her "power" was because her mother-in-law had commanded it and not because she herself had wanted it. Literary sources enumerated several kinds of marriages, ranging from endogamous and arranged marriage to love marriage or marriage by capture. The first – the endogamous arranged marriage – was indubitably the desirable norm and indeed the compulsory practice for high-caste Hindus. Literature sometimes seeks an imagined excess beyond the normative and the actual – so epic and mythological figures need not be taken literally as empirical or historical entities. All the same, the point is that various images of ideal and desirable behaviour and practice for the woman had been constructed and had come to inhabit the public imagination. And the practice of drawing upon or being influenced by such images is, as we know, always something of a factor in shaping the way men and women actually live and relate to each other.

A handful of ancient Indian women had ruled over their kingdoms as regents on behalf of their minor sons – Prabhabati of the Vakataka dynasty in the fourth century CE in the Deccan, and the Kashmiri queen Didda in the tenth century. Razia Sultana, daughter of Sultan Shamsuddin Iltutmish, had ruled an empire in the early thirteenth century, and Noor Jehan, favourite wife of the Mughal emperor Jehangir, was arguably and for several years the real power behind his throne. Several other Muslim queens in the royal and imperial households had commanded a considerable measure of sexual and political initiative and manipulated royal men from within their harems of female seclusion.

A religious vocation could win the woman release from domesticity. Buddhist nuns who lived in women-only monasteries came from all castes, lived without internal social barriers, and lampooned domesticity and conjugality in their songs:

> O free, indeed, gloriously free
> Am I in freedom from three crooked things
> From quern, from mortar, from my crookbacked lord![3]

Peripatetic Hindu women saints from medieval times, and from Saivite and Vaisnava religious traditions, composed and sang songs of their own to express their longing for a beloved deity.

> I am united with the boundlessly expansive
> Channamallikarjuna, jasmine-tender.
> All these husbands who die and decay
> Throw them into the fire, Mother[4]

Or a song that is boldly passionate:

> Go to the fierce lord who roars and mauls . . .
> Tell him I am bloodied. He must heal
> With long caresses, still me in his thrall . . .
> From these very hands I seek
> Fondling[5]

---

[3] From the ancient *Therigatha*, composed by women from the sixth century BC onwards.

[4] Akka Mahadevi, Kannada Saivite Lingayat sect saint of the twelfth century.

[5] Andal, Vaisnava saint from the Alvar sect of Tamil Nadu, *c.* seventh–eighth century.

The space of freedom was however reserved entirely for women whose asceticism was beyond reproach. Life and love, when dedicated to the divinity, allowed daring erotic expression, the woman's single-minded spirituality having seemingly stripped her free of something as base as sexuality.

Two exceptional women saints in western India were tied to the household. Muktabai was a married woman who lived at home and Jahnabai was a "low-caste" servant:

> Jani says, I have become your whore, Keshava
> I come now to wreck your home[6]

A few Mughal princesses in late medieval and early modern times seem to have been talented poets and cultural connoisseurs:

> O Prophet o'er the world . . .
> fragrant flowers are springing from my blood
> And every thorn
> Wherewith my wandering feet are torn
> Turns to a rose . . .[7]

These exceptionally expressive women were precisely that – very exceptional. The lives of Hindu upper-caste women were far more frequently regulated by scriptural injunctions that came to be elaborated in later commentaries and in customary practices. High-caste marriage was sacramental and indissoluble. Widow remarriage was forbidden and pre-pubertal child marriage was mandatory for daughters. If widows immolated themselves on their husbands' pyres, they would supposedly reside in heaven along with their husbands for millions of years.

Over time, these strictures set up a standard of ideal female behaviour even for the aspiring "lower" castes. Transgression spelt enormous social ostracism and penalties. On the whole, however, the rules were somewhat more flexible for "lower-caste" women.

---

[6] Jahnabai, fourteenth century, Maharashtra.
[7] Zeb-un-Nissa, daughter of the emperor Aurangzeb, seventeenth century.

Widow remarriage and dissolution of marriage were permitted to them, even if only to signify their "unclean" status, and as a way of ensuring the continual production and reproduction of labour.

Muslim men were also allowed multiple marriages, though a ceiling of four wives was imposed by Islamic scripture. Muslim daughters inherited a portion of their father's property and divorced wives were entitled to a compensation package – *mehr* – which was fixed at the time of their marriage.

Rosalind O'Hanlon has suggested that a broadly shared conceptual realm bridged gender differences between Hindu and Muslim religious cultures. Whereas some specific rites and codes remained strikingly different – Hindus, royal and ordinary, valorised widow immolation, a practice which troubled the Mughal emperor Akbar, who pleaded in vain with his Hindu subjects to stop it – it would be accurate to say that scriptural laws and conduct manuals for both Hindus and Muslims prescribed similar notions of ideal male and female behaviour: men as providers and protectors, women as obedient and faithful to fathers and husbands. The public world, accessible to men alone, was barred to women – they managed the domestic realm. Medieval Persian conduct manuals and the eighteenth-century Sanskrit prescriptive text *Streedharmapaddhati* show that, when it came to norms prescribed by men for women, the commonalities across the two faiths were more striking than the differences between them.

According to medieval Persian manuals, the royal patrimonial household was the microcosm of an ideal social and political order. The monarch was at once father to all his subjects and husband to the entire kingdom, exercising total authority over both – this being a model which the households of the nobility and gentry followed closely. The good woman was much praised in *akhlaq* (conduct) manuals. By contrast there was the positing of an essentially female nature seen as incorrigibly sensual and wily, her charm being part of her wiles; such a woman was in need of strict discipline.

The genre of *tahzib-al-akhlaq* manuals advised correct male deportment as well – to instil wisdom, temperance, courage, and justice as well as physical strength. They expounded on contemporary medical understandings of bodily and mental health. Then there were *tadbir-al-manzil* tracts which instructed men on household management, clearly investing them with leadership over the domestic sphere. An emperor could also prescribe new rules – according to Abul Fazl's *Akbarnama,* the emperor recommended post-coital baths (instead of the customary pre-coital ones) and believed men should grow beards to preserve their sexual potency. He also advised that all sexual activity be conducted only within permitted relationships. Prostitutes should live outside the city under police surveillance and be barred from moving around the city precincts without the strictest kind of veiling; a stern eye had to be maintained on their relationships with court servants. Akbar was harsh too about homosexuality among his soldiers, as well as among slaves and eunuchs. He insisted on women's obedience and modest deportment and discouraged the marriages of older women to younger men.

We find no references to lesbian practices in these manuals. Surmises about their existence in the enclosed female world of harems, or among segregated Hindu upper-caste women, may not be unrealistic.

The final years of Mughal rule saw the growth of regional powers who acquired – de facto, if not always de jure – independence from the Mughal court. Hindu Rajput warrior kings in North India provided the archetype for martial masculinity. Nayaka warrior kings in South India combined warfare with leadership roles in massive temple complexes that dotted the South Indian landscape. "Low-caste" warriors founded small kingdoms in the eighteenth century and patronised temples and priests to legitimise their authority. Their example would have stimulated notions of manly self-esteem among their "low-caste" soldiers. Later, Dalit and untouchable-caste men drew upon these warrior traditions to construct an empowering martial self-image.

If such rulers required exceptional bravery in warfare from men, they also imposed ideals of death-defying chastity on royal women, especially within the Hindu domain. North Indian Rajput dynasties glorified *jauhar* (collective female suicide) when the men seemed doomed to imminent defeat. This was believed to complement the courage of men at war and preclude the dishonour of sexual captivity by Muslim victors. Legends of *jauhar* burnings are still popular – a recent Bollywood film, *Padmavat* (2015), was a great hit.

Caste and gender were tightly bundled, and any lapse from established gender norms led to loss of caste. In early modern western India the Dharmadhikaris (learned Brahman pandits), astrologers, and noted Vedic scholars presided over *dharmasabha*s (religious assemblies) which deliberated on purity–pollution norms, and on appropriate punishments and penances for violations of these. A man was excommunicated because his wife had dined at a house where a "low-caste" Shudra menial had helped prepare the meal. Another had a "lower-caste" mistress and his entire family was ostracised till the performance of ritual penitence. The daughter of a "low-caste" Shudra man formed a liaison with a man from an even "lower-order" Shudra. Her father murdered the couple since the daughter had polluted their entire lineage. A ritual feast, however, cleansed him of the sin of murder – clearly, cross-caste love was the greater sin. Since the entire family and their lineage suffered from an individual member's "misconduct", the price of transgression was high and surveillance of the family was near absolute.

According to the Hindu codes, however, a high-caste man could have relationships with women from the lower castes and even marry one – despite his wife being of inferior status; but the same option was not open to a high-caste woman who wished to marry a lower-caste man – since the imperative was to keep the woman "pure", the dreaded *pratiloma* or hypogamous form of union was impermissible. Early modern caste genealogies in Bengal show that elopements, cross-caste, and intercommunity liaisons, or "unchastity" among widows, degraded the caste status of an entire kin group for generations.

All cultural systems reserve the zone of licit sexual intimacy exclusively for heteronormative reproductive conjugality. We do have a few Hindu literary and mythological references to powerful emotional friendships between men, and between women, as well as some erotic postures in temple sculpture that are suggestive. Such representations, however, possibly indicate an imagined realm of non-heterosexual intimacy, or could be an exploration of the fabulous and the fantastic. Real-life explicit accounts of such desire or relationships are rare or non-existent in Hindu normative and literary texts despite Hinduism's otherwise remarkable taxonomic zeal for classifying sexual behaviour.

Islamic texts did mention sexual intimacy between men, and between women, but also forbade them. Muslim jurists prescribed severe punishments, though repentance, according to some, could mitigate the sin. Medieval poets, however, wrote stirring tales of love between men. The genre migrated to India with the Muslims, producing romantic Indian variants in songs and poetry. Love for the handsome young boy, usually from a subordinate social strata, was widespread in literary representations.

Courtesans were renowned for their cultural attainments. They enjoyed great wealth, were independent owners of property, and exercised considerable power over men of importance. Men sometimes fell deeply in love with them. We see this in the ancient Sanskrit drama – in the *Mrichhakatikam* (second century BCE), for instance. The Jogimara Cave in the modern state of Chhattisgarh carries an inscription from the third century BCE about a dancing girl: "Sutanuka by name, a *devadasi*... The excellent among young men, Devadinna by name, loved her". Courtesans of eighteenth- and nineteenth-century Lucknow were renowned for their musical, performative, and literary talents and accomplishments. However, Sanskrit normative texts had branded poorer prostitutes – those without significant cultural activities or links with important people to their credit – as degenerate, and this had continued to hold true well into modern times. Veena Oldenburg has composed an attractive portrait of the great *tawaif*s (courtesans) of nineteenth-century Lucknow, who are shown as celebrating their power and freedom from the standard domestic constraints to which most women were subject. This disappeared, Oldenburg says, when colonial ideals of gentility led to a decline in their status. Her convincing celebration of the vitality, vibrancy, and positive self-image of such women does not include discussion of the fate of the ailing, the aged, and the unsuccessful *tawaif*.

A special category of temple dancers, known as *devadasi*s (servants of the gods) and drawn usually from the "low castes", were trained as entertainers in Orissa and parts of South India. They were forbidden to marry or to dance anywhere except at the great temples, and always only in the presence of temple priests and kings. Twentieth-century reformers agitated against this system, though well into our own day a few great dancers, such as Balasaraswati, emerged from among their ranks.

As suggested earlier, the problem of sources as much as the magnitude of the terrain precludes the possibility of any comprehensive comparison between pre-modern and modern gender relations. We have fairly elaborate descriptions of royal and elite households and epigraphic sources and chronicles for Hindu royal dynasties. There is also a body of monastic literature for Jain and Buddhist nuns. Ordinary men and women are, in contrast, relatively invisible. The few references that we have to them show that labouring lives were shaped by poverty, which forced poor women to work outside their homes for survival. So, even if they lived a less restricted life, it was a life framed by extreme poverty and a gruelling work burden at home and outside. The picture is naturally varied: ancient and early medieval literary accounts – especially in Tamil – do describe women artisans and craftspersons engaged in home-based production and in the manufacture of artefacts for the market. We also see tribal and "low-caste" women agricultural labourers toiling in the fields of South India. Presumably, there was everywhere the human need to wrest a little happiness from even within the most dire situations. In Gopinath Mohanty's *Paraja* (1987), a poignant classic of life within a tribal economy in Orissa, singing and the little merrymaking that still remains possible work as weapons of the weak, providing slivers of solace to men and women equally crushed by the pressures of an oppressive world.

This sweeping and simplified survey has tried to give some idea of the immense diversity of gendered historical experiences. It may also alert readers to a range of continuities as well as disjunctures between the pre-modern and the modern.

The British at Home: How Similar and How Different

How different were the lives of British rulers back in Britain in relation to the norms and practices of gender? An understanding of some of the broad features of British gender over the same period would be helpful for us to gauge the degrees of unfamiliarity as well as convergences with what they found in India.

Class hierarchies reigned supreme in Britain: labouring men and women were regarded as "dangerous classes" responsible for crime, epidemics, and insanitary as well as immoral lifestyles. British law courts tended to casually dismiss the complaints of rape that women domestic workers brought against their masters. But if the denigration of labouring people had to varying degrees been quite common to all cultures, there were certain issues in India that appeared unfathomably new to the British.

The infinitely graded caste and purity–pollution rules were initially an unknown and deeply mystifying quantity for them, as were Indian ritual regimes. Widow immolation did not happen at all in Britain, and the discipline of widowhood, though not absent at home, was decidedly less stringent, especially in dietary matters. Widows in Britain could remarry after a "decent" interval. Nor was female literacy frowned upon. But in several other areas of life there was a partial convergence – not so much in the forms that social conventions took in the two countries as in the broad structure of patriarchal values and beliefs that defined social virtue within both locations. In 1869 John Stuart Mill had famously compared the condition of British women with slavery; so had Rammohun Roy for Bengali women five decades earlier. Scottish gender laws and practices were somewhat more advanced than those in England, with the English seeing this looseness or laxity with women as a sign of Scottish backwardness. Indian Muslim women, however, possessed better legal entitlements than British women when it came to inheritance, divorce, dower, remarriage, and property ownership.

An Act of 1836 introduced civil marriage in England as an alternative to the rigidly orthodox ecclesiastical marriage rules which had governed British conjugal life till then. But the change did not become widespread for a long time. Divorce rules were especially unbending – the usual procedure being first a suit at the common law court, followed by an appeal to an ecclesiastical tribunal, and finally a parliamentary bill to grant an individual divorce. Women, totally bereft of control over natal and matrimonial property, and even over self-earned income, found the procedure far too complex and expensive. Before the Married Women's Properties Act of 1882 came into force, the husband controlled his wife's property and earnings even if he had expelled her and her children from their home and had stopped paying for their maintenance.

Despite quite a significant range of male support – even from the Archbishop of Canterbury – several bills failed to ease the path to divorce for abused wives. The efforts, moreover, stoked vast popular anxieties, especially about divorced women marrying again and thereby weakening the institution of marriage.

Finally, in 1857 the government came around to accepting some relaxation in the laws. Married women could now sue for divorce on grounds of adultery – the charge, though, had to be supplemented with several others.

Early schooling for girls merely taught them deportment, embroidery, music, and dance. Women themselves set up the first serious educational institutions from 1848–9. A women's university was established at Bristol in 1876. Before this date Cambridge University had allowed women to study – and later to take the tripos examination – but without awarding them the degree – that continued to be awarded only to male students. In fact, Indian women graduated with proper university degrees ahead of English women. Elizabeth Garrett was the first woman to receive a medical degree and was able to practice medicine from 1865. The first full-fledged hospital for women and children, which also included women doctors, began in the 1870s. Indian women started being trained in medicine merely a decade later.

Victorian feminists faced massive social resistance. When they objected to the Contagious Diseases Act in the 1860s they were accused of mounting a "hysterical crusade". Suffragist campaigns began in the same decade and fought exceptionally tenacious, at times even bloody, battles with the police. Female suffrage was won only in 1928, and the right to equal employment terms came as late as 1975. In comparison, India introduced universal suffrage immediately after Independence, without an upheaval.

As a few windows began to open, the end of the nineteenth century saw new winds of moral panic blowing, especially about homosexuality and women "rampant", challenging family values, colonising the public domain, and seizing functions that had so far been reserved for men. "Anti-buggery" laws, in effect from 1533, had been replaced by the Offences Against The Person Act of 1828, though the death penalty for homosexual acts had been abolished in 1861. A renewed spate of constraints appeared when the Labouchere Amendment of the Criminal Law Amendment Act of 1885 was enacted and persecutions were vigorously pursued.

In 1895 the renowned playwright Oscar Wilde was sentenced to two years in prison with hard labour. England and Wales decriminalised homosexuality only in 1967, Scotland in 1980, and Northern Ireland in 1982.

Indian social regulations, on the other hand, did not formally outlaw non-heterosexual relationships nor laid down penalties, even if homosexuals were certainly ostracised. Clause 304 of the colonial Penal Code finally criminalised homosexuality in 1861 – though, strangely, lesbianism was not explicitly included within its scope.

India was, in short, ruled by a profoundly conservative Britain. Colonial rulers were perhaps rather keener to shore up patriarchal domestic traditions in India than challenge or abolish them, perhaps seeing in them an escape from the feminist struggles and onslaughts at home. Certainly, they would have found several aspects of Indian gender normativity comfortingly familiar. Their rhetoric of colonial rule as a civilising mission hardly ever lived up to its claims. As I will argue later – and my argument runs against the grain of the general run of feminist certainties – the real challenges to existing gender systems in colonial India were thrown up by Indian men and women: the rulers only rather reluctantly and nervously assisted them on a few occasions.

References and Suggested Readings for Chapter 1

Agnes, Flavia, *Law and Gender Inequality: The Politics of Women's Rights in India*, Delhi: Oxford India Paperbacks, 1999.

Anthias, Floya, and Nira Yuval-Davis, "Contextualising Feminism: Gender, Ethinic and Class Divisions", *Feminist Review,* Winter, 1983.

Bandyopadhyay, Sureshchandra, *Smritishastre Bangali*, Calcutta, 1961.

Bourke, Joanna, *Rape: A History from 1860 to the Present*, London: Virago Press, 2008.

Caine, Barbara, ed., *English Feminism, 1780–1980*, New York: Oxford University Press, 1997.

Chakravarti, Uma, *Everyday Histories: Beyond Kings and Brahmans of 'Ancient' India*, New Delhi: Tulika Books, 2006.

Chakravarti, Uma, "Whatever Happened to the Vedic Dasi?", in Kumkum Sangari and Sudesh Vaid, eds, *Recasting Women: Essays in Colonial History*, Delhi: Kali for Women, 1989.

Chatterjee, Kumkum, *The Cultures of History in Early Modern India: Persianization and Mughal Culture in Bengal*, Delhi: Oxford University Press, 2009.

Chatterjee, Partha, "The Nationalist Resolution of the Women's Question", in Kumkum Sangari and Sudesh Vaid, eds, *Recasting Women: Essays in Colonial History*, Delhi: Kali for Women, 1989.

Chatterjee, Partha, *Nationalist Thought and the Colonial World: A Derivative Discourse?*, Minneapolis: University of Minnesota Press, 1993.

Devji, Faisal F., "Gender and the Politics of Space: The Movement for Women's Reform, 1857–1900", in Zoya Hasan, ed, *Forging Identities: Gender, Communities and the State*, Delhi: Kali for Women, 1994.

hooks, bell, *Talking Back: Thinking Feminist, Thinking Black*, Boston, Mass.: South End Press, 1989.

Lal, Ruby, *Empress: The Astonishing Reign of Nur Jahan*, Haryana: Penguin Books, 2018.

Leslie, Julia, *The Perfect Wife: The Orthodox Hindu Woman According to the "Stridharmapaddhati"*, Delhi: Oxford University Press, 1989.

Majeed, Javed, *Ungoverned Imaginings: James Mill's 'The History of British India' and Orientalists*, Oxford: Clarendon, 1992.

Menon, Madhavi, *Infinite Variety: A History of Desire in India*, Delhi: Speaking Tiger, 2018.

Mill, James, *The History of British India*, London: Baldwin, Cradock and Joy, 1817.

Mill, John Stuart, *The Subjection of Women*, London: Longman and Green, 1867.

Minault, Gail, *Secluded Scholars: Women's Education and Muslim Social Reform in Colonial India*, Delhi: Oxford University Press, 1998.

Mohanty, Chandra Talpade, "Under Western Eyes: Feminist Scholarship and Colonial Discourse", *Boundary 2*, vol. 12, no. 3, and vol. 13, no. 1, 1984.

Nandy, Ashis, *The Intimate Enemy: Loss and Recovery of Self Under Colonialism*, Delhi: Oxford University Press, 1983.

O'Hanlon, Rosalind, *At the Edges of Empire: Essays in the Social and Intellectual History of India*, Delhi: Permanent Black, 2014.

Oldenburg, Veena Talwar, "Lifestyle as Resistance: The Case of the Courtesans of Lucknow", in Douglas Haynes and Gyan Prakash, eds, *Contesting Power: Resistance and Everyday Social Relations in South Asia*, Berkeley: University of California Press, 1992.

Oldenburg, Veena, *The Making of Colonial Lucknow, 1856–1877*, Princeton: Princeton University Press, 1990.

Ramaswamy, Vijaya, "Aspects of Women and Work in Early South India", *Indian Economic and Social History Review*, no. 23 (1989), pp. 81–99.

Ramaswamy, Vijaya, ed., *Women and Work in Ancient and Early Modern India*, New Delhi: Sage, 2016.

Rowbotham, Sheila, *Hidden from History*, London: Pluto Press, 1973.

Said, Edward, *Orientalism*, New York: Pantheon Books, 1978.

Sangari, Kumkum, and Sudesh Vaid, eds, *Recasting Women: Essays in Colonial History*, Delhi: Kali for Women, 1989.

Singh, Upinder, *A History of Ancient and Early Medieval India: from the Stone Age to the 12th Century*, Delhi: Pearson Education, 2008.

Stone, Lawrence, *Road to Divorce: England 1530–1987*, Oxford: Oxford University Press, 1990.

Strachey, Ray, *The Cause: A Short History of the Women's Movement in Great Britain*, London: Virago Press, 1978.

Thapar, Romila, "Being a Woman in Earlier Times", in Devaki Jain and C.P. Sujaya, eds, *Indian Women: Contemporary Essays*, New Delhi: Ministry of Information and Broadcasting, Government of India, 2015.

Walkowitz, Judith, *Prostitution and Victorian Society: Women, Class and the State*, Oxford: Oxford University Press, 1980.

Washbrook, David, "Land and Labour in Late Eighteenth Century South India: The Golden Age of the Pariah?", in Peter Robb, ed., *Dalit Movements and the Meanings of Labour*, Delhi: Oxford University Press, 1993.

Zaidi, Annie, ed., *Unbound: 2000 Years of Indian Women's Writings*, Delhi: Aleph Book Publications, 2015.

2

Redesigning Gender Laws

Colonial Lawmaking

A WIDESPREAD NOTION HAS long prevailed about colonial lawmaking in India – that colonial laws deliberately overthrew South Asia's older legal and cultural understandings in order to implant Britain's legal-judicial habits upon the colonised. Recently, however, several historians have modified this large generalisation to argue that, actually, colonial states everywhere practised various forms of legal pluralism. Roberto Unger describes the plurality as "stacked spheres", a domain in which pre-colonial custom continued to play an important role. The pinnacle of this domain was, however, presided over by a modernised colonial apparatus and personnel.

Lauren Benton, on the other hand, emphasises the persistent struggles by colonial subjects to enlarge the status of indigenous legal authorities. A measure of their success was that they ensured the constant diffusion and distribution of colonial laws among many agents. The result was "multicentric legal orders" where the state was one of the major authorities but not always, nor necessarily, the only one.

Julia Stephens observes the preponderance of uncertainties and a degree of incoherence in the formulation and application of laws under the colonial aegis. She suggests colonial lawmaking was torn between the desire for full-scale modernisation and a conviction about the unchanging ways of Indians. I would qualify her interesting suggestion about incoherence. In my own study of colonial "personal laws" I find that, given the state's disinclination to unilaterally intervene in the cultural and intimate spheres of faith and gender, it chose to rely on accredited Indian intermediaries who were famed for their expertise in scripture. From the 1860s, once the colonial rulers had dispensed with the services of court-appointed religious specialists, they drew upon the substantial body of case laws that these specialists had helped to accumulate. They also relied on learned modern intellectuals who knew the scriptures well.

Personal Laws

In 1772 a "Plan for the Administration of Justice in Bengal" laid down that "In all suits regarding inheritance, marriage, caste and other religious usages or institutions, the laws of Koran with respect to Mohammedans and those of Shaster [sic] with regard to Gentoos [Hindus] shall be invariably adhered to."[1] Colonialism functioned at first as a mercantile form of global capitalism under the initiative of the English East India Company (EIC). The joint stock company came to India armed with a royal charter in 1601 and developed close trade links with the Mughal imperial as well as several regional royal courts. However, its relentless effort to exercise control over the production and pricing of certain commodities led to frequent disputes and conflicts between the Company and regional rulers – and eventually to the Company's territorial conquests. By 1818 very substantial parts of India had come under total British control and the shape of an enormously large and profitable empire had begun to emerge.

Soon after it had captured de facto political control over several parts of India, and acquired revenue-extraction and judicial powers

[1] Cited in Ilbert, "The Government of India", p. 278.

in late-eighteenth-century Bengal, the EIC formulated a new legal category – that of "personal laws". These encompassed all matters of caste, divorce, marriage, faith, inheritance, succession, adoption, and dower across their India territories. The entire domain was to be governed according to the scriptural and customary prescriptions of India's religious communities. Since this was legal territory composed largely of familial and gender disputes and issues, Indian religious and cultural norms continued to retain their ascendancy in its sphere.

Notwithstanding large areas of shared habits and customs within India's diversely religious population, the new rubric of personal laws now legally separated religious communities from one another. Buddhists and Sikhs were engrossed under Hindu laws, while Indian Christians and Parsis received their separate law packages quite late in the nineteenth century.

Unlike the later "criminal laws", personal laws did not define or codify legal and illegal conduct; rather, they were composed of guidelines for administering court disputes. Very occasionally, new laws did criminalise ritual practice or legalise prohibited conduct, but *always* as advised by Indian religious experts, and *always* in accordance with some Indian religious precept, textual or customary. Indian religious authorities, therefore, were not mere "native informants". They actively produced a modern social knowledge about India.

In the late eighteenth century few British judges came to India with any legal training – in fact they did not even know the laws of their own country. They were justifiably apprehensive about their ignorance of social and cultural sensitivities in the colony. To alleviate this difficulty the Fort William College in Calcutta appointed reputed Brahman pandits and Muslim maulvis to teach Indian classical languages and texts to British civil servants. The latter in turn commissioned these pandits to investigate important scriptural sources that would advise and facilitate court verdicts. Sometimes the British also translated works considered judicially important into Persian and English.

The Judicial Plan of 15 August 1772 – repeated in the Administration of Justice Regulation of 11 April 1780 and several times thereafter – stipulated that the courts had to appoint *shastris* (Brahman scholars) of the *shastras* (Sanskrit sacred texts), as well as maulvis trained in Islamic jurisprudence to assist judicial pronouncements. A Regulation of 1793 confirmed these appointments at the Supreme Court.

As advised by their pandits, the courts relied primarily on the ancient Hindu law codes, the Dharmashastras, and on late medieval Dayabhaga texts for East India as well as Mitakshara texts for North India, all composed through the early and late medieval periods. Madras came under the Smriti Chandrika school. In practice, though, Mitakshara governed opinions everywhere except in East India.

At first, the courts also sought a usable digest of all the authoritative Hindu laws. Eleven pandits were therefore commissioned in 1773 to prepare a code of fundamental Hindu rules. This was completed in 1775 and the reputed Company scholar-official Nathaniel Halhed translated and published it from a Persian version into English under the title *A Code of Gentoo Laws* (1776). Soon, however, in part because it had been translated from Persian rather than the original Sanskrit, Halhed's work came under critical scrutiny from other pandits who demanded an improved version. A renowned scholar, Jagannath Tarkapanchanan, was put in charge of the new project, and in 1797 another EIC scholar-official, H.T. Colebrooke, translated the pandit's digest of Hindu laws, the *Vivada Bhangarnava* (1794). Strangely, though, neither of these compendiums featured in subsequent discussions around gender laws, and the state came to rely almost entirely on versions of the scripture offered by modern pandits.

The emergence of print culture in the first decades of the nineteenth century enabled cheap publications of ancient Sanskrit texts. This coincided with the maturing of vernacular prose, which for the first time made religious laws accessible to popular under standing through regional-language publications. Gender laws and norms thus became a public matter for the first time in the region's history.

The Judicial Plan of 1772 had acknowledged the paramountcy of a written scripture. A revised Plan of 1776 added legal protection to the "usages and manners of the people" as well. Nearly a century later, Henry Maine's *Ancient Law* (1861) and *Village Communities in the East and West* (1871) also favoured the retention of customary practices in the law. Julia Stephens argues that such regard for local custom came from the fact that custom strengthened patriarchal control over labour and property, especially among the Muslims of Punjab.

Custom, being unwritten, was far more extensive than the sacred texts, immeasurably more variegated and slippery, with its provisions and interpretations often mutually inconsistent. The different communities and castes could and often did cite varying customs pertaining to the same subject between one court case and another. Hindu custom was believed to be of three kinds: related to place – countries/regions/localities (*deshachar*); related to families/lineages (*kulachar*); and related to caste (*jati achar*).

Muslim customary regulations were mostly region- and sect-specific. Of the four Islamic legal traditions, the British selected the Hanafi school of law as the paramount authority for Indian Muslims. In 1791 the British Orientalist Charles Hamilton therefore translated the *Hedaya*, a twelfth-century legal manual which was meant to be extremely influential for Hanafi jurisprudence. Belatedly, however, officials became aware of the existence of unwritten custom for some categories of Muslims. They also realised that, even though many communities lacked written laws, they did possess usages which differed from group to group. "Tribal" (Adivasi) group custom, consequently, earned a belated legal status. Personal laws were trifurcated into Hindu or Muslim scriptural rules; customary law, also supposedly sacred; and statutory laws or state legislations which, too, were derived from Indian sacred traditions. Significantly, all three together tripled the power of faith over Indian lives and conduct.

The new state moved warily in this domain of intimate and sacred matters about which it knew little, recognising that these were extremely sensitive issues for their subjects and mishandling them could destabilise the nascent empire. Indian communities therefore acquired something akin to sovereignty in this sphere. The state intervened only when individual Indians took matters to court, or when individuals or groups specifically asked for new laws based on what they claimed to be authoritative religious prescriptions. In such cases, the state performed a refereeing function, choosing one authoritative interpretation over others.

Personal laws were not, however, frozen within past traditions, and modern judicial procedures gradually changed legal understanding and behaviour. Pandits, maulvis, and increasingly modern reformers and the orthodoxy variously reinterpreted scripture and custom to align them to the diverse designs of gender. Laws, then, became a playground for multiple social imaginaries as well as furious public debates, for here alone lay a terrain within which Indians could try and remake their lives on their own terms. Each group fought tooth and nail to push forward their own versions of authentic community gender norms and laws. The prominence that endless discussions on Indian gender issues acquired in the public sphere was a new and striking feature of colonial history.

When Company rule was abolished after the Great Revolt of 1857 – partly caused, the rulers believed, by state interference in Indian religious beliefs – and India came under the rule of the British Crown, Queen Victoria's Proclamation of 1858 promised tender regard for the religious norms of her native subjects.

Parsis

Followers of the ancient Zoroastrian faith, the Parsis, had migrated en masse to India from Persia between the eighth and fourteenth centuries CE. A small community clustered mainly in western India, Parsis emerged in the nineteenth century as leading cosmopolitan intellectuals, professionals, industrialists, and reformers – so much so that, initially, they were slotted under English laws which applied to British residents in India. In 1835 a Parsi youth challenged the English law of primogeniture and pointed out that Parsis were an autonomous religious community. The community now began to campaign for its own laws.

In 1837 Parsis were exempted from primogeniture under the Succession to Parsees Immovable Property Act (IX of 1837). More importantly, the state now conceded that they were not foreigners like the Europeans but "distinctly Asiatics with an Indian domicile".[2] The Parsi Intestate Succession Act (XXI of 1865) and the Parsi Marriage and Divorce Act (XV of 1865) were amended in, respectively, 1925 and 1940. Parsis from China and Persia were also consulted over the revisions.

Many Parsis were proud of their modern and liberal outlook. Their journal, *Rast Goftar*, advocated women's schooling from 1851, and the Parsi Marriage and Divorce Act of 1865 abolished polygamy, providing for adult marriage and divorce for both sexes. Even though they were preternaturally sensitive about their pure bloodline and prohibited inter-community marriages, men were allowed cross-community sex with prostitutes. Their marriage law did not consider this exception clause as a ground for divorce until a second round of reforms in the mid nineteenth century.

"Tribal" Custom

The word "tribe" was pervasively, if loosely, used in colonial and popular parlance, to be replaced later by Adivasi (original inhabitants) as the politically correct alternative. Good intentions behind the renaming were sadly belied in practice. In colonial as in post-colonial times the Adivasis were victims of massive and forced

---

[2] Whitley Stokes, 1881, cited in Sharafi, *Law and Identity in Colonial India*, p. 87.

displacements, neglect, and repression. Both names, moreover, misleadingly suggest commonalities for extremely diverse peoples – those in hill tracts and forests as well as in sedentary agricultural communities, and, later, labourers working in mines and plantations. The British did not always directly rule over all of them. Some parts of the Khasi-Jaintia-Garo region on the north-eastern frontier, for instance, remained outside the orbit of formal colonial governance for very long, until their incorporation within the new colonial "non-regulation province" of Assam in 1874. In other parts of the North East, the status of the districts was somewhat ambiguous and uncertain under the supposedly indirect political rule by the British – even though British capital penetrated the region and some of the local judicial responsibilities were taken over by colonial courts that functioned with the help of local chiefs.

In 1822 David Scott, political agent of the governor in the North East, had advised that, given the endless varieties of local custom in the region, the British should maintain them "rather than attempt at present to introduce a uniform mode of procedure throughout the whole extent of the frontier."[3] The same attachment to custom also guided judicial conduct in the Adivasi areas within British India.

From the early twentieth century Anthropology entered university syllabi, the Anthropological Survey of India was founded, and ethnographic studies began to appear on tribal clan and kinship, about the sexual division of labour, marriage, divorce, and inheritance patterns. Some authorities believed that, as compared with Hindu gender practices, tribal ones were less rigid and restrictive. But others pointed out the prevalence of witch hunting among some tribes. Some also argued that since tribal widows inherited property, their kinsmen branded them as witches to prevent inheritance – access to property actually therefore

---

[3] Cited in Ray, *Placing the Frontier in British North East India*, pp. 4, 75.

spelt their doom. On the other hand, witch hunting was also known among Santhals in the North Bengal tea plantations – where female inheritance did not apply.

It is usually thought that dowry, when paid to the groom, lowers esteem for the bride because she has to be disposed of with additional gifts; whereas bride price – paid by the groom to the girl's family – signifies a higher social regard for women. But in present-day Arunachal Pradesh bride price coincided with violence and contempt for the woman precisely because she was seen as a bought object. Among eastern Punjab's landowning Hindu, Muslim, and Sikh groups – designated as tribes by the British – bride price and widow remarriage coexisted with levirate marriage – the custom under which the woman married or was made to marry a younger brother of her deceased husband. Families chose this option to keep the widow's labour power and property share within the matrimonial family, and to avoid paying another round of exorbitant bride price for surviving brothers.

Widows were sometimes coerced into marrying their brothers-in-law, and even in a few cases their fathers-in-law. The colonial state, seeking to appease the designated "martial races" who provided substantial manpower to the state's armed forces, allowed this in the name of respecting tribal custom. It also wanted to ensure that landed properties were not fragmented by widows marrying outside the matrimonial family. The state had a stake in this, for its income depended crucially on agrarian revenue.

Garos, who inhabit parts of present-day Meghalaya and Bangladesh, were exogamous, matrilineal, and matrilocal. One particular daughter inherited the property but the others continued to live in their mother's home. Family land – legally the heir's property – was controlled by her husband who, however, could not alienate it. There was thus a split between property ownership and management. No man could inherit property, and if a married man earned something himself the income went to his wife and her female descendants. The divorced man was not entitled to alimony. Marriages followed clan exogamy, but the father found a groom for the inheriting daughter while her sisters married according to their own choice.

Our period saw rapid changes in tribal gender practices and the state found it difficult to align them to traditional custom. From the first census of 1871–2 the British had diligently mined tribal traditions – which they acquired from village elders – to retrieve customary usage for their own judicial purposes, as they had done in their African colonies like Malawi and Zambia. But officials slowly realised how difficult it was to identify tribal leaders once new generations of young men challenged their elders' authority. In especially ambivalent cases, officials circulated questionnaires, or relied on Christian missionaries, local officials, and anthropologists for guidance.

Changing social practices among the Ho, Munda, Oraon, and Santhals in the eastern region of Chhotanagpur proved particularly baffling. Anthropologists used to believe that parentally arranged marriage with bride price was the general custom, but they discovered a parallel practice of marriage by capture, or of love marriage, subsequently sanctified by a ritual fine. Santhal marriages were usually monogamous. But the man could marry again with the first wife's consent if she was childless. From the mid nineteenth century, child marriage proliferated among the Santhals and Oraons when they began to imitate upper-caste pre-pubertal marriage practices. From the late nineteenth century, love marriages, along with premarital intimacy, spread among certain tribes in Chhotanagpur. In a classic "invention of tradition", this was construed by non-tribal observers as the hallmark of traditional tribal libertarianism.

As younger men increasingly asserted themselves in village decision-making, they insisted on non- or extra-marital romances for themselves. Their elders feared this would aggravate adultery, unwed motherhood, and unstable family lives. To counter polygamy, the courts and elders tried to reserve inheritance for the first wife's children. This, however, was contested on the ground that custom entitled children from all marriages to inherit on equal terms.

Change occurred also because some tribes moved towards individual property-holding and inheritance, which led to partitions of family and communal property. Land, consequently, became an uneconomical unit of production. This was exacerbated by the shrinking common access to forest produce – a dominant source of tribal livelihood curtailed by the British enclosure of forests. Women, therefore, came to be perceived as burdens that young men were impatient to shake off.

Courts usually encouraged individual property rights, but they made some exceptions when in defiance of custom sons refused usufruct entitlements to their widowed mothers and unmarried sisters. Judges thought property was customarily divided among the sons within most tribes, while the women were maintained by their male relatives. But when Ho and Munda women filed cases for usufruct or maintenance, they sometimes relented – without, however, making the allowance a legal precedent.

Court verdicts varied. When a Ho woman wanted to leave her matrimonial home to claim a share in her natal inheritance, the judges forbade this as contrary to custom. Elsewhere, a woman willed her property share to her daughter but the court asked her sons to first pay their sister a share of grain instead. When the brothers defaulted and she applied again, the court took her side. Even though patriliny was generally enforced, female usufruct was simultaneously innovated as an antidote. Ho women extended this into a positive right to alienate land via sales.

In late colonial times some eastern tribes began to adopt resident sons-in-law (*ghar jamai*), departing from the usual patrilocal norm. Though this flew against Ho and Santhal custom, the courts allowed the *ghar jamai* to inherit if he had tilled their land and given up his claims to his own family property. Occasionally they allowed the sons of daughters to inherit their maternal grandfather's property – in yet another departure from tradition.

A gap opened up, therefore, between the legal intention to enforce traditional customary law, and actual court practice. Custom evaded fixity and often the courts could find no clear signposts. On the whole, the inclinations of individual judges prevailed, and these, in turn, were shaped by local elders, or by calculations of political expediency.

A surprising number of women accessed the colonial courts despite the expenses, the opaque nature of their procedures, and prolonged delays in the pronouncement of verdicts. Despite their reluctance to go against established norms, the courts did occasionally waive communitarian traditions in the interests of younger men, and for women.

Muslim Laws

The influential Deoband seminary, whose fatwas on proper Muslim conduct were later often consulted by the colonial courts, had decreed at first that foreign courts and laws must be avoided by all good Muslims as they dispensed corrupt non-Muslim laws. Nonetheless, a considerable number of elite and secluded Muslim women did approach the courts to claim inheritance. Kinsmen who represented them in the court were not always reliable, and a balance therefore had to be struck between property and propriety. The courts sent delegations to their homes and the women received them from behind a screen, thrusting their hands out to receive and return documents.

Muslim personal laws involved prolonged conflicts between scripture and custom all through the colonial period. The early colonial rulers had believed that Islam, Indian and global, was a monolithic religion which went entirely by its holy scripture, the Quran, and the Hadith. They placed great reliance on the *Hidayah*, a compendium of significant rules which the EIC Orientalist Charles Hamilton had translated rather badly as the *Hedaya* (four volumes, 1791), hoping thereby to simplify governance. This proved untenable and the Bombay Presidency, the earliest to understand the importance of Muslim custom, made the first breach.

In 1848 a British judge, Perry, tried a case involving daughters' inheritance among the Khojas, a wealthy regional Muslim trading group who identified themselves as Muslim but who withheld the scriptural entitlement of women to their fathers' property. One side argued on behalf of the scriptural right while the other group preferred custom, which denied female inheritance. This posed a dilemma: if the women were to be allowed their scriptural entitlement, the community would have to give up a long-established customary practice. On the other hand if custom were respected, could the community truly be deemed Muslim? Perry accepted the customary rule which disinherited daughters – without, however, disputing their self-identification as Muslims.

The state was now alerted to multifarious customs which sometimes militated against women's rights. It allowed Punjabi Muslim families to disinherit daughters in the name of a regional custom which they shared with Hindu and Sikh landholding families of the region – even though Islam allowed daughters to inherit a portion of their brothers' share of the property. The state also adhered to highly discriminatory divorce laws under the Hanafi school which would not allow women to initiate divorce. On the other hand, colonial interference with *waqf* – religious endowments set up by a donor from which his successors also derived an income – rules threatened the economic security of Muslim women who were often dependent on income from the trust. The British argued that if family members benefited from the endowment, it could not qualify as a charitable religious trust.

Increasingly, a large and mixed segment of Muslim reformers grew sorely vexed by what they saw as non-Muslim accretions to their community custom – caused, apparently, by extensive Muslim social contact with Hindus. Their Indian habitation, these reformers warned, had taken Muslims far from pristine Islamic practices, as was most evident in current gender rules. They looked to the lifetime of the Prophet as a golden era to be retrieved as much as possible. They insisted on a strict adherence to the Shariati scripture and upheld – much like some of their contemporary Hindu reformers – the superior sanctity of the sacred texts over customary practices, the latter seen as violations of the words of the Prophet.

By the early twentieth century Muslims had changed their mind about a strict avoidance of the colonial legal apparatus. They now solicited legal intervention to outlaw several customary practices. By this time a new generation of modernist reformers – including some very vocal and determined women – had joined the demand for legal change. Mumtaz Ali, for instance, advocated in his book that the sharia allowed Muslim women to initiate divorce (*khula*). Such men and women were driven by their anger against gender discrimination, but they too used the language of authentic Islamic legal traditions to argue their case.

In their campaigns against custom, conservative reformers found two unlikely allies – emergent Muslim proto-feminist organisations, and the Muslim League. Begun in 1906 to represent the community in the new electoral arena, the Muslim League was, by the 1930s, keen to establish its undisputed sway over the entire Indian Muslim political world in order to compete with the Indian National Congress – the premier Indian political organisation – which was dominated by caste-Hindus. All three groups sought to make illegal all custom which deprived women of their scriptural entitlements.

Muhammad Ali Jinnah, the uncompromisingly modernist leader of the League, seized the initiative. Even though a Privy Council ruling had allowed *waqf* incomes to be used solely for charity, Jinnah proposed that the donor's family members should also be entitled to their share from it, especially as many indigent women relied on it for survival; the proposal was carried in the Waqf Validating Act of 1913. Jinnah also demanded revision of the inheritance custom among Punjab's Muslims in the 1930s.

The ruling party in Punjab at the time, the Unionist Party, was a conglomeration of landed interests cutting across Hindu, Muslim, and Sikh religious boundaries. It supported customary practices among landholders of all denominations and upheld the common regional practice of disinheriting daughters. To separate Punjabi Muslims from their neighbouring communities and capture this regional Muslim constituency for the League, Jinnah demanded a new law to restore scriptural inheritance rights for Muslim women whereby all Muslims would come to share a homogeneous legal identity. This made sense to many Muslims in a worsening conflict situation which had pitted the different religious communities against one another. After being bitterly and inconclusively fought in the Punjab Legislative Council, the Muslim Personal Law (Shariat) Application Act was, consequently, passed in 1937 in Jinnah's favour by the Central Legislative Assembly. Arguments for community segregation, ironically, came to buttress gender justice. In its final form the Act did not, however, grant daughters a share in their fathers' landed property, even though (or perhaps because) that would have been their most valuable asset.

In the early twentieth century rather a large segment of Muslim women began to threaten apostasy unless they were allowed to initiate divorce proceedings. The Muslim press published alarmist reports of their numbers. This forced the hands of religious seminaries, and Muslim political organisations now feared this might split the community along gender lines. Debates had begun in 1913 when a Muslim man, deserted by his wife, had asked her family to return her to him under the colonial Restitution of Conjugal Rights Act. Her family argued that she had abjured Islam and the marriage was therefore null and void. The court sought the advice of the ulama, and of Maulana Ashraf Ali Thanawi, a powerful voice from the Deoband seminary who had issued a fatwa to decree that apostasy by either partner did annul a Muslim marriage. Now, however, the case assumed a different significance since the community risked a wave of annulments alongside desertions by women from their faith, community, and husbands.

Supported by multiple authorities such as the poet Iqbal – some even came from outside the country – Thanawi revised his verdict. He allowed Muslim wives to initiate divorce under Maliki School rules and also conceded that apostasy need not annul a Muslim marriage. This became enshrined in the Muslim Dissolution of Marriage Act of 1939 passed by the Central Legislative Assembly. In its final shape it allowed Muslim wives to seek divorce on grounds of cruelty, desertion, disappearance, insanity, impotence, or imprisonment. Its remit stretched so far that it displeased many conservative reformers, including Thanawi who had set the ball rolling in the first place.

Feminist reinterpretations of the sacred texts, beginning from the late nineteenth century, sometimes found support in a new political climate within which Jinnah had abandoned his earlier loyalty to the Congress. This was a time when communal tension was pulling the communities apart and also when, paradoxically, a strong and bold Muslim feminist (or proto-feminist) movement had begun to articulate the demand for gender equality.

The Anjuman-i-Khawatin-i-Islam, a progressive women's organisation, passed a resolution against polygamy at its annual conference in Lahore in 1918. This provoked the conservatives. Sharifa Hamid Ali from the influential Tyabji family of Hyderabad, which had thrown up a number of early feminists, prepared a draft marriage contract for Muslims. It included the woman's right to seek divorce as well as "delegated divorce" (*talaq i tafwid*) under which women divorcees retained their *mehr* (dower). She argued that Hanafi laws allowed Muslim wives to seek a divorce if their husbands had married a second wife. *Khula,* as this step was called, also protected the woman from losing her *mehr,* an important source of security for the woman.

Courts occasionally improvised legal usage, and Julia Stephens discusses an interesting controversy. In 1867 a rich Muslim couple from Bengal, Shumsoonnissa and Buzloor Ruheem, took their marital dispute all the way to the Privy Council. The wife suspected her indebted husband of stealing from her inheritance, which, under Muslim law, was her absolute possession. The judges had to identify which aspects of their quarrel concerned domestic issues for them to come under personal laws, and which were purely financial in nature and could thus be adjudicated under non-communitarian civil law. The case first came to the district court under Taraknath Sein, a Hindu judge. He ruled that if she were sent back to her husband's house – as she would be under personal laws – her life could be in danger. So he invoked the principle of a universal religious morality: the protection of human life, he said, was a paramount compulsion, superior to religious injunctions. The British judges at the Calcutta High Court set his argument aside, but, in a somewhat awkward compromise effort, they also argued that since aspects of the Muslim laws were "repugnant to natural justice", their authority could be suspended in this one case. The Privy Council, however, decided to go by Muslim personal laws.

Christian Personal Laws

The state was quite confused about the religious status of Indian Christians. Did relatively recent converts constitute an independent community, or were they to be treated as an offshoot of their pre-conversion identity? Was their change of faith a limited choice, leaving the rest of their social practices and identity definitions intact, and allowing their pre-conversion norms to continue?

Hindu families, branding converts to Christianity as outcastes, usually disinherited them. To circumvent this a new law, Lex Loci of 1850, had ruled that since converts retained their family ties and cultural habits, they must also retain their inheritance. This rendered Indian Christians a double-barrelled or hyphenated category: they were seen as *converts* from another religion rather than full-fledged Christians.

Confusion was evident in a succession dispute involving a multi-religious family at Bellary in Madras between 1854 and 1863. An untouchable-caste man had married a Christian Eurasian (of mixed Indo-European descent) woman after converting to Christianity. When he died, his brother claimed his property under Hindu laws which did not allow the widow to inherit. The brother argued that the deceased's faith at the time of his birth mattered more than his subsequent conversion. The case dragged on over which law should cover the case – Hindu or Christian.

This then raised the possibility of a separate realm of personal laws for Indian Christians – different from both the pre-conversion religious laws to which they had been subject as well as from British laws which covered Europeans residing in India. But then, in cases where both husband and wife were Christian converts, did British Christian legal applications become more relevant than the pre-conversion legal status of such converts? And what of families with a mixed religious lineage?

A court case of 1872 that went up to the Privy Council from the Allahabad High Court involved the custody and inheritance of a minor girl. The father – now dead – was an Englishman. His widow had married another European man, but her second husband already had a wife. The newly married couple converted to Islam to legitimise their second marriage since the man could not have married a second wife under Christian law.

The court decided that the new marriage was invalid. It pronounced that their conversion had not been a genuine religious choice but emanated from bigamous desire. Defined as a concubine rather than a remarried widow, the mother was declared morally unfit to be her child's guardian. The Privy Council upheld the verdict despite the mother claiming – and providing a genealogical chart to back up her claim – that she was born in a family with many Muslim ancestors and been brought up in the Islamic faith, and was thus more a Muslim than anything else; therefore, she was entitled to marry an already married man since Islam allowed bigamy. Moreover, her knowledge of Christianity being scant, as was her daughter's, Christian laws should not apply to them. But the Supreme Court decided that the biological father's faith was the decisive element. The daughter was handed over to her English relatives.

Some scholars argue that because Indian Christians were now made to live under exclusively Christian laws, they lost their anchorage in pre-conversion social and cultural traditions which many of them continued to hold dear. Indeed, several nineteenth-century converts complained that Christian personal laws were a missionary creation, an imposed and artificial implant. Others contend that Indian Christians preferred to have their separate personal laws since most Hindu families disinherited them anyway.

The state eventually enacted four laws between the 1860s and 1870s: the Indian Succession Act, the Indian Divorce Act, the Native Christian Marriage Act, and the Guardian and Wards Act. These did give Christian women larger property entitlements, but marriage was a different matter. The Indian Divorce Act of 1869 stipulated that while the husband could seek divorce on grounds of adultery, the wife could do so only if her husband had also committed incest, bigamy, rape, sodomy, "bestial" practices, and desertion without justification for more than two years.

Church and state allied to negate women's right to dissolve their marriage. To take this issue forward to a much later period, the 1983 Law Commission admitted that Christian marriage rules were discriminatory. Yet it took another decade to strike these provisions down with a Kerala High Court order: only after Mary Sonia Zacharia and E.J. Ammini went to court to claim that the law violated the constitutional guarantee for gender equality. They won their case in 1995.

The Married Women's Property Act of 1874 – applicable also to Parsis and Indian Jews – had allowed Christian women to manage their own property provided they bore liability for their husbands' debts. The Indian Succession Act of 1865 had guaranteed them absolute rights over their self-earned income. In practice, however, its liberal provisions were repeatedly challenged, especially for Christian women. Much later, the new Indian Succession Act of 1925 gave Christian, Jewish, and Parsi daughters equal inheritance rights. An amendment of 1929 extended it to the property they had acquired before their marriage. But this did not extend to cover the spouse who was not a Christian, Jew, or Parsi.

Laws were markedly different in princely states like Cochin and Travancore – both governed by Hindu monarchs. The Indian Succession Act did not apply here, and a widow's inheritance rights were extremely limited if a man who died intestate had lineal descendants. The daughter of such a man, too, had practically no entitlements. In Travancore, for instance, her *stridhanam* (personal possessions given at the time of a marriage) amounted to one-fourth of the son's share if the son's share was not more than Rs 5000. Similar restrictions applied in Cochin. The feminist activist Mary Roy challenged this in 1986. She had married a non-Christian and therefore possessed no *stridhanam*. She later divorced her husband and brought up her children as a single mother. She petitioned the Supreme Court to abolish the Travancore Act as it violated constitutional provisions for gender equality. The court had already struck down the old law with effect from 1951, when Cochin and Travancore joined the Indian Union. Several members of parliament, however, with the help of the Kerala Church Synod for Syrian Christians, introduced a bill in 1986 to prevent the court decision from having retrospective effect. The law was finally modified in 2001, after Christian feminists agitated to ease their divorce rules.

These regulations also applied to Europeans resident in India, as well as to Eurasians of mixed Indo-Western origins. To avoid affronting Hindu sentiments, the Madras High Court ruled that even if both partners had converted to Christianity after going through a Hindu marriage before their conversion, they could not divorce as they remained bound by Hindu laws relevant to matrimonial disputes.

European judges in the princely state of Mysore fully upheld the power of a Hindu husband over that of a Christian wife. Huchi had wanted to convert to Christianity when she was a child but her baptism was cancelled on account of her being too young. Soon afterwards she was forced to marry a Hindu husband. She managed to escape and got herself baptised. But in 1873, when she with the help of her mission applied for divorce, the courts would not allow her to dissolve her pre-conversion child marriage – even though she was now an adult and had converted to Christianity. Some argued that her caste did not recognise divorce, even as others contended that her conversion had in any case resulted in loss of caste. The Lex Loci was now invoked to decide that converts remained tied to their pre-conversion social norms, which included their caste status. So, Huchi was forced to live as an outcaste in her matrimonial home. Her conversion was recognised when it could be used to humiliate her; it was not recognised when she wanted to separate from her husband. Her childhood had been considered a negative factor when she had first wanted to convert, but her conversion did not count when as an adult she wanted to dissolve her child marriage.

Hindu Personal Laws: The War Over Widows

The entire colonial period seethed with controversies around Hindu marriage laws, and we therefore have to devote a disproportionately large space to legal changes in this sphere.

The very first statute that the British had introduced to cancel a much esteemed Hindu ritual was "Regulation XVII of 1829: A Regulation Declaring the Practice of Suttee or Burning/Burying Alive of Hindoo Widows Illegal and Punishable by Criminal Courts". First applied to Bengal, similar regulations were enacted in 1830 for the Madras and Bombay presidencies. They transferred a property of personal laws – immolations being a profoundly sacred ceremonial – to the zone of criminality. The cancellation of sati has a long and acrimonious history behind it, as well as a very important sequel.

Controversies over the scriptural meanings and moral implications of immolations, about correct exegetical methods to authenticate textual citations, and about the lives and deaths of Hindu women now became critical public concerns for the first time in Indian history. The first Indian public sphere debates, too, began with this controversy, helped by modern public sphere resources: print, press, prose literature, associations, and petitions.

The immolation of a widow on the funeral pyre of her husband was a much applauded – though by no means compulsory – ritual endorsed by almost every cardinal ancient scriptural source. The would-be sati was a demi-goddess for large crowds of devout spectators who gathered to avidly watch such spectacular proof of wifely devotion. Most ancient holy texts, like those by the Angiras – a sage prominently mentioned in the Vedas and the Puranas – promised that she would reside in heaven with her husband for three million years, and that her act would pull generations of her paternal, maternal, and matrimonial ancestors out from their sins and release them from hell.

The Bengal Presidency provides particularly rich records of such burnings, though they were also frequent among royal lineages in the Native States – in Tripura, among the Rajput royal dynasties in Gujarat, and in the Maharashtra region. When the Sikh ruler Ranjit Singh (1780–1839) died, several of his wives and concubines were burnt on his pyre. On the other hand Baji Rao, the last Maharashtrian ruler before the British annexed the Peshwa territories in 1818, strongly discouraged the practice of sati. For Bengal, the records reveal that all classes and castes practised immolations.

Going by the annual police reports which were sent to the House of Commons from 1815, at least 350 to 850 widows were burnt alive every year in the Bengal Presidency. Missionaries and officials claimed that many more went unreported. Satis – i.e. immolated widows – came from all castes, though Brahmans provided the single largest category. The "lowly" Shudra subcastes came next, and together they made up the largest cluster. Untouchable Dalits and many Shudra subcastes – supposedly born out of miscegenation among the different jatis and not meant to practise the ritual – often asked permission for their women to perform immolations, and the pandits and the state invariably obliged them. Immolations could well have been a route to "sanskritisation" – upward social mobility – and a way of knitting together deeply stratified castes into a single Hindu ritual community. Although the scriptures prescribed death by burning alone, the caste of Jugis who buried their dead also buried their widows alive. After some reluctance this too was permitted by the state – when pandits urged it to grant permission.

The satis belonged to all age groups, ranging between the ages of four and a hundred. Elderly widows between their thirties and sixties constituted the largest age cluster, perhaps because they were losing their capacity for domestic labour. The women who were burned came from all classes, from substantial landowners to beggars. Rammohun Roy believed that because the Bengal school of Hindu law – Dayabhaga – had provided widows with better usufruct entitlements to the husband's property, well-off families were keen to be rid of them. Yet sati was performed by extremely poor or destitute families too, possibly for the opposite reason: they were too poor to maintain a widow. Polygamy being rampant, sometimes scores of wives burned together and pyres could blaze continuously for days on end.

There were two kinds of immolation, *sahamarana* or concremation, where the widow burned with her husband's corpse; and *anumarana* or post-cremation, which happened when the husband's corpse could not be brought home, or when news of his death reached his home very late. The widow in such cases was burned alone, but Brahman widows were not meant to perform the *anumarana* variant.

Early colonial court records, however, reveal many instances of inappropriate immolations – by a Muslim widow, by a sister, by concubines, and even in one case by a woman who insisted on burning herself since she had dreamt that her husband was dead. Though Baptist missionaries had agitated to abolish the ritual from the late eighteenth century, the state had adamantly refused to engage with the practice in any way. In 1789 a magistrate from Bihar prevented an immolation on his own initiative and the governor general reprimanded him for unwarranted interference in religious matters. Similar instances of independent magisterial intervention, nonetheless, became recurrent, especially when a child widow or brutal coercion was involved. The state, therefore, belatedly felt obliged to discover the authentic scriptural status of the ritual, and in 1797 the Orientalist scholar H.T. Colebrooke reported that it was fully sanctioned by all the important sacred texts.

Prodded nonetheless by officials who were reluctant to allow immolations within their jurisdiction, and by Baptist missionary campaigns for abolition, the state finally asked renowned Brahman pandits to define their proper scriptural scope and form in 1805. By 1812–13 the pandits had retrieved certain scriptural safeguards against rampant burnings: the woman should genuinely consent to burn and should not be drugged or intoxicated, nor be in an "unclean" state (menstruating or postpartum); she should come from the four primary castes or varnas – Brahman, Kshatriya (warriors), Vaishya (traders), and Shudra (menial workers). Pre-pubescent women could not burn, they said, and later added the precise age limit of sixteen. In 1815 an official circular transmitted these conditions to the police and magistrates, asking them to personally check all cases of immolations. In 1817 Mrityunjoy Vidyalankar, chief pandit of the Fort William College, added a scriptural reading which said that the widow could change her mind even after taking the ritual pledge to burn without incurring ritual defilement.

Immolations flourished despite the caution. There were 378 incidents in 1815 in the Bengal Presidency, 839 in 1818, 624 in 1821, 557 in 1823, 639 in 1825, 517 in 1827, and 463 in 1828. The

Sadr Nizamutt Adawlutt, the highest criminal court, confessed in 1824 that many more were burned without informing the police. In sharp contrast to Bengal, the Madras and Bombay presidencies burned far fewer women.

Scriptural safeguards were frequently and flagrantly violated and the British seldom punished violators. Police reports show that, despite the age limit, even four-year-old widows were burned. Reckless violations of the consent clause came to court, but European judges tended to exonerate the widow's relatives or let them off with very light sentences.

In a horrific case before the Gorruckpore court in 1825, Houmulia, a widow fourteen years old and therefore definitely underage – had been forced by her uncle to mount the funeral pyre. Her consent was not verified but was "presumed" by the court – we are not told why. When the flames began to blaze she managed to leap out of the pyre but was caught by the uncle and pushed back on it: "Much burnt, her clothes quite consumed, she again sprang from the pile and running to a well hard by, laid herself down on the watercourse, weeping bitterly. Sheolal (the uncle) now took up a sheet and spreading it upon the ground, desired her to seat herself upon it. No, she said, she would not do this: she would quit her family and live by beggary." Her uncle promised that she would be taken back home. She came back but then was again thrown into the fire. "The wretched victim once more made an effort to save herself."[4] But again she was recaptured and flung into the flames. Eventually, a Muslim was urged to behead her and it is unclear if she died by the sword or by the burnings. The European judge trying the case insisted the uncle was innocent of blame since the girl had sworn the ritual pledge. That done, he had no option but to ensure she burned.

Baptist missionaries played a particularly dynamic role in protesting the immolations. They lobbied parliament, ran abolitionist campaigns in England, mobilised British anti-slavery crusaders

---

[4] Parliamentary Papers, East Indian Affairs, House of Commons, 1830, Proceedings of the Nizamutt Adawlutt, British Library.

and feminists, and publicised Rammohun Roy's arguments against sati in their journals. So did senior police officers, such as Walter Ewer, who argued that immolations contradicted scriptural prescriptions. Governors General, however, retorted that even though the ritual was repugnant to Christian sensibilities, they were obliged to respect Indian beliefs. Ewer complained bitterly that the police presence at immolations provided them the stamp of government approval. He insisted that abolition was perfectly possible without risking an uprising.

When many officials from outside Bengal supported him in increasing numbers, the Company directors grew uneasy. In 1823 they had warned the government, "It is . . . with much reluctance that we can consent to make the British Government . . . an ostensible party to the sacrifice"; they were "averse . . . to the practice of making British courts expounders and vindicators of the Hindu religion." Governor General Amherst, however, thought that, given time, abolition would happen under enlightened Hindu initiative,[5] no doubt alluding to recent publications by Rammohun Roy and hoping that more such would follow. He discouraged legal intervention.

Rammohun had initially feared that an immediate abolition would stoke popular anger, and he advised Governor General Bentinck against it. But Bentinck thought otherwise. Since the burnings were most widely prevalent among the Bengalis, whose numbers were sparse in the British army, most of his civil and military officials assured him that abolition would not affect army loyalty: many Indian sepoys were Muslims and many others came from parts of the country where the ritual was not very widely practised.[6] On 4 December 1829, therefore, Bentinck legally banned the ritual. Those assisting at the burnings were now deemed guilty

---

[5] Ibid., 1825, vol. XXIV, pp. 153–4.

[6] Bentinck Papers, MSS Eur E424, Box 2, Correspondences with European Officials in India, British Library. Also, William Bentinck, "Minute on Sati", 8 November 1829, cited in Major, ed., *Sati: A Historical Anthology*, pp. 102–18.

of culpable homicide, but those using violence to force the woman to burn would face the death penalty.

On 9 December 1829 several thousand upper-caste Hindu landlords and other notables of "Bengal, Bihar, Orisssa, etc." sent a remonstrance petition to Bentinck citing strong religious objections to abolition. The orthodoxy established a modern organisation, the Dharma Sabha, to mobilise Hindu public opinion with journals and pamphlets. They took the case for the preservation of the ritual up to the Privy Council. Abolition, they said, violated their "most ancient and sacred rites and usages" and "the conscientious belief of an entire nation". Rammohun presented counter-petitions to parliament in 1830, rebutting objections to the abolition with scriptural evidence and contradicting conservative assertions.

Widely reputed for his great scriptural learning, Rammohun Roy could offer the state alternative readings of scripture. He argued that the actual form of the practice was customary, not a scriptural requirement. All holy scriptures had instructed the widow to walk straight into the flames, but in practice she had first to be trussed up, then tied to her husband's body, then placed under a huge pile of logs, then set on fire. The accompaniment of loud music rendered her cries for help and struggles to escape unseen and unheard, and her enduring consent – a scriptural precondition – could never be ascertained. This proved to be the clinching argument in favour of abolition: that the customary practice violated the true immolation of the scriptures and that it was in fact "woman murder". Rammohun's orthodox opponent admitted that the customary form departed from the scriptural ideal, but insisted that tying the widow up was nonetheless necessary because while burning her limbs were liable to fall off, and how then would she ascend to heaven?

But Rammohun had also gone well beyond scriptural reinterpretation. The orthodox had argued that since widows who survived would inevitably go morally astray, it was best to burn them. Rammohun said widows should have access to sacred knowledge instead, for it would instil morality. His opponents replied that women were biologically disabled by their gender from receiving true knowledge; Roy retorted by asking them when they had tested a woman's intelligence so that they could conclude women were "foolish". In another tract he argued for absolute inheritance rights for the widow. Not only did he criticise the widow's death, he asked for her life to be secured with property rights and knowledge.

In the process, however, he inadvertently created major problems for future reformers who tried to propagate widow remarriage. Rammohun had cited Manu copiously to bolster his argument: Manu was silent on immolations, and Roy interpreted the silence as active disapproval of immolations. However, Manu was unequivocally opposed to widow remarriage, and this became a major hurdle when later reformers urged its legalisation.

Above all, Rammohun composed a new literary genre and a radically new structure of male sensibilities, a modern critical ethnography of everyday female experiences. An influential feminist historian, Lata Mani, accuses him of using gender as a mere site for religious reform. Feminists persuaded by this view have also argued that Rammohun, as well as British officials who tried to block immolations, in fact infantilised the genuine desire of widows who wished to burn. They are silent on the larger structure of values that the ritual propagated – the fact that when a widow consented to burn herself alive she was voicing the socially inculcated belief that there was nothing on earth a wife should not sacrifice for her living husband. The sati ritual conveyed a stern lesson on her subordinate status – in the shape of sacred conjugal duties – to every Hindu wife. Its message upheld an order of gender that was based on clear sexual double standards: no husband had the reciprocal duty to burn on the pyre of his dead wife. As for the allegation that Rammohun was indifferent to gender asymmetry, let me cite a passage from his second tract on sati at some length because its language and observations have no precedent in our history:

At marriage, the wife is recognised as half of her husband, but, in after conduct, they are treated worse than animals. For the woman is employed to do the work of a slave in the house . . . to clear the place very early in the morning, whether cold or wet, to scour the dishes, to wash the floor, to cook night and day, to prepare and serve food for her husband, her father and mother in law, her brothers in law . . . friends and connections . . . if they commit the smallest fault, what insults . . . After the male part of the family have satisfied themselves, the women content themselves with what may be left, whether sufficient in quantity or no . . . Should the husband acquire wealth, he indulges in criminal amours . . . almost under her eyes . . . As long the husband is poor she suffers every kind of trouble and when he becomes rich . . . a husband takes two or three wives . . . they are subjected to mental miseries . . . lower class women are branded falsely as thieves . . . If unable to bear such a cruel usage, a wife leaves her husband's home to live separately from him, the magisterial authority is generally sufficient to place her again in his hands . . . he sometimes even puts her privately to death . . . What I lament is that seeing the woman thus dependent and exposed to every misery, you feel for her no compassion that might exempt her from being tied down and burnt to death.[7]

War Over Widows: Remarriage

The widow's socio-sexual death became the dominant concern among reformers and the orthodoxy for the rest of the century. The state, now complacently sure of its imperial future, with its territorial and administrative controls secured over practically the entire subcontinent, could afford to be slightly more receptive to liberal interpretations of Hindu texts, albeit only if offered by a Brahman scriptural expert. This, however, proved a rather transient phase, which the 1857 rebellion cut short. By the 1860s, nonetheless, widow remarriage campaigns had spread outwards

[7] Roy, *Second Conference Between An Advocate For, And An Opponent Of, the Practice Of Burning Widows Alive.*

from Bengal to western India and to the Telugu-speaking areas of the South. The law allowing remarriage was enacted in 1856, but its social acceptance remained practically non-existent for a very long time.

Reformers, however, focused single-mindedly on remarriage, which they saw as a panacea for the manifold problems of widowhood. Widows who would not or could not remarry therefore fell outside their ambit, and the harsh ritual, as well as the social and financial mortification of such women, did not seem to dent the singular focus of the reformist project. "Act No. XV, July 1856: An Act to Remove all Legal Obstacles to Marriage of Hindoo Widows" abrogated the accepted scriptural prohibition against remarriage on the basis of alternative interpretations of a specific holy text, the *Parashara Samhita*. It also underwrote the inheritance rights of sons born of remarriage. Widows who remarried, however, forfeited their entitlements to their first husband's property share; nor were they given custodial rights over their children. Even though a colonial legislature – where Indians had as yet no representatives – had enacted the law, the idea had actually originated among a small group of Bengali reformers who had approached members of the Legislative Council with something like a draft bill in 1855.

The Law Commission had briefly considered remarriage in 1837. In order to stamp out infanticide, Governor General Shore proposed criminalising concealed pregnancies, and the Sudder Diwani Adawlut of the North West Province added that such concealment of dead infants, or their secret disposal, should be classified as a "misdemeanour", the assumption being that such concealment hid plans for infanticide. The Commission rejected a provision which made a suspected offence – possible infanticide – into a "positive offence" despite the absence of definite proof. It suggested, moreover, that since most cases of infanticide emanated from illicit pregnancies among widows, a kinder legal alternative would be to enable them to remarry.

But the provincial courts strongly advised against this. The Sudder Court of Madras argued that since all upper-caste brides had to be virgins, Brahmans would now suspect that the state wanted to erase caste differences. R. Macan, Officiating Registrar, Sudder Court, Calcutta, wrote that in the "unqualified opinion of the Court" the law would be "an open violation of the pledged faith of the government," which was to protect the sanctity of their subjects' respective faiths. For Hindus, widow remarriage "involves guilt and disgrace on earth and exclusion from heaven"; it flouts "the usage and obligation of Caste and Custom." Moreover, "the whole framework of the Hindoo Law of Inheritance would be shaken and subverted." The Registrar of the Allahabad Sudder Court reiterated that the widow's "life of chastity and privation" was "both a religious and a moral obligation."[8] When orthodox opponents of the bill later petitioned the government, they added much else to these arguments.

However, whereas official hesitation over abolishing widow immolations had lasted over sixty years, the state moved very quickly on the issue of widow remarriage. In 1855 the renowned Brahman scholar and reformer Ishwar Chandra Vidyasagar approached the legislators Grant and Colville with scriptural citations which, he said, clearly endorsed remarriage. A bill was brought to the Council on 10 November 1855; its first reading began on 17 November, and by July 1856 the Act was in place. Legislators claimed it would merely enable those who believed the scriptures allowed remarriage to live by their interpretation. Unlike the law putting an absolute end to the practice of widow immolation, they said this law on widow remarriage was open-ended and permissive.

They had badly misjudged the situation. Widows, their second husbands, and their friends faced violent intimidation and disinheritance, accompanied by savage and obscene lampooning in the

---

[8] Abstract of Letter from J.P. Grant, Officiating Secretary, Indian Law Commission, to W.H. Macnaughten, Secretary, Government of India, 4 July 1937, Papers Relating to Act XV, Part 1, National Archives of India.

press. Weddings in Calcutta and in Rajahmundry (in the Madras Presidency) were performed under elaborate police protection; upper-caste landlords and their musclemen evicted peasants who supported remarriage; those who remarried were liable to be flogged and expelled from their village. Reformist appeals for help were ignored by Hindu deputy magistrates and the police. Vidyasagar was threatened with death, which he managed to avert with prodigious, strategic gifts to local Brahmans. Widows ready for remarriage were sometimes abducted to distant places by their outraged families. Their lovers and reformist friends had to arrange counter-abductions.

The state, too, had to pay. A year after the bill passed into law, British rule faced a massive insurrection all over North India. Taking stock of their difficulties later, the British felt the law had been one of the precipitating factors. Social opprobrium remained intact and widow remarriages soon lost momentum. In the early 1860s remarriages numbered about sixty in Bengal, while the Andhra reformer Viresalingam's Rajahmundry Association managed forty in the face of huge outrage. Significantly, most remarriages happened in upper-caste families where the prohibition was absolute.

A new civil marriage law was introduced in 1872, providing among other things for widow remarriage. It is quite possible that more widows married under it. In his autobiography a social reformer, Gurucharan Mahalanobis, recalls that, as he was about to marry a widow under the 1856 Act, he was reminded that a new civil marriage was also possible for Brahmos and, as a Brahmo himself, he should use the new law instead. This deeply disappointed his friend Vidyasagar, who had hoped that Gurucharan would marry under the remarriage Act that he (Vidyasagar) had helped to bring about.[9]

Vidyasagar and Viresalingam had to arrange and pay for such marriages themselves. Many soon fell apart in the face of social

[9] Mahalanobis, *Atmakatha*, pp. 56–7.

opprobrium, leaving the widow even more vulnerable. Gurucharan Mahalanobis sheltered twenty-seven high-caste widows at his home for a few years. He did find grooms for some of them, but the others had to return home unmarried. One of the widows joined a midwifery course at the Medical College and, oddly, Gurucharan objected to this: "For that reason, I did not keep her at my home," he wrote, without specifying his objection.[10] Possibly, even the best-intentioned reformers did not want widows to become independent single women who would no longer need a male protector.

In late-ninetenth-century North India Swami Dayanand, founder of the monotheist Arya Samaj, tried to propagate *niyoga* – a rather authoritarian and utilitarian form of remarriage between childless widows and widowers. The Swami believed they could meet at appointed times, only to breed a few children; subsequently they must forgo all mutual contact. At the same time, Dayanand forbade remarriages for high-caste widows. The Arya Samaj was somewhat embarrassed by his proposal and did not try to push it.

The Widow Remarriage Act of 1856 created difficulties for "low-caste" widows who had by custom the right to remarry while retaining their first husband's property share: the Act stipulated that they would lose that entitlement upon remarriage. This resulted in an interesting triangular conflict among Hindu or scriptural law, customary law, and statutory law – this last being the 1856 legislation permitting widow remarriage. North Indian widows in the late nineteenth and early twentieth century often took their inheritance claims to courts, and different courts across the country chose to interpret the legal situation in different ways. The Calcutta and Bombay High Courts followed a combination of Hindu law and statutory law, arguing that, going by the former, widows could not marry at all; and that, if they nonetheless did, under the statute of 1856 they had to forfeit their inheritance.

---

[10] Ibid., p. 68.

In contrast, the Allahabad High Court believed that new laws should eliminate existing disabilities and not add to them. It should allow widows who could never remarry the right to take a second husband. By doing so, they would forgo their share of property. But if a category of widows could, under their specific caste custom, remarry and also inherit something of their first husband's property share, the court should not stand in their way.

The inheritance rights of sons born to remarried widows was a particularly thorny issue. Vidyasagar had insisted that remarriages should follow the Hindu marriage ritual in every detail – barring the obviously transgressive factor of second marriage. This was meant as a safeguard for inheritance rights of widows' sons. The orthodoxy argued that, being of "polluted" and scripturally illicit birth and therefore outcasted – remarriage being invalid, in any case, under Hindu scriptural law – such offspring could not override the superior claims of "pure born" but more distant male heirs. Hindu inheritance being conditional on the performance of funerary rites for ancestors, sons born to remarried widows had no right to perform these rites as they were, by definition, outcastes. Hindu marriage, succession, and inheritance were collective lineage decisions, they argued, whereas the state operated on a narrowly individualistic basis and wrongly assumed that the law affected marriage partners alone.

This raised an interesting question: should marriage be left to the individual will of the partners? If, on the contrary, it was to be a collective familial decision, then how far did religion allow the individual the freedom of decision-making within such a collective?

Beyond Personal Laws: Female Infanticide

Its blanket endorsement of Indian cultural and customary practices posed severe difficulties for the state in the area of female infanticide – a custom widely prevalent among the Rajkumar tribes of Rajputs, and among the Rajbanshees of Bengal. Jonathan Duncan, Resident at Benares, discovered in 1789 that mothers in Jaunpur often starved their newborn daughters to death with not even the pretence of hiding it. It was rare to find more than one daughter in a family – only one village proved an exception in this respect. Duncan thought the heavy pressure of dowry was responsible for the killings; he ordered the communities to sign a covenant renouncing the "horrid practice" and pronounced it irreligious since no scriptural tenets had ever recommended infanticide.

On the grounds that it was not an act of faith, infanticide among the Rajkumars was classified as murder by the Bengal Regulation XXI of 1795 (and extended to the Ceded Provinces by Regulation III of 1894). In 1816 the Rajkumars were still practising infanticide, though more covertly. It also remained widespread among the Rajputs of Cutch and Kathiawar, Mewat and Jaipur. A similar covenant was extracted from practitioners in these locations but proved ineffective yet again: within a single district of 400 families not a single girl could be located.

Act III of 1870 eventually mandated the compulsory registration of births and regular official verification of the daughters' condition for some years after their birth. As we shall see later, the practice remains in force even today – demonstrating the limits of legal remedies in the face of social norms.

Beyond Personal Laws: Civil Marriage

Personal laws instituted – or rather confirmed – an inflexible identification of the individual with her religious community. They embedded the person in a world of obligatory conduct and ritual over which she had no control whatsoever. In the 1860s, with the intensification of the Indian reformist temper, some legislators imagined that many Indians were now ready to live by the dictates of their own conscience. Marriage was an especially rigid institution which prohibited inter-community and inter-caste alliances, and love and personal choice were effaced under the rules of endogamy.

Civil marriage was initially a product of misunderstanding. Its origins lay in religious identity politics, not in a desire for individual freedom. Rammohun Roy had formed an association of Hindus who tried to rid their faith of priesthood, polytheism, and social abuses. First called the Atmiya Sabha and later the Brahmo Samaj, it preached a monotheist, non-idolatrous creed. By the mid 1860s a subgroup had emerged within it, impatient with established Hinduism and keen on radical social reform. This led to a schism in 1866. Keshub Chandra Sen, an energetic proselytising leader of Brahmo dissenters, founded the New Dispensation or Naba Bidhan, as distinct from the Adi Samaj or Original Brahmos led by Debendranath Tagore. Debendranath insisted that Brahmos were Hindus, but Keshub wanted to widen the chasm between Brahmos and Hindus.

Sen's group petitioned the government in 1868 for a separate marriage law just for Brahmos so that they could marry according to their "rites of conscience" instead of being forced into Hindu idolatrous rites. They suggested that the chief commissioners should appoint Brahmo marriage registrars in every district to record marriages among Brahmo couples. Their age needed to be no less than fourteen in the case of the woman and eighteen in that of the man. Only if either party was younger than these stipulated minimum ages would a father's consent to the marriage become necessary. Neither party should at the time of their marriage have an earlier spouse who was still alive. The petition thus implicitly endorsed adult and consensual or love marriage, as well as widow marriage. It also implied the acceptability of inter-caste, though not inter-community, marriage: Sen's suggestions had been meant for the Brahmos alone.

Law Member Henry Maine – progenitor of the concept that civilisations should be measured by their degree of distance between superior status-governed societies and inferior contract-governed ones, and who identified bourgeois individualism as the highest stage of human development – cheerfully took this further in his "Bill to Legalise Marriages Between Certain Natives in India Not Professing the Christian Religion". The last provision, "not professing the Christian religion", was inserted to distinguish marriages under his provisions from the marriages of Indian Christians who had not yet received their own personal laws. Maine was offering civil marriage to all who "objected to be married under Hindu, Muslim, Parsi or Jaina religions". He called it a permissive law – only those who wanted to opt out of existing religious marriage provisions would choose to marry under it.

The draft bill predictably cooked up a storm of protest. James Fitzjames Stephen, who succeeded Maine as Law Member, therefore drafted a second bill in 1871 specifically for the Brahmos, repeating almost verbatim the provisions that the Keshubite section had asked for in its petition of 1868. But Stephen's Brahmo Marriage Bill outraged the Adi Brahmos, who feared that this would irrevocably separate them from Hindus. They considered themselves as reformed Hindus, not as a separate sect.

After a signature campaign from the Adi Brahmos, the bill was drafted yet again. The marrying couple now had to declare they were not Hindus, Muslims, Jains, Parsis, Sikhs, or Buddhists; in Maine's original draft all they needed to say was that they objected to marrying under the existing religious laws. The new version thus amounted to demanding an abdication of faith, inhibiting many who otherwise wished to marry under it.

Under the new bill the guardian's consent became necessary if either partner was below the age of twenty-one. In this respect Stephen's version was harsher than Maine's since it pushed adult men and women under parental guardianship. The compromise had largely resulted from Hindu public outrage and fear that public morality would crash if young people chose their own marital partners. The bill specified the rules of consanguinity under which civil marriages would be forbidden and made bigamy a punishable offence. Couples marrying in a particular district would need a residence qualification of two weeks, and a notice had to be sent to a marriage registrar fourteen days before the proposed marriage date: Maine's bill, by contrast, had specified only five days as the notice period. Moreover the notice would make the intended marriage open to public scrutiny, presumably to avoid bigamous and fraudulent marriages. But, as the anthropologist Perveez Mody shows, it also left the door open for parental pressure to cancel the notice. (To move this subject far forward, the Special Marriage Act of 1954 pushed the age limits upwards to twenty-one and eighteen for men and women, respectively, and extended the period of notice, creating even more problems for adult couples who had eloped to get married.)

Many still believed love would destroy family values and ties, inter-caste marriages would mix pure upper-caste blood with impure blood, and anarchy in bloodlines would follow. In its final form Act III of 1872 opened up at least the possibility of love marriages which could now occur despite family injunctions and familial opposition. It took marriage out of the hands of the community and placed it within the jurisdiction of a state which was meant to be neutral in relation to religion. But in practice the Act worked for far too few. Still, an exceptional minority took advantage of it to plunge into hitherto unthinkable marriages and brave the world. In Bengal, for instance, an upper-caste man married a famous actress – Sukumari Datta – who had been a prostitute earlier and hence an outcaste. Abandoned by their families, the man died abroad in penury and the wife wrote a semi-autobiographical play in 1873 to make a living for herself and her baby daughter. Titled *Apurba Sati*, it was the first Indian play written by a woman to be actually staged and performed.

War Over the Child Wife: The Age of Consent Act of 1891

Though the Prophet of Islam had married a girl of nine himself, he had laid no injunctions on Muslims to marry similarly. The

Hindu sacred texts, in contrast, had mandated the compulsory marriage of pre-pubertal daughters. Since the precise occurrence of puberty could not be known beforehand, parents tended to marry their daughters off as early as possible. The warm Indian climate, it was believed, caused girls to reach puberty particularly early, so the sooner they were married the better. It was also universally believed that once puberty happened, female sexuality grew rampant and forced women to seek out paramours if they lacked a husband to satisfy their longings. Many advocated eight as the ideal age when the "gift of daughters" to a different lineage approximated the gift of a goddess, bringing parents a huge deposit of merit into their afterlife. Though this mandate held true only for the upper castes, Raghunandan, a sixteenth-century Bengali legal authority of great importance, generalised Brahmanical marriage practices to cover the Bengali Shudra castes as well. Solvent fractions of the untouchables, too, sought to improve their socio-ritual status by reaching out in the direction of their social superiors. The *Ethnographic Glossary of Hindu Castes and Tribes in Bengal* for 1891 shows that only tribal groups did not practise infant and child marriage.

Post-pubertal marriages, in the same measure, were deemed a grave sin. Needless to say, this ensured that the child bride was bound to be a virgin; particularly as a considerable number of brides belonged to the 0–10 age bracket, their unblemished chastity at marriage was reassuringly safe. There was no parallel age restriction for the husband, who could even be an old man as well as much married, especially if he belonged to the purest caste of Kulin Brahmans. The age gap between husband and wife was usually absurdly excessive.

Vidyasagar wrote a passionate tract in 1850 called *Balyabibaher Dosh* (Problems with Child Marriage). But he did not try to take the legal route to abolish the practice, knowing full well that it was anchored in far too many authoritative scriptural texts. In 1884 the Parsi reformer Behramji Malabari (1853–1912) sent a *Note on Infant Marriages* to the Government of India in which he argued that Hinduism did not recommend child marriage. By the late 1880s we find two kinds of shifts in the reform agenda. The emphasis moved from the age of marriage to the age of conjugal cohabitation. The centre of the campaigns, for a while, was relocated to England.

Mary Carpenter had founded the National Indian Association in Aid of Social Progress and Female Education in India in 1871. This association ran a journal called *The Indian Magazine and Review*. Malabari made use of these international instruments. He published his *Appeal on Behalf of the Daughters of India* in Carpenter's journal in 1890 and, by way of response, his English friends formed a committee to help his efforts. This committee was not without influence. It included several dukes, bishops, and ex-governors of various Indian provinces. From 1889, therefore, the Indian government was pressurised to solicit Indian public opinion on the age of marriage. Some change, indeed, seemed possible now, especially in view of the fact that from the 1870s the Indian press had sporadically reported on the grievous injuries that many child wives had suffered from marital rape.

Justice K.T. Telang swerved away from Malabari's proposal. Using the reports of deaths from marital rape, he pointed out that what needed immediate change was the age of conjugal cohabitation – not the age of marriage as such. Under the urging of Vidyasagar the Indian Penal Code of 1860 had included a clause which defined cohabitation with girls under ten as rape. Dayaram Gidumal, Malabari's disciple, now proposed that the penal code raise the minimum age to twelve for girls and stipulate that this applied to *all* girls, married or not. The government resolutely ignored these pleas.

In Bengal, where reformist voices had become quite muted – in contrast with the growing virulence of Hindu religious nationalism – a violent episode occurred in 1889 which finally set the scene for legal change. Phulmonee, a girl of barely eleven, had died of a gruesome marital rape in Calcutta. As Viceroy Lansdowne wrote in 1890: "Having had our hands to some extent forced, owing to the Phulmonee case . . ." the state now had to reconsider marital sex with child wives.[11]

According to Penal Code provisions, cohabitation with any girl, married or unmarried, below the age of ten was legally rape. Phulmonee was just above ten. Following the rape she had suffered acute agony for more than ten hours. Her mother, grandmother, and aunt testified in court that her husband had raped her. But because she was just above ten her husband was charged with inadvertent manslaughter and let off with a light sentence.

To prevent the recurrence of similar monstrous injuries to infant bodies, amendments were now suggested to the Penal Code of 1860 and to the Code of Criminal Procedure of 1882. The age of consent for girls, within and outside marriage, was sought to be raised from ten to twelve. Below that ceiling intercourse, even within marriage, would signify rape. The bill covered Hindus, Muslims, and Christians.

Fears now ran very high, particularly among Bengali Hindus, that the law would fatally wound the fundamentals of Hindu marriage. Numerous, massive, and enraged protest meetings and demonstrations exploded against the bill, culminating in the first ever media-driven street agitation against the government. Mammoth processions were held in Calcutta and cultural nationalists introduced the art of well-organised collective action in public spaces. This agitation proved to be the precursor of a full-blown confrontational political nationalism whose echoes were carried into the Swadeshi movement against the partition of Bengal in 1905–8.

The British Indian Association, comprising conservative large-estate owners, opposed the bill. The Indian Association, relatively more liberal, supported it, as did the Central Mahomedan Association. The Brahmo Samaj, champions of reform, also supported the intervention, though in a rather nervous voice in the

---

[11] Lansdowne Papers, Home Confidential, 1890, Correspondence with Persons in England: Letter No. 52, Reay, 25 August 1890, National Archives of India.

face of the growing religious hysteria which now carried a strong nationalist cast. The Arya Samaj was far too preoccupied with the death of its founder Swami Dayanand to pay much attention, but there were some stirrings of discomfort among them even – though the Swami had himself castigated infant marriages.

Bal Gangadhar Tilak, nationalist stalwart from Bombay, added political teeth to the opposition. He turned the situation against his Moderate Congress rivals who were relatively more supportive of social change. Tilak's journals, *Kesari* and *Mahratta*, rebutted Gidumal's suggestions with powerful anti-colonial rhetoric and, from 1885, Tilak presided over numerous meetings to oppose all interference in sacred Hindu marriage rules. Eventually, even the reformer M.G. Ranade, facing enormous outrage, changed his stance and fell quiet. Interestingly, Tilak himself was not really in favour of child marriages: what he contested was the government's right to intervene in Hindu religious affairs. This was a nationalist argument that gathered much resonance and carried great potential for unrest in a context of sharpening colonial misrule. Tilak's efforts resulted in the removal of social reform from the Congress agenda, and the National Social Conference – which functioned as the social reform wing of the Congress – was no longer allowed to share space with the Congress during the latter's annual gatherings.

Several Bombay women's groups, on the other hand, urged in their petition to Queen Victoria that fourteen be made the minimum age of consent. Receiving no response and fearing they had gone too far, they reduced their suggestion to twelve. A Women's Committee from Bombay, which had developed a London branch under the suffragist Millicent Fawcett, sent a pro-Bill petition from 20,000 Indian women to the queen. It mentioned the caste of the signatories but not their names – anonymity was necessary to avert them being attacked.

As the anti-law agitation built up, nervous British legislators as well as liberal reformers in Bombay pleaded that the proposed amendments desist from interfering with Hindu marriage as a whole. They advised merely revising the age of cohabitation within marriage. Nationalists for their part invoked another spectre: even that, they said, would violate the Garbhadhan ceremony, the first of ten fundamental Hindu life-cycle rites enjoining mandatory conjugal cohabitation between husband and wife within sixteen days of her first period. Puberty in a girl, they insisted, occured punctually at the age of ten; therefore, unless wives cohabited with their husbands immediately after puberty as directed by their religion, the consequences would be truly dreadful – by defying the ritual injunction, they would have committed the sin of foeticide. As the anti-Bill controversies surged, liberal Hindus tried to reinterpret the ritual as symbolic act rather than actual sexual cohabitation. They also reinterpreted the marriage ceremony to assert that the sacrament was actually only a betrothal, and that the "real marriage" happened only after the girl attained puberty. Cultural nationalists, in contrast, deployed a highly charged anti-colonial political rhetoric – vivid, hortative, and compelling. Unnerved by the strength of the assault on the proposed changes, the state solicited opinion from European and Indian officials, doctors, and local dignitaries about how widespread and damaging underage cohabitation really was within marriage, and whether it merited legal amelioration.

Most Muslim respondents supported the bill. One said that under Quranic laws the girl's consent was irrelevant if it was a criminal attack on her person. Many flaunted the fact that, unlike Hindus, Muslims were not bound to underage cohabitation by ritual considerations. Infant marriage, they said, became common among Bengali Muslims only because of the baneful influence of Hindus and not because it was favoured by Islam.

Medical testimonies and hospital records, both Hindu and European, cited instances of wife-killings when rape was resisted, or of the wife's death as a consequence of violent intercourse. They added another category of indirect killing, arguing that premature intercourse resulted in premature childbearing, which led to both infant mortality and maternal deaths among child-mothers;

they pointed to medical conditions such as lingering post-puerperal illnesses that were often the cause of early death. Citing traumatic experiences when treating child victims, more than fifty women doctors signed a petition against the practice. Medical evidence, however, left the orthodox cold and unmoved. Of course, neither liberals nor conservatives tried to interpret the consent of the wife in terms of her own genuine desire for sex. The Act of 1891, accordingly, defined the age of consent as that safe age when sex could be borne by a woman without great physical injury.

Matriliny

By the late nineteenth century the British were keen to streamline upper-caste marriage practices across the subcontinent. They found it puzzling that matriliny in the deep South was much at odds with the dominant principles of endogamy, patriliny, patrilocality, and property ownership which elsewhere were always vested in the husband and the father. In parts of present-day Kerala, upper-caste Nayar wives lived in their mothers' home within large jointly held landed households, and the bloodline, as well as inheritance, ran from mothers to co-resident daughters. Marriage, some said, was hypergamous as they married the younger sons of Namboothiri Brahmans; but after the formal marriage ceremony the wife, many alleged, was allowed serial multiple relationships (called *sambandham*s) with other men. Nayar men, however, strenuously countered the allegation. In North Kerala, where the *taravad*s (landowning households) were much smaller, the husband had visiting rights. But his income and property did not flow down to his children, who inherited from their mothers alone. Property was managed by the maternal uncle rather than by the mother.

From the 1870s the British became increasingly puzzled with the plethora of marriage forms among various categories of Indians; they wanted to pull all Hindu marriages under a Brahmanical format which, they thought, should be paradigmatic. By the late nineteenth century young Nayar men, now armed with independent incomes from modern professions, came to resent their lack of proprietorship over household, land, children, and wives. They demanded the partibility of household lands, allowing them to take over their own separate households. From the 1870s there was a movement for marriage reform alongside, and the Malabar Marriage Act of 1896 tried to accommodate some of their demands. It was not very successful on the ground, however, till the agrarian Depression of the early 1930s hit *taravad* fortunes really hard and sapped the foundations of the old order. The Madras Marumakkayathayam Act was passed in 1933, allowing for the partition of landed properties, which now passed into the hands of the husband along with rights over his children. Marriages were made endogamous under pressure from a new generation of both Namboothiri Brahman and Nayar men who were embarrassed about the relative absence of husbandly power and allegations of inter-caste liaisons.

Households in Kerala slowly turned towards husband-governed patrilocality. Malayalam novels and art naturalised and aesthetisised the romance of conjugal love and the beauties of responsible fatherhood. Raja Ravi Varma (1848–1906), the iconic artist, romanticised the change in his 1893 painting titled "There Comes Papa". The picture is of a young mother holding a baby, both looking expectantly outwards, waiting for the man of the family to arrive. The historian G. Arunima says this was emblematic of the entry of the patriarchal father/husband figure into a matrilineal situation.

Property Laws

Property inheritance, as we saw with respect to the widow remarriage and conversion controversies, occupied an ambiguous status. It could fall under the civil law as well as personal laws since inheritance, for Hindus, was conditional on certain ritual and caste observances.

A new controversy erupted from the 1880s about the precise nature of the Hindu Undivided Family (HUF), which was a legally recognised unit of male coparcenaries sharing inheritance rights. Matters became complicated when it came to the HUF's operations as a single economic unit transacting large-scale business operations. Often, individual responsibilities could not be precisely differentiated and the marriage of daughters or deaths in the family left the HUF's membership in a fluid state. Since such occurrences involved the transfer of capital (e.g. during marriages) or debt obligations (e.g. with deaths), the family's business partners were often left stranded in considerable uncertainty. The state too was in a bind when it came to income tax – which was computed on an individual basis.

This situation was of particular concern to Marwari traders whose business networks were enormous and widespread, and who entered into financial transactions with multiple Indian and European firms. Marwaris had steadfastly refused to abide by the contractual regulations of joint-stock companies when deciding on the rights and liabilities of family members. They claimed that the family firm, being an indivisible unit, was not amenable to such rules. From the 1880s they had argued that a contractual regime could not displace customary mercantile conventions. Soon they began to refer to the scriptural – hence sacred – basis of the Hindu family: to argue that the HUF should come under personal laws, not civil ones. To bolster their position they now intervened, frequently and loudly, in public debates on marriage.

Marwari opinion, however, was divided. Their Bombay mercantile associations preferred a liberal stance on the Age of Consent Act of 1891, while the Calcutta Marwaris were hardline conservatives who argued that Hindu marriages lay beyond the scope of legal reform. (Later they also opposed the amended Special Marriage Act of 1923 on the grounds that it inflicted contract upon marriage, thereby radically undermining the unique distinction of the sacramental Hindu marriage.) Since the debates divided the regional mercantile communities, the Marwaris started several associations – for internal social reform, as well as to enforce orthodox positions.

Back to Civil Marriages: The New Century

The Special Marriage Act of 1872 had allowed civil marriage only to Hindus, Muslims, or Christians who had rejected their religious affiliation. Not only did such a marriage oblige them to abandon their faith, it also left them without inheritance rights. Between 1921 and 1923 some Indian legislators, newly admitted to legislatures that had come up under the Montagu–Chelmsford reforms of 1919, had the confidence – which the colonial rulers had so notably lacked – to propose several amendments to the Act. Being Hindus themselves, they possessed the authority to do so. In 1921 Hari Singh Gour introduced an amendment in response to recent judicial decisions which had explicitly stated that not only Hindus, but Jains, Buddhists, and Sikhs too were bound by the Hindu marriage and succession provisions. This meant that members of all these communities needed to declare they belonged to no religion if they wanted to contract a civil marriage. Gour suggested instead that those who said they were Hindu, Jains, Sikhs, Buddhists, Muslims, Christians, and Parsis should enjoy the option of a civil marriage without renouncing their faith. The Select Committee, however, excluded Muslims, Christians, and Parsis from the remit of the bill.

While the Hindu orthodoxy, predictably, was in uproar, the Marwari Association added a fresh twist: it insisted that Hindus contracting civil marriages should not be allowed to inherit family property; and that family trusts, too, as part and parcel of the HUF, should be closed to them. By slyly inserting emergent anti-caste discourses into their argument it suggested that the amendment would add fresh subcastes to the existing ones because those marrying under the new law would be expelled from their ancestral castes and forced to form new subcastes. Eventually, the new law stipulated that Hindus, Buddhists, and Jains marrying under the amended Special Marriages Act would no longer remain a part of their families or have access to inheritance under Hindu personal law: nor would they enter religious offices or offer religious services or manage religious trusts. At the same time, they were exempted from the formal requirement of forfeiting their faith.

Very high costs had to be paid, therefore, for marrying for love.

Back to Child Marriages: The New Century

The enlargement of constitutional reforms from the early twentieth century introduced a greater willingness among Indians to push beyond the limits of scripture. Indian legislators now debated child marriage on the Assembly floor more freely and boldly than ever before. A strong and paradoxical impetus for immediate change, moreover, arrived with the publication of Katherine Mayo's *Mother India* (1927). Its American author, a journalist, was a great believer in empires in general, and convinced of the savage inclinations of the colonised who could only be freed from the primeval darkness in which they lived by Western imperial benevolence. She conveniently disregarded the fact that the initiatives and pressures for social change had so far come from Indian men and women. She wrote obsessively about what she saw as the sexual perversions of Indian men which, apparently, inclined them to abuse young girls – as also to communism, which was no less a scourge. Her grisly portrayal of Indian masculinity led to massive outrage and to a strong desire among Indians to prove her wrong. As Mrinalini Sinha has shown, it also opened up a considerable space for women's organisations to bargain with nationalist legislators about a child-marriage law that was already on the legislative anvil. Ironically, therefore, the book appeared at a moment when each and every one of its stereotypes was proved abysmally wrong.

The Women's India Association had raised the issue of the minimum age of marriage in 1926. The All India Women's Education and Social Conference, formed in 1927, had begun to put strong pressure on Congress legislators. Even though the Deoband group of Islamic clerics believed that a foreign government should not be allowed to intervene in Muslim domestic practices, many Muslim women leaders refused to listen to them. Jinnah had argued that even though Muslim sacred law had not made child marriage mandatory – as Hindu scripture had – the management of domestic matters must still be left in the hands of community leaders. In protest, several women activists wrote a counter-petition entitled "Muslim Ladies Defend the Sarda Act".[12] The wives of Hindu nationalists of an orthodox bent – of Pandit Madan Mohan Malaviya, for instance – persuaded their husbands to endorse the reformed law. Indian women's political-organisational capabilities and agency were no longer in any doubt.

Indian legislators had already presented several bills to raise the age of consent further, within and outside marriage. Gandhi, who otherwise avoided legislative politics, also urged the Congress to support the restriction on child marriage, or its abolition. Married off as a child himself, he knew and feared its effects on a prematurely over-stimulated sexuality. But the bills were blocked by the Viceroy's Executive Council which feared a conservative backlash if the government went too far. Conservatives, moreover, formed a loyalist support base that the government badly wanted to retain, especially at a time when Congress' mobilisation of popular anti-colonial movements had become a real menace for the empire.

---

[12] This refers to the final bill which was brought forward by Har Bilas Sarda in 1929 and which was enacted as the Child Marriage Restraint Act in 1930. It was popularly known as the Sarda Act.

The Council's obstinate defence of child marriage irked British feminists like Eleanor Rathbone, who campaigned for the proposed law in England and in India; so did the women's wing of the British Labour Party. Notwithstanding the pressures, the government vetoed Hari Singh Gour's bill and introduced its own bill in 1925 for a revised age of consent. This was a pale shadow of Gour's proposals. It fixed the age of consent at thirteen for wives and at fourteen for unmarried women. Even the 1891 law had not distinguished between wives and other women in this matter. The official version that was enacted into law did not even mention child marriage.

There was some dithering among nationalists about how far they should accord urgent priority to this legal issue at a time when there was great anti-colonial turbulence in the country. But the publication of Mayo's book left them with little choice. Indian manhood was in the dock, and Mayo had to be proved wrong. So, at long last, and scripture notwithstanding, a bill, introduced by Har Bilas Sarda, entered the statutes as the Child Marriage Restraint Act of 1929 – exactly a century after the abolition of widow immolations. It had first been introduced in the Assembly as the Hindu Child Marriage Bill in 1927 – so Mayo could take no credit for it. It made the marriages of girls below fourteen and of boys below sixteen illegal, though it did not provide much by way of preventive measures if the law was violated. The government also delayed its enforcement, enabling a large number of child or infant marriages before it came into action. It fell far short of the Indian proposals: the All India Women's Conference, for instance, had recommended sixteen as the age of consent for girls within and outside marriage, thus cancelling the official distinction between husbands and males in general. In its final shape the Act stipulated fourteen as the minimum age of marriage for girls and eighteen for men.

In a strange argument, Gandhi suggested in 1935 that Dalits be excluded from its scope. This echoed his conviction that Dalit men were markedly more conservative than caste Hindus, and that Dalit women's interests were therefore more dispensable. This was a most peculiar notion, since, as we shall see later, Phule, Ambedkar, Periyar, and other Dalit and low-caste leaders were far more progressive than Gandhi about gender issues.

Though fairly moderate in nature, the Sarda Act was nonetheless a signpost which registered how far legal reforms had travelled over a century. It marked the entry of new authorities beyond scripture and custom – liberal nationalism, women's organisations, arguments about maternal and infant health, and eugenic imperatives urging a national-modern. The Act also signalled the end of the classic age of legal reform when law was the predominant vehicle of social change, and when religious texts and community authorities took the final call on gender-based laws.

The patterns of change explored elsewhere in this book show corresponding radical transformations in the lives of middle-class men and women in the inter-war decades. As they became drawn into the politics of nationalism, trade unionism, and socialism, and as some chose their partners with a greater degree of freedom, sections of the elite and middle classes learned a new social awareness about the different worlds of gender practices. They constituted a fresh generation of the "New Man" and the "New Woman", a template quite different from that of their nineteenth-century predecessors.

Agitations over Hindu gender and faith continue into our own time. In Kerala, for instance, Lord Ayyappan's temple at Sabarimala has traditionally prohibited women between ten and fifty years of age from entering the pilgrimage site. The Lord, it is believed, will be contaminated by the presence of menstruating devotees. Interestingly, this venue too presumes ten as the invariant age for female puberty. In 2018 the Indian Supreme Court ruled against the temple's ritual prohibition against women's entry, basing its verdict on the constitutional provision for gender equality. But groups of infuriated Hindus – large numbers of women among them – blocked the entry of women who tried to enter the temple. There were clashes, and the women who had forced their way in faced severe penalties from their families.

Very recently, the Gujarat government has introduced a new bill – supported by Opposition parties in the state – which makes parental consent mandatory for love marriages. Inter-faith and inter-caste marriages have come under larger and larger legal and judicial impediments, with families frequently punishing couples with violent death. Love continues to be a dangerous and suspect business in India, best allowed after the safety of marriages arranged or sanctioned by parents who cling to endogamous community-confined rules.

It is time, perhaps, for us to pay more attention to the history of Indian conservatism, and to look beyond – though never excluding – critiques of colonial intervention. I have tried in this chapter to show up the colonial government as a conservative, timid, and nervous institution in these matters, and very far from the rampaging, modernising, and civilising force that its claims have made it out to be.

References and Suggested Readings for Chapter 2

Agarwal, Bina, *A Field of One's Own: Gender and Land Rights in South Asia*, Cambridge: Cambridge University Press, 1994.

Agnes, Flavia, *Law, Gender and Inequality: The Politics of Women's Rights in India*, Delhi: Oxford University Press, 2001.

Anagol, Padma, "Rebellious Wives and Dysfunctional Marriages: Indian Women's Discourses and Participation in the Debates over Restitution of Conjugal Rights and the Child Marriage Controversy in the 1880s and 1890s", in Sumit Sarkar and Tanika Sarkar, eds, *Women and Social Reform in Modern India: A Reader*, vol. 2, Ranikhet: Permanent Black, 2007.

Arunima, G., *There Comes Papa: Colonialism and the Transformation of Matriliny in Kerala, circa 1850–1940*, Delhi: Orient Longman, 2003.

Bentinck, William, "Minute on Sati", 8 November 1829, in Andrea Major, ed., *Sati: A Historical Anthology*, Delhi: Oxford University Press, 2007.

Benton, Lauren, *Law and Colonial Cultures: Legal Regimes in World History, 1400–1900*, Cambridge: Cambridge University Press, 2002.

Birla, Ritu, *Stages of Capital: Law, Culture and Market Governance in Late Colonial India*, Hyderabad: Orient Blackswan, 2009.

Burman, B.K. Roy, "Challenges of Development and Tribal Women", in J.P Singh, *et al.*, eds, *Tribal Women and Development*, Delhi: South Asia Books, 1998.

Carroll, Lucy, "Law, Custom and Statutory Social Reform: The Hindu Widows' Remarriage Act of 1856", in J. Krishnamurty, ed., *Women in Colonial India: Essays on Survival, Work and the State*, Delhi: Oxford University Press, 1989.

Chatterjee, Nandini, *Negotiating Mughal Law: A Family of Landlords Across Three Indian Empires*, Cambridge: Cambridge University Press, 2020.

Chatterjee, Nandini, *The Making of Indian Secularism: Empire, Law and Christianity*, London: Palgrave Macmillan, 2011.

Chowdhry, Prem, *Political Economy of Production and Reproduction: Caste, Custom and Community in North India*, Delhi: Oxford University Press, 2011.

Clark, Alice, "Limitations on Female Life Chances in Rural Central Gujarat", in J. Krishnamurty, ed., *Women in Colonial India: Essays on Survival, Work and the State*, Delhi: Oxford University Press, 1989.

Dalton, E.T., *Descriptive Ethnology of Bengal*, Calcutta: Government Printing Press, 1872.

Datta, V.N., *Sati: A Historical, Social, Philosophical Enquiry into the Hindu Rite of Widow Burning*, Delhi: Manohar, 1988.

Derrett, J.D.M., *Religion, Law and the State in India*, London: Faber and Faber, 1968.

Dodwell, H.H., ed., *The Cambridge History of India*, vol. VI, Cambridge: Cambridge University Press, 1932.

Elwin, Verrier, *Nagaland*, Shillong: Advisor's Secretariat, The Research Department, 1961.

Fisch, Jorg, *Burning Women: A Global History of Widow Sacrifices from Ancient Times to the Present*, trans. Rekha Kamath Rajan, Chicago: University of Chicago Press, 2005.

Fürer-Haimendorf, Christoph von, *Naked Nagas*, Calcutta: Thacker and Spinck, 1933.

Ghurye, G.S., *The Scheduled Tribes*, Bombay: Popular Prakashan, 1963.

Gilmartin, David, "Customary Law and Shariat in British Punjab", in Katherine Ewing, ed., *Shariat and Ambiguity in British Punjab*, Berkeley: University of California Press, 1988.

Gilmartin, David, *Empire and Islam: Punjab and the Making of Pakistan*, Berkeley: University of California Press, 1992.

Heimsath, Charles, *Indian Nationalism and Hindu Social Reform*, Princeton: Princeton University Press, 1964.

Hutton, J.H., *The Sema Nagas*, Oxford: Oxford University Press, 1921.

Ilbert, Courteney, *The Government of India: Being a Digest of the Statute Law Relating Thereto with Historical Introduction and Explanatory Matter*, Oxford: Clarendon Press, 3rd edn, 1915.

Kishwar, Madhu, "Daughters of Aryavarta", in J. Krishnamurty, ed., *Women in Colonial India: Essays on Survival, Work and the State*, Delhi: Oxford University Press, 1989.

Kozlowski, Gregory, "Muslim Women and the Control of Property in North India", in Sumit Sarkar and Tanika Sarkar, eds, *Women and Social Reform in Modern India: A Reader*, vol. 2, Ranikhet: Permanent Black, 2007.

Mahalanobis, Gurucharan, *Atmakatha*, Calcutta: Nirmalkumari Mahalanobis, 1974.

Major, Andrea, *Sovereignty and Social Reform in India: British Colonialism and the Campaigns Against Sati, 1830–1860*, Abingdon and New York: Routledge, 2011.

Mallampalli, Chandra, *Race, Religion and Law in Colonial India: Trials of An Interracial Family*, Cambridge: Cambridge University Press, 2015.

Mani, Lata, *Contentious Traditions: The Debate on Sati in Colonial India*, Berkeley: University of California Press, 1998.

Masud, M. Khalid, "Apostasy and Judicial Separation in British India", in M.K. Masud, B. Messick, and D.S. Powers, eds, *Islamic Legal Interpretations: Muftis and Their Fatwas*, Cambridge, MA: Harvard University Press, 1996.

Mayo, Katherine, *Mother India*, New York: Harcourt Brace, 1927.

Metcalf, Barbara D., "Islam and Custom in Nineteenth Century India:

The Reformist Standard of Maulana Thanawi's *Bihishti Zevar*", *Contributions to Asian Studies*, vol. 17, 1982.

Metcalf, Barbara D., *Islamic Revival in British India: Deoband 1860–1900*, Princeton: Princeton University Press, 1982.

Mody, Perveez, "Love and the Law: Love Marriage in Delhi", *Modern Asian Studies*, vol. 36, no. 1, 2002.

Nathan, Dev, "Gender Transformation in Tribes", in idem, ed., *From Tribe to Caste*, Shimla: Indian Institute of Advanced Study, 1997.

Nongbri, Tiplut, "Khasi Women and Matriliny: Transformations in Gender Relations", *Gender, Technology and Development*, vol. 4, no. 3, 2000.

Pande, Ishita, "Coming of Age: Law, Sex and Childhood in Late Colonial India", *Gender and History*, vol. 24, no. 1, March 2012.

Pande, Ishita, *Sex, Law and the Politics of Age: Child Marriage in India, 1891–1937*, Cambridge: Cambridge University Press, 2020.

Parashar, Archana, *Women and Family Law Reform in India*, Delhi: Sage, 1992.

Prasad, Nita Verma, "The Litigious Widow: Inheritance Disputes in Colonial North India, 1875–1911", in Anindita Ghosh, ed., *Behind the Veil: Resistance, Women and the Everyday in Colonial South Asia*, London: Palgrave, Macmillan, 2008.

Ray, Reeju, *Placing the Frontier in British North East India: Law, Custom and Knowledge*, Delhi: Oxford University Press, 2023.

Roy, Rammohun, *Second Conference Between An Advocate For, And An Opponent Of, the Practice Of Burning Widows Alive*, Calcutta, 1820, in Kalidas Nag and Debajyoti Burman, eds, *The English Works of Raja Rammohun Roy*, Calcutta: Sadharan Brahmo Samaj, 1945.

Roy, Sripati, *Customs and Customary Law in British India*, Tagore Law Lectures, Calcutta: Hare Press, 1911.

Sarkar, Tanika, "A Just Measure of Death? Hindu Ritual and Colonial Law in the Sphere of Widow Immolations", *Comparative Studies of South Asia, Africa, and the Middle East*, vol. 33, no. 2, 2013.

Sarkar, Tanika, "Holy Fire Eaters", in idem, *Rebels, Wives, Saints: Designing Selves and Nations in Colonial Times*, Ranikhet: Permanent Black, 2009.

Sarkar, Tanika, "Intimate Violence in Colonial Bengal: A Death, a Trial and a Law, 1889–1891", *Law and History Review*, vol. 38, no. 1, February 2020.

Sarkar, Tanika, "Resisting Colonial Reason and the Death of a Child Wife", in idem, *Hindu Wife, Hindu Nation: Community, Religion, and Cultural Nationalism*, Ranikhet: Permanent Black, 2002.

Sarkar, Tanika, "Something Like Rights? Faith, Law and Immolation Debates in Colonial Bengal", *The Indian Economic and Social History Review*, vol. XLIX, no. 3, July–September 2012.

Sarkar, Tanika, "Wicked Widows", in idem, *Rebels, Wives, Saints: Designing Selves and Nations in Colonial Times*, Ranikhet: Permanent Black, 2009.

Sen, Asoka Kumar, *From Village Elder to British Judge: Custom, Customary Law and Tribal Society*, Delhi: Orient Blackswan, 2012.

Sen, Samita, "Religious Conversion, Infant Marriage and Polygamy: Regulating Marriage in India in the Late Nineteenth Century", *Journal of History*, vol. 26, 2008–9.

Sharafi, Mitra, *Law and Identity in Colonial India: Parsi Legal Culture, 1772–1947*, Ranikhet: Permanent Black, 2014.

Shodan, Amrita, *A Question of Community: Religious Groups and Colonial Law*, Calcutta: Samya, 2001.

Singh, K.S., "Tribal Women: An Anthropological Perspective", in J.P Singh, *et al.*, eds, *Tribal Women and Development*, Delhi: South Asia Books, 1998.

Sinha, Mrinalini, *Colonial Masculinity: The 'Manly Englishman' and the 'Effeminate Bengali'*, Manchester: Manchester University Press, 1996.

Sinha, Mrinalini, *Specters of Mother India: The Global Restructuring of an Empire*, Durham: Duke University Press, 2006.

Stephens, Julia, *Governing Islam Law, Empire and Secularism in South Asia*, Cambridge: Cambridge University Press, 2018.

Unger, Roberto M., *Knowledge and Politics*, New York: Free Press, 1976.

Viswanathan, Gauri, *Outside the Fold: Conversion, Modernity and Belief*, Princeton: Princeton University Press, 1998.

Xaxa, Virginius, "Women and Gender in the Study of Tribes in India", in Sumit Sarkar and Tanika Sarkar, eds, *Women and Social Reform in Modern India*, vol. 2, Ranikhet: Permanent Black, 2007.

Yang, Anand, "Whose Sati? Widow Burning in Early Nineteenth Century India", *Journal of Women's History*, vol. 1, no. 2, 1989.

3

Redesigning Gender
Reformers and the Orthodoxy

THE CHANGES WROUGHT by social reform – and resisted staunchly by the orthodox – emanated not only from women's sufferings and the desires which a few women began to articulate passionately from the late nineteenth century. They arose also out of a few men's weariness with their own past traditions of masculinity, conjugality, and domesticity, and their hopes of a very different life.

Being reformers rather than revolutionaries, these men and women did not attack all aspects of patriarchal gender, root and branch. They sought instead to initiate sectoral changes in specific areas: companionate marriage with educated wives being one, alongside love marriage, and security for the lives and livelihoods of vulnerable widows. Feminists have tended to criticise the modest scale of these aspirations. Some regard the limited changes as a ploy for new forms of male self-gratification rather than any genuine search for equality, and the reforms as a pale imitation of the Victorian model of domesticity.

Two arguments need to be clearly outlined in order to counter this blanket dismissal. First, in the context of their times, it is necessary to appreciate the overwhelming strength of the opposition that reformers faced. Even their limited ideas for social change were seen as outrageous and wholly unacceptable by society, family, and friends. Those who embraced even these small changes were disinherited, outcasted, isolated, and painfully confined within a tiny coterie of like-minded friends. Any evaluation of their projects therefore needs to be relative and context-specific, sensitive to the enormous social and religious power of the orthodoxy. We require a larger awareness of the ideological context these handful of reformers were embedded in and out of which they sought an exit – an exit which had to be incomplete and tentative given the sheer size and strength of the overarching ideological ecosystem.

Second, in a different reading, the reformist efforts may be called remarkably ambitious: reformers dreamt of fashioning not only a generation of "New Women" but also "New Men" – even if restricted as yet to their own class and caste. But, once begun, the process rolled on beyond their dreams and constituted the contradictory but real beginnings of future Indian feminism. Unless we acknowledge the historic importance of the seemingly small fractures and dents, we cannot account for feminism's emergence. So, while I have bent over backwards to show up the many limitations and failures of these early reform efforts, I have also tried to balance matters by arguing for their potential.

Changes in Tribal Culture

Early colonial ethnographers had assumed that tribes by definition existed in a timeless and self-contained world. Slowly, however, they began to register the processes of social transformation among these communities. Their drift towards Christianity as well as towards Hinduisation or "sanskritisation" – the emulation of "pure" caste habits – meant significant changes in their gender relations as they introduced early marriage for their daughters and prohibited widow remarriage. The Bhil women of Central India, for example, lost their freedom to choose their husbands. Their relative freedom in premarital sexual relations was also curtailed.

From the mid and late nineteenth century conversions to Christianity acted as catalysts for sweeping changes in the north-eastern regions. In some ways, conversions equalised the modes of church worship for women since some Protestant denominations appointed women as deacons, preachers, and trustees. They also became prominent in community work. Mission schools taught their students through the vernacular, which eased their reading and writing habits, and missionaries developed a vernacular script for the Nagas. In what is now the state of Mizoram, government-run schools had used Bengali – a foreign language for the Mizos – as the medium of instruction. Large numbers of students, including girls, therefore preferred the vernacular-medium mission schools. From the early twentieth century missionaries began to send Mizo girls for their higher or vocational education to Shillong or Calcutta, and many of these young women trained for nursing courses.

But conversion also spelt major breaks with earlier cultural worlds, along with the loss of some former freedoms, rituals, and festivals. Missionaries frowned on divorce, for instance, and on premarital intimacy. They also dictated that male and female bodies be firmly gendered by sex-differentiated dress codes. Both sexes were advised to cover themselves fully and stop wearing their hair long. In an interesting contrast, while men took to European dress, women became the chosen bearers of a sanitised ethnic costume which supposedly preserved some elements of the traditional Mizo colours and patterns (*puncheri*). Photographic evidence from the 1890s reveals that Mizo girls took to wearing the sari if they were educated outside Mizoram.

Mizo church services acquired an interesting blend of traditional and Christian cultural elements and Mizos selectively and creatively appropriated aspects of Western culture. A documentary film by Pankaj Butalia entitled *When Hamlet Comes to Mizoram* (1990) reveals a tradition of multiple annual enactments of *Hamlet* in which, typically, Mizo notions of masculinity, filial piety, and a vengeful defence of family honour blend easily within a Shakespearean idiom. Shillong, the capital of Meghalaya, celebrates an annual musical festival dedicated to Bob Dylan. Recently, the city initiated Gay Pride festivals, one of them led by a church pastor.

Between 1876 and 1955 about sixty American Baptist missionaries, including a few women, and hundreds of local evangelists set up churches in what is now the state of Nagaland. They harvested large-scale conversions. These missionaries entertained a certain degree of approval for the "manliness" of warlike Naga men, combined, though, with a stern stigmatisation of Naga head-hunting practices, scanty clothing, supposedly lax sexual norms, and lack of formal modern education. Extensive mission-led social engineering included the setting up of Sunday schools, as also mission schools that focused primarily on Bible teaching and preaching. There was a great emphasis on personal hygiene, sanitation, modest clothing, and deportment to supplant the earlier warlike masculinity and a relatively mobile and confident Naga femininity.

The British had granted *sanad*s (charters; warrants) to the conquered hill states in the western Himalaya region in 1815–16. These included social provisos such as those prohibiting widow immolation and female infanticide, which had been common among the local Rajput and Hinduised royal lineages. But the British did little to enforce these provisos. Nor did the Baptist Mission at Simla try particularly hard to change traditional marriage practices among the agricultural Khash-Kanet communities.

A rather distinctive form of tribal group marriage had long prevailed in the western Himalaya. Several brothers married a single woman and all the husbands were collectively designated fathers of her children. Marriages were easy to break and weddings happened without religious ceremonies. Divorced women remarried under this *reet* system, as it was called, and their new grooms transferred the bride price to the women's natal families.

From the early twentieth century these customs began to invite strong censure from high-caste Hindus who alleged that plainsmen were enticing hill women in order to sell them into prostitution; also that parents encouraged their daughters to repeatedly dissolve their marriage tie to procure themselves a bride price several times over. In 1924 an association of these high-caste Hindus, the Himalaya Vidiya Parbandhani Sabha, petitioned British officials to block such practices. It also appealed to the wives of these officials to persuade their husbands against what they believed was a social malpractice. Protracted triangular discussions followed between the British, the rulers of the native states, and Hindu politicians. Some rulers legally modified aspects of the marriage form, and in some cases group marriages survived by adopting a Hindu ceremonial. The British, however, felt that the Hindu alternative of an indissoluble child marriage was harsher for hill women than the *reet* system. Eventually, a compromise divorce law allowed the dissolution of marriages, but under stringent conditions.

As the twentieth century progressed, customary norms became progressively redundant with tribal land and forests falling under enclosures, dams, industries, and mining – processes hugely exacerbated in the post-colonial era. Massive evictions and dispossession, and radical changes in their environment, livelihood, and community ties forced tribal populations to migrate as cheap labour for factories, mines, and tea gardens. Sometimes they joined the mobile population of construction workers in cities. Their new lives as an urban precariat have not afforded them much access to better employment opportunities. Though cities have provided for girls' education from the early twentieth century, displaced tribal women are seldom able to access such education.

Hindu Reformers and the Orthodoxy

As always, social change proved a far more difficult enterprise than changing state laws. Liberal middle-class and upper-caste Hindu men had pioneered the early reforms and women joined their efforts somewhat later – though from the mid and late nineteenth centuries women's writing provided powerful ballast to reform projects. As they reordered inherited gender practices, reformers also modified, to an extent, conventional notions of masculinity and patriarchal privilege. Modern orthodox Hindus, on the other hand, became acutely aware of the values in which they were embedded, for these had rarely been challenged earlier. As they rallied to defend their norms, they too relied on a new discursive vocabulary and logic to appeal to middle-class opinion. Bhudeb Mukhopadhyay, a modern and highly educated Hindu intellectual from Bengal, for instance, aestheticised each and every aspect of orthodox conjugality and domesticity, bathing it all in a soothing shower of care, beauty, and love, and attributing "scientific" reason to every customary practice. Reformers and the orthodox both mobilised public opinion with modern communication and public-sphere resources: print, novels, polemical essays, the new public theatre, newspapers, and journals. Both founded associations and newspapers to publicise their views.

Liberal and orthodox Hindus were not, however, polar opposites in terms of their personnel and purposes. Radhakanta Deb of Calcutta, staunch defender of immolations and opponent of widow remarriage, encouraged girls' education. Both sides included traditional pandits as well as a modern intelligentsia, and both were high caste. The new intellectuals, whether orthodox or reformist, were equally well trained in the Sanskrit textual and religious traditions. Neither group was openly critical of colonialism. Vidyasagar's campaign for widow remarriage began in the year that a great Santhal rebellion raged nearby against colonial depredations. The reformers ignored the rebellion; it was as if reform and rebellion were happening on two different planets.

Rammohun Roy and Radhakanta Deb, despite the liberalism of the one and the conservatism of the other, represented a new and remarkable generation of polymaths. They were self-taught men, fluent in the classical Indian languages – Sanskrit, Arabic, and Persian – as well as in modern and classical European languages. The Parsis of western India, meanwhile, also played a significant role in the new educational and social-reform projects, not only in their own community but also in those affecting Hindu lives more generally.

This new intelligentsia moved into the modern professions of teaching, law, and journalism, and into the lower and middle rungs of the new bureaucratic and commercial offices, frequently combining work there with an income from landowning. Some from the Bombay Presidency owned mercantile and manufacturing enterprises. With rare exceptions, all came from an elite high-caste or *ashraf* background. Ishwar Chandra Vidyasagar (1820–1891) born in a poor rural Brahman family, profited from the new print capitalism and the publishing industry, and from the introduction of school textbooks, which he wrote copiously.

Perhaps the most remarkable social reformer of this century was Jotirao Phule (1827–1890) who alone reflected on the conjoint oppressions of caste, class, and gender. He attributed the overlapping systems of domination to the power of Brahmans. Born into the Shudra caste of gardeners (Malis), and educated at a Scottish missionary school, he was the foremost founder of Dalit movements in western India. Keenly interested in slavery abolition in the United States, he dedicated one of his books to the American abolitionists. His major work, *Gulamgiri* (1873, in Marathi), equated caste with slavery. Phule was also profoundly disturbed by the plight of peasants tricked and deprived of their dues by upper-caste landowners. In 1873 he founded the Satyashodhak Samaj for caste and gender reform and lent his support to many reformist campaigners who were not necessarily a part of his circle. His wife, Savitribai Phule (1831–1897), was in many ways the equal of her husband: she wrote poetry, campaigned vigorously against caste iniquity, and in 1848, alongside her husband, established at Bhidewada one of the earliest girls' schools. Some regard Savitribai as the first Indian woman teacher. No other Hindu social reformers of the nineteenth century led such a determinedly reformist conjugal life.

Self-confident and cosmopolitan – far more so than the generally insular European officials and missionaries – modern Indian liberals inhabited a vast cultural world, selectively combining

Western and Indian religious and intellectual traditions, and creating a distinctively new idiom for Indian modernity. Rammohun Roy faced massive notoriety for his monotheism, critique of idolatry and Hindu priesthood, and his unorthodox lifestyle – his enemies alleged he had fathered a son with a Muslim mistress. The Brahmo Sabha, founded by Roy in 1828 for socio-religious reform, was followed by similar groups in the Bombay Presidency. The Prarthana Samaj, founded in 1867 by Justice Madhav Govind Ranade (1842–1901), was equally committed to monotheism and gender reform. To advocate women's education and widow remarriage, Ranade gathered together intellectuals and educationists like Dadoba Pandurang, Balshastri Jambhekar, Gopal Ganesh Agarkar, Ramakrishna Gopal Bhandarkar, and Vishnushastri Pandit. A journalist, and later a judge and member of the Bombay Legislative Council, Ranade was excommunicated by the regional religious supremo, the Shankaracharya, for founding the Widow Remarriage Association in 1869. Such reformist associations repurposed the conventional forms of male sociability: patronising or hosting lavish public and private entertainment, displays of piety, and urban factional politics.

Ranade did have to make the occasional compromise. After his wife died his friends expected him to live up to his principles and marry a widow. Instead, bowing to family pressure, he married the eleven-year-old Ramabai, whom he later educated. Intense social pressure, moreover, forced him to boycott the wedding of his friend Vishnushastri Pandit who had married a widow. The Brahmo reformer Keshub Chandra Sen (1838–1884) married off his underage thirteen-year-old daughter into a royal family even while advocating adult marriage. Despite the pronounced anti-bigamy stance of the Brahmo Samaj, Shibnath Shastri (1847–1919), leader of the most liberal branch of the Brahmos, lived with two wives, to one of whom he had been married in his childhood and to the other after having chosen her as his partner in adulthood. A gulf is therefore often apparent between proclaimed values and personal practice, a testimony of the enormous difficulties involved in opposing orthodoxy. The struggle against social norms was in fact a burden so heavy to carry that many laid it down halfway on the journey.

Reformism took an audaciously rebellious turn in the 1830s and 1840s in Bengal when the very young and brilliant Eurasian teacher Henry Louis Vivian Derozio (1809–1831) taught an uncompromising form of rationalism to his Hindu College students in Calcutta, where he told them to question everything that offended their reason and their humanity. More dangerously, he asked them never to practice what they did not believe in. His group – the Derozians, or Young Bengal as they were called – pioneered the advocacy of women's education, widow remarriage, and love marriage. Several of Derozio's students discarded their sacred thread (the signifier of Brahman birth), openly feasted on forbidden beef as well as other such "polluted" food prepared by Muslims and Europeans, and refused to worship their family idols. Forced by his parents to bow down before the image of the goddess Kali, one of these students greeted the idol with "Good Morning, Madam".

This public and spectacular spurning of Brahmanical norms caused an uproar from the parents of several such students. The Hindu College authorities dismissed Derozio quite expeditiously because he also admired French Revolutionary ideals. Radhakanta Deb added homosexuality to the charges against the Derozians. This was a brief Bohemian moment in the reform movement. Ostracised by society and the state, some later returned to the unreformed Hindu fold, others drank themselves to death out of despair and frustration.

From 1840 Bombay's Paramahansa Mandali began to hold secret meetings to propagate widow remarriage, the abolition of idolatry, and, most unusually, caste. A furore broke out when a Gujarati journalist, Karsandas Mulji (1832–1871), exposed the sexual and financial corruption of the immensely powerful and wealthy leaders of the Vallabhacharya religious sect in his newspaper *Satyaprakash*. This developed into the sensational Maharaja libel case of 1861–2 which the sect leaders brought against Karsandas Mulji – who was able to prove his allegations and won the suit. But retaliation was swift and the Vallabhacharya maharajas made their opponent an outcaste.

A new order of masculinity was emerging: bold, irreverent, cosmopolitan, and keen on social change. The New Men were eager to find adult women companions within or beyond the marriage tie. Some earned a reputation for befriending prostitutes, some married adult widows. They wanted to educate their wives, even if it meant severing joint-family ties. In fact, reform for most began at home, before being taken into the public world. Dwarakanath Ganguly (1844–1898), a Bengali reformer who was as active in promoting widow remarriages as in exposing the abuse of Indian labourers by European tea planters in Assam, sent his graduate wife Kadambini Ganguly abroad for medical training. Returning, she built up a busy medical practice while he shared the child-rearing with her. His journal, *Abalabandhab* (1869), reported relentlessly on the atrocities that structured women's existence. David Kopf argues that this was the first journal in the world to devote itself solely to such a cause.

If some wives, such as Ramabai Ranade in Bombay, were coerced into education by their husbands, others like Kailashbashini Debi in Bengal were deeply grateful to their spouse for helping them to learn. Teaching the wife often happened in the deepest secrecy; if discovered, it led to family ostracism. An education secretly acquired became a new form of conjugal bedroom romance, hidden away from the unforgiving eyes of the larger world.

The fate of the Derozians, however, alerted later reformers to the risks of social isolation: taken too far, it would doom their efforts. Vidyasagar had initiated widow-remarriage campaigns, written extensively against child marriage, and as an Inspector of Schools founded several schools for girls. Yet he was careful to live the life of an orthodox Brahman and refused to be drawn into religious debates. In Bombay Ranade, Gopal Hari Deshmukh, Agarkar, and others advocated widow remarriage without overtly violating social norms in their own lives. So, yet another generation of New Men emerged mid century: sober, constructive, trying to persuade society and state about the moral necessity of change rather than indulging in the mockery and defiance that had characterised the Derozians.

In the Telugu-speaking area of Rajahmundry in the Madras Presidency, the poet-reformer Kandukuri Viresalingam Pantulu (1848–1919) started an association in the 1870s to promote widow remarriage. He too disengaged social activism from religious reform, which came late to the Madras Presidency. However, once it began it became an important counter to Hindu revivalism, which went viral across various locations in the late nineteenth century. The Madras Hindu Social Reform Association was set up in 1892 and remained active into the twentieth century even when liberal reformism had declined elsewhere. In 1891 the Madras Legislative Council initiated debates on the Gains of Learning Bill, an important effort to reduce the economic stranglehold of the Hindu joint family over its individual members. Men could now retain their personal income – earned because they were educated professional people. When the bill was enacted in 1900 it enraged the Hindu orthodoxy, which saw it as the end of joint-family-based patriarchal controls.

Widowhood

Social and familial cruelty knew no bounds when it came to disciplining widows – even infant ones. Much of the oppression came from scriptural directives. Hindu scripture had defined the wife as the *ardhangini* (half-body) of her husband, who was believed to live on within her even after his death. The marriage tie therefore supposedly continued even into widowhood, so that any subsequent relationship for a widow was tantamount to adultery. Widowed women followed a regime of harsh and continuous self-flagellation and self-deprivation involving the renunciation of all possible pleasure – sexual, dietary, sartorial, ritual. This applied to widows of all ages, even to infants widowed before their marriages had been consummated and who therefore barely knew their husbands.

Raghunandan, noted earlier as the sixteenth-century authority for the Dayabhaga legal tradition of eastern India, had made the ritual fortnightly Ekadasi fast – during which not a drop of water passed through the widow's lips – mandatory even for the infant or the dying widow: not even medicine could be consumed on that day. A large proportion of Bengali Hindu widows were little girls below ten. Their youth began with their sexuality blocked and every normal pleasure denied: they were condemned to lifelong vegetarianism, restrained from eating food considered sexually stimulating, and allowed to wear only stark white garments (maroon if they were Maharashtrian) without jewellery or other adornments. Considered ritually inauspicious, they were also excluded from all festivities. And yet, at the same time, the widow was a kind of no-man's land, exposed to secret sexual exploitation within the family. If illicit desire involving her came to light, the woman was thrown out of her home while the man went unpunished. In one instance, such a pregnant widow was thrown out of her natal home when her pregnancy was discovered. Living alone with no support, she returned to seek help from the family when childbirth was imminent. Her relatives shut the door on her face. She was found dead the next day, bathed in her own blood, her dead baby beside her, next to her home.

Eighteenth-century Peshwa rulers in western India had issued a formidable set of injunctions on the conduct of Brahman widows. A sacred text of 1735, *Yadi Dharmasthapana,* mandated that the widow be tonsured and allowed only one piece of dark maroon cloth to wear. The tonsure carried great symbolic weight – families which refused to observe it were excommunicated. We hear of a man named Malharpant who would not let his sister face the cruel defacement. He was ordered by the head of the premier regional monastic order not to marry until he had complied. When he continued recalcitrant, he was excommunicated. A father, similarly, was excommunicated for refusing to tonsure his daughter.

On the other hand, to ensure the stable production and reproduction of the labour force, the Peshwas allowed agricultural castes like the Kunbis and Marathas to practice a form of remarriage called *pat*, entered into after paying a monetary fine by the woman's family as well as the loss of certain entitlements to property and over children. Shudra castes in Gujarat could also remarry under an inferior version of marriage – the Nara – as a mark of their caste inferiority.

When reformers – invariably upper-caste men – campaigned for remarriage, they did not know that such marriages were common practice for many "lower" castes. Their ignorance could have been a function of their own high-caste distance from ordinary lives, as well as a result of the fact that prohibition was fast becoming commonplace among the aspiring "lower" castes too. A legend goes that Shudra weavers embroidered verses of praise for Vidyasagar into the saris they wove. Though they were not covered by Brahmanical prohibitions, they had obviously suffered from them and therefore appreciated Vidyasagar's efforts.

Ranajit Guha wrote a remarkable article, "Chandra's Death", about a nineteenth-century untouchable widow impregnated by a male relative. Even though polygamy was widely practised and widow marriages common in her caste, it seems that Chandra's family chose to ignore these options and made her go through a highly risky abortion instead, involving the use of local drugs. Chandra died in horrible pain.

Several Bombay organisations came together to found a joint platform in 1862, as also a journal, *Induprakash,* to campaign for remarriage. In 1865 Vidyasagar's Bengali tract on remarriage was translated into Marathi. There was a public debate at Poona over the issue and the conservatives founded their own organisation, the Hindu Dharma Vyavasthapak Sabha. The Shankaracharya (head of the Karvir monastic sect) presided and the reformers suffered a crushing defeat. This revealed their very limited support base, as the powerful endorsements for the old controls continued to rule. The orthodoxy now resanctified ritual penances against supporters of remarriage. In the ensuing furore the "lower" castes, including the Dalits (the untouchable castes), moved closer to the prohibition than ever before. Even as the reforms spread, the backlash against them gathered greater power.

Vidyasagar tried to disarm the orthodoxy by using their own terms of good and bad conduct. He pointed out the harm that the prohibition did to orthodox morality: secret liaisons, foeticides, infanticides when widows became pregnant in illicit relationships. But he also often and passionately stepped beyond his brief:

> You think their bodies turn to stone as soon as they are widowed . . . that they become immune to desire alas, in this land men have no compassion, no virtue, they do not know what is right and what is wrong they only know what is custom Let no woman be born in such a land any more. Alas our women, for what sin in your past births are you sent to be born in Bharatbarsha?[1]

His query forced out into the open what had been kept implicit: that the rules were different for men and women, and for no obvious reason; and that women have desires which may survive widowhood. Once raised, the issue resounded in the writings of reformers across the country.

Dhondo Keshav Karve (or Maharshi Karve, 1858–1962) married an adult widow who had been the first inmate of Sharada Sadan, an institution he had established to educate young Hindu widows in Bombay. This was a daring act as most remarriages were happening with virginal child widows. Karve revived the Poona Widow Remarriage Association with the help of Vishnushastri Pandit and

---

[1] See Vidyasagar, *Bidhababibaha*.

R.G. Bhandarkar. The orthodoxy led a virulent campaign against his marriage, but, somewhat unexpectedly, Tilak endorsed it since as a ritual it had observed all the orthodox rites – laying bare a fascinating ambivalence because, according to the orthodox, no widow could remarry in the first place. Karve and his wife set up the Anaath Balikashram in 1896, an institution to help and educate indigent widows. Though the ashram itself was separate from his work for widow remarriage, predictably it came to be tarred with the same brush: the orthodoxy alleged that it made unsuspecting inmates go through a second marriage.

Behramji Malabari, the Parsi poet-reformer whom we have seen before and who was much inspired by Christian doctrines, had been complaining from the 1880s that reformers had not gone very far. He had an excellent rapport with British reformers like Mary Carpenter, who was working for prison and educational changes in England and India. Malabari's *Notes on Enforced Widowhood* (1884) asked the government to ensure all widows receive information about the remarriage law, prevent the ostracism of widows who had remarried, and stop the "ill usage" of widows. Most importantly, he asked the state to form a national association for reform since his and K. Natarajan's journals – *Indian Spectator* and *Indian Social Reformer*, respectively – were already working towards that end. The government's response was less than lukewarm: "For one convert that Mr. Malabari may make, at the cost of much social obloquy, among the highly educated classes, Hinduism sweeps whole tribes into its net."[2] Having enacted the remarriage law and faced enormous Hindu opprobrium, it was not keen to invite further trouble.

If liberal ideas grew in strength till the mid nineteenth century, orthodoxy began to enjoy significantly greater ascendancy in its later part. Conservatism aligned or gradually merged with cul-

---

[2] Public Proceedings, November 1886, nos 131–138E, p. 28, Home Department, Government of India, National Archives of India.

tural nationalism, more commonly known as Hindu revivalism. The orthodoxy had earlier sought to block all intervention in the Hindu socio-religio-ritual status quo, while revivalist cultural nationalism now involved an emphatic rejection of modern, Western, or Christianity-derived value. A resounding and triumphalist declaration of the superior glories of Brahmanical civilisation, especially of its marriage rules, was what this amounted to. Their defence of customary and scriptural gender injunctions in the face of reformist ideas and against Western liberal values became particularly pronounced in the Bombay and Bengal presidencies, which had previously been the seedbeds of liberalism.

A curious development was the emergence of social-reform organisations among Marwari entrepreneurs notorious, perhaps unfairly, for their orthodoxy even today. Originally located in Rajasthan and Gujarat, the Marwaris had fanned out all over the country from early modern times to form large interconnected business enterprises that flourished and diversified. While their Bombay association was relatively more open to proposals for education and a slightly higher age of marriage without disturbing the principles of the Hindu Undivided Family, the Calcutta Marwari Association was markedly more conservative. Established in 1898, it invested in education for young men alone. It was opposed to widow remarriage and to raising the age of consent within marriage. At the same time, Gandhi's close association with the prominent Marwari tycoon G.D. Birla ensured that large numbers of Marwari women were drawn into nationalist fund-raising, khadi programmes (preparing homespun clothing), and even protest demonstrations. Inspired by visions of a modern progressive nation of the future, the Marwari nationalist Sitaram Seksaria founded girls' schools and campaigned for widow remarriage at the cost of his stern ostracism by fellow Marwaris. His wife was imprisoned during the anti-colonial Civil Disobedience movements of 1930–2, this being quite scandalous in a community which faithfully observed the stringent rules of seclusion.

Anti-colonial nationalism therefore opened up a few possibilities for rethinking gender.

Rebellious Women

From the mid nineteenth century a few women began to write angry polemical tracts about the Hindu household, while a smaller number defended conservative norms. Kailashbashini Debi, a Bengali woman, bitterly denounced the Hindu household in the 1860s as a place of danger for women, as a cruel tiger-infested forest. In 1881 Vijaylakshmi, a young Brahman widow, was prosecuted at a Surat court for killing her illegitimate child. Responding to this Tarabai Shinde, an educated woman from a well-known Maratha family – her father was active in anti-Brahman politics – wrote a remarkable critique of Hindu marriage titled *Stri-Purusha Tulana*. Later translated as *A Comparison Between Women and Men*, it was also the first published text by a woman in western India. Tarabai Shinde observed that the prohibition of widow remarriage was rapidly spreading among jatis which used to practise remarriage. Much like Jotirao Phule, she saw infanticide as the unavoidable result of prohibiting widow remarriage. She thus transferred the blame from the woman forced to kill her illegitimate child to the social system which had left her no option. She also questioned the notion of the *pativrata* (the chaste wife).

She was an outspoken interlocutor of sexual double standards, an issue which few male reformers openly addressed. Deploying an abrasive tone when providing everyday examples of familial cruelty towards widows, her shrillness was quite deliberately different from that of male reformist voices. Also, unlike most male reformers who tried to bend scriptures to reflect the interests of reform, she took the scriptures to task and made fun of women in the Hindu epics: "All your big talk – you make it all up on the basis of the sastras. But in fact the people who write all these books ought to be ashamed of themselves."[3]

[3] O'Hanlon, ed., *A Comparison Between Women and Men*, pp. 3–6.

Scores of Bombay women had been attending reformist lectures from the 1870s, and in the next decade they formed the Striyancha Sabha, their own weekly association for self-education. Soon this spread to other cities in the presidency. Women learnt about Indian and Western philosophy from Kashibai Kanitkar, Rakhmabai, Anandibai Joshi, and Ramabai Ranade. They also read J.S. Mill's *On the Subjection of Women* and turned traditional ritual occasions, such as the *haldi kumkum* (turmeric and vermilion marks to signify wedded bliss) into group discussions about social and educational issues.

A crop of Bengali women graduates, teachers, doctors, and nurses had emerged by the 1880s. They were remarkable public figures and achievers whose success inspired many others but they were not themselves particularly active in reformist campaigns, serving indirectly as exemplars. In contrast, Bombay's women reformers were the first unabashed Indian feminists to mount an open rebellion against social injunctions. Rakhmabai (1864–1955) offers a most remarkable case in point as her life conjoins gender, caste, and class issues. She belonged to the lowly carpenter or Suthar caste which permitted widow remarriages. When her widowed mother married her stepfather, she passed on the property inherited from her first husband to her daughter. Her liberal stepfather educated her at home and introduced her to the leading reformers of the day, one of them being Vishnushastri Pandit. Rakhmabai therefore had quite exceptional educational and familial resources. But her greatest asset was her own unbending determination, courage, and formidable powers of articulation.

Married off at eleven to a man who turned out to be dissolute and diseased, Rakhmabai firmly refused to live with Dadaji Bhikaji. In 1884 he insisted on his conjugal rights under the Restitution of Conjugal Rights Act of 1877. Several court cases were fought over the next four years, and when the judges asked her to choose between freedom from her husband and imprisonment under the terms of the Act, she was ready to choose imprisonment. Eventually the husband was bought off with a hefty sum of money.

In the meantime, in a powerful series of letters written under the pseudonym "A Hindu Lady" in the *Times of India*, Rakhmabai proved herself to be not only a resolute rebel but also an accomplished polemicist, challenging social conventions with sharp arguments about gender abuses in Hindu society, as well as with impassioned pleas against child marriage, widowhood, illiteracy, and domestic cruelty. She scandalised Tilak and her court cases gained enormous notoriety. Rakhmabai's defence was partly built on the argument that her husband was financially unable to maintain her. It challenged the entrenched belief in the Hindu wife's non-negotiable duties towards a husband who, of course, had no mandatory reciprocal responsibility towards her.

Women's petitions and reformist agitations eventually saved her from the prison sentence and the government now tried to gather opinion from Indian judges about amending Section 260 of Article 14 of the Code of Civil Procedure of 1882. It was for the first time that a lone woman's action had initiated a process of social and legal change. Much reported and hotly debated, the cases revealed the extent of women's defiance of an accelerating social conservatism. The agitation unified Hindu, Christian, and Jewish Indian women as well as English feminists. Rakhmabai later trained as a doctor abroad, became India's first woman doctor, and continued to campaign against Hindu domestic practices.

A spectacular blow to orthodoxy was delivered by Pandita Ramabai (1858–1922), another Maharashtrian woman, born into a Chitpavan Brahman family. Her father taught Sanskrit to his wife and daughter though women were banned from learning the "language of the gods". He founded an ashram where his wife taught Sanskrit to young boys, again in defiance of convention. The family, however, spent much of their time going on endless pilgrimages which sapped their income and led to great poverty, and then to the death of the parents – Ramabai later recalled the waste in searingly scathing terms in one of her last writings, *A Testimony of Our Inexhaustible Treasure* (1907).

Left an orphan and living in the most acute poverty imaginable, Ramabai moved to Calcutta, then a hub of reformism. She had knowledge of Sanskrit as her only capital, which made her famous. She met Keshub Chandra Sen who advised her to read the holy Sanskrit Vedas. Though women were traditionally excluded from this privilege, by this time, clearly, even the orthodox needed to display some degree of concern for women. So not only did they applaud her, they also bestowed on her the title "Pandita".

Ramabai began to go systematically through the scriptures when she was invited to speak about ancient women. This was a time when Hindus were generally scouring their scriptures and history to discover women luminaries in ancient India. Their hopes of unearthing such exemplars boomeranged; as she read the texts, Ramabai became convinced that the real source of women's subordination was in fact the holy Hindu scriptures:

> there were two things on which the Dharmashastras, the Puranas, and modern poets, the popular preachers of high and low caste and orthodox high caste ones, were agreed, that women as a class were all bad, worse than demons. The only hope of their getting liberation was the worship of their husbands. The husband is said to be the woman's god: there is no other god for her. This god may be the worst sinner and a great criminal: still he is her god and she must worship him . . .[4]

Ramabai married a Shudra man in a *pratiloma* (hypogamous marriage), this variety of marriage being profoundly repugnant to Hindus. Soon left a widow with a baby daughter to bring up by herself, she was cruelly excoriated by an outraged Hindu society for her late and unorthodox marriage – she had married at what was then the advanced age of twenty-two under the new Civil Marriages Act – and for her public activism. In the 1880s she founded the Arya Mahila Sabha at Poona to agitate for

---

[4] Ramabai, *A Testimony of Our Inexhaustible Treasure*, pp. 10–11.

women's education and began to plan a home for widows. At first, M.G. Ranade and R.G. Bhandarkar stood by her. But her outspoken criticism of Brahmanical gender led to such a public outcry that Ranade's wife Ramabai found it difficult to befriend her namesake.

Pandita Ramabai turned towards Christianity, seeing in Christ a compassionate saviour of women. Missionaries from the Church of England arranged for her travel to England – at first to study medicine, later to train as a teacher. She was converted by the Sisters of the Wantage Mission (near Oxford), but, when she developed her own individual interpretation of Christianity, they were deeply offended.

Ramabai stuck to her lonely path. She left for the United States and gradually developed close ties with secular feminists and anti-slavery activists like Harriet Tubman, who helped her to set up the American Ramabai Association. The Association developed a number of branches, almost competing with the global following of Swami Vivekananda (1863–1902) who, in sharp contrast, had glorified all aspects of Hinduism as immeasurably superior to anything that the West had to offer.[5]

Ramabai was a close and interested observer of American politics and society and found much to praise there – its widespread levels of literacy even among the labouring classes, its democratic institutions, its social energies. But she also noted that even though American women were freer than women in India, they were by no means the equals of men. She was horrified by the Mormons and found them far more dangerous than the most obnoxious of fraudulent Hindu gurus.

Travel abroad was a difficult and complex enterprise for these early women activists, a lonely and often misunderstood experience even if a space of freedom. When Ramabai returned to India

[5] Vivekananda was at this time *the* icon of a new generation of religious ascetics committed to organised philanthropy and educational work on Hindu missionary lines.

and set up the Sharada Sadan home for widows in Bombay in 1889 – later it moved to Poona – she admitted widows of all castes. They lived together but could practice their separate caste customs if they so wished. Later she founded the Mukti Sadan with the same intention. Her conversion to Christianity, however, had made her a dangerous figure to associate with, even for liberals, and the ashrams had to endure much public calumny.

Ramabai's approach to widowhood reforms was distinctly different from that of male reformers, who had focused single-mindedly on remarriage. In her *High Caste Hindu Woman* (1888) she spoke instead of the disciplinary regimen of widowhood, especially compulsory tonsure, with rage and passion. She provided vocational training to widows to enable them to be financially self-reliant. She suggested a remarkable series of possibilities to the Hunter Commission of 1882, which had been sent out to investigate possible improvements to Indian education. She spoke out on the need to facilitate women's professional and economic empowerment; an indirect offshoot of her insistence on women's medical training was that it influenced Lady Dufferin, who formed the Lady Dufferin Fund, aiming to enhance healthcare for Indian women. In a quite stunning challenge to social conventions, Ramabai also set up a home for prostitutes at Kedgaon.

Though she went much beyond remarriage campaigns, she also supported Godubai, a widowed student who married Maharshi Karve. The Mukti Sadan imparted an entirely non-denominational education and Ramabai never tried to convert its inmates. The institution was nevertheless portrayed as a ploy for converting Hindu widows to Christianity, especially after a few of its residents had converted. Hostile conservative public opinion saw her ashrams as a conspiracy to separate widows from their families, sap family ties, and create a breeding ground for disobedient women. Tempers ran so high that even liberals like Ranade and Bhandarkar resigned from the board of the Mukti Sadan, thus clearing a space for Maharshi Karve's Widows' Home which admitted only

Brahman widows. The state too turned against her when she alleged that, in the name of segregating them from their plague-stricken families, the government's 1897 plague control measures had put women in danger of abduction. Jotirao Phule stood as Ramabai's lone defender.

Ramabai was the most publicised woman of her times and the most wildly denounced. She died in 1922, a lonely and tragic figure who had lost her only daughter and who, at the end of her life, was left with very few friends.

Travels to Western lands opened up new horizons for Parvati Athavale (1870–1955), a young Brahman widow who found some release from her doomed existence when she joined Dr Karve's Widows' Home and later became his close associate. She went to the United States to raise funds but had a difficult time on account of her Brahmanical dietary and clothing inhibitions, as also her lack of personal resources – which made her seek employment at various institutions. When an upper-caste Bengali said he was aghast at a Brahman widow working for other people for money, she proudly invoked her self-reliance and independence. On the other hand she argued with the missionaries she worked with when they chastised her Hindu beliefs.

Women's associations, homes for widows and destitute women, travel across the seas to observe cultural-religious differences, and above all personal rebellion against hegemonic social expectations – these were some of the end-century sites for activism. Sometimes men and women worked together, but all too often women had to struggle on their own against the most tremendous odds.

Educating Women

Even though we associate women's education with schooling, the bulk of women were actually educated at home until the late nineteenth century, either by supportive male relatives, usually husbands, or natal guardians if they came from liberal families that arranged the marriages of their daughters somewhat later in life. A few such women taught themselves to read and write.

Baptist missionaries had formed the Calcutta Female Juvenile Society in 1819, and in 1821 the School Book Society brought Mary Ann Cooke – the first single female missionary sent from England to India – to Calcutta to help educate women. The Church Missionary Society helped with funds and Cooke opened thirty mission schools. Upper-caste families feared these institutions as instruments for conversion, and the missionaries were dismayed to find that only "low-caste" girls attended their schools – they had hoped to convert influential elite families as spearheads for the spread of Christianity. They were more successful in the Madras Presidency, where they founded the first Indian boarding school for girls as early as 1821 at Tirunelveli. Many more followed later. Most students, however, came from Christian families.

J.F. Drinkwater Bethune, Law Member in the Governor General's Council, founded the Hindu Balika Vidyalaya, subsequently renamed Bethune School, in Calcutta in 1849; later, Vidyasagar took it over. Even though prominent families like the Tagores of Jorasanko sent their daughters to it, the school faced cruel lampooning and its bus was attacked on the streets. The orthodox press alleged the place was breeding immorality despite the fact that just one elderly man and some women were the only teachers in the school. Possibly, formal schooling was regarded as an even more dangerous activity than informal systems of education. It took girls away from their homes, gave them an extra-familial identity, and a peer group unconnected with kin circles. The journey to school also meant girls had to travel along public roads which they had not hitherto navigated without a posse of male guardians. At school they were called by their proper names which, too, was a novelty and a route to acquiring an individual identity.

As these schools soldiered on despite the conservative attacks on them, more parents gradually lost some of their apprehensions and educated daughters came to enjoy some value in the marriage market. The change, however, happened within strict limits. Sooner or later, early marriages smashed the brief moment of freedom, leaving only nostalgic memories of schooldays as a distant and fading dream for housewives.

Vidyasagar founded several girls' schools in rural areas, but, since the government was extremely parsimonious, most of his institutions had to survive by private donations. Even if limpingly, these schools grew in number and the circle of their acceptance widened. By the late 1850s there were 626 girls' schools in India, Bengal leading with 288 and Madras not far behind with 256. The conservative Mahakali Pathshala of Calcutta taught ritual and domestic chores to its students. Ironically, its girls were now learning even their homemaking skills at the school, these having in the past been transmitted to them by the older women at home. Clearly, a school degree had become a social ornament which worked as an asset in the marriage market.

In Punjab and the western United Provinces of northern India Swami Dayanand, after meeting modernist religious gurus like Keshub Chandra Sen in Calcutta, founded a new order in 1875, the Arya Samaj. This came to wield enormous influence among large sections of the region's Hindus. An ascetic of the old school, Dayanand's peregrinations across Hindu pilgrimage sites had sickened him because of their rank corruption. Elaborate and pointless ritualism and the innumerable sectarian divisions that besieged Hindus had made him turn away from conventional forms of worship to seek a more rational form of faith. This he found only in the Vedas, and consequently he abjured all other sacred texts. He tried to simplify and rationalise marriage and mourning rituals, opposed child marriage, and advocated widow remarriage – even if along the very idiosyncratic reproductive principles outlined earlier. Dayanand's doctrines and social enterprises brought him into bitter conflict with conservative Hindus who now called themselves Sanatanis, or traditional Hindus. In order to counter the influence of Christian missionaries and prevent conversions to Islam – he hated both – he initiated several organisations which proliferated after his death.

His followers formulated two different kinds of schools for men: *gurukuls*, which provided Sanskrit and religious training only to boys, who were restricted to a strictly disciplined hostel life. The other, a more modernising effort, combined Arya Samajist religious education with curricula largely applied in "Dayanand Anglo-Vedic" (or DAV) schools and colleges. These were so successful and widespread that, all over Punjab and western UP, they became the dominant platform for male education at all levels, reaching much beyond Arya families.

Both varieties of schools initially neglected education for girls. The first girls' school, a *kanya gurukul*, was founded as late as 1936 and followed the more orthodox version of schooling – women's education was, at this point at any rate, restricted to the safe old limits.

Dalit Social Reforms

"Dalit", a word denoting the oppressed (lit. trampled), became the preferred self-description of untouchable castes. Dalit activists formulated the most far-reaching critique of Brahmanical gender. As we saw earlier, the work of Jotirao and Savitribai Phule had begun a tradition of social reform which far exceeded the relatively narrow scope of upper-caste male reformism.

In the twentieth century a remarkable social movement was initiated in the Tamil-speaking parts of the Madras Presidency by E.V. Ramasamy Naicker (1879–1973), popularly known as Periyar (Great Soul). He developed a theory of an egalitarian Dravidian civilisation in the Tamil South which, he said, was racially, culturally, and morally superior to the Aryan and caste-ridden society of North India. Periyar argued that an act of conquest – anterior to British imperialism, and far deadlier – had imposed North Indian caste values and social norms on the Dravidian South. He excoriated

Hindu sacred texts, publicly burnt them, and struggled to free the Tamil language and literature from Sanskrit and Hindi intrusions. Formerly a Congress nationalist, he later opposed Congress as a threat to Tamil distinctiveness and to the Dalits. After Independence his party advocated secession from the Indian Union. An atheist, he was deeply influenced by socialist ideology and founded the Self Respect Movement (Suyamariyathai Iyakkam) in 1925. In 1928 he said: "I have gradually lost faith in social reform. For one who believes in radical change, self respect, equality and progress, the alternative is not mere reform: but radical reconstructive work which would destroy the traditional structures . . ."[6] Most daringly, he advocated marriages that could be dissolved at will and which would be registered as a civic, not a religious, act. He improvised a new marriage rite without religious baggage or sanction and based on perfect mutual equality in all walks of life, public and private. He advocated the woman's right to education, employment, economic independence; and family planning as an escape from unwanted pregnancies. He attacked the very institution of marriage as a conspiracy foisted by patriarchal design to ensure women's subordination. He was particularly harsh on female chastity norms, which he saw as unnatural and a ploy to subjugate women. Most remarkably, he criticised himself as well as his comrades for not fully practising what they preached. Alongside women activists in his movement, he campaigned against the tradition of temple dancers (*devadasi*s), these being young girls who, renouncing family and normal girlhood, were tied for life to "serve" God and temple priests.

Periyar's marriage rites outraged Hindu society, as did the widow remarriages he presided over. Between 1929 and 1932 about eight thousand Self Respect marriages were performed, far exceeding the modest scope of earlier reformism. Women were remarkably vocal in Self Respect conferences and every major conference

---

[6] Speech reported in the Tamil weekly *Kudi Arasu*, 26 November 1928.

was accompanied with a parallel women's conference allowing the development of political skills and voices independently of those of men. Ramamirtham Ammaiyar, Narayani Ammaiyar, Thamaraikanni Ammaiyar, and Munnagara Azhagiyar were especially active in anti-Hindi campaigns between 1937 and 1940. Some of the activists came from a *devadasi* background, and some women even criticised their leader in public. After Periyar's death, however, the movement gradually lost its momentum and dynamism.

Finally, as regards the tallest of India's Dalit leaders, the reformer-intellectual B.R. Ambedkar, I will reserve discussion of the post-Independence legal changes he sought for later and at this point say only that his writings theorised the connection between caste and gender as well as the tyranny of Brahmanical custom and scripture over women. His *Riddles in Hinduism* (1955) also exposed the misogynist values upheld in sacred literature.

Christian Reforms

As early as the 1820s British Protestant missionaries realised that European missionary women must work with Indian women converts to ease and enhance proselytisation if Christianity was to be taken into Indian homes. Several associations were formed to train missionary wives in India for the purpose, as well as single Englishwomen who were interested in mission work in England. This opened up uncharted frontiers in public work for British women: "Wherever there was a missionary wife, a school for girls was established."[7] In 1834 a Society for the Propagation of Female Education in the East began to fund the travels of single women teachers, and for mission wives who wanted to open schools. By 1847 as many as fifty unmarried women were sent to India, Africa, South East Asia, and other countries. Efforts to convert the upper castes proving rather futile, mission schools in India opened their

[7] Haggis, "White Women and Colonialism", p. 52.

doors to subaltern girls. In the 1860s, however, they hit upon the idea of zenana visits to teach high-caste elite women at home, and, through them gain a toehold in the larger family. These attempts did make some headway.

As they began to win more and more converts among the low castes, and their workload increased, they also felt a growing need for more women within their ranks. In 1875 the London Missionary Society decided to recruit prominent women from their congregations. Women missionaries now received a salary and entered the ranks of professionally occupied women, which was something rather rare in Victorian times. The demand for more personnel, however, had to be eventually met by Indian Christian women, most of them from the "low" castes. Such workers were not recognised as full-fledged missionaries and were called Bible women. In South India they were actually as qualified as European missionaries but were never given that designation. Indian Christian women were therefore doubly marginalised – by Indian cultural nationalism which branded them as outcastes and by European missionary agencies that denied them a fair status. They were treated as the recipients of Western benevolence and good deeds rather than as autonomous agents with a clear religious and social perspective – as were high-caste Indian Christian women like Pandita Ramabai, the writer Krupabai Satthianadhan, and Soonderbai Hannah Powar, among others.

In the 1820s the Scottish Board and the Church Missionary Society opened branches in Bombay, and an American Board was set up at Ahmednagar. These gained some early converts from influential Parsi and Brahman families. Educated Hindus sometimes sent their children, including daughters, to their mission schools, which were reputed for excellent standards of teaching. In the 1890s the American Board, the Free Church of Scotland, and the Church Missionary Society, already firmly established in Bombay and Poona, began to spread out to the smaller towns. Early women converts were the wives, mothers, or sisters of well-to-do male converts.

These women were not passive followers of their men – who had mostly been excommunicated by their community and family for converting. Some women willingly abandoned the safer option of staying back with the larger family, even though they understood the price that would have to be paid. Ganderbai Powar, incarcerated by her family when she tried to convert, went to court to plead that she wanted to join her Christian husband. Parental pressure forced Anandibai Bhagat, another convert, to suicide. For some, the husband's conversion opened up new possibilities. For others, like Ramabai and Krupabai, the decision came from their own observation of the conditions of Hindu women – Krupabai wrote two novels illustrating this.

In Punjab "low-caste" and Dalit women were sometimes employed by missionaries to preach from the Bible. They composed their own devotional songs and proved far more adept at reaching mission messages to subaltern women than did missionaries who knew little of the "lower-caste" dialects. Some did not convert at all but lived with their converted husbands, though they dined separately. Some continued to observe Hindu rituals and caste practices even after conversion.

Muslim Reformers

Islamic religious discourses conventionally defined the domestic space as *zaif* – the abode of the weak and the irrational, of slaves, youths, and women who needed constant surveillance. The master of the household was warned against long absences from home lest it collapse into disorder (*fitna*). The *zaif*, moreover, was eroticised space, and the woman, thought to be akin to a living sexual organ, had to be hidden from the male gaze. Even her voice could tempt and corrupt men. The moral stigma associated with Muslim women stood in interesting contrast to the range of rights that Islamic scripture allotted them.

Comprising different schools of the ulama and the modern intelligentsia, late-nineteenth-century Muslim reformers show an uneasy mix – their conventional misogynistic stereotyping existing side by side with notions of female perfectibility on strictly Islamic lines, as well as an acknowledgement that women should be educated even on modern lines: "Women became symbolic, not only of all that was wrong with cultural and religious life but also of all that was worth preserving."[8] Men as diverse as Sir Syed Ahmad Khan from Aligarh, Maulana Ashraf Ali Thanawi from Deoband, and Mumtaz Ali from Lahore were the chief proponents of women's education, though their methods and purposes varied enormously. All blamed domestic custom for distorting the true faith and all saw women as the primary vectors of distortion. Some feared that women, even their speech (*begumati zubaan*), had been contaminated by centuries of proximity with the Hindus, and that this had been responsible for the decline of Muslim power in India. Almost all agreed that men must lead the reforms, which must flow from pristine Islam and not from corrupting Western modernity.

But how to educate elite women who lived in strict seclusion? There were women *ustani*s (teachers) who visited homes to teach women how to read the Quran in Arabic, but they read the text uncomprehendingly since they did not understand Arabic – they merely learned the script. Conservative reformers now planned to make better Muslim women out of them by providing a genuine comprehension of what Islam stood for. They began to write educational books for women's consumption which carried a heavy load of moral and religious content. A robust Urdu print culture had developed from the early nineteenth century and a tradition of Urdu pedagogical fiction began to develop in the later decades of the century to cater to North Indian Muslim women, Urdu being their spoken language. Tracts, novels, and essays encouraged women to shift away from their supposedly lazy, wasteful, self-indulgent domesticity to a disciplined, educated, and spiritual female personality. The ulama hoped that these

---

[8] Minault, "Women, Legal Reform and Muslim Identity", p. 140.

novels would wean women away from cheap and supposedly immoral Urdu romances. Christian missionaries had begun to set up zenana schools from the 1860s, and this perhaps spurred Muslim reformers into vigorous countermeasures.

In 1868 a government notification from Allahabad declared five prizes of Rs 1000 each for suitable vernacular (Hindi and Urdu) books in any branch of science or literature: "Books suitable for the women of India will be especially acceptable and well rewarded."[9] A flurry of Urdu didactic fiction appeared in the wake of this lure, of which Nazir Ahmad's *Mir'at al Arus* (1869) not only won the prize but became something of a blockbuster. It is used as a textbook in many Urdu schools even today and regularly gifted to new brides. An English translation of it, *The Bride's Mirror*, was published in 1884 and a Bengali adaptation was published from Assam in the late nineteenth century.

Originally composed for his daughter in the form of a dialogue between two sisters – one educated, the other lazy, ignorant, and rich – the novel develops an argument for educating women by exposing the hollowness of the strictures that have prohibited her learning. Akbari, the educated sister, predictably turns out to be a model of perfection – modest, able as a housewife, and a teacher to the household.

Maulana Ashraf Ali Thanawi, a powerful religious authority, formulated a complex image for the ideal Muslim woman in the new age. In part he expanded the sense of their self-worth; at the same time, he sought to contain this expansion within the strict limits of a specifically Muslim female piety separated completely from its Hindu counterpart. He wanted the Muslim woman to become "a scholar of Arabic. You will achieve the rank of a learned person and you will be able to give judicial opinion as men do . . ."[10] Reverting to the golden age of Islam in the days of

---

[9] Cited in Naim, "Prize Winning *Adab*", pp. 343–4.

[10] He wrote this in an educational novel for women, *Bihishti Zewar* (Heavenly Treasure), cited in Metcalf, *Perfecting Women*, pp. 8–9.

the Prophet, he unearthed anecdotes about women monarchs, doctors, teachers, scholars, chieftains, and elders who could serve as exemplars for the modern Muslim woman. He even enumerated the feminine virtues of the Prophet himself, describing him as considerate, modest, and gentle. The new conservative woman he imagined was a circumspect and trained housewife but also highly educated in sacred literature, able to write letters, and skilled in household management. Above all, she was to be devout, conscious that her first duty was to God rather than to her family:

> For many years I watched the ruination of the religion of women of Hindustan and was heartsick because of it. I struggled to find a cure, worried because the ruin was not limited to religion but had spread to everyday matters as well. It went beyond women to their children and in many respects even had their effects on their husbands. I have for some time therefore realised that in order to manage women, it is absolutely necessary to teach them the science of religion – even if it must be through the medium of Urdu.[11]

By imagining her as a learned and pious person he hoped to segregate her from syncretic domestic habits and custom, most of which he feared were borrowed from Hindu women. He also situated her firmly and exclusively within her household, her seclusion being seen as feminine virtue and her domesticity invested with noble responsibility – she was to be the reformer within her household.

Abul A'la Maududi (1903–1979), founder of the Jamaat-i-Islami, published an Urdu journal, the *Tarjuman ul Quran*, which was bitterly critical of modern Muslim women who had imbibed a Western education. It mocked them as "Oriental Occidentals", suggesting they were a sort of Trojan horse implanted within Muslim society and intent on corrupting Islam. In his 1935 articles, later published as *Purdah and the Status of Women in Islam* (1972), Maududi argued that Islam had accorded a far better

[11] *Ibid.*, pp. 111–34.

status to its women than had all other religions. But to earn that status the wife needed to happily and completely subordinate herself to her husband, and be content with domestic confinement so as to become "the queen of the household". She could be educated, but strictly on religious lines. She could, however, refuse to marry if she wanted to. Maududi also wanted a replacement of the Penal Code with Islamic criminal laws.

Syed Ahmad Khan (1817–1898) – otherwise a modernist pedagogue and founder of the Aligarh University which aspired to approximate Oxbridge's intellectual standards – was much distrusted by the orthodox for his positive view of Western science. He too opposed a full-blown education for women as premature and favoured a home-based religious education for them. He recalled how his pious mother had fostered his moral impulses over his childhood. He also admitted that seclusion, carried to an extreme, sowed ignorance. In the great days of early Islam women were educated, they inherited and managed properties, they wrote works and knew arithmetic. When Islam declined their rights were abridged by false custom.

We find, therefore, some common threads running through these several discourses – the present state of ignorance and waste in the lives of Muslim women, and their future perfectibility through a religious education that would ensure a willed submission to their families and separate them from Hindu custom. Thanawi gave his ideal woman a more exalted pedagogic activism within the family, whereas Maududi stressed the need for her subordination.

Syed Mumtaz Ali (1865–1935) began with some of these assumptions but went far beyond them to articulate strong aspirations towards equality, even if within the terms of an Islamic protofeminism. In 1898 he founded one of the first Urdu journals for women, the weekly *Tahzib un Niswan*, edited by his wife Muhammadi Begum. This joint conjugal venture opened up a new family enterprise as well as a remarkable vocation for women as journalists and editors. He wrote a book, *Huquq un Niswan*, on women's rights under Islamic law. This was inspired by his Deobandi learning and his arguments with Lahore-based missionaries who had trashed Indian religions for their attitude to women – Mumtaz Ali wanted to prove them wrong as far as Muslim women were concerned.

He too began from the general premise that Islam valued women more than did every other religion. But he broke new and dangerous ground in arguing that women's rights had so far existed only in theory, and that it was time now for practices too to change. To enable such a change, men too must change themselves. Point by point, he refuted the standard views which represented women as an inferior breed. Using logic and common sense, alongside reinterpretations of scripture, he asserted women's ingrained biological, mental, and intellectual parity with men. He urged a broad humanistic education for them, not a narrowly domesticated or religious life. Since both sexes, he believed, had identical moral and rational faculties, education too must be non-gendered; women he felt only needed some additional skills for household management. Seclusion and purdah were indeed scriptural norms, but they had now been taken far beyond their original remit, which had merely advised modest conduct. The veil was not meant to inhibit ease of movement. He suggested marriage reforms, arguing that even though the Prophet had mandated consensual marriage, consent was now merely presumed. Dower, he said, should be fair and precisely spelt out in the contract (*nikahnama*).

All this was too much for Syed Ahmad Khan. When he read the manuscript by Mumtaz Ali, he apparently tore it up in a rage: the author had to retrieve the pieces and stick the pages back together. Eventually, he published it only after Syed Ahmad Khan's death in 1898. It did not find public acclaim, possibly being too advanced for its times.

Mumtaz Ali's wife Muhammadi Begum left behind an unpublished autobiography in which she described herself as a tomboy in her childhood, fond of outdoor games with her brothers.

Growing up, she was trained in the feminine skills too – embroidery, cooking, and household management. Yet at home she also read the Urdu newspapers and books, as well as English grammar. Later her husband taught her Arabic and Persian, an Englishwoman taught her English, a Hindu woman came over to teach her Hindi, and a young neighbour instructed her in mathematics. Her daring example was followed by a host of Muslim women who began to edit journals and agitate for legal reforms – abolition of polygamy and unilateral divorce by men, greater property rights for women, and a woman's right to initiate divorce on the grounds of a husband's cruelty. Ameer Ali, a Bengali Muslim judge, wrote *The Spirit of Islam* (1921), which contained unqualified criticism of polygamy as un-Islamic.

From the late nineteenth century Muslim women began to emerge as prominent reformers in their own right. This can be partly traced back to a few powerful regal women – for instance, the four Begums of Bhopal who reigned in succession. Before them, in the early eighteenth century Fatah Bibi, wife of Dost Muhammad Khan, had defended Bhopal from Rajput and Maratha attacks while her husband was in Afghanistan. Then in 1818 the reigning nawab died suddenly and his eighteen-year-old widow, Qudsia Begum, was appointed Regent by the British Political Agent in 1819 till her daughter, Sikander, came of age and married. Qudsia wore a veil but also learnt riding and military skills. So free was her demeanour that she managed to shock the British Agent. Her great-granddaughter later described her as a "tigress". Qudsia was a devout Sufi and persuaded the important religious leaders in her state to endorse the woman's right to the royal throne. An astute and innovative ruler who had discarded the veil, she started projects to fight cholera with a clean water supply.

She was succeeded by her daughter Sikander Begum (r. 1844–68), who replaced Persian with the more popular Urdu as the court language and made Bhopal a cultural hub, patronising famous poets like Ghalib as well as religious scholars. She wrote a travelogue based on her Haj pilgrimage journey and was the first Indian ruler, men included, to visit Mecca. Closely observing the patterns of British governance in the colonies she passed through, she founded the Victoria School to train girls, Hindu and Muslim, in handicrafts. Her liberal endowment of scholarships helped in the schooling of girls even from subaltern *ajlaf* ("lower-class" converted) families. Sikander did not cover her face, only her head, and did not live in seclusion. She devised an interesting curriculum for women rulers which incorporated subjects like English, arithmetic, and horse riding. She was rewarded for her loyalty to the British during 1857 when confirmed in her right to rule in her own name, not merely as Regent.

The next generations of her female successors broadened her efforts in new directions. They wrote reformist books in simple Urdu for women's education, and patronised architecture, public works, engineering, and traditional *hakimi* medicine alongside Western allopathy. They funded and encouraged schools for girls and in their hands Bhopal became a cultural hub. Together, these queens helped create a rising curve in the history of modern Muslim women, a curve that moved steadily from gender equality for themselves as female rulers to welfare work for women in general.

These royal initiatives were matched, and soon exceeded, by women from modern elite families. Muslim women had already travelled abroad between the late eighteenth and mid nineteenth centuries. One of them, Mariam, accompanied her husband, a government officer, on a scientific-diplomatic mission in 1834, and in 1856 the Begum of Awadh went to England to petition the British government for the return of her son's kingdom. In 1906 Atiya Fyzee (1877–1977), a daring young woman, went much further. She travelled without the veil from Bombay to London on a government scholarship to attend a teacher's training course. Poor health prevented her completing it but she imbibed a great deal of understanding of current Western pedagogical experiments and cultural developments. She travelled widely in Europe and kept a travel diary in the form of letters to her sisters. These came out in the journal *Tahzib un Niswan* (Women's Culture), and were later published as a book, *Zamana i Tahsil* (A Time for Education).

Atiya Fyzee described her encounters with prominent and interesting men – intellectuals, reformers, politicians – and provided detailed observations on Western ways of life: food, clothes, gardens, servants, education. She also wrote about Indian classical music and co-authored plays with her Jewish husband who had converted to Islam to marry her. Her sister, Nazil, Begum of Janjira, published narratives of her own European and Turkish travels, as did several other women from their family.

Travel accounts and diaries became an important sub-genre for these early Muslim women writers, opening up the world to the gaze of homebound women. Atiya was frank about her close friendships with men, both European and Indian, the poet Iqbal being one among them. She gained considerable disrepute for this, especially for her correspondence with Iqbal and Maulana Shibli Numani. The controversies remain alive because the letters revealed prolonged exchanges of thought, both intellectual and emotional. After Partition she left for Pakistan at Jinnah's invitation. Her sisters, too, lived in remarkable freedom. They were photographed with their mother, faces uncovered, playing badminton or rowing a boat.

Women founded their own reformist associations. At its annual meeting at Lahore in 1918 the All India Muslim Ladies' Conference passed a resolution against polygamy, raising a storm of outrage in the Muslim press. They campaigned for "delegated divorce" (*talaq i tafwid*) which was spearheaded by Sharifa Hamid Ali (1883–1971), President, All India Women's Association, in the late 1930s. Born into the famous Tyabji family and married to an ICS officer, she prepared a draft marriage contract to allow women to initiate divorce and retain their *mehr* (dower) if the husband married another woman. Muslim women reformers worked with Muslim League politicians and with the ulama in drafting the Muslim Personal Law (Shariat) Application Act, 1937, and the Dissolution of Muslim Marriages Act, 1939.

After W.W. Hunter's recommendations in 1871, the government took a few tardy steps to initiate modern education among Muslim men, with hostels, grants-in-aid, and special scholarships for students. Towards the end of the nineteenth century, and especially from the early twentieth, there emerged a small but influential group of modern professional men proudly claiming a Bengali Muslim identity and trying to enrich it with their literature and journalism. A spate of Bengali Muslim newspapers and journals appeared from the 1890s, some keen to transform Muslim gender norms.

Bengali Muslim women were doubly marginalised in their religious community by orthodox gender norms and because of their ignorance of Arabic and Urdu. Gradually, a few middle-class women learnt to read and write in Bengali and some began to publish articles in liberal journals like *Nabanoor, Kohinoor,* and *Saogat*. Though they came late to education, they responded to the new possibilities with great alacrity and vigour. Khairunnissa Khatun asserted that religion prescribes equal educational opportunities for men and women. A few decades later Firoza Begum attacked religious leaders who were "the biggest impediment to women's education" – even if she herself saw women as essentially mothers and wives.[12] She dismissed the conventional "molla" (maulvi) strictures that education takes women away from their domestic responsibilities and husbands. Others wrote poems and stories. Masuda Rahman came to be called *Banglar agninagini* (fiery serpent of Bengal) for her sharp polemic against male domination. Her writing expressed anguish for women not even being allowed to understand the Quran, which she said was the "object of my demonic hunger". The woman, she said, had been relegated to cooking and reproducing "like a bitch". She ridiculed

---

[12] Cited in Sarkar, *Visible Histories, Disappearing Women,* p. 100.

men for servility to their foreign masters even as they themselves expected women to be servile to them: no point, therefore, in women asking for rights from their men as they had none themselves.

We may legitimately describe Begum Rokeya Sakhawat Hossain (1880–1932) as the first full-fledged Bengali feminist. Prevented from learning and reading Bengali by her guardians, she was taught secretly by her brother at home. Married off early to a rich widower who supported her in her writing and activism, she wrote "Amader Abanati" (Our Decline, 1904) and its revised version, "Stree Jatir Abanati" (The Decline of Women, 1905),[13] where she compared seclusion to slavery. Most daring was her critique of religion itself, which she said was inimical to women. Whenever women had tried to assert themselves, she said, they had been "crushed with the excuse of the holy texts. Even our souls have become enslaved. Where the bonds of religion are slack, women are as advanced as men. I have to say that 'religion' has strengthened the bonds of our enslavement."[14] Gender injustice was common to all religions, she said, and gave examples of abuse from each.

Her outspokenness incensed men of every community, including some liberals. Her later writings blamed women, too, for colluding with their own oppression because of their "mental enslavement". This then angered women readers as well. Some read her essay as an anti-women piece because it referred to their love of ornaments – "badges of slavery" – and of enjoying a reputation for docility and passivity. "We have been tricked into a weak femininity by indulgent men, we are like pet animals," she says.[15] What she was actually castigating was not, of course, women, but the conventional prototypes of femininity favoured or dictated by men to which women had continued to cling.

[13] Qadir, ed., *Begum Rokeya Rachanabali*.
[14] Hossain, "Amader Abanati", cited in Sarkar, *Visible Histories*, p. 119.
[15] Hossain, "Alankar Na Badge of Slavery?", p. 33.

Widowed at twenty-nine, Rokeya was left a bequest of Rs10,000 by her husband for the purpose of starting a school for Muslim girls. She tried to open one in Bhagalpur but it failed. Persecuted by her matrimonial kin, she moved to Calcutta and in 1911 set up the Sakhawat Hossain Memorial School in her husband's name, in a rented house, with eight students to start with. She had to reassure parents that their children would travel safely on a school bus, discreetly hidden behind heavy curtains. This was an unwilling compromise with social prejudice, and, though the school did flourish later, some parents complained that the curtains were so stifling that their wards had nearly choked on the way to school.

Women's learning began at home, but a new generation of women wanted to take education beyond it. From 1904 an educationist, Sheikh Abdullah (1864–1965), and his wife Wahid Jahan Begum ran a women's magazine called *Khatun* produced out of their home. Begum Abdullah argued that elite girls must go to schools since the *ustani*s who taught them at home were not reliable teachers. She was certain that this would add vibrancy to Muslim elite domestic culture. Along with her husband, she went on to found the Aligarh Zenana Madrasa in 1906. Sheikh Abdullah also started the Aligarh Women's College. The couple needed to raise a lot of funds and persuade reluctant families to send their daughters to school. The husband became Secretary to the All India Women's Education Section of the All India Muslim Education Conference in 1902. To reassure the parents of schoolgoing girls that their daughters need not travel on public roads every day – seen as a dangerous exposure to men on the road – Begum Abdullah set up a boarding school where she kept a careful personal watch over the girls.

Maulvi Syed Karamat Husain established a girls' college at Lucknow in the United Provinces in 1912, which was later named after him. Lucknow being an influential hub of Muslim culture and thought, a college for girls there served as a beacon of attitudinal change in the community vis-à-vis the need for educating grown-up daughters beyond just school.

Many highly privileged women soon turned towards their poorer sisters. *Khatun* carried ads showing how income-generating skills were imparted to women and a Khatun Store marketed their handicrafts. Khairunnissa Khatun, principal of a girls' school in North Bengal, founded a night school for girls and travelled around villages to persuade parents to send their daughters to it. She also participated in the anti-colonial upsurge of 1905. In 1916 Begum Rokeya started the Anjuman-e-Khawatin (Islamic Women's Association) at Calcutta and its members began to help slum women. She also worked with non-denominational associations like the Narishilpa Bidyalay, a school to teach industrial art to poor women.

Their education may have begun late and under as many constraints as existed for other Indian women. But Muslim women came of age as social and political activists with remarkable alacrity, autonomy, and boldness.

We should not assume that the distinction between the older and new generations of women was clear and absolute. They did not inhabit separate worlds, but all kinds of women – old and new, elite and subaltern – lived close together in the same familial space, each influencing and also imbibing the opinions and values of others. Each individual thus represented a rather fluid state of being rather than a sharply delineated one. A remarkable picture of such intermingling that affected all generations within the same home can be found in Attia Hosain's novel *Sunlight on a Broken Column* (1961), set in a time several decades before its publication.

Sikh Reforms

Guru Nanak (1469–1539) had broken away from Hindu polytheism, caste, and idolatry to found a new religion, Sikhism, in West Punjab. Sikhism abjured image worship, adored God as a single and formless presence, and advocated meditation, prayers, and piety in place of ritual. Though it later broke into multiple sects, sometimes locked in bitter internal disputes over the leadership of the community, it preserved its central articles of belief even while interacting with Muslim and Hindu devotional practices.

Though Sikhs were engrossed within Hindu personal laws, some of the Sikh sects began to independently develop gender reforms, not as a part of Hindu efforts but as exclusively Sikh ones. In the mid nineteenth century the Nirankari leader Dayal Das proclaimed that the notions of a post-birth unclean time for women should be junked along with displays of dowry. The Namdhari sect went further, allowing women the rite of initiation and widow remarriage even as it prohibited dowry and child marriage.

Births, Birth Control, and the Spectre of Female Sexuality

Conventional sexual inhibitions and prohibitions began to waver in the inter-war years and the census was a major stimulus for change. The 1921 census had registered as much as a 20 per cent population leap since 1871, and demographic discourses shifted their ground from the "population question" to the "population problem".[16] Malthusianism flourished, with epidemics and malnutrition deaths appearing to be a sad necessity to the many who invariably attributed them to the supposedly reckless breeding habits of the poor. Rani Lakshmibai Rajwade, an early advocate of birth control, warned against overbreeding among "decrepit specimens of humanity". Dr Jerbanoo Mistri advocated total abstinence for the poor.[17]

These decades also saw multifarious political turbulence which seemed to further underline the culpability of the poor. It was a time when "low-caste" movements flourished, working-class strikes proliferated, and peasant struggles against landlords be-

---

[16] Arnold, " Official Attitudes to Population", p. 25.
[17] Ramusack, "Authority and Ambivalence", p. 52.

came endemic. Subalterns had entered elite discourses as a vicious and threatening species. Apart from their allegedly oversexed lives and prodigious fertility, their rebellious tendencies made it all the more imperative to take the challenge of overpopulation seriously: hostile studies of working-class sexuality and breeding became commonplace. Some reformers went around working-class settlements to teach them birth control. Reduced reproduction, moreover, could not be left entirely to Nature because progress in sanitary and medical facilities threatened to lower mortality rates and thereby increase the population. Between the two world wars, therefore, birth control came to be widely discussed in official, medical, missionary, and Indian reformist and political circles. There were debates about whether it should be exercised with contraceptives or through abortion. Predictably, that meant an open engagement with what had earlier been taboo as a subject of public discussion – sexual practices.

The American educator Margaret Sanger toured India between 1935 and 1936, giving lectures and showing films on contraceptives. She met Gandhi in 1935 at his Wardha ashram, and their exchanges were widely publicised. Both believed in birth control, though Gandhi broadly accepted the Malthusian solution – the idea that natural processes and disasters would take care of population excesses. Their approaches could not have been more different. Gandhi advocated total sexual abstinence or "self-control" while Sanger preferred contraception for non-reproductive sex.

Fear of the poor branched out into Hindu communal anxieties about comparative community growth rates and the belief that Muslims, being more fertile, would soon overtake the Hindu majority. But Hindus also began to look inwards as they noticed a lot of Hindu wombs were left unproductive – on account of the widespread reluctance over widows remarrying. The future of the community seemed to be at stake, and Hindu cautionary tracts flooded publishing markets in the United Provinces in the 1920s. In a departure from epiphanies about the unique purity of

Hindu widowhood, now even some of the orthodox Hindu communal organisations began to advocate remarriage for young and fertile widows. They warned that it was a far better alternative to their possible elopement with Muslim men who were, apparently, ever ready to entice them.

Debates around birth control introduced a serious discursive shift. Tracts advised people on intimate sexual practices, this having been a subject unmentionable earlier, especially in the presence of women. Women's magazines discussed contraceptives quite freely and taught their readers the joy of planned families.

Some went further. Padmanabha Pillai, a Tamil Brahman in Bombay who played urgently and insistently on class and caste worries, also advocated contraceptives for the middle classes, arguing that if they had fewer children their offspring would be better nourished. As against nineteenth-century reformers who had restricted themselves to the need for mental compatibility within marriage, Padmanabha Pillai reconfigured the ideal conjugal relationship as a sexually compatible one. He staunchly opposed the view that the wife should be sexually passive and that good women were constitutionally frigid. His *Ideal Sex* (1944) argued that the sexual urge was common to both partners and should be cultivated equally to ensure marital pleasure and bliss. Otherwise, he cautioned husbands, unfulfilled wives would turn to adultery or become a prey to neurological afflictions. Sex education, he said, should begin at school, to minimise the risks of sexually transmitted disease.

Pillai found *coitus interruptus* and condoms pernicious. He preferred female contraceptives. That, however, also appeared as a risky option to his conservative mind. He feared that if women learnt about sexual and contraceptive matters, they would become active and equal partners in conjugal sex. Worse, they might then initiate the use of contraceptives and make the husband merely follow their lead. To minimise such a dangerous inversion of sexual norms, Pillai advised that husbands first learn the required techniques and advise their wives – it would preclude the possibility that female contraceptives might allow the woman fuller control over her own body. A homophobic, he also warned that if "ugly and deformed" women were left sexually unfulfilled, they would turn to lesbianism in large numbers. To avert such a catastrophe, he advised against their being left single. In brief, while recasting the woman as a fully sexed being whose urges needed to be attended to for social and moral stability, Pillai also tried to contain the far-reaching implications of his arguments by keeping sex confined within marital limits.

As noted earlier, the late nineteenth century saw some belated state investments in reproductive and maternal health – effectively, the only spheres as far as women's health was concerned. The traditional Dalit midwife and her supposedly unhygienic and untrained ways were the earliest point of entry into this domain for medical missionaries and doctors, Indian and British. From James Wise, Dacca Civil Surgeon, who condemned Indian childbirth practices in 1871, to later Bengali social reformers, every medical expert criticised the filthy lying-in rooms, the inordinate length of the lying-in period (framed by an elaborate ritual regime), the received wisdom of the midwife and older family women, and childbirth as a public spectacle watched by a bevy of women who crowded a tiny room. There was some truth to these criticisms. A short fictional work by Tagore, "Streer Patra" (1914), provides an almost identical description of childbirth – in line with these critiques – within, surprisingly, an educated and privileged urban household.

Doctors cautioned against older infant-rearing practices such as prolonged breastfeeding and the use of wet nurses. As various brands of baby-food products – one of the popular brands was called Mellin's Food – swept the market, a new child-centric consumerism advised clock-regulated bottle-feeding in the name of modern science.

Indians were suspicious of the early zenana hospitals that medical missionaries had set up. They worried that pregnant women and new mothers, away from their families and physically and emotionally vulnerable, would succumb to missionary preaching in these hospitals. Begum Rokeya wrote a story, "Nurse Nellie", on this theme. In it an upper-class fictional Muslim woman narrator comes across an Indian Christian woman who performs all manner of filthy and degrading tasks at a hospital. The narrator assumes that this woman is from the Methar (scavenger) caste, and is shocked when she learns that, in fact, she is from a well-educated Muslim family and secretly reads the Quran. The narrator shudders at the thought that those same hands, accustomed to handling filth, also turn the pages of the Holy Book. The story is as much a criticism of medical missions as an astonishing revelation of Muslim caste prejudices.

The Calcutta Corporation introduced a scheme in 1916 to provide trained domiciliary midwives, backed by a chain of subsidised maternity homes, for slum women. Despite considerable initial resistance from the urban public and midwives, the system eventually proved fairly successful. In 1922 it handled as many as 3917 maternity cases (more than a fifth of the babies born in Calcutta) and suffered only five maternal deaths – a striking achievement accomplished by just four women health visitors and sixteen midwives who supervised the childbirths on mud floors in slums under appalling sanitary conditions.

Modern doctors, medical missionaries, and governmental as well as non-governmental child and maternal welfare associations worried particularly about women's health issues within domestic seclusion. At first the purdah was criticised for blocking women's access to public health facilities. But the discourse shifted in the early decades of the twentieth century when seclusion was re-described as the very breeding ground of disease: tuberculosis, osteomalcia, anaemia in pregnancy, and eclampsia during childbirth. Some Indian women issued spirited rebuttals. Begum Sultan Jahan of Bhopal, in her *Al Hijab or Why Purdah is Necessary* (1922), argued that confinement at home did not render women more unhealthy than Western women even though the latter enjoyed greater mobility and a bracing climate. In fact, Indian sick women were, she said, ably nursed back to health by experienced family women.

What is clear is that the woman's body, its ailments and sexual needs, had entered the public gaze, inviting interventions from men as well as women. Slowly but surely the female body was becoming a speakable, writable, and readable body.

References and Suggested Readings for Chapter 3

Ahluwalia, Sanjam, "Demographic Rhetoric and Sexual Surveillance: Indian Middle Class Advocates of Birth Control", in Sarah Hodges, ed., *Reproductive Health in India: History, Politics, Controversies*, Hyderabad: Orient Longman, 2005.

Ahmed, Nasreen, *Muslim Leadership and Women's Education: Uttar Pradesh 1886–1947*, Delhi: Three Essays Collective, 2012.

Alam, Aniket, *Becoming India: Western Himalaya Under British Rule*, Delhi: Cambridge University Press, 2007.

Alam, Asiya, *Women, Islam and Familial Intimacy in Colonial India*, Leiden: Brill, 2021.

Amin, Sonia Nishat, "The Early Muslim Bhadramahila: The Growth of Learning and Creativity, 1876–1939", in Bharati Ray, ed., *From the Seams of History: Essays on Indian Women*, Delhi: Oxford University Press, 1995.

Anagol, Padma, "Indian Christian Women and Indigenous Feminism, c. 1850–1920", in Karen Offen, ed., *Globalizing Feminisms, 1789–1945*, London: Routledge, 2009.

Anandhi, S., "Women's Question in the Dravidian Movement: c. 1925–1948", in Sumit Sarkar and Tanika Sarkar, eds, *Women and Social Reform in Modern India*, vol. 2, Ranikhet: Permanent Black, 2007.

Arnold, David, "Official Attitudes to Population, Birth Control and Reproductive Health in India, 1921–1946", in Sarah Hodges, ed., *Reproductive Health in India: History, Politics, Controversies*, Hyderabad: Orient Longman, 2005.

Aryee, Anna, "Gandhi and Mrs Sanger Debate Birth Control: Comment", in Sarah Hodges, ed., *Reproductive Health in India: History, Politics, Controversies*, Hyderabad: Orient Longman, 2005.

Chakravarty, Aishika, *Widows of Colonial Bengal: Gender, Morality and Cultural Representation*, Delhi: Primus, 2023.

Chakravarty, Dipesh, *Provincialising Europe: Post Colonial Thought and Colonial Difference*, Princeton: Princeton University Press, 2000.

Chakravarty, Uma, *Rewriting History: The Life and Times of Pandita Ramabai*, Delhi: Zubaan, 2013.

Chandra, Sudhir, *Enslaved Daughters: Colonialism, Law and Women's Rights*, 2nd edn, Delhi: Oxford University Press, 2008.

Chaudhuri, Rosinka, *Freedom and Beef Steaks: Colonial Calcutta Culture*, Delhi: Orient BlackSwan, 2012.

Chophy, G. Kanato, *Christianity and Politics in Tribal India: Baptist Missionaries and Naga Nationalism*, Ranikhet: Permanent Black, 2021.

Devji, Faisal Fatehali, "Gender and the Politics of Space", in Zoya Hasan, ed., *Forging Identities: Gender, Communities and the State*, Delhi: Kali for Women, 1994.

Forbes, Geraldine, *Women in Modern India*, New Cambridge History of India, Cambridge: Cambridge University Press, 1995.

Geetha, V., "Gender and the Logic of Brahmanism: Periyar and the Politics of the Female Body", in Kumkum Sangari and Uma Chakravarti, eds, *From Myths to Markets: Essays on Gender*, Delhi: Manohar, 1999.

Grewal, Inderpal, *Home and Harem: Nation, Gender, Empire and the Cultures of Travel*, London: Duke University Press, 1996.

Guha, Ranajit, "Chandra's Death", in idem, ed., *Subaltern Studies V*, Delhi: Oxford University Press, 1987.

Guha, Supriya, "'The Best Swadeshi': Reproductive Health in Bengal, 1840–1940", in Sarah Hodges, ed., *Reproductive Health in India: History, Politics, Controversies*, Hyderabad: Orient Longman, 2005.

Gupta, Charu, "Hindu Wombs, Muslim Progeny: The Numbers Game and Shifting Debates in Widow Remarriage in Uttar Pradesh, 1890s–1930s", in Sarah Hodges, ed., *Reproductive Health in India: History, Politics, Controversies*, Hyderabad: Orient Longman, 2005.

Haggis, Jane, "White Women and Colonialism: Towards a Non-Recuperative History", in Clare Midgley, ed., *Gender and Imperialism*, Manchester: Manchester University Press, 1998.

Hardgrove, Anne, *Community and Public Culture: The Marwaris in Calcutta*, Calcutta: Oxford University Press, 2004.

Heimsath, Charles, *Indian Nationalism and Hindu Social Reform*, Princeton: Princeton University Press, 2016.

Hossain, Begum Rokeya Sakhawat, "Alankar Na Badge of Slavery?" *Motichur*, 1907; rpntd Kolkata: Suraha Sampriti, 2010.

Jones, Kenneth W., *Arya Dharm: Hindu Consciousness in Nineteenth-century Punjab*, Berkeley: University of California Press, 1992.

Jones, Kenneth W., *Socio-Religious Reform Movements in British India*, New Cambridge History of British India, Cambridge: Cambridge University Press, 1989.

Jordens, J.T.F., *Dayanand Saraswati: His Life and Ideas*, Delhi: Oxford University Press, 1978.

Kandukuri, Divya, "The Life and Times of Savitribai Phule", *Mint*, 19 April 2019.

Lal, Maneesha, "Purdah as Pathology: Circulation of Medical Knowledge in Late Colonial India", in Sarah Hodges, ed., *Reproductive Health in India: History, Politics, Controversies*, Hyderabad: Orient Longman, 2005.

Lambert-Hurley, Siobhan, *Muslim Women, Reform and Princely Patronage: Nawab Sultan Jahan Begam of Bhopal*, London and New York: Routledge, 2007.

Lambert-Hurley, Siobhan, and Sunil Sharma, *Atiya's Journeys: A Muslim Woman from Colonial Bombay to Edwardian Britain*, Delhi: Oxford University Press, 2010.

Metcalf, Barbara, *Perfecting Women*, Berkeley: University of California Press, 1990.

Minault, Gail, "Saiyyid Mumtaz Ali and *Tahzib un Niswan*: Women's Rights in Islam and Women's Journalism in Urdu", in Sumit Sarkar and Tanika Sarkar, *Women and Social Reform in Modern India: A Reader*, vol. 2, Ranikhet: Permanent Black, and Bloomington: Indiana University Press, 2008.

Minault, Gail, "Women, Legal Reform and Muslim Identity", in Mushirul Hasan, ed., *Islam, Community and the Nation*, Delhi: Manohar, 1998.

Minault, Gail, *Secluded Scholars: Women's Education and Muslim Social Reform in Colonial India*, Delhi: Oxford University Press, 1998.

Naim, C.M., "Prize Winning *Adab*: A Study of Five Urdu Books Written in Response to the Allahabad Government Gazette Notification", in Sumit Sarkar and Tanika Sarkar, eds, *Women and Social Reform in Modern India: A Reader*, vol. 2, Ranikhet: Permanent Black, and Bloomington: Indiana University Press, 2008.

O'Hanlon, Rosalind, *Caste, Conflict and Ideology: Mahatma Jotirao Phule and Low Caste Protest in Nineteenth Century Western India*, Cambridge: Cambridge University Press, 1985; rpnt Ranikhet: Permanent Black, 2010.

O'Hanlon, Rosalind, ed., *A Comparison Between Women and Men: Tarabai Shinde and the Critique of Gender Relations in Colonial India*, Madras: Oxford University Press, 1993.

Pachuau, Joy, and William van Schendel, *The Camera as Witness: A Social History of Mizoram, Northeast India*, Cambridge: Cambridge University Press, 2015.

Qadir, Abdul, ed., *Begum Rokeya Rachanabali*, Dhaka: Bangla Akademi, 1984.

Ramabai, Pandita, *A Testimony of Our Inexhaustible Treasure*, 1907; Kedgaon: Ramabai Mukti Mission, rpnt 1922.

Ramusack, Barbara N., "Authority and Ambivalence: Medical Women and Birth Control in India", in Sarah Hodges, ed., *Reproductive Health in India: History, Politics, Controversies*, Hyderabad: Orient Longman, 2005.

Sanyal, Manaswita, and Ranjan Bandyopadhyay, eds, "Paribarik Prabandha", in *Bhudeb Mukhopadhyay, Prabandha Sangraha*, Kolkata: Charyapad, 2010.

Sarkar, Mahua, *Visible Histories, Disappearing Women: Producing Muslim Womanhood in Late Colonial Bengal*, Durham: Duke University Press, 2008.

Sarkar, Sumit, "Rammohun Roy and the Break with the Past", in idem, *Essays of a Lifetime: Reformers, Nationalists, Subalterns*, Ranikhet: Permanent Black, and New York: SUNY Press, 2017.

Sarkar, Sumit, "The Complexities of Young Bengal", in idem, *Essays of a Lifetime: Reformers, Nationalists, Subalterns*, Ranikhet: Permanent Black, and New York: SUNY Press, 2019.

Sarkar, Sumit, "Vidyasagar and Brahmanical Society", in idem, Ranikhet: Permanent Black, and New York: SUNY Press, 2019.

Sarkar, Tanika, "Wicked Widows", in idem, *Rebels, Wives, and Saints*, Ranikhet: Permanent Black, 2008.

Sarkar, Tanika, *Hindu Wife, Hindu Nation: Religion, Community, Cultural Nationalism*, Delhi: Permanent Black, 2001.
Sen, Amiya P., *Hindu Revivalism in Bengal, 1872–1905: Some Essays in Interpretation*, Delhi: Oxford University Press, 2001.
Singh, Maina Chawla,*Gender, Religion and "Heathen Lands": American Missionary Women in South Asia, 1860s–1940s*, New York: Routledge, 2016.
Thomas, John, *Evangelising the Nation: Religion and the Formation of Naga Political Identity*, London: Routledge, 2015.
Vidyasagar, Ishwar Chandra, *Bidhababibaha Prachalita Hoya Uchit Ki Na Etadbishayak*, 5th edn, 1872, in Vidyasagar Smarak Jatiya Samiti, ed., *Vidyasagar Rachana Samgraha*, vol. 2, Calcutta, 1972.

4

Gendering Work

Work Within Households

A LOT OF DEBATES have swirled around the nature of economic transformations under colonialism and the impact of these on the lives of workers. The changes were indeed multifarious and multidirectional, affecting different categories of workers in diverse ways. Here I look at a few worksites which significantly reordered gender relations.

Indian handicrafts manufacture – especially Bengal's finished cotton goods – had commanded something like a world market in pre-colonial times. Production began to crash as the East India Company introduced cheaper imported yarn and cloth from England. Large numbers of subaltern women lost their traditional occupation in spinning and weaving. Their work had earlier been largely home-based with flexible hours, which had helped them contribute to the family income even as their domestic responsibilities continued. The new factories, when they appeared, precluded this possibility: workers now had to leave home and congregate in the mills for fixed hours. Women found it especially hard to combine factory work with their domestic duties. At the same time, home-based work for income persisted, even if on a reduced scale, and remained the largest area of women's work.

Certain other occupations declined too as bourgeois sensibilities, informed by new moral and sanitary standards, found the presence of "low-caste women" – whom they suspected of dubious morals – offensive in the household and within the sphere of cultural activities. When scientific childbirth techniques became increasingly available, Dalit midwives, for instance, were set aside in favour of modern doctors. Women dancers and singers, redesignated as "immoral" *tawaifs*, were also similarly tarnished by middle-class puritanism which found them obnoxious.

On the other hand, by the late nineteenth century new sites and forms of work had begun to open up in factories, mines, and plantations. Railways and steamships took migrant workers – mostly men, but also some women – to distant parts of the world in search of a livelihood. Many travelled overseas as indentured labourers to work in tea, coffee, and sugar plantations. Such work inevitably separated the home from the workplace, and working women were greatly burdened by their doubled workload when they moved between the two. Of course, the separation of home and workplace also disturbed normative injunctions that had relegated women entirely to the domestic sphere. Unless forced by dire necessity, women therefore refrained from joining waged work outside their homes. Factories often relied on migrant workers from distant areas, making it all the more difficult for women to leave rural homes and resettle in overcrowded urban slums.

The ideal of female seclusion had actually been prescribed for upper-caste affluent families that could do without their women's earnings. But the sanskritising pull of the injunction was so strong that the socially aspirational "lower castes" too tended to stop their women from working outside the home when they could afford the loss of income. By and large, women from solvent middling-caste peasant households no longer worked in the fields – certainly not with the plough. A good deal of agricultural work was, however, finished at home by women – rice husking, for instance.

When they did go out to work, women were sometimes edged into a corner. After several protective labour laws had been rolled out to regulate working time and conditions, employers proved increasingly reluctant to engage women, especially where the work involved using heavy or dangerous machinery. When technological progress rationalised production and induced retrenchment, women were usually the first to fall under the axe.

Slaves, Servants, Artistes

Early modern slavery, bondage, and domestic service overlapped considerably to constitute a rather blurred domain of household work with their respective boundaries indistinct. Slaves, both men and women, were highly diverse in their origins, functions, and status. Some were a part of war booty, others were imported to swell army ranks, many were enslaved due to indebtedness, and innumerable others were bought and sold in the open market. Eighteenth-century Maratha kings employed female slaves to work manually at their hill forts when the families of such women had failed to meet the state's revenue demands. Some women provided unpaid domestic labour, others were cultural performers at royal and elite households, and a few worked in the fields.

Their status varied according to their functions. Cultural performers were highly valued and, in Rajput royal households they sometimes merged with concubines or even, on occasion, with wives. A middle-class master's family sometimes offered a fictive kind of kinship to more privileged upper-caste slaves, especially women who cooked and minded children. Status also depended on caste. A young high-caste Kayastha woman fetched Rs 40 to Rs 100 in the market, but a Dalit Chandal could be bought for as little as Rs 10 to Rs 20. When household slavery was replaced with an expansive domain of paid domestic service, cooking and infant care remained the preserve of relatively privileged upper-caste servants, usually women. As the male infant grew into childhood, he was transferred to the care of a male servant. Alongside expanding urbanisation, domestic service came to provide a more or less acceptable form of work for indigent upper-caste widows whose families had failed to take care of them.

Censuses indicate that domestic work was more widespread in Bengal than in the rest of India. In 1911 servants had constituted 12 per cent of the entire workforce. These were mostly men at the time, especially in households that could afford only one servant. The 1931 Bengal census, in contrast, recorded a huge increase in the number of women workers, who now outstripped male servants – there were four women servants to every manservant. Since household functions and status depended on caste, a rigid internal hierarchy existed among servants. In some instances racial and class relations between European masters and their youthful Indian male servants were partially overturned – as for instance when the master developed an intense emotional dependence on the servant who, nonetheless, remained a servant. Attractive female servants were on occasion elevated as concubines or even wives.

Despite a slew of nineteenth-century regulations for organising the master–servant relationship in most fields of work, domestic service was left outside the purview of the law. The Second Law Commission had, interestingly, advised in the 1830s that domestic service should be made contractual along with marriage. The advice was ignored in both cases. For a long time Chhattisgarh in Central India was the only Indian state to have introduced legal regulations in relation to domestic service. Subsequently, several other states have followed suit.

Factory Work

Bypassing fundamental structural transformations in working conditions and relations, the colonial state occasionally sought a reformist route to provide a minimal safety net for factory workers. It introduced a few legal measures to alleviate the worst abuses, though these were applicable within large formal workplaces, such as registered factories and mines, rather than the vast informal sector, rural and urban. Apart from leaving the bulk of workers out of its protective net, the state also created fresh problems for those that it did try to protect. For women factory workers, protective laws offered an impossible choice – between paid work and shorter hours on the one hand, and loss of employment on the other, since employers often found it expedient to replace them with male workers who were not covered by the new regulations. Women were excluded from several categories of work in mines as it was excessively hard or dangerous: they were not allowed to work at the Kolar gold mines in present-day Karnataka, for instance. Young, single, macho men ruled the mining town, proud of their physical prowess and dependent on prostitutes rather than wives for sexual services. Even though North Indian workers coming to the Bengal jute mills usually left their families behind at home, this was not true of those who migrated from the Madras Presidency: they came with their families and settled down in the jute-mill areas.

The first Factory Act of 1881 had restricted working hours for child labourers. Legislation for women workers followed in 1891. It limited their work time to eleven hours a day and declared Sundays as mandatory holidays for all workers. Prodded by European examples and pressure, the Government of India set up a Factory Commission to investigate working conditions in India, and in the process it recorded the testimonies of workers – their actual words, as spoken by them. These testimonies allow us to hear, for the first time, the voices of several women workers.

Usually, mill work was deeply gendered, women in jute and cotton factories working shorter hours and with lighter machines than their male counterparts – so as to have time to reproduce and nourish the labour force at home. The Bombay cotton mills confined women largely to reeling and winding while men worked in the better-paid spinning department. Women's wages were lower and they formed about a quarter of the total workforce. The fast-growing Ahmedabad cotton mills owned by Indian capitalists, on the other hand, were an exception to the rule: here women constituted about a third of the labour force, joined men in the spinning rooms, and worked on the same machines.

Women themselves were deeply ambivalent about the legislation. They recognised that shorter working hours made it uneconomical for factory owners to employ them; at the same time, they themselves did complain of overwork, which made the shorter hours a necessity. The Commission admitted as much: "The law supposed to be passed for their benefit will inflict serious permanent injury on these skilled millhands."[1]

In a rather astonishing initiative, Ahmedabad's women workers, with the help of a labour activist, sent a petition to the government protesting the law: "Women, who have learnt the art of working the machinery with a great deal of trouble and loss of time, and some of them knew no other profession . . . and if they were turned out of the mill they will be actually starved to death."[2] They referred to rising grain prices which had strengthened the fear of starvation. The petition is a significant revelation of a proud female working-class identity simultaneously conjoined to an image of vulnerability. The women flaunted their hard-earned skills while pointing to looming starvation. Their fears proved right. Large numbers of women were immediately dismissed or put on half-pay as soon as the Factory Act came into effect.

A new Factory Act of 1911 prohibited women from working at night, and the proportion of women workers in the Bombay cotton mills declined between 1911 and the 1930s. In the Bengal jute mills, where women had constituted as much as 20 per cent of the total workforce in the 1920s, the declining numbers became evident from 1930. A rather flexible multiple-shift system of work organisation had helped them to toil more easily on the factory floor because it ensured the occasional break from their routine – as other workers moved in temporarily to take over from them, they could get some rest from time to time. But the transition to the single shift made their mill work considerably more arduous as they now had to work continuously.

---

[1] Cited in Sarkar, *Trouble at the Mill*, p. 234.
[2] Ibid.

Between 1919 and 1939 women had constituted a relatively significant proportion of the Bombay cotton mill workforce, but a decline began from the late 1920s, reaching a peak in 1939. The intervening years had seen the growth of family-budget surveys and enquiries into infant and maternal welfare among the working classes. Clearly, the working-class family had become a source of some anxiety among policy-makers. A Maternity Benefit Act was finally passed in 1929 after several similar bills had been rejected. Because such a bill had already been on the anvil from the mid 1920s, a systematic retrenchment of Bombay women workers began from the late 1920s, the result of a combination of technological advances which led to a rationalisation of the workforce; alongside the aim was to make the male worker the authorised family breadwinner while keeping the woman back at home as breeder and homemaker. Since the exclusion of women from factory work simultaneously enlarged work opportunities for men, this was achieved through an unspoken patriarchal compact between male workers – who seldom struck work to protest women's dismissal – and their capitalist masters.

Radha Kumar attributes women's exclusion to notions of propriety among the millowners. In similar vein, Samita Sen ascribes the strong public discomfort at employing women in tea plantations to investigative reports by Indian labour reformers from the late nineteenth century. These had created something of a moral panic about the sexual exploitation of helpless women workers – many had been misled into migrating to distant tea gardens for plantation work through fraudulent contracts and then trapped in the gardens.

Plantation labourers included large numbers of women whose nimble fingers were in demand for plucking tea leaves. They came from districts and provinces far from Assam, having signed contracts before arriving at the gardens – and thus inadvertently creating the illusion of a free labour market. However, they had often been inveigled by false promises before they signed a contract, and once inside the gardens there was hardly any possibility of exit. Most of these women found their living and work conditions far harsher than what they were given to believe at the time of recruitment. Attempts at escape were brutally punished.

In order to stabilise production rates, the government stepped in and enacted a series of ameliorative laws from the 1860s. It regulated the wages at Rs 5, Rs 4, and Rs 3 for, respectively, men, women, and children. It instituted a nine-hour working day and fixed the period of contract at three years. But within the plantations owners and managers reigned supreme and exercised despotic power – there were allegations of the sexual oppression of women and the laws did not make a great deal of difference on the ground.

Exploitation was, indeed, a vivid reality in the plantations. In Bengal's jute mills, too, the workers usually left their wives in their villages to protect them from sexual encroachment at urban workplaces. Consequently they in turn sexually exploited single women workers. For the few wives who were forced to work in factories, the utter lack of privacy corroded their dignity and the double burden of domestic and factory work exhausted them, especially as their employers did not provide maternity leave or childcare facilities.

At the same time, other motives also pulled women into factory or plantation work. An official report found that men and women who formed extra-conjugal attachments in these places were often "low caste" and were, therefore, less inhibited about norms of propriety. They settled in the mill areas where they brought up their new families: "Illegitimate children of men and women workers . . . and a large number of these women and children . . . are born of temporary unions."[3] Broughton, a British labour reformer, found that several such couples had eloped from their villages, where strict social regulations made inter-caste marriages

---

[3] Gilchrist, *Labour and Land*, p. 10.

or extra-marital relationships impossible. Urban factories offered freedom from severe caste boundaries.

International guidelines began to insist on maternal and child-welfare provisions in the inter-war years – a reduction in working hours, provision for maternal and child welfare around the time of childbirth, and ensuring women's safety in the workplace. At first debated at national levels, then at the Washington Conference of 1919 (the first international labour conference), and, later still by the International Labour Organisation, global standards were gradually firmed up to protect women from overwork and industrial accidents in their workplaces.

This, ironically, made it an increasingly costly business to employ women. Though Indian capitalists fought the labour laws and factory inspection fiercely at first, they eventually navigated the regulations by dispensing with as much of the female workforce as they could. Rajnarayan Chandavarkar, however, points out that women were not entirely, nor always, absent in factories. They had a weaker and more uncertain presence and the "intake" of women fluctuated over time. He argues that they constituted a reserve labour force, to be brought in and pushed out of factories depending on market conditions. Increases in the mechanisation of work, rather than any planned intent to keep women at home, also led to a progressive decline in their numbers. This held true for home-based work as well. Grain threshing was once the preserve of female labour in Bengali households – women operated the *dhenki* (threshing instrument) with their hands and feet. Technological development in rice mills began to take threshing out of the household by the 1930s.

Coal mines flourished from the early twentieth century in the eastern India Raniganj-Jharia region. They were worked by Adivasi/tribal migrant labour – Santhals and Kols – as well as by "untouchable" and "low castes". Till the early twentieth century the work had been divided on a family basis, with women carrying the coal to the pits and men hacking away at the coalface inside the pits. Known as *kamin*s, these women constituted about 48 per cent of the total workforce in the Raniganj mines in 1911, a large number of them toiling even within underground sites. This was acceptable to their employers and to the state, and no one bothered much about their work conditions.

The numbers stayed stable until the 1920s, when the newly constituted International Labour Organisation raised questions about their safety. In 1920 Dagmar Curjel, a Scottish woman doctor from the Women's Medical Services in India, came to investigate how women worked in coal pits. Her report raised huge anxieties about the exceptionally arduous nature of their work and, especially, about childbirths occurring in these dark and dangerous places. According to Kuntala Lahiri-Dutt, however, this was more an exclusionary device to keep women out of the mines.

After many rounds of debates, the state prohibited women from working in underground mines in 1929. But they exempted Bihar, Bengal, Orissa, the Central Provinces, and the Punjab salt mines from its purview – in other words, most major mining regions were excluded. Also as a result of Curjel's report, a Maternity Benefit Bill was introduced in the Bengal Legislative Assembly in 1937. It set up a fund to pay the mother's wages for six weeks after her confinement, the time over which she did not have to return to work. The figures for women's employment in the mines tumbled immediately. Clearly, women's safety could only be purchased at the cost of their livelihood.

Women factory workers – though unrepresented in the unions – were nonetheless very visible during the strikes that took place in Bombay and Calcutta from the 1920s. At the Ludlow Jute Mills in Calcutta, the employers initially brought in women workers to break a strike in 1928. But, undermining their stereotyping of women as a more docile population, the women struck work when the managers refused to meet their terms. The press wrote sporadically of the clashes, bringing women workers into the public gaze. When the police snatched away an infant from the arms of its mother – whom they were arresting – it made headlines even in the Calcutta middle-class nationalist press. Similarly, the press expressed anger when an elderly woman worker fainted under severe police flogging. Public sympathy was occasionally aroused by such victim images. In contrast, women's conditions of work and militancy failed to stir the press or hold its attention.

Between August 1932 and August 1933 alone there were twelve strikes by women workers in the Bombay cotton mills, all directed against retrenchment and wage reduction. In 1935 an even larger number went on strike, demanding wage hikes. Interestingly, they also demanded that a winding master, who was harassing them, be dismissed. The motif of threatened honour was often a spur to their protests.

Life at the factory lines was hard, especially because the unions not only excluded women from the ranks of office-bearers, they also did not press hard for the special facilities that women urgently needed. Marid, a woman working as a winder at a Kanpur cotton mill in the 1890s, started her day at 4 a.m. to finish her housework before the factory siren was heard. She returned home at 11 p.m. Sometimes she even worked on Sundays, cleaning machines. The only earning member in her family, she looked after a sick, jobless husband with no support from elsewhere. Babuniyah, a worker from a Bengal jute mill, complained: "I leave my house at 5 in the morning and go home at 9.30. I come again at 11 . . . if I am a little late . . . the baboos reprimand me. I do not get time for proper cooking . . . I feed my children after 9.30." She demanded crèche facilities and paid maternity leave. Muthialu took her pregnant daughter, who was also a worker, to a mill doctor. "He wrote something and asked me to go to the Sahib. He read this paper and tore it up. We did not know what to do."[4] Her daughter went back to work and lost her child. Going against all the evidence, the managers insisted on the other hand that the

---

[4] Evidence of Babuniyah and Muthialu, Royal Commission on Labour in India, 1930, vol. 5, pt II. Cited in Sarkar, *Bengal 1928–1934*, pp. 62–3.

women workers themselves did not want additional maternity facilities.

The more absolute their work-related degradation, the more strident and uninhibited women workers seemed to become. Women Methranis – untouchable-caste sanitation workers under the Howrah and Calcutta Corporations in Bengal – addressed public meetings, shamed the blacklegs, and incited men to stay on strike during the summer of 1928. During a strike at Howrah the same year they upended pots of excreta on Anglo-Indian policemen who were trying to remove them from the picket lines, turning the filth they were forced to handle into a weapon. The policemen fled, tearing off their uniforms and swearing never to return. But, for all that, women workers' special needs were rarely addressed in the union charters and they found no place in the unions.

An early-twentieth-century song by a Methrani of the Calcutta Corporation is worth citing at length. Her raunchy song, which turns the world upside down, reveals the sense of professional and collective strength that she and her fellow women workers felt, and expressing their absolute irreverence towards upper-caste Corporation babus and employers:

> My name is Hari Methrani
> I am the grandma of the municipality
> If anyone accuses us of being abusive
> We quit work in unison
> Our caste is well bonded.
> But the Babus are different
> They shamelessly lick the half-eaten plates of Sahibs
> . . . And then they retort, "Don't touch us, Methrani"
> . . . Oh we will wed Brahmin priests . . .[5]

Labour Reformism

The growing presence of women workers was matched by the entry of middle-class women, Western and Indian, as specialist

[5] Sur, "Teensho Bochhorer Kolkata", p. 94.

observers of female labour conditions. In the late nineteenth century the British reformer Mary Carpenter had urged factory reforms in India, and this initiated a tradition of labour reportage by women. In 1894 Marie Imandt and Bessie Maxwell, two women journalists from the *Dundee Courier*, arrived to study and write about labour conditions in the Calcutta jute mills. The All India Women's Conference also urged protective and welfare measures. From the 1920s several European women entered the field as labour investigators and reformers: Janet Kelman, G.M. Broughton, R.K. Das, Margaret Read, C.M. Mathieson, Dagmar Curjel, Margaret Balfour. They included women factory inspectors, doctors observing working-class fertility and mortality rates, members from British women's organisations, and factory commissioners. Alongside, Indian male scholars like S.G. Panandhikar and Radhakamal Mukherjee began to take special note of their conditions. The woman worker had clearly emerged as a public figure.

Labour investigation soon led to labour activism. Middle-class women vaulted across feminine stereotypes, befuddled deeply ingrained caste and class taboos that beset upper-caste women, and created a space for themselves that would have been unimaginable earlier. In the Bengal jute belt Santoshkumari Gupta mobilised workers to protest against labour conditions from the early 1920s. In 1928 Prabhabati Dasgupta became president of the Bengal Corporation Scavengers' Union, having prepared the path of labour unionism single-handed by working among municipal garbage and "night soil" cleaners — men and women who suffered the deepest degradation because of caste stigmas and their form of work. She visited them in their slums, drank tea and joked with them: these were all activities forbidden to upper-caste people, and doubly so to an upper-caste woman. Workers began to call her their mother, "Dhangar [scavenger's] Ma". In the 1930s Begum Sakina, an aristocratic Muslim woman of Iranian descent and a Corporation councillor, was also called Dhangar Ma.

Strikingly, these women worked on their own, outside of political party circles.

These early glimmerings of solitary women becoming leading trade unionists faded after political organisations of varied hues captured the labour unions and began to approach workers with a more streamlined, bureaucratic relationship. Women workers became rare figures in labour organisations once the unions were routinised.

New Professions

Cushioned as they were by family affluence, social status, and sometimes supportive families, high-caste middle-class women nonetheless had a hard time when they tried to acquire a professional life. The 1931 census of Bengal, for instance, showed that only 8000 women worked as clerks, cashiers, and accountants, and less than 4000 were employed in government service. Most of those who worked in these capacities would have been Anglo-Indians or Christians. Lacking the push factor of economic distress, other middle-class Indian women faced considerable social resistance when they joined the white-collar workforce. Women doctors, for instance, were shunned as an inferior breed, as unqualified and polluted by their profession since it involved handling bodily effluvia. The Madras Medical College first opened its doors to women students in 1844 but most medical colleges held out against admitting women for quite a while.

Abala Das, a Brahmo woman, and Ellen D'Abrew, an Anglo-Indian Christian, were refused admission at the Calcutta Medical College, such training being regarded as the most unfeminine and polluting of educational activities. They did however manage to join the Madras Medical College. Kadambini Bose, married to the reformer Dwarakanath Ganguly, was in 1888 the first Bengali woman to achieve a full medical degree. She went abroad to study medicine and returned home to practise it while her husband shared some of their domestic responsibilities. As a carriage took her on a round of home visits, she spent some of this travelling time to knit woollen garments for her several children – providing proof that women could when necessary perform motherhood and professional roles simultaneously. However rarely this may have happened, a new world had begun to open up in which men and women started sharing workloads, and outgrowing traditional gender roles to the point of occasionally blurring their boundaries.

The state sought to medicalise childbirth from the late nineteenth century – practically its sole intervention in the sphere of women's health. Missionaries did far more in this respect. The Lady Dufferin Fund – a non-official institution, though heavily patronised by the government – was, as earlier noted, set up in 1885 to expand medical training and facilities for women. It financed Rakhmabai when she went abroad to train as a doctor. It also allowed the Calcutta Medical College to offer certificate courses in midwifery which proved very popular among its low-income students. Lady Curzon established the Victoria Memorial Scholarship Fund in 1903 to retrain midwives in new childbirth methods. Within a decade it had come to cover fourteen provinces and was training 1395 subaltern women.

Modernity slowly reshaped traditional childbirth practices. The Dufferin Fund tried to remedy what modern doctors, at times unfairly, perceived as mismanaged births at the hands of untrained hereditary midwives. There was some truth in their allegations. The prolonged lying-in period, considered ritually unclean, was framed by numerous unhygienic practices – solitary confinement in dark, damp, cramped, and insanitary rooms, excessive heating and hot foods, a kneeling position during childbirth, and so on. Rich and educated families gradually began to prefer home visits by women doctors – or "lady doctors" as they were more commonly called. An additional reason behind the new preference was that the traditional midwives were "untouchables", whereas the doctors were high caste. For all this, there was a huge opposition to the Fund and its doctors – it persisted for a long time and hospital births were avoided till well after Independence. In 1890 a Bengali newspaper abused women doctors as "half-educated good-for-nothings" who expected to profit from the large numbers of medical court cases that revolved around marital rape and premarital pregnancy. They were also seen as missionaries in disguise, bent on destroying Hindu families and values.

From the mid nineteenth century, with the emergence of more and more girls' schools, growing numbers of educated women began to find work as teachers. Women also earned incomes from the books they wrote, even when they were homebound housewives. Rashsundari Debi, a self-taught woman who wrote the first autobiography in Bengali, left instructions to her children about how to spend the earnings from her book sales. Another woman, Muhammadi Begum, edited a journal for Muslim women.

By end-century several educated women were employed in senior administrative positions as "inspectresses" in government schools. The census counted them as government employees and bracketed them with unspecified "Professions, learned, artistic, and minor". The latter category also included sex work since most nineteenth-century female cultural performers came from their ranks. Other professions opened up too as technology advanced. In 1875 the *Hindu Patriot* carried an advertisement seeking a "Hindu Lady" photographer, obviously to photograph women in seclusion. In 1878 the Maharani of Cooch Behar employed a governess on a monthly salary of Rs 50. In the Calcutta census of 1901, 725 women were registered under "professional occupations": school principals, professors, and teachers; administrative and inspecting officials; qualified medical practitioners and photographers; authors, editors, and journalists.

Certain traditional avenues of work and power gradually fell by the wayside as public morality became wary of courtesans (*tawaifs*), who were frequently enormously talented singers and dancers.

This tradition did not, however, completely die out and new forms of performance opened up at the same time. By the late nineteenth century some erstwhile prostitutes had trained to become famous actors – first engaged by the Bengal Theatre in 1873 and then by the Parsi theatre companies that operated from the Maharashtra-Gujarat region. By the early twentieth century, with the large-scale import of gramophones, followed by the arrival of the radio, several of these artistes became renowned singers whose voices could now be heard across the country.

As the film industry developed, Zubeida Begum Dhanrajgir became the first female actor to perform in the first talkie movie, *Alam Ara*, in 1931. Theatre and films made women actors some of the most visible and famous public figures in the country; neither industry could function without women and this opened up a vast and well-paid space for women's employment. All the same, relatively few women have even until very recently emerged as leading producers or directors, two rare exceptions being Kalpana Lajmi of Assam and Aparna Sen of Bengal.

Indian women were not allowed to practice law until 1924. Cornelia Sorabji (1866–1954), a daring and colourful woman, broke new ground several times over. She was the first woman to graduate with a degree from Bombay University in 1888, the first woman to study law at Oxford, and the first female lawyer to practise law in India. Born in a Parsi family to a father who became a Christian missionary, and to a mother who, adopted by a British couple, had several girls' schools at Poona, Cornelia appealed for funds to study law abroad – a subject till then closed to both British and Indian women. She was funded by several British patrons, including Florence Nightingale, and joined Somerville College, Oxford, in 1892. Returning to India in 1894 she decided to help the *purdanasheen* (secluded women) to fight their property suits. Although she could enter their suits in court, she was barred from pleading them because of her gender. She began to petition the India Office from 1902, and in 1904 a new post was created for her as Lady Assistant to the Court of Wards in Bengal. By 1907 she was working in several other eastern provinces as well. Eventually, she managed to help several hundred women in their property suits, sometimes charging them no fees. A single woman herself, she was involved in campaigns against child marriage and befriended Pandita Ramabai. She also was a friend to Katherine Mayo: curiously, as a staunch admirer of Empire, she disliked anti-colonial movements. She wrote several books, both fiction and non-fiction, including her memoir *India Calling: The Memoirs of Cornelia Sorabji* (London, 1934).

Women's work patterns, therefore, were uneven, the strength of women workers and professionals depending on the nature of their work, age, and poverty level, and what was socially prescribed. While upper-caste, middle-class, educated women stepped into the world of paid work in ever-increasing numbers, their subaltern counterparts found many more doors closed against them. The work they found in factories, mines, and plantations was always draining and uncertain, especially because, unlike male workers, they had also to take care of homes and children without help from the state or their employers.

As we will see later, the Second World War and Partition brought rapid changes in women's work possibilities.

References and Suggested Readings for Chapter 4

Arnold, David, *Colonising the Body: State Medicine and Epidemic Disease in Nineteenth Century India*, Berkeley: University of California Press, 1993.

Balfour, Margaret, and Ruth Young, *The Work of Medical Women in India*, London: Oxford University Press, 1929.

Banerjee, Sumanta, *The Parlour and the Street: Elite and Popular Culture in Nineteenth Century India*, Calcutta: Seagull Books, 1989.

Banerjee, Swapna, *Men, Women, and Domestics: Articulating Middle-Class Identity in Colonial Bengal*, Delhi: Oxford University Press, 2004.

Behal, Rana, *One Hundred Years of Servitude: Political Economy of Tea Plantations in Colonial Assam*, Delhi: Tulika Books, 2014.

Broughton, G.M., *Labour in Indian Industries*, London, 1924.

Chandavarkar, R., *The Origins of Capitalism in India: Business Strategies and the Working Class in Bombay, 1900–1940*, Cambridge: Cambridge University Press, 1994.

Chatterjee, Indrani, *Gender, Slavery and Law in Colonial India*, Delhi: Oxford University Press, 1999.

Chatterjee, Indrani, and Richard M. Eaton, eds, *Slavery and South Asian History*, Bloomington: Indiana University Press, 2006.

Dasgupta, Amlan, "Women and Music: The Case of North India", in Bharati Ray, ed., *Women of India: Colonial and Post-colonial Periods*, Delhi: Sage, 2005.

Dutt, Kuntala Lahiri, "Bodies In/Out of Place: Hegemonic Masculinities and Kamins' Motherhood in Indian Coal Mines", in Assa Doron and Alex Broom, eds, *Gender and Masculinities: Histories, Texts and Practices in India and Sri Lanka*, New Delhi: Routledge, 2014.

Fisher, Michael H., "Bound for Britain: Changing Conditions of Servitude, 1660–1857", in Indrani Chatterjee and Richard M. Eaton, eds, *Slavery and South Asian History*, Bloomington: Indiana University Press, 2006.

Forbes, Geraldine, "Managing Midwifery in India", in Dagmar Engels and Shula Marks, eds, *Contesting Colonial Hegemony: State and Society in Africa and India*, London and New York: I.B. Tauris, 1994.

Gait, E.A., ed., *A Census of India, 1911*, vol. 1, pt 1, Calcutta, 1913.

Ghosh, ed., *Claiming the City: Protest, Crime and Scandals in Colonial Calcutta*, Delhi: Oxford University Press, 2016.

Gilchrist, R.N., *Labour and Land*, Calcutta, 1931.

Gooptu, Suparna, *Cornelia Sorabji: India's Pioneer Woman Lawyer – A Biography*, Delhi: Oxford University Press, 2006.

Hodges, Sarah, ed., *Reproductive Health in India: History, Politics, Controversies*, Hyderabad: Orient Longman, 2006.

Jeffrey, Roger, *The Politics of Health in India*, Berkeley: University of California Press, 1988.

Joshi, Chitra, *Lost Worlds: Indian Labour and Its Forgotten Histories*, Delhi: Permanent Black, 2003.

Joshi, Varsha, *Polygamy and Purdah: Women and Society Among Rajputs*, Jaipur: Rawat Publications, 1994.

Karlekar, Malavika, *Poverty and Women's Work: A Study of Sweeper Women in Delhi*, New Delhi: Vikas, 1982.

Kumar, Radha, "Family and Factory: Women in the Bombay Cotton Textile Industry, 1919–1939", in J. Krishnamurty, ed., *Women in Colonial India: Essays on Survival, Work and the State*, Delhi: Oxford University Press, 1989.

Lal, Maneesha, "The Politics of Gender and Medicine in Colonial India: The Countess of Dufferin Fund, 1885–1888", *Bulletin of the History of Medicine*, vol. 68, 1994.

Major, Andrea, "Enclaving Spaces: Domestic Slavery and the Spatial, Ideological and Practical Limits of Colonial Control in 19th Century Rajput and Maratha States", *Indian Economic and Social History Review*, vol. 46, no. 3, 2009.

Majumdar, Leela, *Paakdandi*, Calcutta: Ananda Publishers, 1987.

Mukherjee, Mukul, "Impact of Modernisation on Women's Occupations: A Case Study of the Rice Husking Industry of Bengal", in J. Krishnamurty, ed., *Women in Colonial India: Essays on Survival, Work and the State*, Delhi: Oxford University Press, 1989.

Mukherjee, Mukul, "Women's Work in Bengal: 1880–1930", in Bharati Ray, ed., *From the Seams of History: Essays on Indian Women*, Delhi: Oxford University Press, 1995.

Murmu, Maroona, *Words of Her Own: Women Authors in Nineteenth Century Bengal*, Delhi: Oxford University Press, 2019.

Nair, Janaki, *Miners and Millhands: Work, Culture and Politics in Princely Mysore*, Delhi: Sage, 1998.

Nite, Dhiraj, "The Culture of Safety in the Indian Coalmines, 1895–1970", *Studies in History*, vol. 35, issue 1.

Porter, A.E., ed., *Census of India, 1931*, vol. 5, pt 1, Calcutta, 1933.

Prakash, Gyan, *Bonded Histories: Genealogies of Labour Servitude in Colonial India*, Cambridge: Cambridge University Press, 1990.

Sailer, Anna, "Workplace Matters: The Bengal Jute Industry Between the 1870s and the 1930s", unpublished PhD thesis, Gottingen: Georg-August Universititat, 2015.

Sarkar, Aditya, *Trouble at the Mill: The Factory Law and the Emergence of the Labour Question in Late Nineteenth Century Bombay*, Delhi: Oxford University Press, 2018.

Sarkar, Tanika, *Bengal 1928–1934: The Politics of Protest*, Delhi: Oxford University Press, 1987.

Sarkar, Tanika, "Bondage in the Colonial Context", in Utsa Patnaik and Manjari Dingwaney, eds, *Chains of Servitude: Bondage and Slavery in India*, New Delhi: Sangam Books, 1985.

Sarkar, Tanika, "Calcutta's Underbelly: Corporation 'Methars' and Their Early Strikes", in Sekhar Bandyopadhyay and Tanika Sarkar, eds, *Caste in Bengal: Histories of Hierarchy, Exclusion, and Resistance*, Ranikhet: Permanent Black, 2022.

Sarkar, Tanika, *Words to Win: The Making of a Modern Autobiography*, Delhi: Zubaan, 2013.

Sehrawat, Samiksha, *Colonial Medical Care in North India: Gender, State and Society, c. 1830–1920*, Delhi: Oxford University Press, 2013.

Sen, Samita, *Gender and Class: Women in Indian Industry, 1920–1990*, Delhi: V.V. Giri National Labour Institute, n.d.

Sen, Samita, "Gender and the Politics of Class: Women in Trade Unions in Bengal", *South Asia: Journal of Asian Studies*, vol. 44, issue 2, 2021.

Sen, Samita, "Honour and Resistance: Gender, Community and Class in Bengal, 1920–1940", in Sekhar Bandyopadhyay, Abhijit Dasgupta, and Willem van Schendel, eds, *Bengal – Communities, Development and States*, Delhi: Manohar Publishers, 1994.

Sen, Samita, *Slavery, Servitude and Wage Work: Domestic Work in Bengal*, School of Women's Studies, Kolkata: Jadavpur University, 2015.

Sinha, Nitin, and Nitin Varma, eds, *Servants' Pasts: From the Late Eighteenth to the Twentieth Century*, Hyderabad: Orient BlackSwan, 2019.

Sreenivasan, Ramya, "Drudges, Dancing Girls, Concubines: Female Slaves in Rajput Polity, 1500–1850", in Indrani Chatterjee and Richard M. Eaton, eds, *Slavery and South Asian History*, Bloomington: Indiana University Press, 2006.

Sur, Tinkari, "Teensho Bochhorer Kolkata", in Anindita Ghosh, ed., *Claiming the City: Protest, Crime and Scandals in Colonial Calcutta*, Delhi: Oxford University Press, 2016. See also Malavika Karlekar, *Poverty and Women's Work: A Study of Sweeper Women in Delhi*, New Delhi: Vikas, 1982.

Tagore, Abanindranath, *Apan Katha*, Calcutta: Signet Press, 1946.

5

Gendering Politics

The Queen of Jhansi

MODERN POLITICS, especially the vast sphere of highly organised anti-colonial upsurges, was as much a new domain for men as for women. It reconfigured gender identities, images, self-images, and relationships in startling ways. At the same time, and in a strange paradox, it did not overtly question gender relations and norms in the social world – norms it was rapidly overturning in the political one.

I begin this chapter, however, with two queens from an older order. Rani Lakshmibai of Jhansi, who died in 1858 in a battle with the British, still reigns in popular memory as the most fearless and patriotic of Indian women – almost a non-woman because of her assumed masculinity on the battlefield. The actual history, however, is slightly different.

Jhansi was a small princely state in Central India. After its king died in 1853, a new colonial law prevented his adopted son from inheriting the patrimonial realm. It also left his widow with a relatively small pension. From 1856 she repeatedly petitioned the British for an enhanced pension on account of "the unflinched [sic] faithfulness for which my family has been so remarkable . . . and how I have stretched out my supplicant hands for the protection and favour of the government . . ."[1]

---

[1] Translation of Lachhmi Bai's letter to British Agent, Governor General

The revolt of 1857–8, which began with a mutiny of Indian sepoys in the British army, grew into a massive peasant rebellion, and threatened the survival of the British Empire, brought the Rani the promise of help from several rebel leaders who offered to restore her kingdom if she joined them. She astutely kept her lines of communication open both with the British and the rebels. In June 1857 the Commissioner of Nagpore reported a massacre of British personnel at Jhansi: ". . . all were horribly massacred, men, women and children . . ."[2] The Rani quickly sent two secret messages, concealed in a walking stick, to Major Erskine, a senior British army officer, telling him she had come to know of the massacre very late and deeply regretted it; and that she herself was now a virtual prisoner of the sepoys. They had made her the titular head of the district but she would help the British once they had quelled the rebels. In yet another secret letter to the British in 1858 she promised to send them reinforcements and return them all the districts which the sepoys had handed over to her. But there was a new note of defiance: ". . . should the British officer show displeasure, she will fight to the last."[3] British Intelligence officials concluded she would tilt towards whoever finally won. But they now decided to treat her as an enemy and military conflicts began with her forces.

On 1 April 1858 the Rani heard that Tantia Tope, fellow rebel leader and her potential ally, had been killed. She now had to fight alone. So "the Ranee of Jhansi dressed in manly attire and armed with sword and dagger rides at the head of 50 sowars and 100 matchlock men. She wears a valuable pearl necklace at all times."[4] With her son beside her, she managed to evade the British forces

---

for Central India, 7/1/56, Pol Dept, 28/2/56, cited in Gupta, ed., *Original Documents Relating to Ranee Lakshmi Bai of Jhansi*, p. 289.
 [2] Ibid.
 [3] Ibid., p. 359.
 [4] Ibid., p. 381.

repeatedly, even as she tried to negotiate for peace. She was reported dead, then was heard of again as alive, until Governor General Canning was finally told on 18 June 1858 that "The Ranee of Jhansi is killed."[5]

Even now, popular representations of the Rani stitch together masculine heroism with female vulnerability. A song, composed much later by a woman nationalist, the poet Subhadra Kumari Chauhan, stayed in Indian school textbooks for a long time after Independence and continues even now in many: "How well like a man fought the Rani of Jhansi / How valiantly and well . . ."[6] Her memory surfaced whenever women joined any of the anti-colonial movements. In 1942, for example, Subhas Chandra Bose founded the Indian National Army to fight the British in South East Asia with captive Indian prisoners of war, and with help from the Axis forces. He formed a women's regiment which he named the Rani Jhansi Brigade, a unique all-women battalion the like of which was not to be found elsewhere in the world at the time. Lakshmi Swaminathan (later Sahgal) commanded it and led several hundred young women cadets of expatriate Indian origin. When the Indian naval ratings rebelled in Bombay during the Royal Indian Navy Mutiny in 1946, they approached Aruna Asaf Ali, organiser of the underground apparatus of the Quit India movement, addressing her as the Rani of Jhansi. Far away in India's north-east, as we shall see, the tribal nationalist Gaidinliu was rechristened "Rani Gaidinliu" by Jawaharlal Nehru in an allusion to the Rani of Jhansi.

The same year, 1857, also threw up another royal female rebel – but one who has until recently been ignored by nationalist historians and popular memory. This was Begum Hazrat Mahal, the second wife of Nawab Wajid Ali Shah of Awadh. After the nawab had been exiled to Calcutta, sepoys gathered under her direction

[5] Ibid., p. 416.
[6] Cited in Mukherjee, *A Begum and a Rani*, p. 105.

and for a whole year ventured ferocious attacks on British forces at the Lucknow garrison. Begum Hazrat Mahal personally supervised the military and logistical details of these battles. After all was lost, she issued two proclamations criticising in close detail Queen Victoria's promise of peace and tolerance.

Associations and Movements

The new generation of female political activists were educated, middle-class, high-caste, Hindu, Muslim, Parsi, or Christian women working closely with a few who were British. They formed associations – so far a masculine enterprise – and seized leading roles in social reform. Though some moved into nationalist politics when the Gandhian mass anti-colonial movements began from the early 1920s, feminine reformism continued vibrant.

Prominent initiatives in the reform movement began to reorder gender patterns in public spaces, which now made room for women activists. Sarala Devi, for example, founded the Bharat Stree Mahamandal in 1910, an association for patriotic women which sprouted branches in several North Indian cities. She also organised physical culture centres with Hindu ritualistic symbols to inspire and train strong-bodied male patriots. Her emphasis on physical culture and leadership of a male organisation sharply challenged conventions of female conduct and, interestingly, blurred the boundaries between male and female spheres of action – the more so since physical culture had until then been a typically male activity. Margaret Cousins, an Irish feminist and prominent Theosophist, set up the Women's Indian Association (WIA) in 1915. Restricted largely to Madras, it consisted mostly of upper-caste women. The All India Women's Conference (AIWC) was begun in 1927. Larger in geographical terms, it too was restricted to elite metropolitan women. These associations recommended a gendered yet advanced education for women and opposed child marriage – even if only on the grounds that child marriage had not been prescribed by the sacred Vedas. And though several Muslim leaders had opposed the 1929 Act which restricted child marriage, Muslim women in the organisation supported it, securely ensconced as they were in their alternative community of women.

By and large these women's organisations transcended sectarian identities. The Bharat Mahila Parishad – the women's wing of the National Social Conference – was led by Ramabai Ranade and Mrs Abbas Tyabji. They focused on women's legal difficulties and demanded suffrage based on educational and property qualifications, the reservation of seats for women in legislative assemblies and municipalities, and the inclusion of women in commissions of enquiry. Thus empowered, they argued, women themselves could better address women's needs.

Illustrious women such as Sarojini Naidu, Sarala Devi, Lajjavanti, Muthulakshmi Reddy, Rameshwari Nehru, Ladorani Zutshi, and many others came from exceptionally liberal families in Madras, Calcutta, Lahore, Lucknow – cities that were the hubs of higher education with lively public spheres and cosmopolitan lifestyles. They worked with like-minded men to acquire a wider support base. To ensure that their extraordinary public roles did not lead them into social isolation, they tried to propitiate their religious communities by separating out reform from broader critiques of the religious prescriptions in which gender norms were embedded. In this respect their appeasement was something of a retreat from the nineteenth- and early-twentieth-century feminism which had been bold enough to criticise sacred prescriptions. Nor were these early-twentieth-century organisations concerned about the living and working conditions of women factory workers or agricultural labourers: their attention was restricted to their own class. Educated and public-spirited maternalism rather than gender equality or women's rights was the horizon of their articulations. Yet, paradoxically, even this limited maternal reformism involved breaking entrenched gendered boundaries because it brought women out of their homes and into public spaces.

In 1917 a women's delegation met the British Secretary of State Edwin Montagu to ask for the vote on the same terms as men. Montagu refused them, as did the Indian provincial and central governments. The Southborough Franchise Commission, determined to preserve the colonial image of Indians as irretrievably conservative, and choosing to ignore Indian women's voices and activism, concluded that suffrage "would be out of harmony with the conservative feeling of the country."[7] In contrast, and refuting the charge of Indian conservatism, when Sarojini Naidu brought the demand to the Congress, she received a sympathetic hearing from Indian nationalists. Herabai Tata led a WIA delegation to England to canvass support among British feminists. But there she met a formidable opponent in Cornelia Sorabji, who argued that the vote was a useless adornment because, given the social constraints on Indian women, even the educated and propertied would fail to use it in an independent and informed manner. When the House of Commons dropped the idea for the time being, Madame Bhikaji Cama told the disappointed suffragists that independence alone could resolve women's subordination. Britain itself was passing through the throes of militant suffragist agitations which were fiercely blocked by parliament and public opinion. The Indian nationalist political sphere, in contrast, was relatively receptive.

The suffrage campaign in India went through two phases. The first, which stretched between 1917 and 1928, raised the question of women's vote and representation on the various elected bodies from the municipal to the provincial legislative levels. The second, which lasted between 1928 and 1938, managed to partially achieve both ends. Women's associations had proposed that female franchise be given under the same, rather limited, terms as the male franchise, that is, on terms of the rather high property and educational qualifications which few women possessed at the

---

[7] Cited in Everett, *Women and Social Change in India*, p. 106.

time. Later, when Muthulakshmi Reddy altered this to a demand for universal adult franchise, many others argued for special reservation on the legislative bodies instead. Muthulakshmi Reddy had contended that, given their educational and social vulnerabilities, a female franchise would not indicate free political choices for women, it would strengthen the voices of rich and conservative husbands whose wives alone would acquire the vote under the existing franchise rules.

The Government of India Act of 1935 eventually enfranchised women of property and education – though relatively few women possessed either – giving the vote to about six million. Jawaharlal Nehru wanted women candidates to contest the elections from the reserved and not the general seats. Radhabai Subbarayan, wanting to contest from a general seat, was made to withdraw from the contest. Begum Qudsia Aizaz Rasul, on the other hand, did contest from a general Muslim seat in 1936 to oppose the communalisation of politics and women's seclusion. Though a conservative fatwa asked people not to vote for her, she won by a handsome majority.

There were important debates, too, about desirable relations between the colonial state and women's organisations – a dilemma that has routinely troubled women's movements in other colonial and semi-colonial countries. How far should women seek places on official bodies, how far should they solicit state support for their programmes? The Congress had boycotted the all-white Simon Commission, formed in 1927 to discuss electoral and constitutional reforms. It also boycotted the First Round Table Conference of all parties in London in 1930 which discussed future constitutional reforms. Women's groups were invited to both, and they expected important dividends from them. Now they faced a difficult choice.

The Congress had endorsed female franchise in 1918, though Gandhi insisted that the vote was of no consequence, especially for rural women. Jawaharlal Nehru was more sympathetic, yet somewhat impatient with women's insistence on the removal of legal discrimination. Agrarian reforms should have priority, he thought, and he was uneasy about the role of the state in legal reform.

Many women activists, however, identified more strongly with the massive anti-colonial upsurges that repeatedly rocked the country between 1919 and 1942. They chose to place women's issues on the back burner for the time being. They felt awkward about asking the state for help during moments of acute state repression. Muthulakshmi Reddy resigned her seat on the Legislative Assembly, giving up a hard-won and rare resource. Radhabai Subbarayan and Begum Jahan Ara Shah Nawaz, on the other hand, refused to jettison their shared organisational and gender interests.

When the Muslim League and the Congress pulled apart over constitutional deliberations, and as the Non-Cooperation–Khilafat unity of the Hindu and Muslim anti-colonial movements of 1921 was replaced with communal rioting from the mid 1920s, women's organisations remained islands of non-sectarian unity as long as their agenda was purely gender-based. Once a part of the group moved towards the Congress, the unity fractured and Muslim women too withdrew from the front. This deepened the divisions among political women on community lines.

Recent research has uncovered the caste bias of these organisations. Anjanbai Deshbratar, a Dalit woman, attended the AIWC conference at Nagpur in 1938 and was shocked by the upper-caste women's "distant, cold, mean" attitude towards Dalits, who were kept physically apart from the rest. She felt deeply humiliated. In 1945 a conference of Dalit women inspired by B.R. Ambedkar decided to distance themselves from the AIWC and form their own organisation.

As women joined the nationalist movements in increasing numbers, Jawaharlal Nehru and Subhas Chandra Bose, dynamic young Congress leaders, showed themselves ready to accept female suffrage, social reforms, and the formation of women's wings within the Congress. As their movements intensified, both acted as catalysts to overthrow many of the normative inhibitions against women's public activities. Even if they were disturbed by the public presence and prominence of women, other male nationalists of a conservative stripe could hardly express their reservations, given that these women had made remarkable contributions to the anticolonial movements. In quite a momentous break from their ordained public invisibility and inaudibility, Sarojini Naidu, Ladorani Zutshi, Basanti Devi, Urmila Devi, and many others now began to address political meetings from the Congress podium. So did Bi Amman – mother of the Ali brothers who led the Khilafat movement. She first spoke at a Khilafatist meeting from behind her veil, calling herself not only the mother of her sons but of the entire gathering which had come to listen to her. Having established her virtual motherhood, she unveiled her face as she spoke – a dramatic step made possible by the maternal motif. In a complex coupling of the traditional and the transgressive, motherhood and the idea of a liberation led by the mother figure became a prominent feature of political language for several other movements too. Putative kinship with nationalist leaders, moreover, cushioned the political journey for some women from prominent nationalist families, for it was also the ordained duty of women to follow in the footsteps of male guardians.

Mass Movements

A new phase succeeded the earlier Moderate Congress politics of petitioning the government about various administrative failures and abuses. It was initiated in 1905 when Lord Curzon arbitrarily partitioned the province of Bengal, a decision that had to be retracted in 1911 in the face of tremendous protests which engulfed, in particular, Bengal, Punjab, and Maharashtra. The upsurge anticipated several features of the later nationalist movements – the boycott of loyalists and shops which stored foreign goods, especially cloth; street demonstrations; and, eventually, armed attacks on individual British officials. Though most lower-caste peasants,

Muslims, and Dalits did not show much enthusiasm, large numbers of middle-class women helped the movement from behind their seclusion. They donated their ornaments to the nationalist cadres and burnt their foreign garments. Stirring patriotic songs were composed and sung that particularly addressed and aroused women to acts of sacrifice. The nationalist slogan was *Bande Mataram* (Salutations to the Goddess of the Motherland). The country itself was embodied in nationalist artwork and the poetic imagination as a divine female figure representing the map of Bharatvarsha.

This symbolic tribute to a goddess, however, did not alter the woman's location in her home. Nor did it bring even the most ardent of women patriots out of their homes. *Ghare Baire* (*Home and the World*, first published in 1916), Rabindranath Tagore's controversial novel of these times, captures the paradox: Bimala is inspired by Sandeep, a leader of the Swadeshi upsurge, to imagine herself as the soul of an extreme form of nationalist militancy. Her political ambitions fly high and her language becomes overcharged with nationalist passion. However, all she does for the cause happens within the home – she never takes a step beyond her threshold to join public politics, which still remained the world of men. In Ashapurna Debi's memorable novel *Subarnalata* (1966) a middle-class woman rebukes a young revolutionary: "Your movement is doomed. Try first to save your women from the hell they live in – until then, all your efforts to save the country will go waste."[8]

The situation began to change once the anti-colonial movements began to grow and spread from 1919 – after Gandhi revamped the Indian National Congress to make it an effective instrument for mass mobilisations that reached out far beyond the middle classes. Beginning with the Rowlatt Satyagraha, which protested the extension of wartime restrictions on civil liberties after the

---

[8] Ashapurna Devi, *Subarnalata*, p. 205.

War, the protests gathered increasing momentum in 1920–1 at the time of the Non-Cooperation–Khilafat movements. These called for a boycott of official educational institutions, honours, and foreign goods; they also saw Hindus and Muslims coming together in protests against the abolition of the Turkish caliphate and the massacre of unarmed demonstrators at Jallianwalla Bagh in Punjab in April 1919. Though a few women did become prominent figures in the course of this upsurge, most of them helped the Congress and Khilafat cadres with funds and moral support from their homes. A far more dramatic change, however, occurred from the time of Civil Disobedience (1930–4), which gave a call for preparing contraband salt, disobedience of unjust laws, and refusal to pay taxes.

As is well known, it was Gandhi who first eased the way for women in public nationalism. But what are we to make of the politicisation of women under a leader who himself was explicitly patriarchal and a diehard traditionalist? We should, perhaps, reverse the terms of our enquiry. By pondering over what Gandhi or the Congress movements were doing to women we reduce women's politicisation to the intentions of male leaders. If we ask instead what women did to the movements and to Gandhi – who changed with the movements as much as he changed them – we have a better starting point.

During the Rowlatt Satyagraha of 1919 Gandhi had been reluctant to involve women in the strike action; some, however, joined the protests on their own initiative. In 1930 Gandhi again forbade women to join his long march to the Dandi coast of Gujarat – to make contraband salt and thereby kick-start Civil Disobedience in defiance of unjust colonial laws which had given the state the monopoly for manufacturing salt. Sarojini Naidu nonetheless joined the march, and Kamaladevi Chattopadhyay and Avantikabai Gokhale lit the first fires on which salt was prepared. Gandhi did not object in either case.

Gradually, women became visible in all possible political roles within the Congress movements – in Gandhian rural ashrams, in village welfare work, in picketing foreign goods shops, in rural agitations. They came from rich and conservative Marwari families at one end and from peasant and tribal ones at the other. Marching together and courting arrests collectively led to at least a temporary crumbling of entrenched class barriers, an enlargement of social horizons for both rich and poor. But while these mass movements constantly opened up new frontiers for women, no one seems to have initiated any serious discussion of Indian gender inequities. This, too, was an unintended or non-explicit fallout of the Congress movements: like gender relations, class relations attained a temporary, almost unreal, equality in the world of politics, even as inequalities remained fixed in the social worlds of labour and property relations.

The Congress soon realised the tactical value of placing women in leading positions in political militancy and certain kinds of action became the preserve of women – who more than justified the political trust placed on them. The Congress had, in particular, entrusted the picketing of shops that stocked foreign goods to women and children, in the hope that their moral appeal, displayed in public places, would inspire passive onlookers on the streets to join the struggles. The street-level processions were either mixed, women being placed on the frontlines, or there were women's own demonstrations in the expectation that the presence of women and children would soften the fury of police attacks on demonstrators. An official report on Bengal for the second half of June 1930 noted that, as a women's procession marched and mounted police confronted it, women fell on the ground in front of the police "clutching their legs and by catching the reins of mounted police horses."[9] Surprisingly, many of these women came from elite Calcutta families, including Jyotirmoyee Ganguly and

---

[9] Intelligence Bureau, file no. 90 of 1928, Secret: Fortnightly Reports on the Political Situation in Bengal, 2nd half of June and 2nd half of July 1930.

Urmila Debi, sister of the nationalist leader C.R. Das. One even assaulted a European assistant. "On 26 July, a large number started out from the headquarters of the Women's Civil Disobedience Committee and marched to Burrabazar in North Calcutta to picket foreign goods shops. Stopped by a police cordon, they sat down in front of shops till midnight."[10] They blockaded the law courts and roads in the remote East Bengal district of Noakhali. Inhibitions and conventions treasured for ages practically melted away at the touch of nationalism and women now glaringly transgressed the boundaries of approved feminine conduct in full public view. Many, however, were shielded from social disapproval of their unfeminine behaviour by the approval of their nationalist relatives.

Prisons lost their terror for women, so much so that by February 1931 officials made "every endeavour to avoid arrests, especially of women and boys from processions . . . The Policy followed is to separate the women and then to disperse the boys vigorously." But the relentless police repression did eventually affect middle-class morale. "In many districts, middle classes are avoiding demonstrations and many of the women and boys in the processions belong to the lower classes." Subaltern women, clearly, bore the brunt of police attacks with more confidence and courage. The police offered a cynical explanation: "They [lower-class women] would probably have no objection to be fed in jail."[11]

Villages in south-west Bengal refused to pay *chowkidari* (village policing) taxes even when the police tortured and arrested large numbers of their people, distrained their properties, and set fire to their standing crops. This bore down very heavily on middling and poorer peasants already badly damaged by the agrarian depression which had begun to hit farmers from 1929. Sometimes whole families hid in the nearby forests as policemen went on the

---

[10] Ibid., 2nd half of July 1930.
[11] Ibid., Fortnightly Reports, first half of March 1931.

rampage against their homesteads. The costly resistance to such brutality would have been impossible to sustain without the consent and courage of peasant women. More and more men were put behind bars and peasant women now became the "dictators" of local Civil Disobedience committees. Many came from the "low" Shudra castes: Urmilabala Paria from Midnapore was the district's first woman martyr.

From 1930 onwards Gandhians began to attract women from the wealthy peasant and upper-caste landed families at Pandaul, an estate of the Maharaja of Darbhanga in north Bihar. Seclusion norms were particularly rigid here and upper-caste women seldom stepped out of their homes. Social reform and nationalism now overlapped in conjoint anti-seclusion movements and Gandhian khadi programmes, Gandhi having decreed the spinning of cotton – khadi – a compulsory activity for all nationalists. An example of the changed circumstances for women is Janaki Devi, who ran away from home when her father arranged a match for her – to join the Congress: Gandhian ashrams and rural constructive work began to offer shelter to women who wanted to bypass marriage and domesticity. Janaki Devi went on to open schools for village girls.

Many young high-caste Pandaul landlords also joined the Gandhian ashrams, which emerged as spearheads of social change in a particularly orthodox place. They brought their wives into the nationalist campaigns and into the ashrams, in the process tearing apart family-centred lives and domestic conventions. Jagadamba Devi, Rajkishori Devi, Neeras Chaudhury, and other high-caste women established the Magan Ashram where, in a revolutionary departure from the rules of caste commensality, high-caste men and women dined with untouchable Chamars and Muslim artisans taught them the art of weaving. The ashram was controlled by young Gandhian men who encouraged their wives to join in the rallies in violation of upper-caste purdah rules. As a result, control over women slipped away from the extended family and older male guardians to young husbands who fashioned new gender norms within the political movement. Not everything changed, of course, and many young unmarried women remained homebound – in this respect Janaki Devi was an exception, and even she advised women to spin khadi at home. Women could join nationalist work only after they were safely married and once their children had grown up, which was when they were deemed to be of a "safe" age.

The Quit India movement of 1942, the third and most intense phase in the Gandhian struggle, sanctioned even the use of violence. The Congress was banned and prominent leaders, including Gandhi, imprisoned. The circumstances required women replacements and Aruna Asaf Ali emerged as the premier organiser of the underground resistance. Born into a rich Brahmo family in Bengal and working as a teacher, she had joined Gandhian politics in 1940. Daringly, she had married a left-leaning Muslim Congress activist, Asaf Ali, twenty-three years older than her. He supported the British war efforts while she opposed them. Jailed for her violation of the Defence of India Rules, she spread political education among her fellow women prisoners. Once out of prison in 1942, she led a procession, braving teargas attacks at a protest rally in which thirty-four people were killed. Facing a warrant of arrest, she went underground to organise the resistance movement, moving rapidly around – with the help of friends among senior Indian bureaucrats – to befuddle the police searching for her. A hefty reward was announced for her capture, and though the Criminal Investigation Department were hot on her trail she successfully evaded arrest.

Sucheta Kripalani, similarly, was always on the move, posing as a student and sheltering with rich families who were above suspicion. Once, her group sheltered at a Bombay clinic, pretending to be patients. Their underground movement was financed by prominent Indian bankers and industrialists like Birla and Walchand Hirachand. While they certainly took fantastic risks, their social background did cushion them up to a point and facilitated their courage. It was a totally different story for subaltern activists. Matangini Hazra, a poor rural woman, for example, was killed while leading a peaceful procession.

Aruna Asaf Ali later joined the Congress Socialist Party, a radical wing of the Congress. Her husband worried about his young wife who had struck out a dangerous path all by herself while he was relatively safe inside prison. She decided not to have children, cut her hair short, and made her politics spill over into social rebellion.

In the 1937 Assembly elections four women were elected from reserved constituencies in Bihar: the anti-colonial struggles were visibly enabling women's claims to political and electoral equality. When female franchise was granted after Independence, it was given to all women, not just to the propertied and the educated. Indian suffragists did not have to endure the intense state and public repression and violence that their British counterparts had suffered for many decades. Yet, as long as the struggles continued, their leading roles were usually reversed once state repression was relaxed — at which point the men returned to the movements to decide their course. Nor did women, however privileged or active, ever occupy the pinnacles of nationalist organisations. And the multi-class and caste character of these movements notwithstanding, all the renowned women leaders came from privileged social locations.

Nationalist movements did not explicitly envision or advocate a radical repositioning of women within domesticity — separate spheres for men and women remained the unquestioned ideal. Gandhi exalted women as ideal satyagrahis but did so precisely because they were selfless, non-violent, and innately chaste — or so he believed. While this gave them a moral edge and an iconic status within the movements, they purchased the privilege with a redoubled affirmation of their traditional image, and of the woman's lot. Gandhi's close disciples were obliged to observe stern celibacy within their marriage, he being the exemplar. He had already taken a vow of chastity in South Africa in 1906 – without consulting his wife. Inspired by him, Sucheta and J.P. Kripalani pledged themselves to a sexless marriage. Gandhi attributed a surplus of moral energy to widows precisely because they were perforce celibate. He believed this helped them to sublimate their sexual passion as nationalist ardour. Volunteers were told to either eliminate the sexual urge or be ashamed of it, and their sternly austere leader kept an eagle eye on interactions between men and women in his ashrams. He opposed child marriage because it led to a premature and excessive expenditure of sexual energy – as he recalled from his own conjugal experiences. He found the compulsory segregation of purdah repugnant but also thought that women should face a world of men only once they had fortified themselves with impregnable chastity. His was therefore a most complex approach to gender, a compound of unprecedented liberation in the political sphere and impossible demands for sexual self-denial.

Two significant features of the Gandhian movements eased the unprecedented entry of women into the turbulent world of mass politics. Gandhi's political action included traditional domestic ritual and women's work. The spinning wheel, for instance, operated by women at home, had been made a compulsory nationalist activity. The boycott of foreign goods similarly depended on women's decisions about domestic consumption. Who else, moreover, better understood the great significance of salt during the salt satyagraha – a campaign to manufacture salt in defiance of the law – than women who handled it every day in their cooking? The anti-liquor agitations, too, had special resonances for women, beleaguered as they were by bankruptcy and domestic violence from loutishly drunk husbands. Gandhi told women to defy their men if they were loyal to the British; in other ways the woman's defiance of the man was, of course, out of the question. Conversely, what men did in the non-violent satyagraha replicated women's strategies against domestic tyranny – that is, unflinchingly facing police assaults without retaliating. The logic underpinning Gandhian activism therefore blurred the divisions between the domestic and the political, between spheres that had for long been separated as male and female.

Being perceived as a saint, a moral and spiritual force more than the politician that he also was, Gandhi recast nationalism as a religious vocation rather than as politics. This too made politics hospitable to women, since religion was to them a familiar terrain. The nation appeared as the family writ large, and men and women could worship together at its shrine.

Nationalism did, nonetheless, change women in ways that Gandhi himself might not have approved. Manmohini Saigal asked Congress women from respectable families to do the unthinkable – to socialise with prostitutes in prisons. Some who followed her suggestion returned home from the prison transformed. Sir Ismail Mirza found his wife excessively self-assertive after her brush with politics.

There is thus a tension between Gandhi's proclaimed ideology of separate spheres and the political equality which became a reality within his struggles, between what he asked of women and what women in fact came to do, between his moral precepts and political praxis. Eventually, he could not control all the consequences of what he had unleashed. Even when social norms remained outwardly unscathed, the very fact of politicisation was in itself a momentous departure. When I asked an old Gandhian woman from a Calcutta slum why her ways did not change after her political life was over – a child-widow, she had remained tied to Brahmanical widowhood norms – she chided me: "The woman who came back from the movement was not the one who had gone out. How can she possibly be the same person? She had been making History in between."[12]

Perhaps the paradox climaxed when Gandhi took a number of young Hindu women – unarmed and unprotected – along with

[12] My interview with Sudha Mukhopadhyay, Calcutta, June 1989.

him on his peace mission to riot-torn Noakhali in 1946, where many Hindu women had recently been raped. He asked Ashoka Gupta, the wife of a senior bureaucrat and the mother of young children, to stay on at this dangerous place on her own after he departed with his team. At the same time, he reprimanded the rape survivors there for not committing suicide. He alleged that, had they been truly virtuous, no one could have raped them – they were modern "Juliets" who must have lost their virtue and therefore could not protect themselves. He also constantly tested his own chastity with bizarre sexual experiments at Noakhali, sleeping naked with his teenage grand-niece Manu, for instance. Gandhi's gender ideology and what his politics offered to women were enmeshed in what now seems a strange and complex interface.

Women also played a significant role in autonomous anti-colonial movements which lay outside Congress control. At Kachar in the north-eastern region of present-day Nagaland, Gaidinliu (1915–1993) led the Civil Disobedience and No Tax movements. Later called "Rani Gaidinliu" by Jawaharlal Nehru, she was "at the time of her death a national figure, with admirers and followers comparing her to the Rani of Jhansi . . ."[13] Gaidinliu had in fact followed only in the footsteps of her cousin Jadonang, a sectarian nationalist leader who had led Civil Disobedience in Manipur. After he was executed as a rebel by the British, she shifted her base to the North Cachar Hills, among the Zeliagong tribal people. She led them in an anti-colonial movement against compulsory porterage levies – called *begar* in Garhwal, this was a form

---

[13] Chophy, *Christianity and Tribal Politics*, p. 259. Clearly, by this time in the nationalist mind every politically brave woman was a variant on the Rani of Jhansi. As Chophy puts it: "It was Nehru who bestowed on Gaidinliu the title 'Rani', which then became the honorific prefixed to her name. The two leaders had first met while Gaidinliu was serving life imprisonment in Shillong Jail . . . The honorific, not even remotely related to traditional Naga usage, became Gaidinliu's trademark as her fame spread far beyond the landlocked hills of Tamenglong." Ibid.

of forced labour. The colonial government tried many ruses to capture her but she escaped arrest for months by hiding in jungles.

Robert Reid, Governor of Assam, had complained in 1939: "Manipuri women are notorious for their independence..."[14] The "First Women's War" known locally as Nupilal, occurred in the small north-eastern princely state of Manipur in 1904. It happened when the British political agent demanded that local people rebuild the government bungalows which they had supposedly destroyed by arson. Sturdy resistance forced Reid to retract his order. A second Nupilal exploded in 1939. Women had traditionally dominated the main market at Imphal where they freely bought and sold their wares: they were, therefore, particularly sensitive to price fluctuations and the export of goods. They reacted sharply when the British as well as Marwari traders began to export rice from Manipur to serve military demands and sell it at inflated rates elsewhere. Following on the heels of floods and bad harvests in late 1939, prices escalated dangerously and the ruling dynasty did nothing to obstruct the outflow. The market women, now bereft of their control over rice sales in a situation of deepening hunger, appealed to the political agent to ban the exports. Dissatisfied with his response, thousands of women mobilised for a remarkable protest movement all by themselves. This involved a boycott of the market, and peaceful but extremely determined blockades of government offices despite severe police and army manhandling. Their resistance lasted for a year, aggravating popular anger against the British agent and the Marwaris, and discrediting the puppet princely dynasty.

Armed Revolutionaries

From 1908 revolutionary "terrorists" began to plot secret assassinations of British officials and European men in India. Occasionally, they organised large-scale uprisings as well. During the First World

---

[14] Cited in Arambam and Parrott, "The Second Women's War and the Emergence of Democratic Government in Manipur", vol. 2, p. 196.

War the Ghadar Party, recruited from Punjabi migrants in the United States and Canada, planned to return home with foreign arms and stage an insurrection. They were arrested en route. In 1930, at Chittagong in Bengal, revolutionaries planned to take over the town by disrupting transport and managed to immobilise the local administration for a few days.

Revolutionaries threw up a new ideal type of political masculinity and initiated a cognitive shift in Indian social and cultural perceptions which otherwise valorise age and experience. Youth was their most valued asset, instead. Since many were arrested, tortured, exiled to the dreaded Andaman Cellular Jail, or hanged, an aura of martyrdom bathed even the living, for death was always awaiting them just round the corner. All took the vow of celibacy till freedom came, and many left home to avoid marriage. They repudiated the conventional goals of life, such as material success, family ties, procreation. Surya Sen, legendary leader of the Chittagong raids of 1930, abandoned his wife as soon as he was married, even though he later told his young women followers that "your courage and your dedication made me change my mind."[15] The compliment related to their capacity for armed action

So ubiquitous was the renunciation of marriage that revolutionaries occasionally disguised themselves as married men and women because the police, aware of the chastity resolution, always hunted for the single and the unmarried. There could also have been a hidden motive for some – a distaste for heterosexual relationships and a strong urge for the homosocial intimacy that these secret groups offered. There were pragmatic and strategic reasons, too, for hardening oneself against familial and married love. Impending martyrdom threatened to leave a trail of young widows, and affection for parents occasionally tempted captives to betray comrades when the police tortured their families.

[15] Dutt, *Chittagong Armoury Raiders*, p. 31. The cited sentence is my own translation.

Additionally, celibacy was supposed to be a source of moral and physical strength and resolve. Here, ironically, Gandhian non-violence and revolutionary violence – polar opposites otherwise – met and agreed.

Bhagat Singh (1907–1931), a young Sikh revolutionary from Punjab, left home to avoid marriage. In 1928, along with Ashfaqullah, Chandra Shekhar Azad, and others, he founded the Hindustan Socialist Republican Association (HSRA) – socialism being a most unusual addition to the usual revolutionary ideological repertoire. The admission of a Muslim man into their secret ranks was also a rather unique decision since most other such organisations kept Muslims out. On the run from 1928, and disguised as a Sahib, Bhagat Singh was captured in 1929 and executed in 1931, becoming the most iconic revolutionary martyr whose radiance shines bright to this day. The commemorations, however, ignore his later turn to atheism, his repudiation of the revolutionary goal, his embrace of Marxism, and his interest in Russian anarchist traditions.

Simona Sawhney emphasises the way in which the inevitable sacrifice of the self – in life as in death – knitted together a masculine and feminine impulse among these revolutionaries. They sacrificed their lives – as women sacrifice themselves perpetually – in the cause of a sorrowful and vulnerable Motherland; but they also used violence as men, as the conquerors of foes.

Women were rarely permitted to join revolutionary circles but they did sometimes inspire violence. Urmila Devi and Basanti Devi, sister and wife of the Bengal Congress leader Chittaranjan Das, were front-ranking Congress workers. After Lajpat Rai was killed by the colonial police in 1928, Basanti Devi issued a public challenge: "I, a woman of India, ask the youth of India: what are you going to do about it?"[16] The HSRA responded with a plot to

---

[16] Cited in Maclean, *A Revolutionary History of Interwar India*, p. 31. Also Maclean, "What Durga Bhabhi Did Next".

assassinate J.P. Saunders, a policeman who they thought had taken part in the attack which killed Lajpat Rai – a mistake, because the lathi charge had in fact been ordered by Saunders' immediate senior. Bhagat Singh killed Saunders and was, ironically, executed in 1931 for assassinating the wrong man.

The dazzle of Bhagat Singh's martyrdom, and that of his comrades, has obscured the role of the women who acted as their logistical support base, took enormous risks, and even engaged in direct terrorist action in North India. Along with her left-leaning husband, Durga Devi Vohra, a teacher at a Lahore college, helped revolutionaries to make bombs. The fact that she had a small son misled the police, who thought a mother could not possibly risk manufacturing incendiary devices. After the Saunders killing she helped Bhagat Singh with funds and facilitated his escape by posing as his wife. Commonly known as Bhabhi (sister-in-law), the name indicating a fictive kinship with Bhagat Singh, she shot at a European couple in 1930, mistaking the man for the governor of Punjab. She escaped arrest but continued to collect funds for Bhagat Singh's defence. In 1932, however, depressed and increasingly disheartened about the future, she surrendered. After her release she shifted to the Congress.

From 1930 a number of Bengali revolutionary women became full-scale comrades-in-arms, this being somewhat unique to Bengal. The Congress had earlier set up several women's associations to train women for volunteer work. The Chhatri Sangha, for instance, was a wing of the nationalist women students. While they organised pickets and demonstrations, a secret core nested within, testing and preparing students for the assassinations that were to follow. They were trained in lathi, dagger, and sword combat, while a chosen few learnt to make bombs and use guns. In 1931 two teenaged schoolgirls, Shanti and Suniti, assassinated the district magistrate of Comilla. Pritilata Waddedar led an attack on the Chittagong European Club the same year, killing several members. Kalpana Dutt, another member of the Chittagong group, followed Surya Sen into a prolonged underground existence. Dressed as a man and living in the deepest secrecy of forests and hill tracts with male comrades, she was captured in 1933. Bina Das had earlier fired at Bengal's governor, Stanley Jackson, at a Calcutta University convocation in 1932. She spent seven years in prison – where she once had a curious dream. Lenin appeared in it to reproach her for just plotting killings when there was so much else to do – even within her prison walls. She could teach ordinary women convicts to read and write and thus atone for her class privileges. It was an unexpected dream for someone so deeply into revolutionary politics. Perhaps the subconscious guilt that had inspired the dream in the first place later made her work among ordinary labourers under Congress auspices after her release. She went back to prison during the Quit India movement.

Women, more than revolutionary men, had to account for their rejection of family ties, the defiance of their guardians, their violent actions, and intimate comradeships with men. These constituted a far more painful as well as violent transgression of their gendered identities and sensibilities. Despite their celibacy vows, romance blossomed among some. Kalpana Dutt and Tarakeswar Dastidar fell in love, but Surya Sen constantly policed their conversations. After Pritilata Waddedar died, the police found a photograph of Ramakrishna Biswas, another member of the Chittagong group, on her person: she had clearly been in love with him, abandoned a family which was dependent on her salary, and gone against the family loyalties which always framed the woman's world. Her last letter speaks of times of extraordinary upsurges that require extraordinary sacrifices from women.

The motif of sacrifice, and the assurance that violations of the norm happened only because of an emergency, therefore foreclosed new gender roles for women in general, even when the activists themselves inhabited them. The blurring of gender boundaries and equality in combat had to be restricted to moments of violence, and these heroic women spared little thought for ordinary women. In her confession Bina Das says her action was "an outrage against my nature . . ." But she did it "to die, to die nobly, fighting against the despotic system of government which has kept my country in perpetual subjection." Her possible death mitigated and redeemed her wish to kill: "Would not the immolation of a daughter of India and a son of England awaken India? A slave cannot realize God . . . My sense of religion and morality is not inconsistent with my sense of political freedom . . . freedom is originally connected with religion." She also referred to her sister Kalyani Das, a Congress student activist who suffered a year's rigorous imprisonment for supposedly harbouring revolutionary leaflets. Interestingly, it is Kalyani's humiliation, primarily described in class and caste terms, that had awakened Bina's resolve to kill British officials. Though she belonged to a "well off, respectable family . . . Kalyani had been subjected to the ignominy of the jail uniform and the prison diet and even had to spend sleepless nights among criminals."[17] Bina Das compared her own act with self-immolation, thereby recuperating revolutionary work within the tradition of sati and sacralising the political.

Women nationalists and revolutionaries came out of broad social developments during the inter-War period when middle-class lives were being radically refashioned. Their political work should be read as a part of this larger canvas. While professional male wrestlers and athletes had always trained themselves at the *akharas* (special training schools), nationalism broadened and generalised the urge among young people of the middle classes as well. Revolutionaries taught them combat skills and the use of weapons. The urge equally engrossed young women from nationalist families – they too eagerly took to physical exercise and combat training, learning for example to wield the dagger and the lathi. They were often taught by young men. Bina's brother testified that

---

[17] Das, *A Memoir*, p. 80.

"Both of my sisters, Miss Kalyani Das and Miss Bina Das, had many girl and male friends."[18] Cycling and other forms of athleticism were a sign of this, as was intimacy with young men. Shanti Ghosh and Suniti Choudhury, the two young girls who assassinated Magistrate G.B. Stevens of Comilla in 1931, met him on the pretext of being acclaimed swimmers who wanted his permission to demonstrate their skills in a public event. Clearly, Stevens did not find this an unusual request. Accustomed to modern dress and cosmetics, both asked for "snow, hairpins, sari, chemise, blouse, and towels" when they were incarcerated in Alipore Central Jail.

Politics did not constitute a stand-alone sphere – it was connected with a broader social transformation that encompassed higher education, staying in hostels and the consequent independence from family controls, athleticism, and romances that did not always lead to marriage. Altogether, it represented a fresh generation of the "New Woman" who turned her class, caste, and educational privileges towards autonomous personal and political choices.

Gender on the Left

In 1939 the Tinkonma peasant movement against the Maharaja of Darbhanga in North Bihar was inspired by left-wing anti-landlord slogans. Peasants banded together to seize crops from the maharaja's land. "Lower-caste" and Muslim women, who had worked in the fields since the agrarian depression of the early and mid 1930s, were remarkably active and visible in their red saris, the colour of Left politics.

From the early 1920s a few educated middle-class women began to work in the slums of Calcutta and Bombay to build unions and organise strikes. Occasionally, they worked with the Workers'

---

[18] Confession of Bina Das, sent to Special Police Superintendent, Calcutta, 10/7/1939, IB Records 172/32, Part 2, Intelligence Bureau Archives, Calcutta.

and Peasants' Party, the mass front of the Communists, but they almost always worked on their own. A few women who had married communist men were similarly drawn into working-class militancy. Ushatai Dange had already made a small social revolution when she, a Maharashtrian Brahman child-widow from a ferociously conservative family, defied custom and guardians by falling in love with and marrying S.A. Dange, a young Brahman communist. She had leadership thrust upon her when her husband was in jail and the Girni Kamgar Union of the Bombay Textile workers went on strike. Otherwise a timid housewife, Ushatai was virtually dragged out of her home by workers who wanted her to lead their strike as Dange's wife, and once among them she felt exhilarated. Women workers took care of her baby while she made fiery speeches.

Ascribed motherhood enabled women to move among distant social classes and castes. Manibehn Kara, Parvati Bhore, and Ushatai Dange found in their motherhood a language and emotion that they could share with women workers who, in other respects, lived in a totally different world. But, in general, trade unions neglected their women workers, and women leaders too worked primarily with male unionists.

The Communist Party of India was founded in 1925 but women began to join it only from the late 1930s and early 1940s. Godavari Parulekar was sent to organise the landless tribal labourers of Worli in Maharashtra against a system of unpaid labour. She has left a rare description of Worli family life and homes, along with an account of their labour and employment terms. Even as she worked with tribal men, she critically described their "witch" trials.

Several feminist studies have underlined the marginalisation of women activists in the Communist movements. Communist ideologues did not theorise gender issues, seeing them as epiphenomenal in relation to class. Nonetheless, in their own lives they often refashioned domesticities, familial worlds, and gender practices. Love marriages were the preferred norm, and the 1940s saw daring experiments with communes into which individual families were submerged within these larger collectivities, all the families living in the same residence. Party offices were regarded as a haven for rebellious young women who sometimes ran away from home to avoid arranged matches.

At the same time, women were not placed in leading, decision-making positions, nor were they encouraged to engage in ideological theorisation. Another constraint was the absence of a specifically women's front where they could spread their wings in relative freedom. In 1942 the Mahila Atmaraksha Samiti (MARS) was formed to recruit party as well as non-party women for constructive welfare work among the poor. During the Bengal famine of 1943 MARS came into its own, organising famine relief, generating small-scale employment schemes, and providing rehabilitation to famine victims. Women played a leading role, too, in the theatrical and musical productions of the Indian People's Theatre Association (IPTA), which took political plays to villages and cities to raise funds for famine relief – the devastating famine in Bengal and Bihar of 1943 shocked women from many rural and urban conservative families into joining relief programmes.

Only occasionally did women overstep their prescribed roles. Ila Mitra, a renowned athlete in her early youth, was a legendary leader of the peasant sharecroppers' struggles at Nachole in East Bengal in the late 1940s. This was a movement of sharecroppers for a larger share of the harvest, transmutation of the produce rent into cash rent, and the attainment of tenant status. Captured and placed in an East Pakistan prison shortly after Partition, Ila Mitra suffered savage sexual torture.

Tribal women worked closely with local party cadres in the Tebhaga sharecroppers' movement in North Bengal. Being poor and tribal, they were spared neither by the police nor by the armed retainers of the tenure holders, and even pregnant women were shot or kicked to death. Women became most prominent during the peak points of repression, when the men went into hiding or were imprisoned; their prominence predictably waned when male leaders were back in position to reassert control.

Gender on the Right

Women's politicisation was not restricted to emancipatory politics. In 1936 the Rashtriya Swayamsevak Sangh (RSS) – the hard-right Islamophobic cultural organisation founded in 1925 – opened a women's wing in 1936 called the Rashtrasevika Samiti. The Samiti set up daily training centres for largely urban, upper-caste, and middle-class women with physical and combat training and ideological teaching. The intent was twofold: first, to strengthen the upper-caste female body so that future Hindu sons became invincible in conflict; and second, to cultivate mothers in communal political values so that they would transmit ethnic hatred and ethnic pride to their children at home. Though the Samiti was founded in 1936, its women played no role in the mass anti-colonial movements, nor in progressive women's organisations that worked on gender issues. Lakshmibai Kelkar, its founder, had been refused by the RSS leaders several times when she proposed a separate wing for women supporters of the Sangh. That it materialised at all was a sign of her insistence, which finally prevailed despite an obdurate male leadership. Samiti branches, rather few and quite low-key in colonial times, ran parallel to the RSS *shakha*s (branches), with an identical ideology and organisational apparatus that was primarily pedagogical. Their leaders, like the full-time preachers of the RSS, were celibate full-time women workers (*pracharika*s) who co-ordinated their activities in relative distance from the RSS which was, and remains, exclusively male. RSS leaders constitute the apex body of the Sangh and relegate Samiti leaders to a subordinate status, allowing them day-to-day autonomy within their own branches.

Though the RSS prescribed domesticity for its mothers and

wives, the very fact that women had stepped out of their families to join it and train in all-women centres added something important to their lives. It bestowed a novel political role on women from orthodox families, increasing their bargaining power at home and allowing them to navigate public spaces and roles with greater confidence. Simultaneously, their possible dissatisfactions with patriarchal control at home were tamed by what they learnt at the Samiti: that Muslim men were on the hunt for Hindu women, and that Muslim women were subordinated to an incomparable degree by their men. In short, the Samiti benefited its women recruits by providing them a degree of self-confidence and public roles that routine domesticity had never allowed them, even as it drilled into them the patriarchal ideals of womanly submissiveness, conjugal duty, and maternal care that were supposedly sacred and beyond challenge.

The home too was rendered a political base of RSS operations, as advised by M.S. Golwalkar, the second supremo of the RSS. He instructed the mothers and wives of RSS men to seek out poor and low-caste women in the neighbourhood, bring them home, make them literate, invite them to family meals, and generally draw them into the family circle. This would enlarge the circle of people receptive to RSS messages. Golwalkar also advised Hindu families to help young low-caste students with their studies. Keeping clear of all reformist endeavours that might confront caste discrimination, and even of overt critiques of caste, this was an extremely astute method for developing the Hindu home as a mass base where women could play a key role in the reproduction and construction of the ideology of Hindutva.

The demand for Pakistan brought Muslim women out into agitational politics in large numbers, but in this case there had been important antecedents. Several Muslim women had participated in the Khilafat movement. In 1924 women had been barred from the Mahomedan Education Conference which was debating women's education – and an enraged Atiya Fyzee had gate-crashed the conference and spoken from behind a curtain until the embarrassed organisers had invited her in to speak. Sayeeda Bano, an eleven-year-old girl, had led and made speeches at a women's demonstration, demanding admission into the conference.

The demand for Partition energised far larger numbers. A Muslim Girls' Students' Federation was formed in 1941. It was launched by Lady Abdul Qadir, Fatima Begum, and Miss M. Qureshi, who travelled around women's colleges to mobilise female support for Pakistan. From 1942 Jinnah began to refer to gender problems within the community, blending communal divisiveness with gender equity. Women, likewise, took their songs to rural areas, adding a markedly communal politics to the theme of women's subordination. The League's Central Committee formed a subcommittee to study Muslim women's conditions. In 1943 its women members helped Bengal famine victims.

In 1943, 5000 women attended the League's annual session at Karachi. A Women's National Guard was formed with uniforms of white *pyjama-kurta* and green *dupatta* – later adopted by the Pakistani Girl Guides. Women contested as Muslim League candidates in the 1946 elections and campaigned energetically in rural constituencies. When the League was prevented from forming a government in Punjab, where it had won only 79 out of a total of 175 seats, Muslim women came out en masse to protest. The government banned the National Guard and arrested its women leaders, and many others then courted arrest in solidarity. Several women's demonstrations were teargassed. Girls broke into the jails, shouted slogans, and hoisted their flags. One replaced the government flag in an official building with the League flag.

At first such turbulence was confined to Lahore and Karachi, but a communal civil war in 1946 – which the League chose to call Civil Disobedience – demanding the creation of Pakistan saw it spread to the North West Frontier Province. In 1947, for the first time, Pathan women unveiled their faces in public processions. They scaled ladders and braved police attacks to get into jails and hoist the League flag. A women's secret organisation was formed which named itself the War Council. It set up an underground radio station in 1947 and called it the Pakistan Broadcasting Station.

Partition inflicted untold suffering on women, both Hindu and Muslim. It left a permanent residue of bitter mutual vindictiveness on both sides of the border. But there is no doubt that it also quickened Muslim female political activism.

War, Independence, and Partition

Male combatants and indentured labourers had served in foreign lands in the Great War, their wives left behind to cope as best they could in the absence of the male breadwinner. There are colourful accounts of how Indian soldiers were feted by French women during the First World War while their wives wrote anxious letters about survival problems at home. The Second World War came closer to the Indian borders. As Japan dropped bombs on Calcutta in December 1942, occupied the Andaman Islands, and marched towards the north-eastern borders, British and American soldiers flooded into Indian cities. Severe shortages of essential goods occurred following the requisitioning of essential commodities to serve the army's needs. A scorched-earth policy in case of an invasion by Japan made the British destroy all modes of river transport in Bengal, blocking the movement of goods even as the imports of Burma rice dried up when Burma fell to Japan in early 1942. This was among the reasons for the catastrophic Bengal famine of 1943. Villages emptied out as the men migrated in search of jobs and food in cities, leaving their wives to fend for the children. Babies were sold off and many women prostituted themselves to feed their infants. The *Birmingham Mail* reported the sale of a Bengali girl to a British officer for Rs 2. Eventually, men, women, and children trekked to the cities to beg for gruel. Dead bodies piled up along pavements, too numerous to be cremated or buried. About two to three million people, mostly peasants, starved to death in Bengal. In the end the Congress, especially the communist women within it, came forward to organise food kitchens and agitate for fair-price shops for famine survivors.

Soldiers' wives faced severe problems when their husbands went missing for long periods. Nazir Begum, wife of the sepoy Jhelum, told his commanding officer that he had not sent her a penny for four years. She begged to be released from the marriage tie *in absentia* if he continued to withhold remittances. The British were reluctant to intervene in these cases of marital discord, fearing it might affect the recruitment and morale of Indian soldiers. When the women themselves initiated separations, they invited social censure. District soldiers' boards were flooded with their pleas for terminating marriage contracts and the return of dowers. The boards, sympathetic to the soldiers and indifferent to their wives, said the amounts the wives demanded were exaggerated. Love affairs bloomed between lonely wives and other men. Many such women had barely been married before their husbands left to fight in the war. Unwanted and illegitimate children arrived as an inevitable and considerable problem: *Kismet,* a popular Bombay film of 1943, depicted this difficulty.

The influx of foreign solders into Indian cities and villages played havoc with the moral order. Brothels sprang up wherever they camped; American soldiers were especially notorious for their wild behaviour in public places. Fear of the spread of venereal disease was pronounced: until 1943 soldiers were court martialled if they failed to declare sexual contact with prostitutes without using prophylactics. This rule was subsequently waived, but doctors continued to make random checks to ensure sexual health. The dreaded disease also spread among Indian soldiers, who transmitted it to their wives when they returned home. Calcutta-based troops saw the highest incidence of venereal disease. This was accompanied by a loosening of inhibitions about interracial sex, so that sailors made ports like Karachi notorious for prostitution. A spate of anti-prostitution propaganda films arrived as cautionary tales.

By and large, the racial divides remained in place. After Burma fell to the British, leading to its evacuation by British and Indian personnel, Indian soldiers were abandoned to their fate and European nurses were forbidden to attend to them. Many nurses did so nonetheless, out of compassion and professional commitment. Women – white, brown, and of mixed race – worked together, often taking over men's jobs. They relaxed together too, in bars and dance halls. More than 11,000 women joined the Women's Auxiliary Corps which was founded in 1942; English-speaking skills being favoured, the bulk of those recruited – as typists, telephone operators, filing personnel, and clerks – were mostly Anglo-Indians and Anglo-Burmese, with a sprinkling of Indian Christians. A few Indian women from princely and middle-class families also signed on, seeing in such service the potential for liberation from domestic chores and controls.

At the other end of the scale were women labourers hired on war contracts. About a thousand were put to work in the coal mines of central and eastern India, with practically no maternity leave – this was raised at one point in the House of Commons. They were also dragged into the back-breaking work of road building and construction, earlier the preserve of men.

Anglo-Indian women were valued as competent typists but they also acquired some renown for their social flair and daring interest in fashion. A bemused British businessman's wife who had joined the typists' pool at Karachi remarked of one such fashionista: "She typed with speed and accuracy yet she had the longest nails for a working girl I have ever seen."[19] In the major Indian cities, war work was tempered with hectic shopping, cinemas, dances, bars, fashion, jazz, and the latest American pop songs. Varieties of old and new consumer goods, especially the frigidaire and tinned items, invaded Indian markets to cater to changing domestic consumption habits.

[19] Khan, *The Raj at War*, p. 354.

War accelerated social change. Educated women worked in anti-aircraft direction plotting, parachute inspection, and packing; they were appointed as cipher clerks and operators, as well as in the more traditional catering or housekeeping duties of army canteens and government offices. Highly qualified women became intelligence officers, translators, and radio mechanics. Women's militias and guards units were raised where British and Indian women joined on fairly equal terms, the pressures of war being something of an equaliser. This troubled those in Whitehall who feared that at this rate Indian women might soon be issuing commands to European soldiers.

As Independence approached alongside a blood-filled Holocaust in Europe and Partition in South Asia, there were two parallel developments pulling women in very different directions. The Constitution, finalised in 1950, conferred full adult franchise on all Indians, and all women now became formal citizens of the republic. In 1955–6 there followed a revision of Hindu personal laws – discussed later – that sought to improve women's social and marital status.

On the other hand, Independence arrived amidst great brutality against women. Recent feminist work reveals that this violence did not always emanate from the rival community. The families of wives and daughters who were abducted, raped, or converted all too frequently shored up the ethos of patriarchal cruelty. Few, sometimes none, would take such women back when they were rescued. Fathers killed daughters to deny men from other communities access to them, and collective family and community memory honoured the killings. When the two new states, India and Pakistan, worked out the division of properties, they agreed that Hindu women abducted by Muslim rioters would be returned to India, and vice versa. This decision – made over the heads of women – remained in place even when some women were reluctant to go back to their old homes and abandon their new families, where in the meantime they had found affection. Surprisingly, even though both Jinnah and Nehru proclaimed secularism as their national ideal, they did not doubt that an abducted Hindu woman had to belong to India and a Muslim woman to Pakistan. Even before abortion had been legalised in either country, pregnant abducted women were compelled to undergo the trauma of an operation, and their consent or lack of it was immaterial to state decision-making.

In this subcontinental version of the Holocaust, women's bodies were freely scarred, marked, ravaged, and sometimes branded with patriotic slogans: *Pakistan Zindabad* (Long Live Pakistan), and *Jai Hind* (Victory to India). Even more painful, perhaps, was the woman's dread of being rejected by her family after being rescued by relief workers. Durga Rani, a young Hindu woman, recalled the callousness: "Their families said, how can we keep them now? Better they are dead."[20] About a third of the total number of women who were recovered from both communities were less than twelve years old, and most came from village homes. Many were sold or "gifted" to new families. Some lived as servants, others became new wives.

On the other hand, a new sphere opened up for women's activism as relief and rehabilitation work among refugees, especially among women, was largely entrusted to women social activists. Begum Anis Kidwai of Lucknow came from a Muslim Congress family; her husband was a civil servant who did not desert his post to return home, even though he was at risk from both the League for his Congress loyalties and from communal Hindus for his religion. Soon enough, he was killed. Anis Kidwai joined Congress relief work and left behind a remarkable diary filled with searing eyewitness accounts.

Ironically, out of the carnage, the uprooting of huge populations, the loss of homes and homelands, important new spaces of mobility and freedom began to emerge. Homeless refugee women looked for any jobs that they could get, and working women

---

[20] Ibid., p. 134.

gradually became a familiar feature in urban public spaces and workplaces.

Women's politics and the profound transformations in gender relations were braided processes, but the relationship was complicated. Women were activated as political subjects by movements that refused to engage with gender issues, which upheld the doctrine of separate spheres, and which ignored the specific needs of women comrades. In some ways politics created yet another site where women's subordination was reinvented. Yet, at the same time, women did gain a whole new world and unprecedented roles therein, alongside male political activists, albeit within an overarching framework of male supervision and leadership. Now that women were also fellow activists, even the general structure of their obedience to male leadership allowed new gender relationships to be forged.

It is necessary to plot the relationship between gender and politics as well as chart transformed lifeworlds with careful attention to nuance, to small shifts and modest changes, and to revisit old terms that could mask new meanings.

References and Suggested Readings for Chapter 5

Alter, Joseph, *The Wrestler's Body: Identity and Ideology in North India*, Berkeley: University of California Press, 1992.

Arambam, Saroj N., and John Parrott, "The Second Women's War and the Emergence of Democratic Government in Manipur", in Sumit Sarkar and Tanika Sarkar, eds, *Women and Social Reform in Modern India*, Ranikhet: Permanent Black, and Bloomington: Indiana University Press, 2008.

Asaf Ali, Aruna, *Fragments from the Past: Selected Writings and Speeches of Aruna Asaf Ali*, New Delhi: Patriot Publishers, n.d.

Bacchetta, Paula, "Communal Property/Sexual Property: On Representations of Muslim Women in a Hindu Household", in Zoya Hasan, ed., *Forging Identities: Gender, Communities and the State*, Delhi: Kali for Women, 1994.

Basu, Aparna, and Bharati Ray, *Women's Struggle: A History of the All-India Women's Conference 1927–1990*, Delhi: Manohar, 2003.

Basu, Aparna, *Mridula Sarabhai: Rebel With a Cause*, Delhi: Oxford University Press, 1998.

Bhasin, Kamala, and Ritu Menon, *Borders and Boundaries: India's Women in Partition*, Delhi: Kali for Women, 1998.

Burton, Antoinette, *Burdens of History*, Chapel Hill: The University of North Carolina Press, 1994.

Butalia, Urvashi, *The Other Side of Silence: Voices from the Partition of India*, Delhi: Penguin Books, 1998.

Chakravartty, Renu, *Communists in Indian Women's Movement: 1940–1950*, Delhi: People's Publishing House, 1980.

Chattopadhyay, Kamaladevi, *Inner Recesses, Outer Spaces: Memoirs*, Delhi: Navrang, 1986.

Chaudhuri, Nupur, and Margaret Strobel, eds, *Western Women and Imperialism: Complicity and Resistance*, Bloomington: Indiana University Press, 1992.

Chophy, G. Kanato, *Christianity and Politics in Tribal India: Baptist Missionaries and Naga Nationalism*, Ranikhet: Permanent Black, 2021.

Custers, Peter, *Women in the Tebhaga Uprising: Rural Poor Women and Revolutionary Leadership, 1944–46*, Calcutta: Naya Prakash, 1967.

Das, Santanu, *India, Empire, and First World War Culture: Writings, Images, and Songs*, Cambridge: Cambridge University Press, 2018.

Das, Bina, trans. Dhira Dhar, *A Memoir*, New Delhi: Zubaan, 2010.

Debi, Sarala, *Jibaner Jharapata*, Calcutta, 1958.

Devi, Ashapurna, *Subarnalata*, Calcutta: Mitra and Ghosh Publishers, 1966.

Dutt, Kalpana, trans. Arun Bose and Nikhil Chakraborty, *Chittagong Armoury Raiders: Reminiscences*, Bombay: People's Publishing House, 1945.

Everett, Jana, *Women and Social Change in India*, New York: St Martin's Press, 1979.

Forbes, Geraldine, "Votes for Women", in Vina Mazumdar, ed., *Symbols of Power*, Bombay: Allied Publishers, 1979.

Forbes, Geraldine, "Women of Character, Grit and Courage: The Reservation Debate in Historical Perspective", in Lotika Sarkar, Kumud Sharma, and Leela Kasturi, eds, *Between Tradition, Counter Tradition and Heresy: Contributions in Honour of Vina Mazumdar*, Kochi: Rainbow Publishers, 2002

Gandhi, M.K., *Women and Social Justice*, Ahmedabad: Navajivan, 1954.

Gupta, Ashoka, *In the Path of Service: Memories of a Changing Century*, Calcutta: Stree, 2005.

Gupta, Sudha, ed., and Bhagwandas Gupta, compiled, *Original Documents Relating to Ranee Lakshmi Bai of Jhansi (1839–1859)*, Delhi: Manohar, 2015.

Hingorani, Anand T., *Gandhi for 21st Century: The Role of Women*, Bombay: Bharati Vidya Bhawan, n.d.

Joshi, Pushpa, ed., *Gandhi on Women: Collection of Mahatma Gandhi's Writings and Speeches on Women*, Ahmedabad: Navajivan, 1988.

Kaur, Manmohan, *Role of Women in the Freedom Movement, 1857–1947*, Delhi: Sterling Publishers, 1968.

Khan, Yasmin, *The Raj at War: A Peoples' History of India's Second World War*, Delhi: Penguin Random House, 2015.

Kidwai, Anis, trans. Ayesha Kidwai, *In the Shadow of Freedom*, Delhi: Zubaan, 2004.

Kishwar, Madhu, "Women and Gandhi", *Economic and Political Weekly*, 5 and 12 October 1985.

Kumar, Radha, "Women in Bombay Cotton Textile Factories", unpublished doctoral thesis, Jawaharlal Nehru University, Delhi, 1992.

Lahiri, Abani, *Postwar Revolts of the Rural Poor in Bengal: Memoirs of a Communist Activist*, Calcutta: Seagull, 2001.

Lalita, K., *et al.*, *We Were Making History: Life Stories of Women in the Telangana People's Struggles*, London: Zed Books, 1989.

Loomba, Ania, *Revolutionary Desires: Women, Communism and Feminism in India*, Delhi: Routledge, 2018.

Maclean, Kama, "What Durga Bhabhi Did Next: Or, Was There a Gendered Agenda in Revolutionary Circles?" in Assa Doron and Alex Broom, eds, *Gender and Masculinities: Histories, Texts and Practices in India and Sri Lanka*, New Delhi: Routledge, 2014.

Maclean, Kama, *A Revolutionary History of Interwar India: Violence, Image, Voice and Text*, London: Hurst and Company, 2015.

Menon, Visalakshi, *Indian Women and Nationalism: The UP Story*, Delhi: Har Anand Publications, 2003.

Minault, Gail, *The Extended Family: Women and Political Participation in India and Pakistan*, Delhi: South Asia Books, 1990.

Mukherjee, Janam, *Hungry Bengal: War, Famine and the End of Empire*, London: HarperCollins, 2015.

Mukherjee, Rudrangshu, *A Begum and a Rani: Hazrat Mahal and Lakshmi Bai in 1857*, Delhi: Penguin, 2021.
Mukherjee, Sumita, *Indian Suffragettes: Female Identities and Transnational Networks*, Delhi: Oxford University Press, 2018.
Mumtaz, Khawar, and Farida Shahid, eds, *Women of Pakistan: Two Steps Forward, One Step Back?* London: Zed Books, 1987.
Nair, Neeti, *Changing Homelands: Hindu Politics and the Partition of India*, Ranikhet: Permanent Black, and Boston: Harvard University Press, 2011.
Oberoi, Harjot, "The Inner Life of Bhagat Singh and the Making of a Maximal Self", in idem, *When Does History Begin: Religion, Narrative, and Identity in the Sikh Tradition*, Ranikhet: Permanent Black, 2021.
Panjabi, Kavita, *Unclaimed Harvest: An Oral History of the Tebhaga Women's Movement*, Delhi: Zubaan, 2017.
Parulekar, Godavari, *Adivasis Revolt: The Story of Warli Peasants in Struggle*, Calcutta: National Book Agency, 1975.
Patel, Sujata, "Construction and Reconstruction of Women in Gandhi", *Economic and Political Weekly*, 20 February 1988.
Ray, Bharati, ed, *From the Seams of History: Essays on Indian Women*, Delhi: Oxford University Press, 2000.
Rege, Sharmila, *Writing Caste/Writing Gender: Narrating Dalit Women's Testimonies*, Delhi: Zubaan, 2013.
Roy, Anupama, *Gendered Citizenship: Hisory and Conceptual Explorations*, Delhi: Orient Longman, 2005.
Roy, Anwesha, *Making Peace, Making Riots: Communalism and Communal Violence, Bengal 1940–1947*, Cambridge: Cambridge University Press, 2018.
Sahgal, Lakshmi, *A Revolutionary Life: Memoirs of a Political Activist*, Delhi: Sage, 1998.
Sarkar, Sumit, *The Swadeshi Movement in Bengal 1903–1908*, 1973; rpntd Ranikhet: Permanent Black, 2011.
Sarkar, Tanika, "Introduction", in Amrita Basu and Tanika Sarkar, eds, *Women, Gender and Religious Nationalism*, Cambridge: Cambridge University Press, 2022.
Sarkar, Tanika, "Nationalist Iconography: The Image of Women in Nineteenth-century Bengali Literature", in idem, *Hindu Wife, Hindu Nation*, Delhi: Permanent Black, 2002.

Sarkar, Tanika, "Politics and Women in Bengal: The Conditions and Meanings of Participation", in J. Krishnamurty, ed., *Women in Colonial India: Essays on Survival, Work, and the State*, Delhi: Oxford University Press, 1998.

Sarkar, Tanika, "The Woman as Communal Subject: The Rashtrasevika Samiti and the Ramjanmabhoomi Movement", *Economic and Political Weekly*, 31 August 1991, rpntd in idem, *Hindu Nationalism in India*, Ranikhet: Permanent Black, 2020.

Sarkar, Tanika, *Bengal 1928–1934: The Politics of Protest*, Delhi: Oxford University Press, 1987.

Sarkar, Tanika, *Hindu Nationalism in India*, Ranikhet: Permanent Black, 2022.

Sawhney, Simona, "Bhagat Singh: Sacrifice, Suffering and the Tradition of the Oppressed", in G. Arunima, *et al.*, eds, *Love and Revolution in the Twentieth-century Colonial and Postcolonial World*, Palgrave Studies in the History of Social Movements, London: Palgrave Macmillan, 2021.

Sen, Manikuntala, *In Search of Freedom: An Unfinished Journey*, Calcutta: Stree Publishers, 2001.

Sen, Samita, *Women and Labour in Late Colonial India: The Bengal Jute Industry*, Cambridge: Cambridge University Press, 1999.

Singer, Wendy, *Creating Histories: Oral Narratives and the Politics of History Making*, Delhi: Oxford University Press, 1997.

Sinha, Mrinalini, ed., *Selections from Katherine Mayo's "Mother India"*, Delhi: Kali for Women, 1998.

Southard, Barbara, *The Women's Movement and Colonial Politics in Bengal: The Quest for Political Rights, Education and Social Reform Legislation, 1921–1936*, Delhi: Manohar, 1995.

Vaidik, Aparna, *Waiting for Swaraj: Inner Lives of Indian Revolutionaries*, Cambridge: Cambridge University Press, 2021.

Valdameri, Elena, "Physical Education and Femininity in India: Global Trends and Local Politics towards Crafting Women Citizens", unpublished research paper.

6

Holy and Unholy Gender

NOTIONS OF MALE and female holiness were interestingly redefined in modern times. Deep anxieties grew alongside over "deviant" or abnormal behaviour which threatened existing sacred social and familial templates as well as state interests. Society and state had to find new definitions as well as devise different regulations and institutions to manage the change.

Holiness

Contrary to Max Weber's contention about a disenchanted modern world from which faith has fled, modern India did not become a secularised polity and society. Rather, multiple versions of faith and worship proliferated so densely in all Indian communities, and their respective gurus, sects, and institutions remained so powerful, that we could well call modernity a newly enchanted universe. This is a very large and overworked terrain, so I will only mention a few developments — and even those very sketchily.

Brahman priests are by definition holy men, and they continued to preside over household worship and ritual as well as over temples, which never stopped multiplying. Mosques and religious schools guided the religious lives of Muslim men while Sufi *pir*s (Muslim mystic saints) spoke freely to devotees, offering them solace, cures, and amulets against mundane dangers. As Urdu print developed in the early nineteenth century, the Deoband seminary began to publish a variety of fatwas and advice manuals for ordinary Muslims.

Many of them outlined ideal domestic conduct and proper life-cycle rituals. *Dargah*s (the burial sites of *pir*s) were holy places where men and women prayed for earthly benediction as well as divine grace. Some of these sites, famed for their miracle cures, attracted Hindus as well. Men and women from both communities, especially Hindus, also converted to Christianity in fairly large numbers.

Some Hindu saints, however, dispensed with miracle-making claims and shifted to advising householders on spiritual quests and domestic piety. Ramakrishna Paramahansa (1836–1886) spent his mature life in the vicinity of Calcutta, often in the company of prominent modern intellectuals, even though he himself was practically illiterate and came from a rustic background. Deeply tolerant, he saw the different religions as so many paths to God, separate but equal. His earthly parables, spoken daily to large followings of learned as well as lower-middle-class men and women, taught people how to live a genuinely religious life even when remaining enmeshed in apparently fruitless domestic and job responsibilities.

Ramakrishna regarded female bodies with visceral horror and found sexual activity repugnant. He never consummated his own marriage. He admitted women – including his wife – among his devotees by turning them into mother figures and warned male disciples against sexual passion and love. Women, nonetheless, flocked to him in large numbers: perhaps his messages resonated with their own experiences of marital and domestic cruelty. His advice to the many householders who also worshipped him was to regard their material and familial obligations as an outer and less relevant cover for an inner spiritual life.

Ramakrishna's close disciple Swami Vivekananda (1863–1902), on the other hand, sought Hindu unity alongside moral and physical self-strengthening. He looked outwards, seeking to make the world bow down before a presumed Hindu spiritual and moral greatness. Interestingly, he inverted the imperial connection by drawing a number of Western disciples into his circle; American women, in particular, found him immensely inspiring when he visited the United States.

A vigorous, cosmopolitan, and highly educated modern man, unlike his gentle and illiterate guru, Vivekananda founded a Hindu monastic order, the Ramakrishna Mission, along an entirely new vision. He founded modern philanthropic and educational institutions, jettisoned ritualism in favour of a transcendentalist and intellectual approach to faith, and looked forward to community self-strengthening with trained male bodies that carried cultivated and spiritual minds. Unlike Ramakrishna, who respected all faiths, Vivekananda preached the great superiority of Hinduism at the Chicago Conference of World Religions in 1893. His resounding oratory won him many Western devotees, including the Irish-woman Margaret Noble – later renamed Sister Nivedita – who followed him to India to work for his cause. She, however, was not allowed to join the Mission, which remained an all-male sect. Vivekananda's evangelism and social messaging sought to develop a muscular Hinduism along the template of certain strands in contemporary Western Christianity.

If Vivekananda was the emblem of a powerful masculinity, Swami Dayanand (1824–1883), founder of the Arya Samaj sect – which spread all over Punjab and the western United Provinces – threw up a different ideal of ascetic maleness. He was born in an orthodox family, entirely distant from metropolitan and cosmopolitan influences. Learned in traditional but self-selected religious texts, he developed a sternly rationalist streak and gradually came to abhor image worship, polytheism, ritualism, and religious sectarianism which, he thought, had weakened and divided Hindus. Castigating the conventional sects as greedy and corrupt, and most sacred texts as inauthentic, he eventually saw the ancient Vedas as the only true textual tradition for Hindus. He tried to unify the multifarious sects of Hinduism under a single creed and formulated a simpler version of Hindu life-cycle rites – which enraged the orthodoxy who now defined themselves as Sanatanis or devotees of the eternal, immutable faith. He taught himself the rudiments of Islam and Christianity, both of which he detested, but he had no intellectual exchanges with Western thought or people.

Unlike Vivekananda's self-designed elegant saffron robes and headgear, Dayanand clad himself in the traditional garments of the ascetic. At first he discoursed in Sanskrit, much later he shifted to Hindi. Though, unlike Ramakrishna or Vivekananda, he had no important female disciples, he revised and partially reformed certain conjugal and family codes – wedding and mourning rituals in particular. As noted earlier, he also advocated a strange form of widow remarriage. Vivekananda, on the other hand, though he had many acerbic things to say in private about the Hindu norms of child marriage and sex with child wives, stayed away from gender reform, while Ramakrishna was opposed to social reform per se, preferring to focus wholly on spiritual uplift.

Women monks and saints, as we have seen, had from ancient and medieval times carved out a non-domestic space for themselves. In modern time we find a new version of female sainthood, with organised groups of devotees cohering around the cults of individual holy women. In contrast with the more enduring sects founded by male saints, these seldom outlasted the lifetime of the women saints. But like the male guru, the woman saint combined the formal authority of the preceptor – who initiates and directs religious lives – with warm personal interactions among followers who were instructed on solutions to their everyday problems. Such gurus fashioned a form of sacred maternalism, but their fame also relied greatly on legends of their miraculous powers.

Piro, a mid-nineteenth-century religious woman, formerly a Muslim prostitute, followed Gulabdas, a dissident Punjabi Sikh guru who preached a distinctive version of monism, quite different from traditional Sikh monotheism. She became his romantic partner as well as co-leader of the Gulabdasi sect. Hers was an unusually unconventional and controversial life, full of adventures – military, romantic, and devotional. Her life fascinatingly combined holy and unholy elements, the stigma associated with her early life being eventually transcended by her association with Gulabdas.

Another such religious figure, Gauri Ma, was born in mid-nineteenth-century Calcutta and became a celibate devotee of Ramakrishna Paramahansa. Though she had a modern middle-class upbringing and was educated at an Anglican school, she rejected both and resisted marriage to become a wandering ascetic even before she met Ramakrishna. Like him she had a frenzied desire to encounter Kali, the fierce Hindu goddess, face to face. Later, she gathered her own following, became a public figure, and set up a widows' home dedicated to Ma Sarada, Ramakrishna's wife, who herself had acquired a saintly reputation after her husband's death. Gauri Ma's home offered religious education but did not address the social problems of widows or set them on the path to economic independence. A social conservative, she firmly rejected liberal reform.

Another woman saint came to enjoy a massive India-wide following which included some members of the Nehru family. Unlike Piro and Gauri Ma, she achieved her success all by herself, without leaning on a man. Anandamoyee Ma was married off at twelve in eastern Bengal to a poor Brahman but refused to accept the conjugal tie. Her husband acknowledged her sainthood and became her first disciple. News spread rapidly of her ecstatic trances, which soon attracted a growing number of followers. As her reputation for saintliness and miraculous powers grew, she began to travel widely. Widowed in 1938, she continued to move with a larger entourage that lavishly catered to all her needs. And yet, for all this, she retained the holy mantle of the renunciate. After 1926 she was always fed by her disciples, never using her own hands to feed herself – a striking departure from the womanly duty of feeding others. She spoke in tongues when in a trance and cross-dressed playfully to enact the role of Krishna as divine incarnation and epic hero. Her whimsicality, personal warmth, and homely parables elicited passionate adoration in her devotees.

Illiterate all her life, she discoursed orally and extensively on faith and social values. Her religious practices had certain peculiarities: she always referred to herself in the third person, as "this body". Her devotees believed she was a divine incarnation, that her body was beyond gender. She taught a simplified version of monism, preaching the view that anyone could become God if they acquired the right qualities. Her followers set up chains of ashrams and charitable foundations in her name, though she did not herself particularly advise them to help the poor. An inner core of women devotees always surrounded her, enjoying close tactile contact with the saint. Going against orthodox norms, she bestowed the sacred thread on several male Brahman devotees – normally, women gurus never did so. At the same time, she was a social conservative, staunchly upholding the Brahmanical order.

A very different sect, made up largely of women living celibate lives, is the Prajapita Brahmakumari Ishwariya Visvavidyalaya. Though its headquarters are now situated at Mount Abu in Rajasthan, it has a global spread. Founded in the 1930s by Dada Lekhraj, a Sindhi businessman who predicted a nuclear holocaust after which the world would be renewed and perfected, it had a millennarian beginning. Interestingly, its concept of future perfection also included gender equality – something that no contemporary woman saint had asserted. The sect, largely made up of women, practices yoga and vegetarianism, and avoids tobacco, alcohol, and sex. It names itself after Brahma – the Creator of the universe in Hindu mythology. Lekhraj claimed he himself was Brahma's incarnation, though Brahma has no incarnation in myths.

In the early days of the sect Lekhraj attracted huge numbers of women, which many critics attributed to his sex appeal. Others believed it was due to the unhappiness of the wives of Sindhi businessmen, whose husbands often lived abroad to conduct business and developed extra-marital connections while away. Upon joining this sect, its members are deemed dead to their families and given new names. Everyone who signs on, moreover, is supposedly reborn as a Brahman. They live highly regulated and segregated lives within the order.

The sect tells its women members that they are the victims of their men and families, that marriage is a trap and husbands incorrigibly immoral. Women can avoid their sorrowful fate by abjuring sex, family attachments, and conjugal obligations – that is, by turning into the very opposite of their socially ordained role. There is a larger reason for abjuring sex: the end of the world is near and it is the special responsibility of women to stop procreation to accelerate its arrival. If they are not renunciates and already have children when they join the order, they are allowed to care for them – but they must not add to their number. Though sex must cease, chaste love is believed to be possible between men and women. Every woman member is deemed reborn as a virgin at the time of her religious initiation, even if she joins the order after a long married life.

After Lekhraj's death in the 1960s the order came into the hands of two women, and women are now its moving force. Sometimes they organise séances and act as mediums through whom dead souls speak.

The lives of most of these modern saints, men and women, show that many are no longer content solely with spiritual quest, mystical union with the Divine, or search for transcendental Truth and sacred knowledge – though these elements also persist. Predominantly, their trajectories suggest involvement with the world here and now, with the lives of their householder devotees, and with the strength and standing of their respective communities or sects.

Modernity bestowed enormous visibility on Hindu women saints. (There were also Muslim women of legendary piety, but they did not emerge as prominent religious leaders and guides outside their families.) It also gave them control over large organised followings. Unlike their pre-modern predecessors who lived lonely, peripatetic lives, the new religious gurus acquire power, prominence, and sometimes enormous material wealth. Their sainthood is most often confirmed by their recoil against sex, distanced or severed family ties, and above all by trances and miracles. Though all have themselves tended to live lives against the grain of conventional gender norms, they endorse these norms for their lay followers. In this they resemble the Hindu deities – who are not meant to be exemplars for their devotees but who are worshipped precisely on account of the radical difference between their lives and those of ordinary mortals. The one sect that has questioned aspects of patriarchy – Lekhraj's – has been, ironically, founded by a male leader.

*Devadasi*s, a category of women previously believed to uphold a sacred tradition, have in the twentieth century been denigrated as unholy. Mandated to be unmarried female servants of the gods, from their early years they perform dances dedicated to temples and priests. They proliferated mainly in three locations: Orissa in eastern India, the princely state of Mysore, and the Madras Presidency. Despite their considerable cultural skills, Devadasis came to be perceived in modern times as nothing more than the sexual slaves of venal temple priests and royals, a slur on Hindu moral purity.

The "native state" of Mysore, ruled by a Hindu dynasty, effortlessly banned the system as anti-Hindu in 1909. British India, on the other hand, was nervous about outlawing a profession connected with temple traditions. In 1929 Muthulakshmi Reddy, social reformer and the first woman legislator in British India, moved a bill for abolishing the system in Madras. She argued on the basis of sanitising her faith and cleansing the moral disorder that the *devadasi*s apparently represented. The British government was reluctant to interfere for a long time, lacking the confidence that a Hindu monarch possessed; the practice was abolished only in 1947.

Folk religious cults flourished in colonial India, drawing on strands of Sufi and pre-colonial Hindu devotional traditions. Many were dissident organisations which practised deviant sexual behaviour, and most challenged conventional religious and caste divisions. Many sects had low-caste leaders who refused to abide by Brahmanical purity–pollution taboos and questioned the fundamentals of caste beliefs and practices: the Ad Dharam in Punjab, the Adi Hindu sect of Swami Acchhutanand in the United Provinces, and the Matua sect in Bengal. Most were monotheistic and some believed that God lies hidden in our own selves.

One of the most interesting holy figures was Lalan Fakir, who is believed to have lived sometime between 1772 and 1890. He became iconic within Bengal's remarkable folk tradition of the Bauls, which still flourishes among ordinary people in many parts of West Bengal and Bangladesh – their mystical songs and dances attract crowds of middle-class urbanites to their festivals. They also have large numbers of Western patrons. Bauls express their religious thoughts primarily in songs of exceptional beauty and spiritual depth – the songs of Lalan are still the most treasured part in their repertoire. Scholars think that their mystical language masks coded subtexts about sexual practices. Legends have proliferated about Lalan Fakir's life, suggesting a Hindu birth but discipleship under a Muslim fakir. He denounced organised religious establishments and even the conventional understandings of faith itself: "Lalan says I do not know what religion looks like . . ." Emphatically and sardonically, he dismisses caste divisions: "Caste (*jaat*) is the source of all evil, it is a fraudulent trickster that gambles with our lives." Not surprisingly, he was denounced as a false prophet by the Hindu and Muslim establishments of his time. He sought Truth within the human body, love, and mind. God for him was "*maner manush*", an intimate but forever unreachable friend who visits the human mind but evades final union, "a strange bird that flits in and out of the cage – if only I knew how to put the chain of my heart around it . . ."

Lalan Fakir was one of the rare folk spiritual leaders who became well known among the contemporary Bengali *bhadralok* (modern, upper-caste middle classes). Rabindranath Tagore's brother Jyotirindranath sketched his only extant portrait, and his songs inspired many of Rabindranath's own. Many women joined Lalan Fakir's group as valued members, and several women singers and composers have earned local fame as Baul figures since then. Interestingly, however, no woman has become the leader or founder of a relatively libertarian sect.

Unholy Gender – Beyond the Two Genders

The world seen through British Victorian eyes was strictly bi-gender and heteronormative, sex being restricted within the boundaries of conjugality and ideally meant for procreation alone. Anything that troubled this order of things was considered an abomination, a sin, and a crime against nature. Inter-sex people whose gender attributes were either not clearly marked, or who chose to reject their original sexual identity to assume that of the opposite sex, or those who clinically changed the sexual attributes they had been born with were uniformly designated as *hijra*s (eunuchs). They were a particularly suspect category. Their gender was considered unnatural, their transvestite dress codes unseemly, and their peripatetic habits akin to those who belonged to the "criminal tribes". It was widely suspected that they kidnapped infants as they travelled around, castrating them and forcing them to become a part of their community. When the Criminal Tribes Act was passed in 1871 they were forced to register themselves under Part II of the Act, which defined them as castrated or impotent males, impotence being perceived in nineteenth-century colonial circles as a cause of effeminacy in men. They were also accused of sodomy, which had been outlawed by the Penal Code provisions of 1860. They represented, therefore, a sum of many "unnatural" proclivities, "malevolent" intentions, and criminal activities.

The 1871 Act was enforced in the North West Frontier Province from 1872, in Oudh (Awadh) from 1877, and parts of it were applied in Punjab. This suggests the British were particularly fearful about their presence in areas which supplied army personnel. The regulations prohibited public transvestism and *hijra*s were debarred from the guardianship of children as well as from making wills. The police were required to monitor their movements and, in the process, frequently molested them. The rest of India, however, was exempt from the scope of these regulations despite the pan-Indian ubiquity of *hijra*s.

In part the British were echoing Indian sentiments in this terrain of sexual identity, but they also intensified them and gave them a legal and penal form. The North West Frontier Province of India had seen several upsurges of panic from the 1850s directed against small *hijra* groups, usually of male-born castrated persons who chose to dress like women. In the two decades that followed in the wake of the 1857 upheaval, the state began to recruit its soldiers in increasing numbers from those designated "martial races" in North India. Consequently, they were preternaturally anxious about any departures from the conventions of masculinity, especially among potential army recruits. Soldiers, British and Indian, being the acknowledged protectors of the honour and strength of the Raj, had to appear as ultra-male. This was also a time of anxiety about sodomy in prisons, juvenile reformatories, and penal colonies like the Andamans.

Troubled by the sexual and gender ambiguities of the *hijra*s, who described themselves to census officials as neither men nor women, the authorities, keen to slot them into either of the two genders, chose to classify them as men. They were ordered to dress as men and medical officials tested them for impotence. But it could not escape their notice that some of them possessed incipient female biological features. This of course troubled their fixed definitional categories.

Mainstream Indian society, too, abhorred such folk because they were castrated and suspected of stealing children. Sir Syed Ahmad Khan accused the government of not doing enough to banish such people from public spaces and society. He demanded that they be systematically rounded up and incarcerated. Nonetheless, *hijra*s continued to perform ritual functions in Hindu and

Muslim marriages and childbirth ceremonies. They formed their own households, consisting of gurus and disciples. Like an untouchable caste, they were allowed to be themselves – but only in order to occupy a stigmatised position in society.

Courtesans, Concubines, Sex Workers

Some scholars have provided rather romanticised notions about a presumed pre-colonial tolerance towards professional dancing women and singers who could also double up as the courtesans of rich men. Veena Talwar Oldenburg's compelling study of the famous *tawaif*s of Lucknow, and their eventual loss of status under a westernised morality, is a somewhat rosy picture of female sexual power over male clients, their skill in manipulating men and bending them to their will. Rosalind O'Hanlon disagrees sharply. She says that by providing an alternative sexual space such women actually reaffirmed orthodox norms in the larger social sphere. Nor does their ability to manipulate men indicate anything like genuine autonomy and agency. Moreover, the focus on successful *tawaif*s alone deflects attention from the run-of-the-mill sex worker who had few resources apart from her body, and who often lived in dire poverty as a daily wage earner at the mercy of ruthless pimps and brothel-keepers.

Records of crime, disease, sexual deviance, soldiery, and law that supposedly framed the existence of sex workers came together to create a formidable archive on venereal disease among Indian and European soldiers. As the East India Company built up its Indian army, it was haunted by the spectre of "mercenary love" which threatened to undermine the moral and physical health of their empire. Though a racial stereotyping described Indians as sexual savages, ordinary European soldiers, because they came from the subaltern social ranks, were assumed to be similarly prone to drunkenness and debauchery. The Army Sanitary Commission actually noted the relatively low incidence of venereal disease among Indian soldiers. They attributed this to their diet.

Since soldiers were not allowed to bring wives into the barracks, some contact with Indian prostitutes was inevitable. The state was therefore in a bind. It had to tolerate sex between prostitutes and soldiers while throwing the blame for venereal disease on the prostitutes rather than their male clients. Since no effective medication was known in the nineteenth century, efforts to keep the disease in check meant reducing sexual contact. Some Indians, however, feared that such restriction would lead to social anarchy and put their wives and daughters at risk from a soldiery running amok. As the *Almora Akhbar*, a Hindi weekly, said in 1888, "Not to provide women for European soldiers who are drunk and mad with lust would be like letting loose beasts of prey."[1]

Janaki Nair concludes that the imposition of Victorian prudishness led to the criminalisation of sex workers, while Ashwini Tambe offers a more nuanced approach to colonial policies, describing state interventions as targeted regulation that did not intend abolition. More than narrow moralism, the British in India were guided by pragmatism. Sodomy and masturbation, supposedly debilitating, were seen as greater dangers to the soldiery and, properly monitored, prostitutes could become a healthier resolution to male sexual needs. Tambe also emphasises the gap between the language and the actual practice of the law.

The state recruited prostitutes for the military encampments and set up regimental brothels in bazaars that catered to the army camps. Cantonment authorities appointed midwives to check them for venereal disease and specialist hospitals in the army barracks confined and treated infected women. The treatment was horrific: it included rubbing mercury into their genitals. By the 1860s, however, it was clear that the measures were not working. The Cantonment Acts of 1864 now provided for the compulsory medical examination of all sex workers who served soldiers. There were regular

---

[1] Ballhatchet, *Race, Sex and Class*, p. 166.

check-ups and those who failed to report the illness faced penalties. That sex workers would find the measures shameful, painful, and humiliating never seems to have troubled the authorities.

The Contagious Diseases Act was first enacted in Bombay in 1870, following upon an Indian Contagious Diseases Act of 1868. It was suspended after a year, reintroduced in 1880, and stayed in place till 1888. The Bombay Act tried to tackle some special problems for a city which was both a port and a military garrison. Because soldiers and sailors tended to spill out all over the city in search of sex, it tried to monitor all sex workers and not just those who served the barracks. It demarcated areas where prostitution could be legally practised and prescribed measures for diagnosing the disease in them. The Act made it compulsory for prostitutes to register themselves with the police, undergo medical check-ups every week, and face confinement in a hospital if found infected. This ensured an unprecedented level of surveillance, allowing the police considerable power for checking, reporting, and punishing defaulters.

Bombay, with its floating migrant population, proved particularly difficult to monitor, and police regulations dating as far back as 1812 had been riddled with inconsistencies: while the measures had tried to control unruly brothels, brothel-keeping itself had not been made an offence. In 1827 the enticement of women into brothels was criminalised because it was seen as snapping the control of fathers and husbands over their women. Similar laws in northern and eastern India shared the same premise – that the women trafficked were not the injured party but their male guardians were. The Penal Code of 1860 had broadened the definition of enticement, which now included the buying, selling, and kidnapping of children for prostitution. This came in part because in 1838 a judicial officer in Monghyr, Bihar, had leased out two infants to a brothel-keeper.

Prostitutes, however, devised innovative ways of evading controls, bribing the police being their favoured method. The Bombay municipality, established in 1865, also resented the laws as an undesirable intrusion into its own authority and refused to pay for their enforcement. Nationalists criticised them as an encroachment on the freedom of Indians – obliquely admitting, rather uncharacteristically, sex workers as citizens of the nation.

European prostitutes were racially hierarchised. Antisemitism being rampant in officialdom, Jewish prostitutes occupied the lowest rungs. By the mid nineteenth century the first generation of European prostitutes came to settle in the Kamathipura and Kolaba districts of Bombay, cheek by jowl with Indian working-class settlements. The League of Nations began to monitor the trafficking of European women from the 1920s, especially those who were young and virginal. Many were deported.

Brothels were dangerous places and prostitutes were frequently murdered. The brutal killing of Akkotai became a well-publicised criminal case in 1917. Afflicted with venereal disease Akkotai had refused to entertain her clients. When one of them forced his way into her brothel she tried to escape but was caught and beaten to death by the brothel keepers, both male and female. Hers was by no means an unusual predicament.

A Police Act of 1902 delegalised brothel-keeping and soliciting in Bombay city. Many sex workers were arrested under it for soliciting but, one way or another, the brothel-keepers escaped arrest yet again. From 1921 prominent Indians began to agitate against the presence of sex workers in public places, and to allege that the government was deliberately ignoring the problem in order to give Indian cities a bad name. This led to an official enquiry and more curbs. An Act of 1923 restricted pimping, soliciting, procuring, and detaining women forcibly in brothels but, once again, it did not criminalise brothel-keepers and owners – presumably respect for property had trumped moral concerns. The police, however, hardly ever enforced the legal provisions, thereby exposing what Tambe identifies as the gap between laws and law enforcement. The entry of Indians into the Legislative Councils eventually changed the situation. Their pressure brought forth an Act in 1930 which considerably tightened law enforcement in areas where soliciting was common.

The inter-War years saw a spate of middle-class women's campaigns against deviant sexual relationships. The WIA, the AIWC, and the National Council of Women in India repeatedly demanded the prohibition of the *devadasi* system of temple dancers. Gandhi strengthened the trend when, in 1921, he rejected the appeal of 350 sex workers who wanted to join the Congress-led Non-Cooperation Movement. Some, however, did manage to enter it covertly, and Gandhi was furious when he discovered this. He threw them out at once.

Interracial Relationships

The British did not enact formal laws to forbid interracial marriages, perhaps because racist stigma made such relationships near-impossible in any case. There were far too few opportunities for developing a long-term relationship which could blossom into marriage, given that racial segregation inhibited Indo-European social intercourse, especially post-Mutiny. Before 1857, because their wives did not accompany them out to India, many Europeans harboured one or more Indian concubines in their households. Some of them enjoyed a coveted status.

Before the mid nineteenth century, British households in India included large numbers of Indian servants, men and women, the dividing line between young women servants and concubines being rather hazy. Even without a formal marriage tie, Indian concubines were treated as legal partners by the courts and many received hefty bequests after their master's death. Their children were often sent to their father's home in England. For example, John Deane, a civil servant, asked the executors of his will to maintain a trust for "beebee Mussummaut Matloob Brish who has lived with me for nearly 20 years and whose kindness and affection towards me during the whole of that period has continued unadulterated, the sum of Rs 100/ per month as long as she lives."[2] For their six children,

---

[2] See Robb, *Sex and Sensibility*.

born out of wedlock, Deane set aside £ 2000, to be received when they turned twenty-one.

The same woman could also inherit from several European patrons at different times. The bequests declined after 1800, but they did make the fortunes of several Indian women. Many became rich enough to draw up their own wills. A notable instance was Begum Samru, born Farzana (1751?–1836). A Muslim dancing girl, she was at first a companion to Walter Reinhardt, an Austrian mercenary whose private army and landed estates at Sardhana, near Meerut, she later inherited. She became a political figure of considerable importance, fascinating Europeans with her military and diplomatic skills and penchant for cross-dressing.

It was a different story with the domestic servants in European households, who sometimes brought criminal charges against their masters for physical cruelty. In *Rex v Betty and Peggy* (1777), Betty and Peggy, companions of an Englishman in Calcutta, accused him of scalding a young slave girl with oil and killing her. The court reduced the charge to manslaughter. Rape cases involving Indian female servants rarely received proper justice. When adjudicating, the courts deliberated on the virginity, age, and puberty of the victim. This was common practice for rape cases in Britain as well, but in India judges also speculated on how far the servant had made herself sexually available to the European master; their presumption was that since Indian women "ripened" very early, they inevitably became sexually promiscuous too – the rape charge therefore should not be admitted. Half a dozen such cases between 1770 and 1840 were tried without resulting in conviction. Not that the servants or slave girls were any safer in the Indian households. In 1828 a Muslim noblewoman was charged with beating a slave girl to death with the help of three other slave women. Though the three accomplices were immediately arrested, the proverbial long arm of the law proved very short and did not touch the mistress.

After the 1857 uprising, when racial barriers became quite impenetrable, "fishing fleets" of hopeful British women sailed to India to look for prospective husbands. Most settled down as memsahibs to form colonial households, but a lot of them returned home with their children once their offspring were ready for school. Memsahibs set a racist tone in their households, socialising only among themselves; the only Indians that most of them knew were their servants. Of course interracial marriages did sometimes happen when love prevailed over prejudice. Quite often this happened between Indian royal family members and Europeans. White skin and royal blood could more easily conjoin to overcome deep-rooted prejudice.

Occasionally, ordinary Indians and Europeans married. A British woman recalled in the 1970s that "My father's grandfather, he was out in India, in the army, and he married an Indian girl, evidently, very young – but they did that sort of thing out there . . . and they came back to England."[3] The couple lived in the East Anglian village of Grislea, and their descendant recalled her Indian ancestry without a trace of embarrassment.

A few European wives became illustrious figures. Nellie Sengupta, the British wife of the veteran Congress leader J.M. Sengupta, emerged as a leading nationalist in her own right in the 1930s and 1940s. Subhas Chandra Bose, iconic leader of the Bengal Congress and founder of the Indian National Army, married an Austrian woman. This, however, was a well-kept secret in his lifetime and his spouse, Emilie Schenkl, played no role in Indian politics.

It is remarkable that even though the British would not allow inter-caste marriages, they enacted no law to prohibit interracial unions despite the profound racism that otherwise marked their regime.

Beyond Heteronormativity

British rule in India coincided with a sharpening of homophobia and the criminalisation of homosexual practices in Britain. This influenced Indian criminal laws which were remade in the early

---

[3] Oral testimony of Meg Ladell, who was fifty-one when interviewed by Mary Chamberlain in the 1970s. Chamberlain, *Fenwomen*, p. 42.

1860s on an Anglicised model. Section 377 of the Indian Penal Code criminalised sodomy and defined homosexuality as "unnatural sex", so that "Whoever voluntarily has carnal intercourse *against the order of nature* with any man, woman or animal, shall be punished with imprisonment for life or with imprisonment . . . for a term which may extend to ten years and shall be liable to fine." Intercourse, which supposedly defied the proper order of Nature, was defined as penal penetration. The provisions obviously intended to proscribe all manner of same-sex activity but, curiously, lesbian sex slipped through the loophole created by the term "penetration". The word, however, was not precisely defined, which left the door open for possible measures against lesbians as well. The Penal Code was otherwise elaborately detailed in its description of each type of criminal action. It seems likely therefore that lesbian sexual activity would have been explicitly mentioned had the state seriously intended criminalising it.

No reliable research has as yet assessed the actual number of prosecutions and convictions or the mode of their legal-judicial handling. Once again, it seems that enforcement of the law proved to be rather lax. The police apparatus was not intensive and extensive enough to monitor intimate behaviour unless families and neighbours brought matters to court. Moreover, several senior colonial officials were gay men themselves and would not have wanted such complaints investigated too closely.

Law seldom kills desire. Eighteenth- and nineteenth-century Urdu poetry had dwelt on homoerotic themes despite strong religious and imperial disapproval. Early Urdu poetry was suffused with the love of young boys in adult men.

> Your face with down on it is our Quran
> What if we kiss it – it is a part of our faith.
> – Mir Taqi Mir[4]

The nineteenth-century Urdu poetic tradition of *rekhti* has men poets appropriating the woman's voice. Their verses usually expres-

---
[4] Vanita and Kidwai, eds, *Same Sex Love in India*, p. 184.

sed a woman's erotic longing for her absent beloved in colloquial diction, quite distanced from the language of lyrical romanticism. But sometimes the poems also indicate same-sex love. By the twentieth century, however, the Urdu literary canon was redirected into more conventional paths and *rekhti* became a rather repressed genre in the high culture of this literary tradition.

Autobiographies, biographies, fiction – high and low – can be usefully explored for hidden subtexts about same-sex love. A lot of the time homosexual transgression was overshadowed by other, socially more threatening, forms of "deviance" which disturbed the normative fabric of family life, especially marriage. Ignorance could, moreover, provide a safe cover for homosexuality and the boundary between emotional friendship and same-sex love was blurred; intimacy could be read as intense companionship even by its practitioners.

A short story written by an early-twentieth-century Bengali novelist, Prabhat Kumar Mukhopadhyay, clearly reveals the uncertainties. It is, significantly, titled "Priyatam" (Beloved), a mode of address typically used by women for the men they love. A love-starved widow in an upper-caste family develops an intensely strong attachment for a married woman friend. She writes unsigned love letters to her, calling her *priyatam*. Her family intercepts the letters and can only conclude that she is conducting an illicit love affair with a man. Faced with social ostracism, the widow kills herself. When her friend discloses the truth, the relatives repent, persuaded now of the widow's innocence. This is an interestingly layered story of misrecognition, a tragedy of errors. On the surface, an innocent friendship has been misconstrued. The subtext, however, clearly reveals an exceptionally intense erotic longing between two women. The fact that the author hints at but does not openly call it sexual desire indicates that such relationships existed as an unnamed and unnameable possibility.

Homebound women could seek same-sex love within families, kin groups, neighbourhoods. Twentieth-century homosexual men found new sanctuaries: students' hostels, schools and colleges, working men's hostels, public toilets; even prisons became the possible sites of homosexual encounters. Even if banished from classical literary domains, as the *rekhti* was, new forms of cheap print and pulp fiction sometimes narrated them. In the 1920s a Hindi booklet, *Chaklet* (Chocolate), for instance, became notorious in the United Provinces for its graphic descriptions of homosexuality. Sensational bazaar literature sometimes tried to make these depictions respectable in the guise of homophobic warnings. However, even as such they invariably stoked the appetite for lurid description. What was banished from the realm of an acknowledged literary tradition found a new habitation in cheap and increasingly accessible pulp.

A more serious literary genre also represented homosexual love in a cautionary mould. In *Shabdangal*, a Malayalam novel of 1947, Vaikom Muhammad Basheer depicted transgender desire between a vagrant ex-soldier and a man disguised as a woman. Though a novel of warning – associating gay love with the underworld and sexual disease – it allowed minute descriptions of forbidden sex.

In Urdu novels and short stories such as Ismat Chughtai's "Lihaf" and Siddiqa Begum's "Taare Laraz Rahein Hain", neglected wives in upper-class households seek comfort in same-sex love. The descriptions are explicit, but the sexual relationship itself is propelled by the boredom of a neglected wife rather than by genuine love. More recent Indian authors writing in English about same-sex love as well as cultural figures include Suniti Namjoshi, Mahesh Dattani, Nisha da Cunha, Leslie Noronha, Bhupen Khakhar, and S. Rangarajan. Section 377 was scrapped as late as 2018, after prolonged and organised agitation from the 1990s. Same-sex marriage is still not legal.

Section 497 of the Indian Penal Code defined adultery as a criminal offence. This was deeply problematic for the "low castes", some of whom permitted extra-marital connections under certain customary qualifications. Women, however, were exempted from the penalties, which were reserved for male lovers – but on the dubious ground that adultery constituted an offence against the husband's property rights in the wife. Moral sanctions and social penalties nonetheless ensured that the adulterous woman was socially ostracised, not the man. In a notorious criminal case of 1873, a Bengali Brahman murdered his young wife. She had been forced into a relationship with a powerful and lecherous religious leader (*mohunt*) at a pilgrimage site. The husband received a life sentence, to be spent in the Andamans Island. Hindu public opinion, expressed in numerous contemporary plays, tracts, and petitions, depicted him as a hapless and innocent victim of colonial misrule: he had merely done what any wronged husband ought to have. Faced with a huge public outcry, he was set free in 1875.

Prisons and Lunatic Asylums

Male and female convicts were herded into building the dreaded Cellular Jail on the Andaman Islands. This incarcerated a large range of criminals, from habitual thieves to murderers to political figures considered especially dangerous by the state. The British liked to import female convicts to the Andaman Islands and marry them off to male convicts once they had served their term of hard labour and been classified as "Self Supporters" – meaning convicts who could eke out a living for themselves. The aim was to enhance the production levels in the islands and transform erstwhile dangerous liabilities into hard-working labourers.

Inside the jail, female convicts often faced great violence from male convicts – torture, mutilation, even death. The prison authorities turned a blind eye, describing the violence as attacks which went out of hand and were not intended to inflict grievous injury. Themselves the target of extreme cruelty from the authorities, male prisoners received a modicum of sympathy on this issue.

Before the beginnings of psychiatry and psychological research in the nineteenth century, Western women were considered more prone to mental illness than men. European doctors like James

Wise, however, found a very different situation in India. Once lunatic asylums began to assemble the statistics for their patients from mid century, they found that men outnumbered women by a very long margin. In Bengal, of a total of 56 Hindu inmates in 1865, 47 were men and 9 were women. Among 58 Muslim patients, there were 51 men and 7 women. To avoid public stigma, families usually chose to keep such women at home when they could. Most inmates were destitute people – the dividing line between vagrancy and lunacy being thin.

Everywhere, asylums found it impossible to understand the causes of madness as they had no access to case histories. Most female inmates were picked off the streets and perforce remained anonymous. Even when their relatives had them admitted, they could say little about their life history or explain the possible causes of their illness. Such men and women generally came from poor agricultural families and "low castes". Many women packed off to an asylum had been caught begging on streets. At the Dullunda Asylum in 1875 there were, apart from peasants, 1 fisherwoman, 1 housewife, 8 prostitutes, 3 domestic servants, and 1 washerwoman; 22 others belonged to "unknown castes". Many were widows. The families of better-off women could afford to maintain widows at home.

Doctors guessed at a whole range of possible causes – tropical climate, epilepsy, the use of hemp, puerperal fever, uterine defects, hereditary illnesses. Catamenia – the disruption of regular menstrual flow – was also a prime suspect, and younger women were supposed to have a better chance of eventual recovery after menopause. Some attributed women's medical problems to "asthenia", a vague umbrella term for all manner of disease with inexplicable causes and effects. James Wise found that grief, particularly at the death of a son, often caused it, while others believed that loss of property brought it about. The symptoms ranged between profound melancholia and passivity to severe anxiety attacks to outbursts of wild speech and violent action. Some patients exhibited all these symptoms in turn. Musammat Omrah, aged thirty, who had tried to burn down a house before she was admitted, maintained absolute silence. Musammat Alta, on the other hand, regularly tore her clothes and blankets into shreds. Musammat Ropee, fifty-six years of age, a beggar from the untouchable Chandal caste, was usually silent, but when she spoke she did so unstoppably and with incoherent passion. Asylums provided rudimentary medication, such as treatment with silver nitrate, but had no provision for therapy. They merely herded women with different degrees of illness and provided them a roof over their heads.

My grandmother, afflicted with deep melancholia from when she would have been in her late twenties, lived at home. She spent more than three decades in a small room, mostly forgotten, hardly ever speaking, never disturbing the normal rhythms of her family life. Married to a very successful civil surgeon, she received neither treatment nor counselling – apart from a disastrous spell at an asylum from which she had to be rushed back home; asylums sometimes only make an already difficult mental problem far worse. Homes, if affluent and spacious, gave the "mad woman" a bit of space, even when giving her little else. My grandmother spent her days reading the same page from a book over and over again.

Families and the state proved equally futile with regard to those they regarded as mad. Madness, a blanket category, became an excuse for neglect and indifference, if not positive annoyance, rather than for greater care and understanding.

References and Suggested Readings for Chapter 6

Anderson, Carol S., "The Life of Gauri Ma", in Karen Pechilis, ed., *The Graceful Guru: Hindu Female Gurus in India and the United States*, New York: Oxford University Press, 2004.

Babb, Lawrence, *Redemptive Encounters: Three Modern Styles in the Hindu Tradition*, Berkeley: University of California Press, 1986.

Ballhatchet, Kenneth, *Race, Sex and Class Under the Raj*, London: Weidenfeld and Nicolson, 1980.

Biswas, Somak, *Passages Through India: Indian Gurus, Western Disciples and the Politics of Indophilia, 1890–1940*, Cambridge: Cambridge University Press, 2023.

Carritt, Michael, *A Mole in the Crown: Memoirs of a British Official in India Who Worked with the Communist Underground in the 1930s*, Calcutta: Rupa Publishers, 1986.

Chamberlain, Mary, *Fenwomen: A Portrait of Women in an English Village*, London: Routledge and Kegan Paul, 1983.

Dalrymple, William, *White Mughals: Love and Betrayal in Eighteenth Century India*, London: HarperCollins, 2002.

Das, Debjani, *Houses of Madness: Insanity and Asylums of Bengal in Nineteenth Century India*, Delhi: Oxford University Press, 2015.

Ernst, Waltraud, "Feminising Madness, Feminising the Orient: Gender and Colonialism in British India", in B. Pati and Shakti Kak, eds, *Exploring Gender Equations: Colonial and Post-Colonial India*, Delhi: NMML Publications, 2005.

Ghosh, Durba, *Sex and the Family in Colonial India: The Making of Empire*, Cambridge: Cambridge University Press, 2006.

Gupta, Charu, *Sexuality, Obscenity, Community: Women, Muslims, and the Hindu Public in Colonial India*, Delhi: Permanent Black, 2002.

Hallstrom, Lisa Lassell, *Mother of Bliss: Anandamayee Ma 1896–1982*, Delhi: Oxford University Press, 1999.

Harris, Ruth, *Guru to the World: The Life and Legacy of Vivekananda*, Harvard: The Belknap Press, 2022.

Hinchy, Jessica, "Troubling Bodies: Eunuchs, Masculinity and Impotence in Colonial India", in Assa Doron and Alex Broom, eds, *Gender and Masculinities: Histories, Texts and Practices in India and Sri Lanka*, Delhi: Routledge, 2013.

Jones, Kenneth, *Arya Dharm: Hindu Consciousness in Nineteenth Century Punjab*, Berkeley: University of California Press, 1976.

Jordens, J.T.F., *Dayananda Saraswati: His Life and Ideas*, Delhi: Oxford University Press, 1978.

Malhotra, Anshu, *Piro and the Gulabdasis: Gender, Sect and Society in Punjab*, Delhi: Oxford University Press, 2017.

Metcalf, Barbara D., *Islamic Revival in British India: Deoband, 1860–1900*, Princeton: Princeton University Press, 1982.

Mukhopadhyay, Prabhat Kumar, "Priyatam", in *Galpa Samagra*, vol. 1, Calcutta: Mitra and Ghosh, 2015 reprint.

Nair, Janaki, "The Devadasi, Dharma and the State", in Mary E. John, ed., *Women's Studies: A Reader*, India: Penguin Books, 2008.

Nandy, Ashis, *Exiled at Home*, Delhi: Oxford University Press, 2005.

Nandy, Ashis, *The Intimate Enemy: Loss and Recovery of Self Under Colonialism*, Delhi: Oxford University Press, 1984.

O'Hanlon, Rosalind, "Issues of Widowhood: Gender, Discourse and Resistance in Colonial Western India", London: Institute of Commonwealth Studies, University of London, 1989.

Oldenburg, Veena Talwar, "Lifestyle as Resistance: The Case of the Courtesans of Lucknow", in Douglas Haynes and Gyan Prakash, eds, *Contesting Power: Resistance and Everyday Social Relations in South Asia*, Berkeley: University of California Press, 1992.

Robb, Peter, *Sex and Sensibility: Richard Blechynden's Calcutta Diaries, 1791–1822*, Delhi: Oxford University Press, 2011.

Sarkar, Sumit, "Kaliyuga, Chakri and Bhakti: Ramakrishna and His Times", in idem, *Essays of a Lifetime: Reformers, Nationalists, Subalterns*, Ranikhet: Permanent Black, 2017.

Sarkar, Tanika, "Talking about Scandals: Religion, Law and Love in Late Nineteenth Century Bengal", in idem, *Hindu Wife, Hindu Nation*, Delhi: Permanent Black, 2003.

Sen, Satadru, *Disciplining Punishment: Colonialism and Convict Society in the Andaman Islands*, Delhi: Oxford University Press, 2000.

Tambe, Ashwini, *Codes of Misconduct: Regulating Prostitution in Late Colonial Bombay*, Minneapolis: University of Minnesota Press, 2009.

Thatcher, Mary, compiler, *Respected Memsahibs: An Anthology*, London: Hardinge Simpole, 2009.

Urban, Hugh D., *Songs of Ecstasy: Tantric and Devotional Songs in Colonial Bengal*, New York: Oxford University Press, 2001.

Vanita, Ruth, and Saleem Kidwai, eds, *Same Sex Love in India: Readings from Literature and History*, London: Macmillan.

Vatuk, Sylvia, "Bharattee's Death: Domestic Slave-women in Nineteenth Century Madras", in Indrani Chatterjee and Richard Eaton, eds, *Slavery and South Asian History*, Bloomington: Indiana University Press, 2006.

Wald, Erica, *Vice in the Barracks: Medicine, the Military and the Making of Colonial India 1780–1868*, London: Palgrave Macmillan, 2014.

7

Writing and Performing Gender

THE IMMENSE PLURALITY of dreams, hopes, visions, and political projects that always revolve around gender issues was nowhere more abundantly expressed than in the many worlds of modern culture. Never had so many cultural genres been made so accessible to such a diverse spectrum of readers, spectators, and listeners; nor had so many different categories of people joined the ranks of culture producers.

There were material reasons behind the expansion of the cultural field – the cheapness of the printed book, the blossoming of the vernaculars, the developed art of translation, the proliferation of diverse literary genres, and the new audio-visual spectacles provided by the public theatre, radio, gramophone, and later cinema. All these knitted together a collective that partially transcended class, caste, gender, and regional barriers. As a result, more and more Indians from varying social segments became aware of one another. Benedict Anderson has written of the effects of print capitalism which helped produce an imagined nation: the cultural supplements of print made the nation visible and audible as well.

Alongside, the lines of division also expanded and intensified, using precisely the same public sphere resources. Communal ideologues used them to mobilise a mass base for their hate campaigns, and the orthodoxy gathered an ever-increasing market for their conservative outpourings against social reform. Paradoxically, the vast wealth of modern cultural production makes it impossible for me to do any kind of justice to them. I have, moreover, neither the resources nor the competence to tackle it all and have limited myself to a select few instances in the hope that what I outline suggests the richness and plurality of Indian modernity.

The World of Printed Books

There is a common sense assumption that modernity led to a thoroughgoing erasure of older cultural traditions, that if the older forms survived at all they were attenuated, frozen, or robbed of vitality. Although there is some truth in such assumptions, we must recognise that there were countervailing tendencies. Actually, the older popular traditions not only survived but "many plebeian forms ... benefited rather than declined with modernity."[1] Colonial modernity, especially nationalism with its urge to draw closer to compatriots of all stripes, came to value the plebeian, the oral, and folk forms as a precious part of the nation's heritage. Some scholars began to collect and preserve folktales and songs, and study local forms of art.

Heritage building had begun under the auspices of the Asiatic Societies. From the early nineteenth century the Asiatic Society's journals had started collecting and publishing old texts, especially the sacred literature in the classical languages. Soon, British officials of an antiquarian bent extended the search into the domain of popular legends. James Tod published his *Annals and Antiquities of Rajasthan* in the 1830s. This included ballads about past kings, queens, and the battles of the region – some were subsequently reshaped by Indian fiction writers as historical novels. Once classical Sanskrit literature came to be published alongside vernacular translations in the course of the nineteenth century, and was thereafter incorporated into the syllabi of new colleges and universities, readership and

---

[1] Sarkar, *Modern Times*, p. 386.

knowledge of the Indian literary past was much extended and greatly influenced modern vernacular languages, imagination, and expressive forms.

Christian missionaries, on the other hand, were more interested in the spoken languages of common folk. The Reverend James Long assiduously collected Bengali proverbs from the mid nineteenth century and set a trend for future compilations of vernacular proverbs, riddles, verses, and songs. In the early twentieth century a historian, Dinesh Chandra Sen, sent out assistants to Bengal villages to collect old manuscripts (*puthi*s). Folk or plebeian culture also attracted the middle classes. Rabindranath Tagore asked his wife to write down the fairy tales that she remembered from her childhood, though he decided against taking the idea further when Dakshinaranjan Mitra Majumdar published his famous collection, *Thakumar Jhuli* (Grandma's Tales), in Calcutta in 1907.

These printed editions probably stifled the diversity of the oral tellings, but I remember my mother singing lullabies to me when I was a child in the late 1950s and early 1960s, and our cook telling me fairy tales that were very different from those in *Thakumar Jhuli*. Later I repeated the stories and songs to my infant son. Even now, a lot of children's books carry different versions of the same nursery rhymes. The oral tradition probably died out in late postcolonial times: when I asked my students at Ashoka University in 2022 if they had *heard* any nursery rhymes or fairy tales in their childhood, they all said they had not. Sumit Sarkar mentions the Nautanki, the most popular folk entertainment form in North India, as actually receiving a major boost from print. Cheap printed collections of Nautanki songs proliferated from the 1860s, and their numbers increased constantly as fresh songs came to be recorded.

Many of these folk tales, proverbs, nursery rhymes, and lullabies were women's oral compositions; frequently, they were expressions of grief – at parting as a child from playmates and parents at marriage, at cruelty in the new home, at sharing a husband with co-wives. Bhojpuri folk songs from eastern India articulated women's pain as their men were driven out to distant places in search of a livelihood. Modernity added several new expressive registers to the older corpus but also retained quite a lot of its sentiments.

Popular culture frequently reflected on modernity in a satirical idiom. Kalighat paintings, sold at temple bazaars in late-nineteenth-century Calcutta and later refurbished by woodcut technology, represented the modern man and woman comically but also mocked traditional ascetics and gurus as well as mythological figures. Popular theatre and pulp writing discussed contemporary urban social and sexual scandals in a satirical vein, sparing no one, traditional or modern, reformer or conservative. This found a resonance in elite dramatic productions – Michael Madhusudan Dutt's play *Ekei ii Boley Sabhyata* (1860; Is This Civilisation?) made fun of ultra-modern reformers while his *Buro Shaliker Ghare Ron* (1860; Ways of an Old Rake) exposed the hypocrisy and immorality which may lurk behind orthodox piety.

New ways appeared, too, for representing the new world. With the maturing of vernacular prose literatures from the mid nineteenth century, even the semi-educated – whose ranks now included growing numbers of women – could read and write in their familiar mother tongue. Consequently the range of authors and readers expanded vastly: they could access with ease the new literary genres – modern poetry, fiction, polemical essays, autobiographies. Diverse literary inclinations and tastes ensured an enormously variegated cultural production ranging from scurrilous pulp to serious modern classics. Men and women could reimagine themselves in unexpected ways as they read and wrote, even if reordering their actual lives remained difficult.

Modernity witnessed an astounding problematisation of gender. This acquired plural forms, some transcending or challenging the familiar prescriptive order, others defending it, and yet others reserving a degree of uncertainty and ambiguity in relation to it. While Bengali men began composing prose works from the 1820s, several middle-class women, educated at home or self-educated, began publishing work from the late 1850s. The gender gap was prominent in terms of output and recognition but not insuperable: the fact that women too found publishers and markets suggests a widespread male appetite for understanding the distinctive experiences of women who had so far been hidden from, or been opaque to, the male gaze.

The woman writer was a disturbing figure nonetheless, and men sought several coping mechanisms to adjust to her. Reformers saw in her a validation for their own agenda. Conservatives, on the other hand, lampooned her. A misogynist Marathi satirical genre emerged from the late nineteenth century, provoked by the boldness of the early Maharashtrian feminists. Rakhmabai, for instance, found a barely disguised comical reflection in the writings of Narayan Bapuji Kanitkar. There were savage portrayals of eager young widows, apparently all seeking liaisons in notorious hotels. Pulp fiction quite often used tropes of crude obscenity to castigate the modern, educated, self-willed woman. Other genres were cautionary in nature, warning against extra-marital, non-marital, and homo-sexual relationships. Purporting to shore up virtue and morality, they frequently dripped with sexually overcharged language and misogynist pornographic content.

The first generation of women writers of Malayalam literature from Kerala was soon forgotten, and the few who were remembered – Lalitambika, K. Saraswati Amma, Madhavikutty, and Sarah Joseph – were misrepresented by male reviewers who, for instance, bypassed Lalitambika Antarajam's sharp critiques of gender in favour of her other writings – which they celebrated for their non-disruptive image of motherhood. Some women authors were admitted into "male homo-aesthetic circles" but their dissident content was often transformed into an amenable version of "the universal feminine".[2] Rashsundari Debi's Bengali autobiography, which subtly but powerfully critiqued her life-world, was reviewed by contemporary male literary figures as the work of a contented

---

[2] Devika, *Womanwriting, Manreading?*, pp. 9–12.

and pious housewife. The misrecognition was strategic – women authors became digestible only when their writings could be twisted into an endorsement of patriarchal values.

Several early writers composed critical polemical reflections on social conventions. Most urged at least some degree of education for women. A few women, however, wrote in a contrary vein, arguing that serving a husband and his family should be the wife's chosen vocation, not educating herself. A very early Bengali autobiography was composed by a housewife from a conservative upper-caste landlord family which abhorred the idea of female literacy. Rashsundari Debi was a timid housewife who had fearfully taught herself to read and write in the deepest secrecy of her kitchen. She stole pages from one of her son's books to learn the letters – even as she cooked for twenty-five people every day, nursed the sick, gave birth to eighteen infants, and brought up twelve children. Much later in life she produced the first full-length Bengali autobiography, mastering this modernist genre even before Bengali men.

Written in 1868 and first published in 1875, *Amar Jiban* (My Life) went through several editions. Its author disguised and legitimised her defiant learning as an unquenchable thirst for reading holy books, even as she discussed domestic cruelties and insensitivities in a guarded doublespeak. But she also exuberantly and explicitly welcomed modern times and compared the older ways most unfavourably with them. Interestingly, her narrative is filled with reflections on God and faith – by no means always epiphanic – and about her miraculous access to the Word. It says relatively little about her family. Autobiographies as a genre indicate modernity and women contributed a significant number. Self-revelation, however, required a particularly bold effort for them and they adopted a variety of strategies to justify the boldness, often clothing their narrative in "womanly" modesty.

Important Marathi-language women's autobiographies began to appear from the early twentieth century, some marked by a "proxy patriarchism".[3] Ramabai Ranade, the wife of the reformist Justice M.G. Ranade, wrote a widely read autobiography, *Amchya Ayushyatil Kahi Athavani* (1910, Reminiscences of Our Lives). Kashibai Kanitkar, wife of a senior bureaucrat, wrote an untitled autobiography which was posthumously published in 1937, and Parvatibai Athavale published *Majhi Kahani* (My Story) in 1928. Some of these women writers expressed their sense of an abject, inadequate selfhood, valorising the husbands who had educated them and in the process saying more about the worth of their husbands and their husbands' lives than their own.

We also begin to find some autobiographies written by men famous for their literary or political work, Premchand and Rahul Sankrityayan among them. Sometimes the less-known wives of such figures published their life narratives as well. Comparing how these men and women thought of their mutual relationships at home suggests very rich possibilities for understanding gender, conjugality, and family from a doubled perspective. Fatherhood, for instance, emerged through them as a domain of male reflections and discussions.

Reflections on love and physical desire, always a staple of courtly literature, continued to dominate modern lyrics and poetry. In pre-modern Hindi-Urdu poetry, *ishq* (passion) and *muhabbat* (love) had revolved around non-marital or premarital love, and true passion was usually located in the figure of the courtesan – her accomplishments and beauty making her an irresistible yet never fully obtainable object of desire. Love, therefore, was seen as intense but elusive. Nineteenth-century Hindi and Bengali poetry, songs, and lyrics, in contrast, introduced celebrations of conjugal love. Most, though, were carefully cleansed of overt eroticism; most also rejoiced in the "safest" form of love – heterosexual, conjugal, and occasionally premarital love which did not eventually culminate in conjugality. Such expressive forms of love in the literary-

---

[3] Kosambi, *Crossing Thresholds*, pp. 33 and 41.

public domain – self-chosen and not imposed – began to enjoy a powerful literary endorsement.

Religious lyrics continued to dominate poetry and a whole modern genre revolved around the illicit and tragic love of the mythological figures Radha and Krishna, pre-modern devotional songs having celebrated their love for centuries. Others expressed adoration for the goddess Kali – including the mid-twentieth-century Muslim poet Kazi Nazrul Islam – or for the epic hero Ram. Tulsidas' sixteenth-century re-creation of the *Ramayana* epic found new performative expressions that were aided by the innovations of loudspeakers and print.

Gender relations have always been central to fiction, the genre which the novelist Henry Fielding once described as domestic history. Each such work aims at a distinctive narrative form, content, and language, which necessarily involve the production of variegated gender imaginaries. Fiction, moreover, probes psychological interiorities, describes emotional shifts and crises, and imparts to each of its characters a unique inner nature. These generic requirements produced multiple configurations of men, women, and relationships, some of which showed transgressions of the normal boundaries of norm-driven lives – even if the excess was also criticised. From the late nineteenth century men and women increasingly published such novels and short stories expressing understandings of each other, and of gender and family, in ways that set up a mutual dialogue or even confrontation.

Novels situated love, even illicit love, as the central focus of lives and emotions – a love now made difficult by a multitude of social constraints. Sometimes the overt message seemed to indicate a denunciation of forbidden love, but a simultaneous subtext either interrogated the social constraints or, at the very least, made their compulsive power evident. Whereas the older songs about Krishna and Radha's illicit love had focused on the lives of gods, these feelings and desires were now transferred to contemporary relationships; the transgression was therefore bolder. When men wrote about women's love, they were also reimagining themselves, coming to grips with the larger social relations that contained and constrained love, and indicating the ways in which they longed to be loved.

Unexpectedly, a European Christian woman pioneered the first Indian-language novel in India. Hana Catherine Mullens (1826–1861), born and educated in Calcutta, who married a missionary, wrote a Bengali tale of two Christian rural women, *Phulmani o Karunar Bibaran* (1852). A didactic novel, it explained how to run a virtuous Christian household. Krupabai Satthianadhan (1862–1894), a Tamil Christian woman, wrote two major novels on Christian lives, *Kamala* (1894), and *Saguna* (serialised 1887–8, published posthumously, 1895). After her death her husband Samuel married a much younger woman called Kamala, who later co-authored a collection of Tamil short stories with him, *Stories of Indian Christian Life*, published from Madras in 1898. This sub-genre, then, primarily sought to familiarise majority-community readers with the lives of their Christian Others.

Bengali novels, especially those of Bankimchandra Chattopadhyay, experimented with conflicting registers of love from the late 1860s. Even inter-community love was represented – doomed yet noble and heart-wrenching. From historical situations he shifted in the 1870s to contemporary domesticity, depicting conjugal passion as well as extra-marital desire, such as the love of and for a widow. While he conveyed this in a cautionary vein, he did sensitively articulate the passion which suffused it, allowing the power of descriptive language to contradict his conventional social message, thereby suggesting the chasm between passion and social prescription. Bankim's female protagonists are invariably more complex and more powerful than his male characters.

His enormously influential and much-translated novel *Anandamath* (1882) was arguably the first work of Indian political fiction. It inaugurated a momentous literary departure by imagining the country/nation as a Hindu goddess who commands the total destruction of Muslims. The novel's communal patriotism ignited a religious and political tradition which became incredibly powerful as the century wore on. The Motherland as a holy – perhaps the holiest – female icon gained enormous visibility and value in subsequent patriotic literature.

Hindu widowhood, now problematised by social reform as well as its adversaries, acquired multiple and contradictory literary figurations. Some, as we saw, lampooned her sexual desire which had found an outlet in the remarriage law. Others depicted her deprivations with some sympathy. Govardhanram Tripathi's Gujarati novel *Saraswatichandra* (1887) represented the thwarted love between a man and a woman which survived her marriage to another, and her subsequent widowhood; eventually, their forbidden love has to be sublimated in selfless social work. In *Chokher Bali* (1903, lit. an irritation in the eye) Rabindranath repeated the motif of sublimation but added new dimensions to the perennial theme of the barren passions of the young widow with descriptions of the oppressively possessive maternalism of an elderly widow.

His *Gora* (1909) and *Ghare Baire* (1916) critically reflected on cultural and political nationalism and on what they did to love. *Ghare Baire* also offered a strikingly new image for masculinity. A gentle, self-reflexive husband ponders over whether his wife is his property. He concludes that he cannot and should not have a monopoly over her mind, body, and passions, regardless of what this acknowledgement may cost him.

In a much-criticised short story, "Streer Patra" (1914; The Wife's Letter), Rabindranath imagines a married woman who abandons her marital home because of the callousness of her husband's family towards an impoverished relative, a young girl whom they had married off to a mentally disturbed man. The girl committed suicide, which proved the last straw for the sensitive protagonist who had long resented her patriarchal household. Pitted against husband and household, the woman's mind and heart – her moral identity, integrity, and independence – acquire a new significance that was revolutionary in its day.

A related though different difficulty arose when novelists addressed the new relationship between love on the one hand and social and political revolution on the other. Rabindranath in *Chaar Adhyay* (1934, Four Chapters) and Saratchandra Chattopadhyay in *Pather Dabi* (1930, The Call of the Road) – a book that was immediately banned – situated desire against revolutionary turbulence, juxtaposing patriotic and human love against each other and presenting an almost impossible choice between two equally compelling yet contrary passions. In both novels, political as well as emotional complications are expressed primarily by women protagonists.

Women activists had, as noted earlier in relation to Bhagat Singh, helped the Hindustan Socialist Revolutionary Association in the 1920s and 1930s, at considerable risk to themselves. At the same time, their comrades feared their subversive sexual potential. A debate about love and revolution arose in their ranks when the revolutionary leader Chandra Shekhar Azad ordered that Yashpal – another revolutionary – be put to death for his love for Prakasvati Kapur, who was also a comrade. Later, when Yashpal was in prison, Prakasvati and the poet Harivansh Rai Bachchan were suspected of a romance. All three wrote of these events in their autobiographies and novels. Yashpal's novel *Dada Kamred* and his autobiography *Sinhavalokan* (A Lion's Eye View), were published in three volumes in the 1950s; Prakasvati's *Lahore Se Lucknow Tak* (From Lahore to Lucknow) was published belatedly in the 1990s, and Bachchan's *Kya Bhooloon, Kya Yaad Karoon* (What to Forget, What to Remember) appeared in 1963. They represented those stormy times and relationships through three quite different lenses.

Udaya Kumar's study of autobiographies in colonial Kerala tracks the complex emergence of anti-caste political identities along with spiritual and literary reflections on desire and salvation. Love was indeed put to a range of services, one involving reflections on the ideal family format wherein it could flourish best. The first major Malayalam novel, *Indulekha* (1889) by O. Chandu Menon, was critical of the older familial arrangements. Menon celebrated the setting up of a nuclear family by a loving married couple, this reflecting a new Malayali male desire for a home harbouring the nuclear family unshackled from matrilineal control. In C. Kesavan's Malayalam autobiography, *Jeevitasamaram* (1990), a husband smuggles a blouse into a matrilineal household governed by his mother-in-law – the blouse here being a forbidden, non-traditional garment. His desire to refashion his wife's body stokes parallel longings in her. Rejecting her mother's control, she takes secret but intense pleasure as she puts on the blouse and finds herself a "new person", a different object as well as a new subject of desire. The account disputes matrilineal norms by reinventing male and female bodily dispositions and pleasure.

The first Punjabi-language novella, *Naval Sundari*, was published in 1898 by Bhai Vir Singh with special messages and images for the modern Sikh woman. It remains enormously popular even now, having gone through its forty-ninth edition in recent times. Situated in the eighteenth century, it touts a rather conventional morality and forms of masculinity and femininity, along with a communal Othering of Muslims. It refurbishes a Sikh male self-image derived from the colonial stereotyping of Punjabi men as martial. Sikh men in the novel are selfless and heroic warriors while their women match the masculine virtues with their flawless chastity and purity.

Social realism emerged as a much used genre to reflect on subaltern lives and class exploitation – this too was a modern preoccupation. It found an early and powerful depiction in Fakir Mohan Senapati's Oriya novel *Chamana Atha Guntha* (1897, Six Acres and a Third). Depicting as its central protagonist a subaltern figure, this is a story about a poor low-caste weaver couple whose tiny plot of land is expropriated by the landlord. The novel made subaltern family life as well as class oppression vivid for middle-class readers.

In 1901 Kamala, co-author with her husband Samuel Satthianadhan of *Indian Christian Lives,* founded an English-language journal called the *Indian Ladies' Magazine*, which in 1905 published Begum Rokeya Sakhawat Hossain's pathbreaking small fiction, *Sultana's Dream*. Apparently, when the book arrived from the press Rokeya's husband read it at one go while standing transfixed on a staircase and exclaimed it was an amazing act of women's revenge. In a curious dream sequence within this work, an upper-class woman is magically transported to a land ruled solely by women. Women cultivate crops and gardens, they administer the realm and lay down the law, they fight wars with rival male-ruled kingdoms; all the while their men sit at home, cooking and nursing babies. The land is rich, well governed, environmentally innovative and militarily powerful. It is especially strong in scientific and technological achievements. Begum Rokeya imagines a world turned upside down, a society which has reversed conventional male and female functions and capabilities. The argument is that if women were in fact to do men's work, they would achieve far more. Generally regarded as outlining a feminist utopia, her book can also be seen as an ironic, tongue-in-cheek inversion of the ways of the world, bringing out the absurdity of the conventional gendering of spaces, work, and capabilities.

A striking crop of left-wing women began to write Urdu fiction from the 1930s. Their writings were scandalously bold for their times, as explicit about women's bodily functions and sexuality as about class inequities. Rashid Jahan (1905–1952), the daughter of reformist educators, was a doctor who married a communist and became a Party activist. An impetuous and recklessly defiant woman, she emerged as a prominent member of the leftist Progressive Writers' Association (PWA), founded in the mid 1930s by writers of the United Provinces. She faced outrage and death threats when *Angarey*, a collection of plays and stories by a group of four youthful left-wing authors – Rashid, her husband Mahmuduzzafar, Sajjad Zaheer, and Ahmed Ali – appeared in 1933. The book was soon banned under popular pressure. The works of these writers explored feudal and bourgeois decadence, psychological perversion, and patriarchal insensitivity. As the sole woman in the quartet, Rashid bore the brunt of the public and clerical attacks, but these did nothing to affect her language and style, nor moderated her assaults on the tyranny of faith and men – her explorations of women's bodies, diseases, and childbirth continued unabated. Her short story, "Parde ke Peechhe" (Behind the Veil), probed the crabbed lives of secluded elite women who are shown as little more than the sexual slaves of their husbands. "Woh" (That One) describes a meeting between a teacher and a sex worker horribly disfigured by venereal disease: it was the kind of theme that no respectable woman could mention then, or even be allowed to know about. Ismat Chughtai, a towering fiction writer of the next generation, said of Rashid, "She shook me up . . . the handsome heroes and pretty heroines of my stories, the candlelike figures, the lime blossom . . . all vanished into thin air . . . the earthy Rashid Jahan simply shattered my ivory idols into pieces . . ."[4]

Ismat Chughtai (1915–1992), who had trained as a teacher, was later affiliated to the PWA. Her fiction offered a sharp exposé of middle-class hypocrisy and cruelty as well as the miseries of subaltern lives – without, however, sentimental idealisations of the poor. She made waves with her short story, "Lihaf" (1941, The Quilt), which portrayed lesbian sex between the pampered wife of a rich landlord and a servant girl, the sex scenes being watched by a hidden and uncomprehending child narrator.

The Urdu and Hindi world of the PWA, accompanied by the leftist theatrical group the Indian People's Theatre Association (IPTA), have sometimes been accused of circulating conservative gender values even if their expressions were bold to the point of being offensive to social conventions. Priyamvada Gopal disagrees: "Each writer thought . . . gender in relation to their own complex subjectivities as writers, political thinkers and social beings. Out of this emerged a body of fiction where gender came to have constitutive rather than a mere thematic importance."[5]

[4] Tharu and Lalita, eds, *Women Writing in India*, p. 118.
[5] Gopal, *Literary Radicalism in India*, p. 5.

Gender in the Modern Journals

Women's journals bloomed from the late nineteenth century. They renovated the images and self-images of women as they struggled to enter modernity – without, however, letting go of the traditional virtues. Most Hindi journals superimposed nationalism upon social reformism. They refashioned domesticity for elite women with new information about maternal health and childcare, cooking, household management; they created templates for emergent nationalist families. Their popularity soared as they entertained women readers with short stories, serialised novels, biographies, poetry, reproductions of traditional oral and folkloric traditions, and "Grandmother's Tales". The editors of these magazines often came from distinguished families. Rameshwari Nehru, editor of *Stree Darpan* and married into the illustrious Nehru family of Allahabad, was proud that her journal had inculcated a deep love for Hindi literature among women. Managed by Kamala Nehru, Jawaharlal's wife, it conveyed the Congress' political views without becoming a party mouthpiece. It advocated a strong public profile and equal rights for the new woman, who was described as the fount of patriotic motherhood.

Chand, edited by a married couple, Ramrakh Singh and Vidyavati Devi, was extremely popular, and the journal most committed to social reform. While enlightened domesticity was its chief agenda, it also advised the woman to work outside the home. *Grihalakshmi* too was edited and published by a husband-wife duo, Pandit Sudarshan Acharya and Gopaldevi. It included pieces on non-domesticated Western women like Joan of Arc, side by side with Indian mythological figures celebrated for their fabulous chastity. It represented an eclectic mix of ideal womanly virtues, Western and Indian.

Arya Mahila, published from a religious organisation and edited by Surath Kumari Devi, was the mouthpiece of hard orthodoxy. It opposed remarriage even for infant widows, valorised

Brahmanical caste practices, and glorified ancient times when Hindu women supposedly behaved like goddesses and were regarded as such.

Some magazines specifically addressed young girls, some were motivated by anti-colonial nationalism, others by Hindu cultural nationalism. Rameshwari and Roop Kumari Nehru edited *Kumari Darpan* for a few years from 1916. The journal taught patriotic morality through stories and verses and provided general knowledge to supplement the school syllabus. *Kanya Manoranjan,* founded in 1913 by Pandit Omkarnath Bajpeyi, on the other hand, was Hindu-sectarian in its orientation.

The pioneering Urdu women's magazines have been discussed earlier. Among them, Muhammadi Begum used her journal, *Tahzib un Niswan*, to selectively modernise household relationships. It advised the upper-class woman on her domestic roles and duties and taught ideal Muslim etiquette for the new times – how to behave at tea parties, for instance. But it also circulated educational news, helped raise funds for schools, and described prize-giving ceremonies at girls' schools in Lahore. After her death in 1908 her husband continued the journal and it found more and more women contributors, some of whom wrote a highly polished prose. This journal discussed the Khilafat–Non-Cooperation movement with sympathy.

Ismat, edited by a well-known novelist, Rashidul Khairi, was a magazine for aristocratic (*sharif*) women. It taught them history, science, and literature and also provided lessons in womanly modesty, chastity, honour. In 1909 an article in the more assertive *Khatun* reacted strongly against such views, arguing that the homilies in *Ismat* were actually authored by conservative men who wrote under female pseudonyms.

Gender on the Stage

Judith Butler has famously described gender values as regulations that need to repeatedly perform themselves: they change gradually in the course of reiterated performances. We may take performance in a very literal sense when we look at developments in the new theatres that came into existence over this period.

Scholars generally assume that modern sanitised bourgeois tastes drove out traditional women cultural performers from public view because they came from the ranks of courtesans or sex workers. The scale of displacement has perhaps been exaggerated for such women never entirely disappeared. Some, moreover, moved into the modern cultural professions that the public theatre, and later the gramophone, the radio, and the cinema introduced from the late nineteenth and early twentieth centuries. Some recordings by the London Gramophone Company from 1902 were marked by a great prominence of women singers from the traditional performing castes and professions. As their popularity grew, middle-class and upper-caste women began to join their ranks. From the early twentieth century new music schools opened their portals to young women students from the middle classes. Later, a few began to participate in national music conferences.

Starting a new tradition in 1873, the Bengal Theatre in Calcutta employed four sex workers as actresses. Though this made the theatre anathema to a number of puritanical reformers, soon all the companies began to replace male actors playing female roles with women. Some of these women became highly educated and accomplished, earning independent incomes and, notwithstanding their socially despised backgrounds, enjoying considerable power over male theatre personnel. The director and the producer, the controlling figures, were of course always men.

The Bengal Theatre also provided screened-off seating arrangements for respectable women viewers from the 1870s. This took housewives into a varied audio-visual worlds that they would never otherwise see – of goddesses and queens, of prostitutes and immoral women. To meet their Others in flesh and blood on the stage would have set up complicated circuits of desire and resentment among some of these hitherto homebound viewers. The visual realism offered by the proscenium stage brought home different social and emotional experiences that were otherwise unfamiliar, even unimaginable, to the audience. This was particularly so for women spectators who had had few or no chances of meeting the world outside the home. These new staged realities expanded and complicated their limited personal experiences and disturbed inherited certainties.

Binodini Dasi, sometimes compared with the great English actress Ellen Terry, completely captivated audiences at the Bengali theatre; European viewers too enjoyed and reviewed her performances. She was, however, forced by the renowned playwright-director Girishchandra Ghosh to abandon the stage and become the mistress of a rich businessman who had offered to fund a new theatre company for him. Binodini was promised that the company would be named after her, but Girishchandra soon dropped the idea, depriving Bengali theatre of a brilliant actress, and Binodini of her hopes and creativity.

Another leading actress, Golap – later renamed Sukumari Dutta – wrote a play, *Apurba Sati Natak*, in 1875. Born a prostitute, she married a high-caste actor under the Special Marriages Act of 1872. Widowed early, she had an infant daughter, and, abandoned by both families, wrote this autobiographical play to earn an income; it was the first written by a woman to be staged. Daringly, prostitutes in her play emerge as loving and lovable figures, in sharp contrast to heartless and hypocritical social bosses. Her language was bold and outspoken: it articulated women's desire and denounced socio-sexual double standards.

Love was central also to the Parsi theatre, but here it often took a sacrificial shape, being shown as an emotion born only to be given up for a higher and more conventional duty. Sometimes, the premarital romance culminated in the safe haven of marriage. Mythological and social plays – the two staples of the early theatre – similarly valorised marital love. As Anuradha Kapur puts it: "By domesticating the mythology and mythicising the domestic . . .

Parsi melodrama mediated the transition from courtly culture to the new domesticity and nationalism of the emerging middle classes."[6]

Mythological and historical themes dominated much of the theatre, while the earliest dramatic representations of modern gender relations were often satirical or didactic. The classical-modern genre of paintings, too, relied much on these themes but they were generally more didactic than satirical. Ravi Varma's splendid and elaborately detailed oil paintings portrayed richly garbed mythological heroines alongside a few nationalist women. Abanindranath Tagore painted "Bharatmata" (Motherland) as a watercolour, representing the nation as a beautiful, ethereal woman encompassing the map of undivided India. Nandalal Bose's "Sati" re-aestheticised widow immolation by providing no room for the horror of a woman being burned alive, replacing the grotesquerie with a spectacle of tranquillity, grace, and beauty. Women seem to occupy a much larger space then men in these paintings, but we find very few instances of women painters – Sunayani Debi from the affluent Tagore family being a rare exception.

All through the nineteenth and for much of the twentieth century men and women struggled with uncertainties thrown up by the encounter between the old and the new. A clear choice was impossible for most, especially in colonial times, when Indian traditions were frequently lampooned or dismissed as trivia by the rulers. To overcome the imperial slur, modern creative forms developed the category of the "modern-traditional", which entailed investing past traditions with great aesthetic and moral value. At the same time, modernity was inescapable, presenting Indians with the possibility of confronting their problems along the old ways, or else tempting them to explore and try out the alternative ways of being that had become available. To a degree, the new cultural genres combined both impulses. The outcome was interesting

---

[6] Kapur, "Love in the Time of Parsi Theatre", p. 3.

precisely because no choice between the traditional and the new was entirely clear-cut. The persistence of unresolved ambiguities remained clear well into the decades after Independence.

References and Suggested Readings for Chapter 7

Bagchi, Barnita, "Towards Ladyland: Rokeya Sakhawat Hossain and the Movement for Women's Education in Bengal, c. 1900–1932", *Pedagogia Historica: International Journal of the History of Education*, vol. 45, no. 6, 2009.

Bakhle, Janaki, *Two Men and Music: Nationalism in the Making of an Indian Classical Tradition*, Ranikhet: Permanent Black, 2002.

Banerjee, Sumanta, *The Parlour and the Street: Elite and Popular Culture in Nineteenth Century Calcutta*, Kolkata: Seagull, 1989.

Banerjee, Swapna M., *Fathers in a Motherland: Imagining Fatherhood in Colonial India*, Delhi: Oxford University Press, 2022.

Bhattacharya, Rimli, ed. and trans., *Binodini Dasi: My Story and My Life as an Actress*, Delhi: Kali for Women, 1998.

Dalmia, Vasudha, "The Spaces of Love and the Passing of Seasons: Delhi in the Early Twentieth Century", in Fransesca Orsini, ed., *Love in South Asia*, Cambridge: Cambridge University Press, 2006.

Dasi, Dayamoyee, *Patibrata Dharma,* Calcutta, 1870.

Debi, Rashsundari, *Amar Jiban*, Calcutta, 1868.

Devika, J., *Womanwriting, Manreading?*, Delhi: Zubaan and Penguin Books, 2013.

Devika, J., ed., *Herself: Early Writings on Gender by Malayalee Women: 1898–1938*, Kolkata: Stree, 2005.

Ghosh, Anindita, *Power in the Print: Popular Publishing and the Politics of Language and Culture in a Colonial Society, 1778–1905*, Delhi: Oxford University Press, 2006.

Gopal, Priyamvada, *Literary Radicalism in India: Gender, Nation and the Transition to Independence*, Routledge Research in Postcolonial Literature, London and New York: Routledge, 2005.

Guha-Thakurta, Tapati, *The Making of a New 'Indian' Art*, Cambridge: Cambridge University Press, 1992.

Gupta, Charu, *Sexuality, Obscenity, Community: Women, Muslims, and the Hindu Public in Colonial India*, Delhi: Permanent Black, 2001.

Jain, Jyotindra, *Kalighat Painting: Images from a Changing World*, Ahmedabad: Mapin Publishing, 1999.
Jalil, Rakshanda, *A Rebel and Her Cause: The Life and Work of Rashid Jahan*, Delhi: Women Unlimited, 2014.
Kapur, Anuradha, "Love in the Time of Parsi Theatre", in Francesca Orsini, ed., *Love in South Asia*, Cambridge: Cambridge University Press, 2006.
Kosambi, Meera, *Crossing Thresholds: Feminist Essays in Social History*, Ranikhet: Permanent Black, 2007.
Kumar, Udaya, *Writing the First Person: Literature, History, and Autobiography in Modern Kerala*, Ranikhet: Permanent Black, 2016.
Loomba, Ania, *Revolutionary Desires: Women, Communism and Feminism in India*, London and New York: Routledge, 2019.
Lutgendorf, Philip, *The Life of a Text: Performing Tulsidas' Ramcaritmanas*, Berkeley: University of California Press, 1991.
Majeed, Javed, "Literary Modernity in Colonial India", in Douglas M. Peers and Nandini Gooptu, eds, *India and the British Empire*, Oxford: Oxford University Press, 2012.
Malhotra, Anshu, "Bittersweet Imaginings: Form, Gender and Religion in Bhai Vir Singh's *Sundari*", *Sikh Formations: Religion, Culture, Theory*, online publication, 18 February 2020.
Metcalf, Barbara, "Islam and Custom in Nineteenth Century India", *Contributions to Asian Studies*, vol. 17, 1982.
Metcalf, Barbara, "The Making of a Muslim Lady: Maulana Thanawi's *Bihishti Zewar*", in Milton Israel and N.K. Wagle, eds, *Islamic Society and Culture: Essays in Honour of Professor Aziz Ahmad*, Delhi: Manohar, 1983.
Minault, Gail, *Gender, Language and Learning: Essays in Indo-Muslim Cultural History*, Ranikhet: Permanent Black, 2009.
Minault, Gail, *Secluded Scholars: Women's Education and Muslim Social Reform in Colonial India*, Delhi: Oxford University Press, 1998.
Murmu, Maroona, *Words of Her Own: Women Authors in Nineteenth Century Bengal*, Delhi: Oxford University Press, 2020.
Nijhawan, Shobna, *Women and Girls in the Hindi Public Sphere: Periodical Literature in Colonial North India*, Delhi: Oxford University Press, 2012.
Orsini, Francesca, *The Hindi Public Sphere, 1920–1940*, Delhi: Oxford University Press, 2002.

Pandey, Gyanendra, *Fragments of Family: Men at Home in Colonial and Post Colonial India*, forthcoming.
Pinney, Christopher, "The Material and Visual Culture of Colonial India", in Douglas M. Peers and Nandini Gooptu, eds, *India and the British Empire*, Oxford: Oxford University Press, 2012.
Sai, Veejay, *Drama Queens: Women Who Created History on Stage*, Delhi: Roli Books, 2007.
Sarkar, Sumit, *Beyond Nationalist Frames: Relocating Postmodernity, Hindutva, History*, Delhi: Permanent Black, 2002.
Sarkar, Sumit, *Modern Times: India 1880s–1950s*, Ranikhet: Permanent Black, 2014.
Sarkar, Tanika, "Talking About Scandals", in idem, *Hindu Wife, Hindu Nation*, Delhi: Permanent Black, 2003.
Sarkar, Tanika, "Performing Power and Troublesome Plays", in idem, *Rebels, Wives, Saints: Designing Selves and Nations in Colonial Times*, Ranikhet: Permanent Black, 2009.
Sarkar, Tanika, "The Birth of a Goddess", in idem, *Hindu Nationalism in India*, Ranikhet: Permanent Black, 2021.
Sarkar, Tanika, "The Child and the World", in idem, *Rebels, Wives, Saints*, Ranikhet: Permanent Black, 2009.
Sarkar, Tanika, *Words to Win: A Modern Autobiography*, Delhi: Kali for Women, 1998.
Sinha, Nitin, "When Women Sang in the Age of Steam", https://thewire.in/the-arts/railways-bhojpuri-folksongs, 31 July 2016.
Tharu, Susie, and K. Lalita, eds, *Women Writing in India: The Twentieth Century*, London: Pandora, 1993.

8

Post-colonial India

O N 15 AUGUST 1947 India gained independence from British rule: "At the stroke of the midnight hour, when the world sleeps, India will awaken to life and freedom", announced Jawaharlal Nehru, the first prime minister, in a memorable radio broadcast just before midnight.[1] Millions of ecstatic Indians had their ears glued to the radio set that night as wild jubilation and celebrations burst out all over the country. Terrible communal violence had preceded the event, but on the day of independence Hindus and Muslims embraced one another in the streets.

As the country gained freedom from colonial rule, vast numbers of Indians lost their homes and homelands, and many their lives: a paradoxical moment of triumph, then, shot through with violence, loss, and suffering of unimaginable proportions. If Indians had waged the largest anti-colonial mass struggles known to history, the world also saw the largest forced mass migrations of refugees who trekked like lost souls across the new borders between India and Pakistan. If under Gandhi's leadership the freedom struggles had been, by and large, non-violent, the process

---

[1] Strictly speaking, India still remained a part of the imperial dominion until 26 January 1948, when the formal transfer of power was finalised.

of decolonisation was accompanied by the most savage ferocity between Hindus and Muslims. In his broadcast, therefore, Nehru also reminded his compatriots that any recurrence of mutual hatred would vitiate the future of independent India. He envisioned a secular state where citizens of every faith, sect, gender, caste, and class would enjoy equal rights. Ironically, so did Jinnah in his early utterances after Pakistan was created, despite his striving for a pure Islamic nation.

So while India and Pakistan celebrated their independence, masses of refugees struggled to come to terms with their new country. Gandhi spent the day of Independence alone, at his spinning wheel. When asked for a message for the great occasion, he simply said "I have run dry of messages."

On 30 January 1948, shortly after the birth of the sovereign nation-state of India, Gandhi was murdered by Nathuram Godse, a Maharashtrian Brahman member of the Hindu Mahasabha earlier trained by the far-Right Hindu RSS. A man of peace *par excellence*, Gandhi's unparalleled moral force and charisma could, on occasion, draw the most inflamed of hearts towards non-violence and he had stopped several terrible conflagrations with fasts unto death or by travelling through the troubled areas, unarmed and unprotected.

A truncated India emerged from bloody civil war and the decolonisation process to face formidable responsibilities – of constructing a brand-new post-colonial economy and polity, rehabilitating refugees who arrived in recurring waves, and pulling into its fold as many erstwhile-independent native states as possible. Worst of all was the problem of how to deal with the terrible memories of fratricidal violence – memories continuously inflamed by communal propaganda, rioting, and hostilities with Pakistan. While colonial India already had a Hindu majority, the strength of the majority community was exponentially expanded after Partition: its numerical strength matched its political, material, and electoral ascendancy. The religious minorities, now attenuated further by the loss of the Muslim-majority regions, were correspondingly rendered even more vulnerable.

Enough has been written on Nehru's socialist ideals, industrialisation drive, and his solidarity with the decolonising countries of the world as well as with the Palestinian cause. They are only tangentially relevant here; in the sphere of mass education, however, his regime left a lot to be desired. While educational institutions proliferated, widespread illiteracy was not adequately addressed, and women's literacy, particularly, remained in a pathetic state. The Constitution, drafted by Ambedkar, stressed gender and caste equality and freedom of expression and reserved educational and job quotas for Dalits and Adivasis in government institutions. But its remarkably liberal promise was nowhere fully realised in practice.

India fared badly in the Sino-Indian war of 1962. It was a personal blow to Nehru, who died shortly thereafter. The sudden death of his successor Lal Bahadur Shastri in January 1966 led to a succession battle and a split in the Congress. A caucus of senior leaders chose Nehru's daughter Indira Gandhi as the next prime minister, in the hope that, politically inexperienced as she was, she would remain under their thumb. Mrs Gandhi, however, adroitly manoeuvred herself into a position of supreme strength. She nationalised the banks, abolished privy purses for India's princes, and soon acquired the aura of a relatively progressive and daring leader. When in 1971 her decision to assist East Pakistan against West Pakistan resulted in India's victory and the creation of Bangladesh, even her staunch right-wing opponents saluted her as a warrior goddess.

In response to the United Nations' International Decade for Women (1975–85), Mrs Gandhi commissioned a renowned feminist scholar, Veena Mazumdar, to compile a report on the status of Indian women. A Centre for Women's Development Studies was founded in 1988. In 1989 the Panchayati Raj Bill reserved a certain proportion of seats for elected women members in village self-governing bodies. There was no such reservation, however, in the national and state legislatures.

Belying Indira Gandhi's triumphal progress, a crisis was nonetheless brewing. India's Second Five Year Plan had concentrated on heavy industries and the agrarian sector was dangerously neglected, as was the vast informal sector of small-scale manufacture where most women labourers worked. Welfare measures for the poor were minimal and corruption in the Congress Party ranks rampant. As consumer prices spiralled, agitations started in many parts of the country and women played a prominent role in them.

Faced with the huge protests, as well as a court case alleging electoral corruption on her part – a case that she lost – Indira Gandhi declared a National Emergency in 1975. It suspended civil and democratic rights and muzzled the press with brutal censorship. Helped by her son Sanjay Gandhi, she ordered a programme of forced sterilisation that severely impacted subaltern men and subjected them to sexual humiliation.

Despite her assassination in 1984 by Sikh bodyguards who supported Sikh secessionism, Indira Gandhi had by her strength, determination, ruthlessness, and political intelligence proved herself the equal of India's powerful male politicians. Yet she did not distinguish herself at all by bringing about substantive gender reforms.

The Communist Party of India, the leading party of Opposition in parliament, had formed the government in Kerala – the first elected communist government anywhere in the world. Nehru had had it arbitrarily dismissed in 1959, the Party had split in 1964, and one of its two factions, the pro-Soviet Communist Party of India (CPI), moved close to Mrs Gandhi. The other faction, the CPI (Marxist), proved far more confrontational. The two parties, however, came together with several other smaller parties to form a

United Front government in West Bengal in 1967. The same year, following clashes between the state police forces and tribal peasants of Naxalbari in north-western Bengal, a further split occurred within the CPI (M) as its dissident members chose an insurrectionary politics rather than the embrace of parliamentary politics. Bands of young men and women joined the new CPI (Marxist-Leninist) in 1969 to attempt class struggles in rural areas as well as to follow the "urban guerrilla" line of exterminating what it termed "class enemies". Facing enormous repression, Naxalites nonetheless spread out over parts of eastern and southern India. Several bouts of severe state violence have eroded its bases over time, though not completely.

After the Left Front led by the CPI(M) won a decisive victory in West Bengal in 1977, vibrant campaigns for the release of political prisoners, including the Naxals, secured freedom for those who were still alive. On their release, women activists gave searing testimonies of the sexual torture they had faced in prison. The CPI(M)-led Left Front won elections continuously over the next three decades in West Bengal, and frequently formed governments in Tripura and Kerala as well. Wherever the Front held state power, their women's wings grew rapidly. While these focused primarily on women's livelihood issues, non-Party feminist groups too began to flourish, uncovering and underlining patriarchal oppression and women's sexual autonomy. Many such independent feminists arranged relief and rehabilitation for Sikh victims of the 1984 genocidal violence that followed in the wake of Indira Gandhi's assassination. *Manushi*, a feminist journal edited at the time by Ruth Vanita and Madhu Kishwar, brought out a remarkable exposure of the riots, as did *Delhi Riots*, an investigative monograph jointly written by two independent feminists, Uma Chakravarti and Nandita Haksar. The first feminist publishing house, Kali for Women, was established in Delhi in 1984.

At the other end of the pole the right-wing Bharatiya Jana Sangh – renamed the Bharatiya Janata Party (BJP) in 1980 – also began to contest elections. The political front of the staunchly male-dominated RSS, it was backed by the formidable cadre base of the RSS. Undeterred by an eighteen-month ban after Mahatma Gandhi's murder in 1948, and unnoticed by most political pundits, the RSS had been quietly and methodically expanding its cadre base and range of activities, forming affiliates and sub-affiliates which worked through more and more mass fronts. One of their chief tasks was the inculcation of hatred for and distrust of religious minorities, especially Muslims. Apart from the Rashtrasevika Samiti, its women's front, it formed a large chain of schools and trade unions. In 1964 it added a religious wing, the Vishwa Hindu Parishad (VHP), which became very powerful from 1984. It organised a formidable movement of Hindu extremists for the demolition of the sixteenth-century Babri Mosque which it alleged had been erected on the ruins of a temple that stood on Lord Ram's birthplace. As the movement gathered national and global momentum, the mosque was completely demolished in 1992. Various women's wings of the RSS-BJP-VHP had been formed in the 1980s and 1990s. They work tirelessly to block inter-community marriages and expand Islamophobic messages in schools, households, workplaces, and kin groups.

Gendering Births and Deaths

I began this book with the skewed sex ratio in India, the discovery of which had created a positive environment for critical feminist research. The demographic imbalance, identified as early as the 1871 census, persisted after Independence. From the 1970s it caught the attention of economists and demographers who debated the reasons behind the phenomenon of "missing women".[2]

---

[2] Amartya Sen used the term to argue that the gap between the numbers of women in *women-deficit* areas in Africa and Asia – India providing a particularly glaring example – and *women-excess* areas can be called a case of "missing women", i.e. women who should have been in existence but were not allowed to be for man-made reasons. See Sen, "More than 100 Million Women Are Missing".

According to the 1991 census, only forty-two Indian districts – one-tenth of the total number – showed a ratio that favoured women. The gap was most marked in women's earliest years, in the 0 to 6 age group. Even in Tamil Nadu, where women generally attain high levels of education, the ratio dips below the age of 7. Whereas the all-India ratio for the "girl child" in that age group is 950 women to 1000 men, it is 945 in Tamil Nadu. Barbara Harriss-White has called this "gender cleansing".

An inordinately strong son-preference in India ensures that daughters are deprived of adequate nutrition and healthcare in their earliest and most vulnerable years. Female infanticide, which is still quite rampant across diverse social levels, may provide another explanation. Since this happens in the deepest secrecy, we cannot fathom its actual extent. In a documentary film, *The World Before Her,* women from two very differently situated families narrate the pressures that drive parents to kill their daughters at birth. They talk about it as something to be entirely expected, if also deplored. One is a highly educated middle-class mother from Bombay who chose to leave her family with her second daughter – instead of killing her, as advised by relatives. Another is a lower-middle-class, unsophisticated girl from a small town in Madhya Pradesh. She is deeply grateful to her rather brutal father simply because he allowed her to live.

Killing daughters actually begins in the womb. The First Five Year Plan of 1951–6 made population control a matter of great urgency, and in 1966 the Ministry of Health set up a family-planning department. While contraceptives are indispensable if women are to gain control over their bodies, family planning had a different consequence. An obsessive state insistence on the two-child norm – subsequently incorporated under the Panchayati Raj Acts in many states – made many families resort to sex-selective abortions with amniocentesis and ultrasonography techniques, so that unwanted daughters could be identified and disposed of before birth. At Ludhiana in Punjab, as Monica Das Gupta's research in the 1980s shows, most female foetuses were systematically destroyed after the birth of the first daughter. Even after they were banned in 1994, the tests continued to flourish at backstreet facilities. Female life-expectancy figures are disturbing. Between 1971 and 1980, given a general average of 52 years of life, Madhya Pradesh showed 47.5 for women, Orissa 46.0, and Uttar Pradesh 41.9, whereas male life expectancy is higher in every case. This strains against the global trends where women generally outlive men. Das Gupta reveals that families in Ludhiana spent twice the amount on sons' nutrition than on daughters'. Kerala – at an average life expectancy of 66.3 for women – however, showed an excess of females over the male population.

The gender imbalance is most acute in the northern states of Punjab, Haryana, Delhi, Uttar Pradesh, and Rajasthan, and in parts of Madhya Pradesh. It is more marked in urban locations, though rural areas too show a declining ratio for women. Surprisingly, it is very common amongst the educated and affluent middle classes. For the poor, the daughter may even be a precious source of labour rather than the commodity for exchange at marriage that she sometimes is in the richer families. In some villages of Tamil Nadu, on the other hand, where landownership and moveable properties are thickly concentrated in a few hands, and where poverty is therefore widespread, female child deaths among the poor have been increasing from the 1980s.

A common sense view is that exorbitant dowry demands weed out daughters before or after their brith. This is a valid but not sufficient explanation. In their 1984 study, Randeria and Visaria found that the sex ratio hardly differed between dowry-paying communities and bride-price-paying ones in northern Gujarat. Leela Gulati tried to establish a correlation between female work participation and enhanced life chances in the 1970s, and Pranab Bardhan found that in wet-rice-cultivation zones – these being more female-labour intensive than wheat-growing ones – women are more numerous. Maria Mies, on the other hand, attributed the gap to the growth of capitalist production relations in India which bear down heavily on the country's urban and rural economies and prove especially damaging for women. Whatever the contributory or proximate causes of missing women may be, the enduring roots certainly lie in an entrenched patriarchal culture which devalues daughters to the point of causing their deaths.

There is another category of execeptionally vulnerable women, mostly born to those in subaltern families that cannot afford to give them the care they deserve. The special needs of disabled – or differently abled – women have only recently come to the attention of the state and public, even if rather inadequately. Some disabilities are caused by medical neglect or malnutrition. The 2001 census identified over nine million such women in India.

Gendering Labour

The affluent middle classes, enjoying political and cultural dominance, have remained hegemonic in post-colonial India, so much so that the poor in general, and labouring people in particular, have all but disappeared from mainstream public concerns and historical scholarship. With a few exceptions, historians continue to focus on industrial workers in colonial times, largely bypassing their fate in the post-colonial world.

This applies especially to labouring women, whose unpaid domestic chores fail to count as work. Before certain methodological changes were made in 1991, censuses classified wage labour in large factories and the market-oriented manufacture of commodities alone as proper work. Those kinds of work, however, exclude what is produced for the workers' own consumption. Even home-based piecemeal manufacture, which earned an income, was deleted from earlier definitions of work. So were certain kinds of agricultural work that did not involve the use of the plough or heavy tools, or were finished at home by women. The consequent invisibility of women as productive workers concealed their prominence in subsistence activities such as dairy work, fishing, cattle care, fruit and vegetable gardening, fuel gathering, fodder collection, harvesting water and forest products, cooking and cleaning, and caring for children, the sick, and the elderly.

Amrita Chhachhi argues that, earlier, factory production mainly involved the manual assemblage of components which rarely necessitated sharp gender distinctions. In fact, women – supposedly docile and a bulwark against male militancy – were sometimes preferred as employees. We have, however, already noticed a decline in women's workforce numbers from the 1930s, and the trend continued and intensified steadily after Independence. Many women lost their jobs in textile mills between 1950 and 1956 on account of a systematically gendered retrenchment. By 1956 women made up only 7 per cent of the workforce. Formerly a fourth of all jute workers, they were reduced to a mere 2 per cent by 1971. At a time when trade unions expanded rapidly, women occupied only a tiny corner: 2.4 per cent of the total union membership in West Bengal. Naturally, they greatly resented the loss of factory jobs, their identity as skilled workers being important for their self-esteem, economic independence, and mobility. Men monopolised the union posts as well, depriving women of yet another cherished aspect of working-class identity.

Women at the Budge Budge jute mills in West Bengal were predominantly employed to weave jute yarn and make gunny bags. Many pretended to be married to the men they lived with. They worked to send remittances back to their village homes even as they acquired another family on the mill lines. They – and not the men they lived with – were castigated for immorality, even in their own circles. Male co-workers called the women's department *maagi kol*. Literally signifying machines where women work, *maagi* is also a sneeringly contemptuous term for women. The unions, male-dominant, did not fight women's retrenchment because it furthered male employment chances. Leela Fernandes calls this a patriarchal compact between master and male worker.

A few women did participate in trade-union struggles. Phoolmayanand Dilmaya, a tea-garden worker, joined the "Red Flag" union established in 1946 and helped to mobilise women workers. Chameli and Shelly Tamang, also tea-garden workers, joined the All India Trade Union Congress of the CPI. In January 1955 Mouli Soba Raini, a woman union leader, died in an incident of police firing at Darjeeling. Dukhmat Didi was an important leader in a jute-mill union in West Bengal.

From the late 1980s the state began to liberalise trade and investment regulations, and open up Indian markets to multinational investments and imports. Under this new economic regime mobile multinational capital, searching for new sources of cheap labour, arrived as a major employer. The result was a fragmentation of the production process into decentralised units of informal work. Employment now moved away from large factories to home-based workplaces, and production was subcontracted among individual workers. The impact of this change on women's work possibilities has been much debated. Some argue that it enlarged the room for work available to women, others track a decline. Those who favour the feminisation-of-work model – a term much used since the late 1980s – suggest that women have actually replaced men in certain sectors of work. From the 1980s young women from Kerala, and from Delhi and its hinterland, for instance, migrated in search of factory jobs to other parts of India, enabled by their secondary-level education degrees which were now obligatory for factory employment. But this was not a general trend. The ratio of women workers within the total workforce declined from 36 per cent in 1983 to 34.5 per cent in the early 1990s. A masculinisation of the industrial workforce and a simultaneous feminisation of rural labour advanced rapidly thereafter.

Between 1981 and 1991 the largest expansion in women's work occurred in the agricultural sector, especially in those regions where women were already prominent: Andhra Pradesh, Madhya Pradesh, Maharashtra, Tamil Nadu, and Uttar Pradesh accounting for two-thirds of India's women agricultural workers. Their participation remained static in West Bengal while the introduction of large-scale agricultural machinery in Punjab and Haryana led to a decrease in their numbers.

Several unusual features marked women's agricultural labour at Nellore district in Tamil Nadu: non-bonded women farm-servants exceeded male servants until the 1950s. There were female supervisors of farm labour (*malata*s) and upper-caste women also worked as farm servants. This may be explained by the large extent of landlessness among all castes which forced even some upper-caste women into rural labour; also by the large-scale migration of men to Madras city for urban and factory work. Male migration generally left the field open to the greater entry of women labourers. Surprisingly, Kerala registered a sharp decline in precisely those areas where women were numerous elsewhere: paddy cultivation, cashew and coir manufacture, handloom manufacture. In 1981 it ranked fifteenth in female work participation rates on an all-India basis.

As famine, war, riots, and Partition washed over India, and over West Bengal in successive tidal waves till the end of the 1950s, they left behind a detritus of devastated and destitute people. Widows with small children poured into West Bengal from East Pakistan, bereft of their men and a livelihood. A later exodus consisted chiefly of low-caste peasant refugees whose families were stranded on railway platforms; government relief measures could hardly keep pace with the relentless inflow. Rehabilitation planners eventually tried to transform these refugees into productive workers for the new nation. Many peasant families were packed off to settle on the Andaman Islands and spead agriculture there. Some were made to migrate to other states to work at "developmental" ventures – to build dams and clear forests for agriculture. Single women in refugee camps were taught handicrafts that the government marketed.

Early generations of refugees lived a tough and dangerous life. Some resisted their forced exile to inhospitable lands and insisted on returning to Bengal. In the mid 1970s a large number of men and women – mostly low caste – began to trek back from the Dandakaranya forests in Madhya Pradesh–Orissa to West Bengal. With the help of local communities they formed settlements in the remote and wild Sunderbans area of Bengal. In 1979, in the name of preserving the local environment, the Left Front government sent forces to evict them. Those who resisted were killed.

Uprooted refugees flocked to the cities to form an urban precariat of "pavement dwellers". They survived by begging, doing odd jobs, or living off petty crime. Many young women were trafficked into prostitution; others settled in the suburbs and boarded early-morning trains with sacks of vegetables and grain to sell in Calcutta. Penniless women filled up the domestic service sector in large numbers while lower-middle-class women with a smattering of education crowded into minor clerical jobs: in offices and schools, in milk booths, in shops. Slowly, the working woman became a familiar figure in the urban landscape. But the city was not too comfortable with her. Either she was stuck with social stigma, or else she was pitied as a tragic figure who had been forced into waged work which should never have been her lot.

Colonial tea planters had used fraudulent contracts to tempt rural men and women into the remote gardens of North Bengal and Assam. However, the planters – rather like their antebellum American counterparts – encouraged the labour force to reproduce itself. The costs of importing labour being exorbitant, they used pro-natal policies, including rewards for the birth of healthy babies. They also aspired for a healthy child-labour force since a child's delicate hands are useful in leaf-picking. Consequently, maternal health in the gardens was somewhat better than in mines and factories.

Post-colonial tea estates now fragmented into a mosaic of small family-owned plantations, large Indian corporation-run estates, and multinational enterprises. Marwari traders became the major investors and owners, and English planters ceded their place to Indian managers – these were the new Sahibs, trained in public schools, often from an army or business background. The ownership and management of these estates remained stubbornly male, even as new advertising images featured middle-class women sitting in posh parlours, serving tea in elegant cups, and presiding over a sophisticated domesticity. Other ads displayed the tea-plucking "coolie" woman as a happy and sexy labourer, as inviting in her physical presence as the commodity she produced.

Labouring women, made famous for nimbly plucking tea leaves, worked the gardens while higher-paid men monopolised tea processing in the factories, their work regulated by clock-time and the factory siren. Women's labour was relatively more flexible: they could bring their babies to the workplace and feed them during the breaks. Daughters learned on the job as they followed their mothers into the bushes. *Aurat chaprasi*s (senior women labourers) supervised the plucking of tea leaves. On occasion, if menfolk moved into better jobs outside a tea garden, some women were able to become part-time shopkeepers. Pia Chatterjee's ethnographic research for the 1990s shows women organising their post-work social, cultural, and ritual lives well away from the domination of masters. This partial autonomy, however, should not obscure the internal hierarchy and customary regulations in their own ranks, nor their back-breaking labour in extreme heat or cold, their long hours of work, and the triple burden of domestic work, childcare, and waged labour.

The environmentalist scholar-activist Vandana Shiva argues that violence against Nature and against women are interconnected because women are naturally more sensitive to ecological conservation. Though her faith in this special relationship is disputed, women undoubtedly work intensively with natural resources in India – in relation to forests, cattle, and waterbodies.

The Nehruvian era embraced a vision of industrial development which involved massive deforestation as well as the depletion of land and water resources. The trend has only grown since then. The large-scale construction of canals, alongside big dams and mining, led to the privatisation of erstwhile community resources. They also devalued women's traditional knowledge systems.

Ground-level research in histories of western Himalayan environmental activism by Shekhar Pathak and Chandi Prasad Bhatt shows several courageous instances of women's defence of such resources connected with the Chipko movement. The struggles began in 1972–3 in the Chamoli district of north-western India. Village women protested en masse against the auctioning of forests of ash trees to a sports-goods manufacturer. They hugged or pressed their bodies (*chipko*) to the trees designated for felling. Women's songs in the region showed their different priorities:

> Foresters: "What do the forests bear? / Profits, resin and timber."
> Women: "What do the forests bear? / Soil, water and pure air."[3]

Their argument against loggers habitually took shape as poems, slogans, and songs in their vernacular, Garhwali:

> *"Dharm ki ladai chhidige, jungle bachhon,*
> *kanwalandi dali koo paran chhati se chipkoon"*

(This is the fight for our rights. Save the jungle, hug the young tree to your breast and save its life.)

Children remembererd these slogans and the women recalled the songs.[4]

The Garo hill tribe in present-day Meghalaya had traditionally lived off shifting cultivation (*jhum*) and forest produce. They began to shift to wet-rice cultivation and fruit-and-nut orchards from the early twentieth century, and the trend strengthened from the 1960s. This aggravated economic stratification, and its effect worsened matters for women by eroding their former prominence in *jhum* – plough-based agriculture now excluded them from the production process. Men became the primary producers, and

---

[3] Shiva, *Staying Alive*, p. 484.
[4] Pathak, *The Chipko Movement*, p. 218.

women mere helpers. Unable to sell the produce they used to gather from uncleared *jhum* land and jungles, they also lost their cash earnings from petty trade, which now passed into male hands. As land came to be increasingly privatised, the government granted *patta*s (ownership titles) to men alone, bypassing the tradition of Garo matriliny.

It is difficult to decide whether to place Dalit women's work under labour or under caste since they inhabit both spaces: their caste adds fresh twists to their gendered location within labour regimes, and vice versa. They have, however, always been ready to fight for their rights. As she lectured on African-American women's struggles in the US to a group of landless Dalit women at a farm in Maharashtra in 1971, Gail Omvedt was told by her audience, "Women are the most ready to fight, the first to break through police lines, the last to go home."[5] This notwithstanding, their existence within a controlling ethos of patriarchy almost always prevents them organising or leading working-class and agrarian movements.

Omvedt, however, found a rather unusual situation among Dalit municipal women sweepers at Pune. Militant trade unionists there asserted: "The union is our mother."[6] Founded in 1930 by a Dalit man, this union had won them repeated pay rises, wage parity with men, maternity and sick leave, the bonus of two saris a year, and municipal housing. It also guaranteed them protection from harassment by their supervisors. Since no other caste cares to do these apparently demeaning jobs, Dalits enjoy a monopoly over street sweeping and sanitary work. However, since their women also shoulder domestic responsibilities, most of them are reluctant to work outside the home once their men procure better jobs.

Dalits everywhere find it hard to move out of their caste-designated occupations. For women, the glass ceiling proves even harder

[5] Omvedt, *We Will Smash This Prison*, p. 2.
[6] Ibid., p. 25.

to break through. Some Balmiki-caste male municipal sweepers in Delhi have moved to better jobs, but not the women sweepers.

Gendering Property

Governments of all political stripes have signally failed to address women's pleas for landownership rights. The Sixth Five Year Plan for 1980–5 promised women basic entitlements in education, health, and food resources, but not in landownership despite repeated petitions from women since the 1970s for separate or joint titles to land. This issue was not even placed on the Seventh Plan agenda. Nor did Left parties help women when they formed their governments in various states. The Left Front government in West Bengal granted land titles to erstwhile sharecroppers from the late 1970s under their radical programme "land to the tillers". Women, classified as non-cultivators because they did not manually till the land, were left out of the loop. In 1960 a communist government in Kerala introduced the Kerala Agrarian Relations Bill which was eventually enacted under a Congress government. It imposed a ceiling on landownership, fixed the terms of tenure, and allowed the purchase of ownership rights by the tenant-cultivator. Surplus land was redistributed among the poor and the landless. Since most peasant women did not physically work on land, they failed to benefit from this reform too. Single women who were running households on their own petitioned the state saying their only source of income was rent from land – which they now stood to lose. Their plea was ignored.

The Hindu Succession Act of 1956 had allowed absolute ownership and full testamentary rights over property to female heirs. At the same time, it had also stipulated that if a Nayar man of Kerala died intestate, his properties, including self-acquired ones, would devolve equally upon all heirs, male and female. Undoubtedly egalitarian in its intent, this nonetheless reduced women's special entitlements within matrilineal arrangements that had earlier prevailed in the community. In Cochin, southern Malabar, and Central Travancore, ancestral land and the larger *taravad*s (homesteads) could still be matrilineally inherited, but the inheritance of cash, small houses, gardens, and orchards now passed to men as well.

On the rare occasions when women did achieve ownership rights in land, they did so through their own struggles. In the early 1980s, when surplus land was being redistributed at Bodh Gaya in Bihar, the Chhatra-Mazdoor-Yuva Sangharsh Vahini, a far-Left organisation, launched a campaign for independent ownership titles for peasant women. The possession of land had always been the staple of peasant dreams and struggles, and women were no exception. In this instance, they demanded their own titles to protect themselves from male abandonment and abuse.

They won the battle and celebrated their victory with a song:

> We had tongues but could not speak
> We had feet but could not walk
> Now that we have the land
> We have the strength to speak and walk.[7]

We habitually discuss inheritance in the context of wealthy families with substantial properties. But property titles are far more vital for subaltern people, for whom even a minor tenancy right to land makes an enormous difference to livelihood. They are even more critical for rural women, who suffer from immense social and economic discrimination.

Gender in Households

Non-feminist scholars generally depict the household as a homogeneous unit working for the welfare of all and sustained by the efforts of each member. There is some truth in this assumption since, in the absence of state and other social safety nets, the family is often the sole source of survival, especially for its more vulnerable constituents. Yet the ideal type requires considerable

---

[7] Cited in Agarwal, *A Field of One's Own*, Preface.

demystification. As we saw in his *Second Treatise* on immolations in the early nineteenth century, Rammohun Roy sharply segregated male and female worlds within the household: the former, a place of privilege and power; the latter, a site of deprivation and abuse. Feminist scholars have argued from the 1980s that the widespread assumption of a common household purpose and interest is a chimera.

Rajni Palriwala studied 272 households in the Sikar district in Rajasthan in the early 1980s to see why women cherish the very family structures that oppress them. She found that the head of the household – the seniormost man – was in absolute charge of the family budget, income pooling, allotment of resources and tasks, and investment decisions. All other family members deferred to him. Women, additionally, deferred to the seniormost woman in the family, usually the household head's wife or mother who controlled the daily household consumption and the distribution of domestic tasks among servants as well as among the junior women of the family. Most women in such families therefore laboured under a triple yoke – of the male head, of the seniormost woman, and of their own husbands. Beyond this, senior women's control over the household's grain stocks was limited to the food that was brought into the home, and even that privilege could be undermined. Palriwala found two occasions when the men sold off the grain to buy themselves drink, flogging any woman who objected.

Women bear with a profound lack of autonomy because they are dependent on the general good-will of the household. Even when they earn an income of their own, the family remains their chief source of support. Social morality, moreover, prescribes unquestioning obedience on pain of social ostracism for the slightest lapse. Whatever their other accomplishments, women's primary personal status in much of India depends on their reputation as docile and competent housewives.

At the same time, women gain status with age – as they become senior women and mothers of earning sons. An important point remains implicit in Palriwala's ethnography – that "woman" is not an undifferentiated, unitary category. Rather, she becomes a different person with highly differentiated entitlements or deprivations, depending on her changing life-cycle stages and life circumstances: as a young sonless widow from a poor natal background, as a wife or a widow from a rich natal family, as a senior widow with mature and affluent sons, as a wife whose husband is poor and dependent, as a wife whose husband earns the bulk of the family income. Even when all her status co-ordinates are derived from her relationship with men, and even if the household proves indifferent to her welfare, the matrimonial family still remains her dominant resource for survival and security. More importantly, it offers her the prospect of power at some point in her life.

In Palriwala's account consumption was hierarchically arranged and the daily meals unerringly confirmed a patriarchal ideology. Men of the core family had priority in food consumption in terms of both quality and quantity, with the household head and primary earners enjoying even greater priority. Senior male members and children came next, their claims deriving from past and prospective services to the family. Pregnant women and lactating mothers enjoyed special consideration. The youngest daughter-in-law, who usually cooked the food, ate last. She had to put up with relentless criticism if her cooking failed to satisfy the family. The bright spot in women's lives was their occasional brief visits to natal homes where, for a short interval, they were treated like queens.

Palriwala's account of peasant women in Rajasthan in the 1980s resembles to an uncanny degree the life of an upper-caste wife in a rich landlord household in mid-nineteenth-century Bengal. The basics of a woman's condition have stayed remarkably stable across India's vast temporal, regional, and social divides.

In passing, let me refer to a cluster of Facebook posts in 2023 from a group titled Purono Kolkatar Golpo (Tales from Old Calcutta). A surprisingly large number of the contributions, from both men and women, fondly recall their childhood in identical terms:

mothers, aunts, and widowed grannies working in stuffy kitchens all day and late into the night, bent over smoking coal ovens to produce enormous and delectable meals for children, men, and unexpected guests. Ever happy to be assigned this task, they did not even keep back for themselves any of the delicacies they were making. Their backbreaking labour, with scant or no personal rewards, is bathed in a glow of nostalgic affection and gratitude – and enormous approval. We may also cite an alternative recollection of a widowed aunt in the Kolkata of the 1970s:

> I never saw my aunt eat the fish curries she made . . . How did she cook what she must have forgotten the taste of? She made egg and mince-stuffed cutlets, prawnmalai, hilsa, and waited looking at us until we took a mouthful and told her how it had turned out . . . She was even forbidden anything with onion or garlic in it. She had to ensure she didn't eat food that made her feel over-energetic . . . Starved of the delights she cooked for us, I wonder now about the memories on which she fed to sustain her spartan frame . . . There were many women like her among our extended family.[8]

The woman is still what she cooks.

Dalit men and women live precarious lives without secure jobs or work that brings dignity and security. Purity–pollution taboos related to untouchability are practised by all castes, top to bottom, as the jatis observe "graded inequality" – the deprived always looking down upon the even more deprived – and so on to the "lowlier" jatis – to acquire a modicum of relative status for themselves. A Bengali novel, *Ashtam Garbha* by Bani Bosu, about a post-Partition Calcutta household vividly narrates the numerous rules that regulate an upper-caste kitchen – which servant from which caste can touch which utensils and perform which tasks, everything laid out in the minutest detail and in strict line with their respective status. Sanitary cleaners in urban households usually have a separate entrance and an employer was chastised in the 1950s for a

---

[8] Roy, "Cooking Women".

violation of untouchability – he had handed over his salary to a sanitation worker whereas he should have thrown the money down from a safe distance.

Social Work for Gender Reform

The constitutional reforms of 1935 gave the vote to a third of the Indian population. The Congress Party won the elections in most provinces, with a thumping majority in several. It set up a National Planning Committee in 1938; a rather minor advisory sub-committee of women with strong public profiles, but with no special expertise in economic planning or ideas, was attached to it. Envisaging women primarily as producers and reproducers of the labour force, it prescribed that they should participate more in the industrial and plantation sectors. Progressive laws, it hoped, would empower middle-class women with legal rights and skill-development programmes. But it did not suggest labour laws to help women workers. Its 1947 report, entitled *Women's Role in Planned Economy*, sought to combine traditional and modern images of Indian womanhood – the latter being reserved for middle-class women. The woman as an equal citizen was blended uneasily with the family's paramountcy.

Though the Left government in Kerala was dismissed by Nehru on rather spurious charges in 1959, the communists have frequently come back to power since then. The "Kerala model" became a byword in India's welfare vocabulary. Let us look at some significant statistics between 1971 and 1980. Whereas the all-India sex ratio was 933 women per 1000 men, it was 1032 women in Kerala. Undoubted poverty levels notwithstanding, Kerala also achieved remarkable levels of female literacy, in contrast to most other states. Where the all-India figure was 24.8 per cent, 65.7 per cent of Kerala's women achieved full literacy.

Mission schools had laid a solid foundation for women's education, and community-based enterprises like the Nayar Service

Society had also worked hard in this area from the 1950s. The high-caste monopoly over government schools began to wane from the early twentieth century, and women from diverse castes now received at least literacy and some education. This bore farreaching consequences for their employment, welfare, and children's health. Kerala's excellent schools came to be largely run by women teachers, and educated mothers helped reduce infant mortality. Nursing, too, was a popular vocation. In the 1950s the new state of Travancore-Cochin, made up of two princely states, and later integrated with the state of Kerala, had 400 nurses. By 1981, their number was 4894.

Some matrilineal families had been using contraceptives from the 1930s, and Margaret Sanger's 1934 visit was a major spur to the birth-control movement. The chief activist was Anna Chandy, Kerala's first woman advocate, later a High Court judge. The clinics angered the Catholics and they overruled the young socialists from Malabar who had been elected to district boards and were keen to fund birth-control clinics. In 1939 the Congress, too, had opposed birth-control measures in the Madras Presidency.

All this changed after Independence and political parties now raced to set up clinics. With early starts in Travancore-Cochin in 1954–5, the CPI government appointed a full-time Family Planning Officer and an advisory Family Planning Board in 1957. By 1959, 2000 men and 1500 women were working in them. First among the Indian states, the Left government tied the programme to maternal and infant healthcare provisions: distributing free milk, cod liver oil, and multivitamin tablets to mothers and children. By the 1960s even some Catholics had come around to birth control, so the scheme continued regardless of the government in power. Accompanied as it was with material resources for women, this signified not a fear of daughters but a greater regard for them. Its success released the woman from excessive childbearing but did not involve a decline in Kerala's female sex ratio.

In contrast, the West Bengal communists at first suspected birth control of being a Malthusian ploy to prevent births among workers. A large population, it said, was actually a national asset. One woman activist, Manikuntala Sen, delivered many speeches to this effect to working-class women. To her dismay, they often secretly came up to her, begging that she do something about their unwanted energy-draining pregnancies.

After Independence various state governments initiated programmes to enhance political, administrative, and work skills among women. These helped state-sponsored female constructive activism: middle-class women taught subaltern women to play an active role in their immediate environment. After the government enacted laws to enforce Panchayati Raj (rural self-governance), and a quota was reserved for elected women members, women's associations (Mahila Samakhya Samitis) sought to train women to become effective panchayat members. Some feminists, however, fear that these were but cosmetic changes which actually provided undeserved legitimacy to a state which had failed to introduce structural transformation in gender relations.

Not all reforms were undertaken by government agencies, and a well-known exception has been the Self-Employed Women's Association (SEWA). Envisaged as an extension of Gandhian rural uplift programmes, it was founded by Ela Bhatt and Renana Jhabvala in the early 1970s. They described it as a trade union of self-employed women and called it India's second freedom movement. Most of their branches remain located in various parts of Gujarat, with membership rising to more than 200,000. SEWA provides co-operative banking facilities to self-employed women in the informal sector, maternal and child care, and insurance plans in collaboration with insurance agencies. Women are trained to become the managers of these programmes. The broad aim is to enhance women's economic agency, security, efficiency, and understanding of markets and self-governance in order to strengthen their domestic status and bargaining power.

From the 1980s, Muslim educational institutions renewed their efforts to educate women. School enrolment figures show that, up to the primary school, Muslim girls, even the poorer ones, enjoy parity with Hindu students. But the figures weaken subsequently. Several reasons, varying from region to region, may explain the disparity. The general and relative poverty of the community as a whole means that Muslim men have not been able to compete for jobs with high educational qualifications. This failure produces resentment and a fear of educated wives among them. The growing communalisation of India's politics, which makes communally mixed schools inhospitable to Muslim students, has also kept young Muslim girls at home. Often, they avoid schools and colleges for fear of attacks on them in public spaces. Interestingly, there is a good argument to the effect that the custom of purdah does not significantly obstruct education.

The Arya Samaj had pioneered women's schools in colonial Punjab and western Uttar Pradesh, and their women became prominent educationists after Independence. In the 1970s and 1980s J.E. Lewellyn studied the Arya Samaj women religious preachers, teachers, and their women's journal, the *Sarvadeshik*. He discovered a complex ideology at work. One Arya Samaj adherent, Surya Kumari, excoriated the Deorala sati episode as shameful and un-Hindu, and also condemned the religious institutions which supported it. At the same time, she glorified collective immolations (*jauhar*) among Rajput royal women in past Hindu wars with Muslims. Arya Samaj teachers broadly valorised the high status of ancient Hindu women which, they believed, had been nullified by Muslim invaders and their alleged abductions of Hindu women. They thus pressed communalism into the service of Hindu women, seeking to advocate modern reforms while justifying past orthodoxy in the name of Muslim outrages against Hindu women. They also retained a basically domestic ideology for educated married women. Most asserted that, being educated, the woman makes a better homemaker, mother, and wife. The Arya Samaj's women preachers, always celibate, had struggled hard against their own families to escape marriage; yet, having escaped, they advised ordinary women to dedicate themselves to domesticity.

The post-Independence state policy of quota-based reservations in government jobs and education for the designated Scheduled Tribes have allowed well-off tribal families to educate their children, including their daughters, and some have entered white-collar professions. This has caused further changes in their social practices. Their middle-class men now prefer educated but domesticated wives, and, in imitation of non-tribal caste communities, there is among them a growing shift away from bride price to dowry. There is also great anxiety and resentment in rural areas when tribal women marry outside the community. Apart from the cultural stigma associated with exogamy, and fears about a possible tribal demographic decline, there is the additional worry over the loss of her property share, which she will now take outside family and community control. This apprehension is especially acute where land is held collectively by an entire lineage – under the *khuntkatti* system in contemporary Jharkhand, for instance.

Though many scholars tend to romanticise Adivasi gender relations, Tiplut Nongbri argues that it is a mistake to identify the relative autonomy of Adivasi women in production as a necessary indicator of their high social status. By and large, tribal women are subordinate to men. This is so even in matrilineal tribes where women have formal rights over land but where men enjoy the managerial powers – among the Khasi, Jaintia, Garo, Lalung, and Koch tribes, for instance. Ho and Oraon women are forbidden to touch the plough and are, consequently, excluded from landowning. Bihar and West Bengal have seen a growing incidence of "witch hunting": since 1950 there have been forty-six cases of killing "witches" in just the Malda district of West Bengal.

Tribal women play a relatively small role in managing community resources, or in public affairs conducted by the village council. Even when they are elected to the panchayat, they arrive there with little training. Contrary to popular belief, child marriage, forced marriage, and polygyny are also widely prevalent among the tribals. Bride price actually enables men to treat women as purchased – and therefore as disposable – commodities. Naga and Khasi women seeking divorce have to return the bride price to the husband.

Political turbulence in the North East aggravates tribal conservatism. Women marrying outside the tribe are castigated as a threat to the community's beleaguered economic, cultural, and ethnic interests, and children born of such unions are rejected by both communities. A Ho woman may lose her right to land. A recent political group at Shillong in Meghalaya threatens to punish prostitutes, drunken women, those "indecently" clothed, and those dating non-tribal men. Naga and Mizo insurrectionary groups have issued similar warnings.

Meghalaya's tribes tried to change their matrilineal custom into a patrilineal one in 1961. In 1978 the Meghalaya Tribal Youth Organisation called for the suspension of the inheritance rights of Khasi, Jaintia, and Garo women who married outsiders. Ka Syngkhong Rympei Thymmai, an urban professional organisation, formulated plans for widespread changes in traditional kinship patterns to deprive women marrying outsiders of all property claims.

Virginius Xaxa argues, on the other hand, that Adivasi gender relations and labour patterns are actually more diverse than Nongbri's work indicates, and that gender intersects with age. Women gain in status as they grow older. The organisation of labour and gender is therefore fluid and variable. In Jharkhand, where under the traditional *khuntkatti* system the land belongs to the entire lineage, the question of separate male or female ownership does not arise. An earlier scholar, the administrator K.S. Singh, pointed out that because Ho women surpass men in numbers, the community has a large surplus of single women. Men therefore oppose women's customary maintenance claims because they result in highly uneconomic subdivisions of landholding in a situation of land scarcity.

However, the material and political rationale for the loss of tribal women's rights does not remedy ground realities for women, which, by and large, show a decline in their rights.

Legal Reformism

Cardinal legal issues, much debated in colonial times, have persisted after Independence. Widow immolations, for instance, have not completely disappeared even in the twenty-first century; rather, their memorialisation has become a large and highly organised industry. Snatches of the older orthodox rhetoric are still heard, but now couched in a seemingly sophisticated modern political idiom.

Immolated widows had long been worshipped as lineage goddesses in the massive Rani Sati Mandir complexes of Rajasthan. A managing committee was formed and a religious festival begun in 1912 to strengthen sati commemorations. The committee built numerous temples between 1917 and 1936 and raised huge funds for their sati festivals. Though the temple at Jhunjhunu in Rajasthan is the nerve-centre of the movement, hundreds have sprung up all over India – twenty-five in Calcutta alone; even New York and Hong Kong are graced with several. A Rani Sati Girls' Primary School was set up in 1961, and a new section added to the older temple in 1986, which received vast donations of gold.

Such commemorations gained a fresh lease of life in 1954 when Taradevi, a young widow with infant children, from a modern, well-educated family, apparently decided on her own to perform sati at Jhunjhunu. Thousands flocked to the spectacle and miracle tales sprang up instantaneously. The burning site turned into a major pilgrimage centre and donations from devotees poured into her family's coffers. The woman belonged to the Marwari Jalan family, which was proud of having performed twelve earlier satis.

Though many Hindu communities worship satis, the Marwaris, who are mostly wealthy traders, financiers, and industrialists, and who see themselves as culturally ill-used, are the pre-eminent organisers of the sati cult. They have in fact adopted it as a defining feature of their community identity. Annual festivals, religious publications, posters, tracts, and cassettes sold at sati temples preach Nari Dharma (the Religious Duties of Women) and disseminate deeply conservative messages. The temples are also the hubs of local religious, educational, and charitable enterprises. Several management committeees, keen to present a modernist self-image, have tried to prevent actual immolation efforts. However, since immolations are stimulated by their celebrations, it is impossible to wholly distinguish them from their commemoration. Even when some do try to prevent an actual immolation, the widespread respect for the ritual reinforces the structure of values which had always been the raison d'être for the burnings.

In the Shekhawati region of Rajasthan, three upper castes have made concerted efforts to revive historical immolation memories – Rajputs (supposedly of royal lineage, now large landowners), Banias (traders), and Mahajans (moneylenders). Brahman chroniclers (*bhat*s; *charan*s) sing stirring tales of Rajput widows who, through the ages, have immolated themselves most willingly before the Muslims could conquer their realms. The ideology of sati performs several political functions for them: it elevates the Rajput and Marwari communities in popular perception: community glory then broadens out into narratives of Hindu heroism embodied by Rajput warriors and self-immolating women. Sati celebrations moreover function as an everlasting and self-renewing reminder of Hindu–Muslim wars of the medieval past.

In 1987 an eighteen-year-old Rajput widow, Roop Kanwar, performed sati in Deorala village, Rajasthan. Some claimed her relatives had forced her, but in any case a cult developed immediately around her name, with attendant festivals. This called forth a counter-movement of feminist protests which managed to bring about a legal ban on commemorative acts of this kind. The ban did not prove very effective: Calcutta's Marwaris called for a twelve-hour-long general strike to protest the ban on sati festivals and took the matter to court. The Calcutta High Court allowed several state restrictions to continue but confirmed the right to worship at sati temples. The conservative backlash was as intense and far better funded and organised than the feminist demonstrations.

Challenged by feminist protests against the promotion of patriarchal legends, modern Marwari leaders mounted a strong counterattack. Dinesh Nandini Dalmiya, a Marwari woman writer of note, stated that "there has never been a ban of glorification, nor can there be any. Along with temple construction comes the question of our citizenship rights and freedom – and how can you stop that?" Nandalal Goenka, another proponent of sati, insisted that "Jhunjhunu's Rani Sati was a brave and sacrificing woman who inspires us . . . This is a question of our faith."[9]

A new crop of scholarly analyses emerged around these burnings. None explicitly endorsed them, but some objected rather more forcefully to the prohibition of sati worship as an onslaught on tradition and faith – and not merely a ritual event. Ashis Nandy and Veena Das criticised feminists as blind adherents of a modernity which, they said, was in itself a form of obscurantism, the slavish imitation of a colonial mindset. Sudesh Vaid and Kumkum Sangari, on the other hand, offered a persuasive materialist explanation of the belief in terms of contemporary Marwari self-assertion and leadership over other local castes, and family investments and profits from the cults.

The events at Deorala stimulated interesting revaluations of ritual meanings. Paul Courtright pointed out that the colonial criminalisation of immolations had not eroded their moral power, which had reinvented itself in a modernised context. Unlike Das and Nandy, who described the feminist protests as modernity striking

---

[9] Cited in Hardgrove, *Community and Public Culture*, p. 248.

a blow against inherited culture, Courtright emphasised the specifically modern purposes of the new immolations. Hardgrove on the other hand criticised feminists for ignoring the complicated processes through which ritual meanings are regenerated and re-purposed. She described the immolations as exemplars for Marwari domesticity.

Endorsements of sati celebrations object to the feminist denial of the apparent agency – of willed deaths by burnings – of past widows. They ignore the crude fact that the will was actually generated by a climate of temptations and injunctions, of social expectations and a profound gender asymmetry. It contributed to the subordination of women and a devaluation of their pain and lives, not just for the satis, but also for living wives and widows.

Some of the values of Brahmanical widowhood have also stood the test of time, even though the exremes of the widow's ritual discipline have declined. A renowned Bengali historian who married a widow in the 1950s had to face such disrespect in his peer circle that he was forced to leave Calcutta and join the University of Delhi. The number of Indian widows, meanwhile, remains remarkably large. As late as the 1991 census it stood at more than thirty-three million, constituting 8 per cent of India's total female population – the largest figure anywhere in the world. This no doubt indicates the low incidence of widow marriages.

According to Martha Alter Chen's sample survey for North Indian landowning families in the 1990s, 51 per cent possessed usufruct over their husband's property share while 11 per cent enjoyed some rights in natal property. Brothers-in-law seldom allowed widows to manage their own property. If the widows objected, they were expelled from the village or even murdered. Their property rights were restored only if they had produced a son – and when that son reached adulthood.

Some childless widows did of course remarry. Out of a sample of 562 widows, 13 per cent in North India and 6 per cent in South India had married again: interestingly, customary levirate marriages accounted for the larger northern numbers. Of the 52 remarried widows in the sample, 24 came from the Dalit castes, 22 from the so-called Backward Castes, and only 6 were upper caste: and all the upper-caste widows were Rajput Brahmans from the Garhwal Hills where levirate unions are common. Castes which customarily practised remarriage, therefore, still provide the bulk of remarried widows and levirate accounts for a large proportion of remarriages.

Widowhood has been sporadically ameliorated here and there, but for the bulk of India it continues to spell enormous economic insecurity. State welfare provisions in the country were practically non-existent till the 1990s. Many states did have pension schemes, but these fell far below subsistence levels. Most widows relied on family and community charity and dared not offend those they perforce relied on. Since India does not possess a uniform civil code, the widow's inheritance prospects are still controlled by community custom. Many widows have to provide for their children entirely on their own, and only if they have borne sons – and such sons are earning a living – do they achieve some measure of security. Chen's sample survey found that most widows suffer from psychological stress and trauma. The sexual needs of young widows are a matter of great unease to their families, who closely police their lives.

Sarkar and Banerjee found a similar situation in their study of thirty-six Hindu and tribal widows in the Bankura district of West Bengal. Both communities clung to their customary laws, under which widows with young sons have trusteeship rights till their sons have grown up. Widows with adult sons, on the other hand, are entitled to some basic maintenance from their sons. Childless widows have no rights to land at all, and most such women are driven back to their natal villages.

Bela Bhatia studied the rehabilitation packages of widows whose land was submerged by the Sardar Sarovar Dam in Gujarat. Those who lost their land before 1980 were not counted as heads of their households, but were classified as dependants no matter what their actual status. So, even if they had been landowners earlier, they now lost both their home and their land. Rural widows in Gujarat are generally not allowed to work outside the home, and this compounds the difficulties of widowed land losers.

Matters are no better for widows elsewhere: they constitute the most vulnerable category among home-based women by lacking access to credit, skills, markets, and alternative occupations. Waged workers are also precariously positioned. Stone mining, for instance, is done by a husband-wife team and widows cannot continue to work as single women. Even when they manage to attach themselves to other families, they receive far lower wages for the same work.

The legal reform of Hindu marriage became a national preoccupation immediately after Independence. As noted earlier, the state, not wanting to disturb Muslim loyalties so soon after Partition, restricted its focus to Hindu legal reform; existing Hindu marriage laws had, moreover, lagged behind Muslim laws in several respects – so there was a greater urgency about improving them.

In 1941 the colonial government had appointed a committee of four Hindu legal experts and jurists to review women's property rights. They said, "We ourselves think that the time has now arrived to attempt a code of Hindu law."[10] The committee – with just one woman member on it – chose two essential ritual aspects out of the entire elaborate marriage sacrament, and decided that these two were sufficient to legalise a marriage: *agnisakshi* (the sacred fire) as a witness to the marriage, and *saptapadi*, the term for a couple circling the fire seven times. Most families, however, continued with the full ceremonial panoply for arranged endogamous marriages, even as match-making procedures changed with urbanisation and enhanced communication methods.

---

[10] Report of the Hindu Law Committee, cited in Newbigin, *The Hindu Family*, p. 120.

In 1944 the government reactivated the Hindu Code Committee to prepare a draft code on succession, maintenance, marriage and divorce, minority and guardianship, and adoption laws. The draft was widely translated and circulated before being presented to the Assembly in 1947. But Independence intervened, the Constituent Assembly was formed, and Nehru referred the draft code to a Select Committee under Law Member B.R. Ambedkar. A second woman was now added to the committee. Ever suspicious of conservative religious injunctions in general, and of caste customs in particular, Ambedkar sought to generalise the proposed gender-just laws by sweeping aside caste and local customary differences, replacing them with equal property rights for women, divorce under specific conditions, and the abolition of customary laws as well as of all restrictions on inter-caste marriage. He had underestimated the strength of Hindu orthodox opposition and overestimated the powers of the new state. Conservative Hindus swung into battle mode, campaigning fiercely against what they saw as an onslaught against their religion.

The earlier committee had already included the 1872 civil marriage provisions on prohibited degrees of intra-lineage marriages. Ambedkar retained the restrictions but stipulated that they applied to religious and not to civil marriages. He was widely accused of encouraging incestuous marriages. Congress luminaries like Sardar Patel and J.B. Kripalani reacted violently against divorce and property rights for individual women as defying the Hindu Undivided Family inheritance rules. The right-wing Hindu Mahasabha under N.C. Chatterjee and Syama Prasad Mukherjee ran a smear campaign against Ambedkar, as did the *Organiser*, the mouthpiece of the RSS. President Rajendra Prasad threatened not to sign the bill. Outraged that Hindu marriages were now made compulsorily monogamous whereas Muslims retained polygamy, Ambedkar's opponents saw the law as "racial suicide".[11] They argued from the bizarre arithmetical premise that polygamy results

---

[11] Som, "Jawaharlal Nehru and the Hindu Code", p. 254.

in increased progeny – disregarding the fact that since a woman can only bear one child at a time, the number of wives her husband has is irrelevant.

Several women members of parliament were also unhappy about the proposed changes. Some objected to the erosion of caste-custom and scriptural guidelines, others because married women deemed "immoral" would lose the right to alimony. Several objected to the provision that alimony would have to be given by a divorced husband. Others pointed out that agricultural land remained beyond the pale of female inheritance.

Nehru backtracked. Not wanting to antagonise the Hindu electorate before the impending national elections of 1952, he postponed the discussions indefinitely. Ambedkar resigned in 1951, bitterly disappointed by Nehru's procrastinations, calling the deferment "a great shock, a bolt from the blue" and squarely blaming the prime minister: "I have never seen a case of a chief whip so disloyal to the Prime Minister and the Prime Minister so loyal to a disloyal whip."[12] After the Congress won a landslide electoral victory, the bill was reintroduced in 1952, now broken up into four segments. The Hindu Marriage Act (1955) was followed by the Hindu Succession Act (1956), the Hindu Adoption and Maintenance Act (1956), and the Dowry Prohibition Act (1961). The Marriage Act enabled wives to seek divorce; an amendment in 1976 introduced divorce by mutual consent. The Hindu Adoption and Maintenance Act enabled wives to reside separately and yet be maintained by their husbands.

Several provisions remained on paper because they did not stipulate the penalties for non-compliance. Some introduced fresh problems. Since polygamy was criminalised, a polygamous husband could waive maintenance claims from his second wife on the grounds that his second marriage was invalid. Equal inheritance for daughters was also largely notional – the inheritance only applied

[12] Ibid., pp. 261–2.

to the father's self-earned income, not to joint-family property which enjoyed tax relief. If a husband died intestate his widow, notwithstanding her contribution to the household through paid and unpaid work, received the same amount of inheritance as her children. She could even be willed out of the estate by the husband since she had been a "beneficiary" of the property during her married life. Only in 2005 was the right of residence in the matrimonial home finally ensured by the Protection of Women from Domestic Violence Act. Hindu husbands, legally bound to monogamy, flouted the law with impunity, while allegations of adultery and immorality were routinely hurled against wives, making the marriage appear invalid and rendering children illegitimate. Clauses in the Criminal Procedure Code linked a wife's maintenance entitlements to her sexual morality.

A new Special Marriage Act was passed in 1954 to legalise civil marriages, whatever the religious affiliation of the couple. They no longer needed to abjure their faith in order to marry. The law now provided against bigamy through the compulsory registration of marriages. At the same time, it invalidated marriages between first cousins, even though Muslims, Christians, and Parsis were able to marry their first cousins. Since South Indian Hindus had traditionally allowed marriage between a maternal uncle and his niece, an amendment was introduced in 1963 to restore their customary practices. This then showed a clear preference for exclusively maintaining Hindu custom. In 1976 amendments to the Special Marriage Act introduced additional concessions for Hindu men. If a Hindu couple married under it, they were excluded from the Indian Succession Act of 1925 and brought under the Hindu Succession Act to ensure that male coparcenaries retained their privileges; but a Hindu man who married a non-Hindu forfeited those privileges. Inter-community marriage as well as free choice in marriage thus came at a high cost.

An Adoption Bill was introduced in 1972, but the Parsis, Muslims, tribals, and Dalits asked to be excluded from its remit. The

Bill was reintroduced in 1980 conceding the Muslim demands, but was then abandoned when Parsis too claimed exemption.

The Dissolution of Muslim Marriages Act of 1939 had not specified the extent of economic relief for the divorced woman – a serious flaw, since the dower (*mehr*) had become merely notional over time. In 1973 the law which had earlier granted deserted or destitute wives a fixed sum as maintenance extended it to divorced Muslim wives. Subsequent judicial verdicts helped put her maintenance on a secure footing.

In 1985 a huge controversy about Muslim divorce and maintenance rules burst over India, setting far-reaching social and political consequences in motion and undoing past gains. Mohammad Ahmad Khan, an affluent advocate, had married Begum Shah Bano and divorced her – because he had taken a young woman as his second wife – when she was sixty-two, after she had borne five children. She filed a case for maintenance and the Indian Supreme Court heard her plea sympathetically. However, while upholding her suit the judge, Justice Chandrachud, made critical remarks against Islam, urged the government to introduce a uniform civil code, and obliterate Muslim Personal Law provisions. Supporting his suggestion, Hindu communalists organised a vicious anti-Muslim campaign.

Enraged by these communal slurs, the Muslim orthodoxy loudly protested the judgment. They deployed Article 25 of the Constitution, which promises religious freedom, and argued that the court had mounted an assault on their constitutional right to faith. The resultant outcry forced Shah Bano to drop her claims. The Indian government led by Rajiv Gandhi, trying to appease orthodox Muslims, passed the Muslim Women (Protection of Rights on Divorce) Act of 1986 so that the provision for the maintenance of a divorced Muslim woman was removed from the relevant law. This was done in the teeth of opposition by many women's organisations, including those of liberal Muslims, alongside the All-India Shia Personal Law Board, all of whom protested vociferously in defence of the divorced woman. The new law restricted the divorced woman's maintenance rights to a mere ninety days – the *iddat* period which covers three successive menstrual cycles – after the divorce.

Since Hindu communal organisations chose to read the Act as a concession to Muslim husbands rather than as an injustice against Muslim wives, the government sought simultaneously to appease them. It opened the locks on the doors of the controversial Babri Mosque at Ayodhya in Uttar Pradesh, thus allowing Hindu worshippers inside a shrine that had long been shut precisely to pre-empt Hindu–Muslim conflagrations. By trying to pacify the extremist elements in both communities the government actually ignited intense communal agitations, vitiating community relations beyond repair.

The Committee on the Status of Women had recommended in 1975 that family disputes be adjudicated at special matrimonial courts. These were set up in 1984. Flavia Agnes argues that Indian feminists mistakenly assumed that these courts would be gender-just; in practice, they frequently endorsed family controls on women. They assumed for instance that a functional family was always a two-parent one. This created difficulties for single parents, and single mothers found it a problem to assert their custodial rights.

A new and intense wave of women's agitations from the 1980s brought about a slew of changes in criminal laws. The rape law was amended in 1983, the Dowry Prohibition Act in 1984 and 1986, the domestic abuse of wives was made a cognisable offence in 1983, and a special section dealing with dowry deaths was incorporated in the relevant law in 1986. "Dowry death" refers to the killing of a wife by her husband (or by him and his family) when the woman's natal family fails to meet their dowry demands – a phenomenon persistent across class, caste, and political affiliation. Matrimonial families cover up the death as accidental and the police, notorious for amenability to gratification, are "persuaded". A bundle of diverse motives – and not dowry demands alone – actually underpins these killings. From the mid 1970s, independent feminist groups began to collect evidence of such murders, took them to the police and the press, publicly named and shamed the families responsible, performed street plays in front of their homes, and followed up with consciousness-raising discussions with bystanders and neighbours.

Beginning in Hyderabad, from the late 1970s anti-dowry activism reached Delhi, which grew into the storm centre for this activism. When a woman named Tarvinder Singh died in Delhi in 1979, feminists alleged it was murder. The Mahila Dakshata Samiti, the Stree Sangharsh, and the Indraprastha College Women's Committee (formed in 1978 to protest against molestations of women on public transport) organised huge demonstrations and initiated investigations into each possible case of murder. *Om Swaha*, a street play, was performed in front of Tarvinder Singh's matrimonial home and women formed neighbourhood committees to unearth police complicity.

Judges finally began to reverse their earlier tendency to classify such deaths as mere accidents. In December 1983 the Criminal Law (Second Amendment) Act added to the Indian Penal Code by making cruelty to wives – including mental torture – a cognisable, non-bailable offence punishable by three years in prison and a fine. The Evidence Act was amended to incorporate abetments to suicide, shifting the burden of proof from the complainant to the defendant. The Criminal Procedure Act was likewise amended to provide for compulsory post-mortem examination if a woman died under suspicious circumstances within seven years of her marriage.

Changes or modifications in rape laws also followed upon intense feminist agitations. Rape had long been an ambiguous and slippery social and legal category, eluding precise definition. Family, society, judges, even the victims themselves often believed it was more a crime against the male guardian than against the woman, or that the woman must prove her "chastity" and virtue before her rape charge could be entertained; a woman of "loose morals" or one with premarital sexual experience could not be deemed raped as she was no longer an "innocent" person. Hyderabad-based feminists from the Stree Shakti Sangathana (Women's Liberation Organisation) initiated debates on rapes by landlords which spiralled into redefinitions of rape in general. They also brought custodial and police rapes into focus.

The debates fed on atrocities. In 1972, for example, Mathura, a teenaged tribal domestic help who wanted to marry against her family's wishes, was dragged by her brothers to the police station at Gadchiroli in Maharashtra. The siblings asked the police to dissuade her. While they waited outside, two policemen raped the girl inside the station. A case was lodged by some women's groups on her behalf and taken through several courts until the Supreme Court acquitted the rapists. The defence lawyers argued that since Mathura had a boyfriend, she was an immoral person; and an unchaste woman cannot be raped. Four senior lawyers signed an open protest letter against the perverse logic of this judgment. A Bombay-based feminist organisation, Forum Against Rape (later renamed Forum Against Oppression of Women), agitated for a retrial. There were mammoth nationwide demonstrations on International Women's Day in 1980. Mathura herself, however, was not too enthusiastic about the retrial, which led to much feminist soul-searching. Should they respect her decision or see rape as a violation affecting all women and not just a single victim? What could explain or justify their moral and social distance from Mathura? The campaign eventually went ahead. After the National Federation of Indian Women organised a demonstration of women's groups before the Supreme Court, the Bombay government finally lodged a retrial plea.

In 1978 Rameeza Bee, wife of a rickshaw-puller, was gang-raped by Hyderabad policemen who murdered her husband when he tried to stop them. Thousands of men and women gathered at the police station with his corpse. They stoned the station and set it on fire, and the police in turn fired on the protesters. The agitation peaked when the chief minsiter of Andhra Pradesh was surrounded by protesters and the whole city immobilised by a general strike. Curfew was declared and nine people were killed in the clashes. Eventually, the army had to be summoned to quell the agitations and the government was forced to set up an enquiry committee.

In 1980 Maya Tyagi was stripped, raped, and paraded naked along a public thoroughfare by the Haryana police at Baghpat. She had been travelling with her husband and his friends when the police shot the men dead. Feminists forced Home Minister Zail Singh to go to the site, and ten women members of parliament joined the protests. At long last the government instructed the Law Commission to formulate a rape bill. It placed custodial rape in a separate category, requiring special penalties. The law now encompassed sexual assault by employers and state functionaries at workplaces, with offenders facing ten years in jail. It also introduced additional categories which covered mass rapes and gang-rapes.

Blatantly absent, however, was any mention of marital rape. Rather, a difference was inserted into the age of consent for unmarried and married women, respectively. For the former, intercourse below the age of sixteen was classified as rape, while for the latter it was fifteen. Simultaneously, and despite feminist protests, the burden of proof was placed on the woman. Eventually, a truncated version was enacted in 1983 which shifted the burden of proof to the accused for custodial rape but ignored the other Law Commission recommendations. Civil Rights groups subsequently discovered to their dismay that rape charges were often brought against a man who had eloped with a perfectly willing girl who genuinely wished to marry him.

Even though the 1970s were a time of intense legal reform for women's groups, incidents of rape remain just as commonplace as always. This has made several feminist groups question the efficacy of legal redress. Yet the waves of fury that break out over each such case – finding their boiling point in the gang-rape, torture, and killing of Jyoti Singh in Delhi in 2012 – have repeatedly freshened and intensified awareness and anger against gendered violence. Exposing in visceral detail the foundational cruelty underlying Indian gender systems, these protests have also de-naturalised and problematised male impunities which have thus far been taken for granted by most men and women. Such battles for legal redress have invigorated feminist mobilisations and made men and women probe different aspects of patriarchal ideology and practice; they have sharpened self-understanding, even if the concrete results of activism have not borne immediate results.

Women's Political Activism and Feminist Politics

A large part of women's activism on behalf of women's interests and issues has been the work of groups affiliated to the mainstream Leftist parties. Ironically, they have rejected feminism as a divisive political label, misunderstanding the term as struggles against men – including Leftist and working-class men. All the same, a distinctively feminist consciousness has emerged and coalesced among independent women's organisations from the late 1970s. This has added other facets to women's survival and livelihood: a recognition of women's access to sexual pleasure, control over their own bodies, multiple sexualities, and the infinite modes of subordination where class, caste, community, and gender intersect and overlap. Women and progressive men began to question – along with homosexuals, lesbians, and transpersons – the discipline of compulsory heteronormativity.

Growing AIDS awareness made homosexuality a public issue, and something of a moral panic built up around it. But this also introduced gay-lesbian and trans perspectives and voices into debates and the public domain. It enabled gay-rights organisations and movements to gain visibility and publicise their viewpoint, which in turn gained them some social and moral legitimacy from the late 1980s. Gay-lesbian agitations peaked in the 1990s and early 2000s, but homosexual relationships were decriminalised only in 2018. Gay marriages have not yet found legal sanction.

Two formidable mass movements began in late colonial India and continued after Independence. The Tebhaga movement in Bengal had started among rural sharecroppers who demanded one-third share of the harvest. Communist women's brigades (Nari Bahini) went to North Bengal villages where the Party helped peasants snatch crops from landlords and tenure holders. Clashes ensued and the landlords' musclemen, with police help, wreaked havoc on the peasants, sometimes killing even pregnant and old women. Middle-class women activists also came under fire, and Ila Mitra, leader of the Nachole movement, then in East Pakistan, was monstrously tortured in jail. Communist Party women maintained shelters and kept lines of communication open between Party headquarters and ground-level activists. Village women insisted that they add domestic abuse to the Party's class-based agenda. One scholar has suggested that rural women were able to exert their autonomous initiative in this movement every time male leaders were arrested, but lost the advantage when the men came back.

The same years saw a huge anti-Nizam uprising in Telangana, in the Andhra region. The All India Women's Conference had been formed there in 1916, followed by the Andhra Mahila Sabha in 1930. Associations of elite upper-caste women with a reformist slant, these had nonetheless challenged the profoundly feudal ethos which even allowed landlords to prey on their tenants' wives as a matter of right. A broader Mahila Navjivan Mandal was formed in the late 1930s, composed of "ranis and begums,"[13] as well as Congress and RSS women. Developing a left-wing cast, it later began to advocate widow remarriage, divorce, and property rights

---

[13] Pramila Tai's testimony in Stree Shakti Sangathana, *We Were Making History*, p. 8.

for women. Many members, including a few Muslim women, subsequently joined the Andhra Communist Party. By 1940, predictably, a clear rift separated the leftist women from the rest.

In 1946 the Nizam of Hyderabad, the head of India's largest princely state, banned the Communist Party in his domains; in 1947 he refused to join the Indian Union, unleashing his armed forces, known as the Razakars, upon Congress and communist activists who favoured Hyderabad's integration with India. The communists called for an armed uprising against the Nizam and began to seize and redistribute land among the peasants. They built up guerrilla resistance in district after district, bestowed land rights on the tenants, and gave control over trees to toddy-tappers. They also abolished untouchability in the areas under their control and added a women's wing to the Party, the Andhra Mahila Sangham. The Congress government sent the army into Telangana to crush the Nizam. Soon, though, it redirected its forces, targeting the communists: Home Minsiter Sardar Patel pledged to wipe them out. The Communist Party inititated armed struggles in 1948 but called them off in 1951.

Numerous peasant women had joined the guerrilla struggles, leaving their families behind, carrying guns, going into hiding, undergoing tremendous privations – material and emotional – and repression. Many were raped, others suffered the pangs of hell when their leaders asked them to give away their infants upon joining the resistance or when their husbands went underground. At the same time, the Party imposed rather puritanical moral codes on these women, sternly berating them for presumed sexual lapses and making them feel as if they were "untouchables" within the Party. As soon as the movement was disbanded, the women were told to go back to their kitchens – their activism and sacrifices ignored and made to seem of little consequence.

Some male leaders of this time later repented their insensitivity. Rajeshwar Rao admitted: "We praised women when they came but we did not do anything to encourage them to come because their protection was a problem."[14] P. Sundarayya cited a letter from a woman comrade whom he had ignored at the time but who clearly haunted his recollections:

> We women are still being looked upon with the old outlook that we are inferior. Any slip or mistake we commit, our leaders come down very heavily upon us. It becomes a subject of open gossip and scandal. We must be guided and improved and not derided. If we move a little freely, we are watched with suspicion. Why have you not allowed any woman to participate in actual guerrilla raids on the enemy?[15]

He felt especially guilty that the Party had ignored the question of their children.

Communists are not usually in the business of admitting their mistakes, and these admissions therefore carry exceptional value. Years later, women spoke bitterly about what they had suffered. But they also remembered those days as "That magic time... When we were making history." Women's understanding of their relationship with History is an important issue and one worth probing at length.

Communist women were initially a part of the Congress-affiliated All India Women's Conference (AIWC) which enjoyed much leverage among the new ruling circles. In 1954 the CPI formed its own women's wing, the National Federation of Indian Women (NFIW). When the Party split in 1964 the NFIW also began to splinter. The CPI(M) formed the All India Democratic Women's Association (AIDWA) in 1981; its Tamil Nadu unit had already formed a separate women's wing in 1973.

The AIDWA was more confrontational than the NFIW vis-à-vis state power, especially after two successive United Front governments in West Bengal – in which the Left had played a major role – were dismissed by the Congress-led central government.

[14] Cited in Stree Shakti Sangathana, *We Were Making History*, p. 17.
[15] Sundarayya, *Telangana Peoples' Struggle and Its Lessons*, p. 24.

The CPI and its NFIW, on the other hand, were close to the Congress. When the Emergency was declared in 1975, the AIDWA women planned their own strategies of resistance since most of their male comrades were imprisoned or had gone undergound. Coming from different directions in Calcutta, individual women would arrive at a pre-arranged destination, their handbags concealing posters and banners. Having converged, they quickly unfurled the banners, made a short speech for onlookers, and dispersed just as quickly, before the police got its act together. Despite bouts of repression, the CPI(M) remained much the larger party, and its women's wing, too, has continued more powerful and dynamic.

Raka Ray and Amrita Basu have explored the CPI(M) women's organisations. Ray focused on Calcutta and Bombay in the 1970s–80s while Basu studied their rural organisations in Maharashtra. They looked, especially, at relations between the mainstream leftist organisations and autonomous feminist groups. The latter had raised issues of sexual and domestic violence, while the Party-affiliated organisations had focused more on women's livelihood and rejected the feminist tag. Manjari Gupta, president of the AIDWA's Calcutta unit, attributed rapes to state and class violence, not to patriarchal power. Malini Bhattacharya, a prominent MP, ascribed these to presumed criminal tendencies among the lumpen classes. The Bengal unit could sometimes be quite conservative. Their members asked Raka Ray why she wore her hair short and did not wear a sari and a *bindi* – the hallmark of approved Hindu female facial make-up. At the same time, since they enjoyed enormous power in Bengal, they successfully introduced safeguards ensuring the property entitlements of divorced women. Basu argues that the AIDWA had a greater capacity for struggling alongside rural women in Maharashtra – where the communists did not enjoy state power – than it did in West Bengal, where it was a part of the ruling party and had to obey its directives. The relative prominence of Dalit organisations in Maharashtra, as against their absence in Bengal, allowed the Maharashtrian unit to engage with a larger range of social issues. This did not happen in West Bengal, where Dalit politics was low-key.

Kerala was initially reluctant to encourage political women. The first women's magazine, *Keraleeya Suguna Bodhini*, had promised in 1892 that it would "publish nothing related to politics." This began to change from the 1920s. An exceptional figure was Akkamma Cheriyan Varkey (1909–1982), a Syrian Christian woman who joined the Congress in the late 1930s and suffered frequent spells in colonial prisons. She was elected to the Travancore Assembly in 1948, but, because her sister was a communist, she had to resign in 1952. Kerala's much-valorised gender model was therefore somewhat uneven in its functioning.

The Congress and the communists both preferred that women not raise gender issues within their parties. But women, especially the communists, became increasingly strident, as was Gouri Amma, who lost the 1948 Travancore elections by a slender margin and who raised demands for women's employment; and Susheela Gopalan, who worked for women's legal rights. Since Gouri Amma later chose to join the CPI(M) while her husband remained with the CPI, the couple decided to separate. However, the CPI(M) found her too assertive for its liking and she later left the Party. By the end of the 1960s women had gained some political space in Kerala, though often by "ungendering", de-feminising themselves in the public eye by abandoning the signs of feminine adornment – a burden that political men did not have to bear.

Mass movements began from the late 1960s in the cities of Maharashtra, Gujarat, and Bihar against a terrible price inflation. Mrinal Gore from the Socialist Party, and Ahilya Ranganekar from the CPI(M), formed the United Women's Anti-Price-Rise Front in 1973. Housewives marched on the streets, banging cooking utensils to enact a militant and public domesticity. Village women and their husbands joined the Sramik Sangathana in Maharashtra to protest landlord oppression. Soon, however, they began to raise gender issues as well, especially their hostility to male alcoholism.

They raided liquor shops and destroyed the tills, they marched across villages and held meetings on domestic abuse. They had learnt the art of political mobilisation and agitation within a joint movement which addressed the shared problems of class power. They then formed their own plank within the organisation, which often turned against their own men in the larger unit. The writings of Shekhar Pathak and Chandi Prasad Bhatt show a parallel situation for the same period in the Kumaon and Garhwal regions of the western Himalaya, where village women's participation in both the Chipko Movement and numerous anti-alcohol agitations was very impressive.

Maharashtra had a large range of autonomous women's groups, working among rural, tribal, and urban subaltern women from a broadly leftist persuasion – a large number coming from independent leftist organisations. The Lal Nishan Party, the Shetkari Sangathana, the Peasant and Workers' Party, and the militant Dalit Panthers provided important alternatives to mainstream Left Party lines from the 1970s. The Stree Mukti Smarak Andolan Samiti, founded in 1979, was formed as a shared platform for the Party as well as non-Party organisations to struggle against sexual abuse, sex-determination tests, communalism, and religious fundamentalism. Under pressure, the state introduced the Regulations for the Use of Pre-natal Diagnostic Techniques Act in 1988 to curb random sex-determination tests. Maharashtra was the first state to set up a state women's commission which other states later adopted.

Dalit feminists raised new and interesting issues. A Dalit Marathi journal, *Janwedana,* brought out a special women's issue in which the title page carried Mao Zedong's famous statement, "In the Third World, Women Hold Up Half of the Sky". Their feminists formed the Mahila Samta Sainik Dal. Unlike many such groups, they also developed a critical perspective on religion and caste, explaining male domination not only in economic terms but also as men's desire to extract sexual pleasure by instrumentalising women's bodies and making women their sex slaves. Some groups wanted to raise gender consciousness within trade unions and peasant associations, while others wanted separate socialist-feminist organisations for workers and peasants. Maoist groups among them advocated armed struggles against the state, capitalists, and feudal landlords. In the 1970s the Progressive Organisation of Women (POW) at Hyderabad, and the Purogami Stree Sangathana and Stree Mukti Sangathana in Maharashtra brought together anti-state, anti-patriarchal, anti-feudal, and anti-bourgeois activism. The POW manifesto challenged the sexual division of labour as well as its cultural apparatus.

Also in the 1970s, Naxalite-Maoist activists had launched armed combat groups – first in the villages, then in the urban areas. These worked clandestinely, always at the edge of capture, torture, sexual violence, and death. Since women – peasants as well as urban students – engaged in all their forms of action for over two decades, it seemed that they came to occupy a markedly more equal status than women in other struggles and organisations. Some scholars, however, argue that the Maoists, no differently from every other ideological grouping, believed that the revolution would automatically overthrow patriarchy without requiring separate struggles. They too dismissed the concerns about gender as an irrelevant bourgeois luxury and were uncomfortable with matters pertaining to female sexual desire, branding women's sexual self-assertion as promiscuity. In their political recollections, most Naxalite men ignore the contributions of women from their ranks.

Between 2003 and 2004 Srila Roy interviewed twenty ex-Naxal Bengali women and sixteen men. All were Hindu, many from the lower-middle classes in small towns, and several from the families of Partition refugees. Interestingly, their children's courage and idealism sometimes influenced mothers who followed them into hiding, as if enacting, in real life, the literary inspiration of Maxim Gorky's *Mother*, or Mahasweta Devi's *Hajaar Churashir Ma* (The Mother of 1084). Naxals cherished both novels and greatly valued mothers who joined their movement. They also respected tribal women as natural warriors. But their sensitivity did not extend to younger women from their own class – the women were suspected of being more mortgaged to their social milieu than men. The men conveniently overlooked the residues of old values within themselves — their indifference to caste, or their imagined vanguard role vis-à-vis peasants.

Middle-class women Naxalites faced different sets of problems which were neither acknowledged nor addressed by the movement. Even when they lived identical lives to men in village hideouts, they stood out as non-familial outsiders in the families they stayed with. They could be more easily spotted by the police and hunted down. Occasionally, they faced sexual attacks from their rural hosts. Almost invariably, the younger women were sexually tortured in police custody. Sometimes male comrades, brutalised by risks, fears, and the imminence of death, exploited them physically. The cult of blood and violence, suffused with something like an erotic charge, primarily signified male virility rather than sexual desire or emotional bonding. Certain conventional values also persisted. Most men viewed marriage as the ideal social norm, with only a few choosing not to register a partnership. Women found it exceptionally hard to speak of these events, even after a gap of decades. While this prolonged dance with death exceeded the experiences of older Left revolutionaries, as well as of the armed revolutionaries of colonial times, the Naxals did not entirely sever their umbilical cord with either. A few women abjured politics after their release, some joined independent women's groups, and others became active in civil rights movements.

In the early twentieth century Dalit reformers and religions of protest such as the Adi Hindu described their women as strong and militant rebels. Some even imagined a history where Dalit women had fought alongside royal heroes against the British in the 1857 uprising. Dalit women in western India joined politics chiefly under Ambedkar's inspiration. In 1927 they joined his Mahar satyagraha, during which Dalits forced their way onto public roads adjacent to temples where their presence was strictly forbidden. Women also participated in the conferences of the Scheduled Castes Federation in the 1940s and organised Buddhist Mahila Mandals in the 1950s – after Ambedkar converted to Buddhism with half a million Mahar-caste Dalits in 1956. Savitribai Borade and Ambubai Gaikwad were appointed on the executive committee of *Janata*, the periodical that Ambedkar edited in 1930. It specially solicited articles from Dalit women. Women later recalled Ambedkar's initiation into Buddhism – the *diksha* ceremony – as a magical moment that seemed to transform them from despised Dalits into full-fledged human beings. Wearing white saris, they came to the ceremony in very large numbers. When white saris ran out, they dressed themselves in the white dhotis that are normally worn by men.

Ambedkar had laid special stress on educating Dalit women in his creed of Organise, Educate, Struggle. Women felt especially empowered when he excoriated Brahmanical gender practices, including widow immolations, endogamy, and child marriage; they learned to value the difference of their Dalithood from the identity of caste-Hindus. In 1977–82 they joined huge agitations around the renaming of Marathwada University as Babasaheb Ambedkar University. The political momentum, however, began to decline after the 1970s. There was a brief resurgence in the mid 1980s, when young Dalit feminists formed Mahila Sansads (women's parliaments) to discuss gender problems within their own community. There was yet another revival of Dalit feminism from 1995, when women organised themselves under the National Federation of Dalit Women.

Gendering State Repression

After Independence, the boundaries of Assam were redrawn and the erstwhile native states in the region were pulled into the Indian Union. Between 1947 and 1950 they acquired statehood – Manipur, Arunachal Pradesh, Nagaland, Tripura, Mizoram, and Meghalaya, apart from Assam itself. Manipur had already formed its independent government when the British left and had to be "integrated" within India, which sometimes involved state coercion and tribal resistance. To counter their aspiration for freedom from the Indian Unon, a draconian Armed Forces Special Powers Act (AFSPA) was imposed on the entire region in 1958, even though only the Naga areas were then affected by separatist insurrections. The Act authorised extraordinary powers of surveillance and violence for the armed forces.

As each new state included multiple tribal groups, all contending for dominance, cross-cutting sources of violence from state and non-state agents came to shape the everyday lives of women – a violence emanating from the armed forces, insurrectionary groups, intra-tribal rivalries, and domestic violence. Women also faced sexual attacks and hardships because of forced displacements, land loss, and the phenomenon of "disappeared men" – men who vanished during bouts of violence.

In 1974 young Rose Machui Ningshen of Ngaprum village in Manipur committed suicide after some men from the Border Security Forces raped her. The women of the Tangkhul community in the region formed the East District Women's Association to resist such attacks; it was subsequently renamed the Tangkhul Shanao Long (TSL). Improvising constructive activism against army and domestic abuse, especially male alcoholism within the family, this body organised itself into vigilante groups, sounding the alert against attacks from all possible directions. First called the Prohibition Movement, it was later renamed Meira Paibi (women torchbearers).

The Madras and Mahar regiments were brought into Manipur in 1980, when the state was declared "disturbed". To block armed risings by the Naga, Meitei, and Kuki tribes for a state of their own, within or outside the Indian republic, these regiments conducted drastic counterinsurgency operations; the repression was at times so intense that even non-partisan bystanders were subjected to gross violence. In 1986, in a village of the Ukhrul district of Manipur, a young woman called Luingamla was working in her garden where she was allegedly raped and killed by two army officers. Though her sister found her corpse with the officers standing right next to her, the evidence was ignored. The army blamed and attacked the villagers for her rape and death. The community lodged court cases – knowing that these would prove ineffective. But they also devised novel forms of defiance. The TSL led the protests, followed by several political organisations and students' groups from all over the state. They decided to observe 11 March as their Unity Day.

Women created a calendar with Luingamla's picture in order to stamp her face on every heart. Its pages carried symbolic motifs to depict their search for justice. People raised funds by donating one day's pay from their wages or by selling poultry. They eventually collected Rs 15,000, a considerable sum for a cash-strapped community. The army tried to stop her memorialisation and alleged that the protesters were funded by a Naga insurrectionary group. Women, however, had kept meticulous records of the funds and the evidence finally silenced the army – her killers were court-martialled in 1988 and jailed. Manipuri women also wove the traditional Tangkhul female sarong to embroider and thereby memorialise the story of Luingamla.

A massive counterinsurgency effort, Operation Bluebird, was launched in 1987 by the Assam Rifles. It covered thirty contiguous Naga villages, supposedly aspiring for independence and using violent means towards it. Repression was stepped up when the armed forces were attacked by the insurrectionary National Socialist Council of Nagalim. The army allegedly used terror tactics when they interrogated village women – threatening to rape, kill, burn, and skin them alive if they did not disclose the hideouts of the rebels.

Kashmir has been the country's hotspot of tensions, clashes, and wars since Independence. In 1944 the National Conference under Sheikh Abdullah had issued a Naya Kashmir Manifesto declaring Kashmir an independent secular, socialist state, and promising equality for women. He was arrested by Kashmir's Hindu Dogra king who later acceded to India. After his release Abdullah was for a while very close to the Congress; the state of Jammu & Kashmir was granted special status and rights under Article 370 of the Indian Constitution. A plebiscite was also promised to the Kashmiri people so that they could decide whether to remain with India, or join Pakistan, or form an independent state. This was never held and there is no prospect now of any such plebiscite.

By the end of the twentieth century perhaps 70,000 Kashmiris were reckoned to have been killed through insurrections, warfare, displacement, and counterinsurgency; 4000 were believed to be in detention or had simply disappeared. The state repression targeted Muslims who were branded as terrorists, and Kashmiri Muslim terrorists drove away hundreds of Hindu pandits from the Valley in retaliation. The militancy and repression left Kashmir's women in a particularly helpless position as they faced attacks from both state and militants. As men died or disappeared in larger and larger numbers, Kashmir was besieged by the strange problem of "half widows" – women whose husbands had gone missing and who therefore could not remarry. Widows and half-widows numbered perhaps 15,000; many of them had also lost sons to bullets. The situation took a radical turn for the worse in the 1990s – in 1990, the state was placed under the AFSPA, plunging it into a recurrent cycle of violence and counter-violence.

Gendering Pogroms

A rather distinctive form of communal violence appeared after Partition, when Hindus came to form an overwhelming numerical and political majority, with pre-Partition religious minorities now much reduced in India because of the creation of Pakistan and the ensuing migrations. This created a pattern conducive to highly unequal combat, and, increasingly, pogrom-like events where the majority community often enjoyed considerable state and social impunity. Starting with the Nellie massacre of Muslims in Assam in 1983, majoritarian communal violence has from the mid 1980s been usually directed at Muslim communities.

Hindu communalism found a new target in the Sikhs. Thousands were killed brutally after Indira Gandhi was assassinated by her Sikh bodyguards in October 1984. In Delhi alone the vengeance resulted in about 3000 Sikh men being killed, many of them burnt alive. Across forty other cities the casualties totalled between 8000 and 14,000. The victims were neither a part of the conspiracy nor necessarily anti-Congress. Many were poor.

Since young able-bodied Sikh men were the primary targets, they left large numbers of fatherless children and young or middle-aged widows. Many of the Sikh families affected in 1984 had earlier suffered displacement over Partition. Many women of the community had migrated from Pakistan and managed to pick up the threads of their lives; the horrors of 1984 destroyed not only family life and relationships but also the existing modes of livelihood managed by Sikh men. Members of the Congress Party, complicit in the rioting, were never properly investigated or punished. The wound has festered to this day, since subsequent non-Congress governments have shown no real willingness to ensure justice for the families of murdered Sikhs.

Of the 1200 or so women rendered widows in Delhi, many were stranded in relief camps where social workers provided them some training in income-generating skills. One of these workers, Jaya Srivastava, studied sixty such widows at the Tilak Vihar rehabilitation centre in West Delhi, which trained them in tailoring. Government aid was sparse and difficult to obtain, and NGOs were the major source of relief. Economic difficulties were compounded by social problems and aggravated by family cruelty. To facilitate family survival, elderly women revived the custom of levirate and forced grieving widows to remarry surviving younger brothers-in-law. One 22-year-old woman was ordered to marry her somewhat demented 14-year-old brother-in-law: somehow or the other she managed to survive her refusal. Others were forced to marry elderly brothers-in-law. Local community panchayats excluded women from their deliberations, so that decisions about their lives were taken over their heads – unless they managed to bribe someone from the panchayat.

The late 1980s and 1990s were filled with anti-Muslim pogroms, during which rapes were not uncommon. Rape was an instrument for inflicting what was perceived as the supreme dishonour on designated enemies: majoritarian sexual violence is now customarily represented as "revenge rape" by perpetrators.

Re-Presenting Gender: Literature

The many worlds of fiction, which had already queried social and sexual boundaries and moral norms in colonial times, acquired far more varied and experimental forms after Independence. Women's writings won regional and national acclaim as India's states strove to present a liberal self-image by honouring them.

Some of the women writers were not formally educated but their social observations – flowing from their experiences of life – were acute, and their literary style highly polished. Though they came from the middle classes, their work was suffused with remarkable sympathy and fellow feeling for suffering subalterns. Rajam Krishnan (1925–2014) wrote forty Tamil novels and much else besides, winning the Sahitya Akademi Award in 1973 for her *Verruku Nir* (Water for the Roots). Emerging from a middle-class rural Brahman background and married early into a conservative patriarchal family before she could be given a formal education, she initiated Tamil writings on labouring lives which she observed minutely: salt-pan workers, fishermen, child labourers in match factories, tribal communities, temple dancers.

Ashapurna Debi (1909–1995), a towering Bengali fiction writer, had no formal education either. Born in a middle-class family with an educated and cultured father, she learnt the letters from books that her brothers studied. Married off early and burdened with domestic duties, from the 1930s she nonetheless began to publish fiction for adults as well as children. Her work brought her prominent literary awards. *Pratham Pratishruti* (1964), the first volume in a trilogy, won her the highly presitigious Jnanpith award in 1976. The trilogy tracked the difficult journeys of three generations of indomitable women towards liberation from patriarchal conventions. The women face defeat after defeat as they struggle for self-expression. The novels, therefore, are not exactly in the *bildungsroman* genre, where obstacles are eventually resolved and a vastly strengthened self emerges out of the struggle. Not altogether a feminist, Ashapurna formulated a worldview which was often multiplex and complicated, tilting occasionally towards a romantic nostalgia for feudal-patriarchal values, but sometimes also composing a remarkably bitter critique of the old ways which she knew very well. The self-contradictory tensions in her work reveal an interesting and incomplete struggle to understand and evaluate women's lives, past and present.

Some others were far more uncompromising critics of traditional gender. Krishna Sobti (1925–2019), born in Gujrat (Punjab), emerged as the leading light of the Hindi fictional world, receiving numerous awards. She astounded the literary world with her novel *Mitro Marajani* which explored the sexual defiance of a married woman. She also wrote essays and short fiction.

Mrinal Pande (b. 1946), daughter of the famous Hindi woman novelist Shivani, writes Hindi novels and musical drama. Much acclaimed even as a young author and journalist, she depicts working women, mostly those who are self-employed. Her short story "Hum Safar" describes the train journey of a very poor woman and her little son. While young women in the compartment suffer lascivious male comments and rich passengers devour delicacies, the poor woman and her son have nothing to eat. The mother's rage against injustice suddenly boils over but it is taken out on her son, whom she beats up for accepting leftover food from the rich passengers. A single compartment on the train holds up a mirror to the inequities and cruelties of the world at large.

Manjul Bhagat (b. 1936) is the author of *Anaro* (1977), a novel about a part-time maidservant serving several households. It describes her small longings and constant disappointments as well as her unquenchable will. On a parallel plane live her employers – insensitive husbands and wives with empty lives.

Unlike the Urdu writers, Bengali left-wing authors have remained on the margins of the communist literary world. Mahasweta Devi (1916–2016), however, was an exception. A non-Party left-wing activist for tribal rights, and a novelist of revolutionary politics, she burst upon the fictional world with an outspoken boldness and passion in her language and themes, especially with her novels *Hajar Churashir Ma* and *Aranyer Adhikar* – both about the Naxalite uprisings, rural and urban.

Autobiographies are designated a typically modernist genre which have waned in the post-modern cultural climate. Dalit autobiographies, on the other hand, have emerged and flourished precisely in that moment. Baby Kamble (b. 1929), born in an "untouchable" Mahar family in western India, was the first Dalit woman to compose an autobiography. She does not mention her husband and marriage in the text, though she does discuss both rather critically in an interview. She writes of Mahar villagers, about food, hunger, caste oppression, daily humiliations, and relentless poverty in visceral detail – a characteristic of many Dalit writings which focus mercilessly on the ugly and repellent particularities of their everyday lives to drive home the Dalit condition. Kamble describes how her village children would in lean years eat thorns mixed with grime and snot, as well as filthy leftover food thrown at them by the upper castes whom they served. She writes also about the stunning and transformative impact of Ambedkar on Dalit lives. *Jinu Amucha* (My Life) was published in 1987, a work that has been followed by many other such life narratives.

The feminist autobiography *Ente Katha* (1973), by Kerala's Madhavikutty (known as the poet Kamala Das in the English-speaking world), was an immensely controversial literary event debated intensely by Kerala's literary modernists. Madhavikutty broke with several modern conventions to discuss gender in a way quite distinct from the pervasive feminist idiom. Instead of making feminism purposeful and inordinately serious about rights-oriented struggles, she acknowledged the beauties and satisfactions of the feminine as well as its constant frustrations and disappointments. She made maternalism playful and pleasurable, foregrounded the joys of frivolity, and dwelt on female eroticism.

On the whole, there do not seem to be very many substantive differences in the writings of men and women, either in terms of content or language use: the commonalities arise from a shared caste and caste context. Gender, as the unresolved problem and as a world of future possibilities, is a much used theme in both. Beyond this, women authors have shown themselves keenly alive to themes outside the gendered universe. They have written of the problems of class and caste divisions, contrasting subaltern and middle-class lives, and political struggles – usually of a leftist and egalitarian cast. Many have continued the autobiographical tradition: Lakshmi Sahgal, mentioned earlier in the context of Subhas Bose's Rani Jhansi Brigade, which she led, published memories of her army experiences in 1997. Others wrote semi-autobiographical fiction – *Sunlight on a Broken Column* by Attia Hosain has been much hailed as a remarkable English novel portraying in close and vivid detail the changing texture of a multi-generational elite Muslim family in Uttar Pradesh. Household servants have as significant a presence in her novel as elderly conservative men and women, a new generation of Anglicised fashionistas, young women students interested in nationalist and leftist politics, and their male cousins and friends with whom they converse in ways intimate and unthinkable for their still-living elderly relatives.

Some, like the novelist Nayantara Sahgal – Nehru's niece and an outspoken opponent of Indira Gandhi as well as authoritarianism more generally – have frankly spoken about the political and cultural elites of post-Independence India in light of their own intimate experiences. All have pondered on the meanings of Independence and nationhood, reflected on Partition and the problems of citizenship, and on difficult political choices.

Gender in the Cinema

Although theatre remains popular and creative, it is the post-colonial cinema, more than anything in the world of the spectacle, that has decisively reordered the audio-visual experiences of multifarious consumers. Driven by a gigantic market, popular cinema in Hindi and a few regional languages, most notably Tamil, has come to command a global presence. Bombay cinema or Bollywood now produces the largest numbers of films in the world. Urdu-language cinema – or films that used predominantly Urdu idioms – has gradually waned because of aggressive Hindi linguistic supremacism, which has basically driven away Urdu-derived words from cinematic dialogue. A rare exception in this respect was *Garam Hava* (1974), directed by M.S. Sathyu. A remarkably delicate and poignant depiction of the Muslim experience of staying on in post-Partition India (specifically Agra), the searing film was disrupted by right-wing Hindu groups during a show at a Delhi cinema hall: Indira Gandhi had to intervene to allow the screenings to continue.

Some films from the parallel art cinema received international recognition, especially Satyajit Ray's *Pather Panchali* (Song of the Road), released in 1955. In several films that followed – *Aparajito, Apur Sansar, Debi,* and *Charulata* – the woman's face and gestures, more than her words, underpin cinematic action and meanings. In *Pather Panchali* a layered and complicated mother–daughter relationship unfolds in a context of son-preference, made sharper by scarcity and want. It dictates an insensitive disciplining of the daughter, in contrast to the obvious maternal adoration of the son, till the moment when the little girl dies and the mother's walled-up love finds expression in a single freeze-shot of wild but mute grief as she holds her dead daughter in her lap – the image of an Indian Pieta. In Ritwik Ghatak's *Meghe Dhaka Tara* (1960) and *Titash Ekti Nodir Naam* (1973), too, the woman's face and words embody the effects of ecological, social, and emotional devastation more heart-wrenchingly than anything imaginable.

In films coming out of Tollywood – headquarters of the Bengali cinema in Calcutta – romantic scenes and songs sometimes couch serious themes of class and familial cruelties as well as religious prejudice: Ajoy Kar's *Saptapadi* (Seven Steps, 1961), for instance, dwells on a Hindu father's adamant refusal to let his son marry a Christian woman whom he loves deeply. The father's objection throws both young lives out of kilter.

Beginning from 1953 and continuing upto the late 1960s, two Bengali heartthrobs – Uttam Kumar and Suchitra Sen – brought a doubled charisma to the countless films in which they acted together. Suchitra Sen often portrayed a strong female personality – forthright, outspoken, and independent – thus opening up a space for a strident femininity which contrasted sharply with the more usually docile and coy females of the film world.

Malayalam cinema had an interesting beginning which contrasts with the apparently woman-friendly culture and politics of Kerala. Its early cinema of the 1920s used mythological themes where women's boldness and desire were vested in female demons – demons being the visual embodiments of their sexuality. Till the 1950s no woman could emerge as a star. In 1928 the pioneering filmmaker J.C. Daniel searched in vain for six months for a Malayali woman who would play the lead role; he eventually asked an Anglo-Indian actor to star in his *Vigathakumaran*, the first Malayalam film. The love scenes so enraged the audience that they often attacked the screen or filled the hall with catcalls.

From the 1950s, with the growth of communist influence in Kerala, a new thematic came to shape the literary and cinematic worlds – both began to represent class and caste oppression, political radicalism, and social abuses. This was apparent in *Jeevithanuka* (1951), *Neelakkuyil* (1954), and many others. Marriage, however, remained of paramount importance, so that women were shown to dominate the domestic sphere but never the world outside.

The 1970s brought a very powerful and creative "new wave" cinema to Kerala which experimented with visual form and language, drawing on features from world cinema. Much of this variety of cinema represents a dark or darkening world of rural class oppression where tensions build into a social apocalypse and where politics becomes increasingly complex: the Party splits, the state is besieged by economic problems. This is often highly sophisticated cinema focusing on subaltern lives, and it captured the interest even of viewers from villages and small towns: avid discussion groups formed around the viewings. Such surprisingly widespread reception of "high art" cinema coexists with a separate cinematic realm of popular soft porn and conservative values.

Feminist critics have argued that, even in the realm of high art, conventional representations of women and gender did not change substantially. The woman remained bifurcated between the idea of the nurturant mother and the enticing vamp. The Malayalam world's Adoor Gopalakrishnan, an iconic director in this line of work, constructs each of his scenes with meticulous attention to detail, brilliance of conception, and superb directorial control. But even in his celebrated *Swayamvaram* (1972), as well as in his later films which have been particularly attentive to gender problems, women seem to lack strong agency. Feminists complain that the bold and talented directors of the 1970s and the 1980s built their films around an essentially male gaze which instrumentalised the woman's image.

Bombay's renowned Bollywood was cross-fertilised by diverse sources: mythological, historical, and domestic romances as well as influences from the Parsi theatre and the leftist theatrical ventures of the Indian People's Theatre Association of the 1940s. Several directors from the latter joined the Bombay film industry, bringing certain left-wing values and themes into it, albeit recast in popular motifs: *Kisan Kanya* (1937), *Mother India* (1938), *Do Beegha Zameen* (1953), and, much later, *Coolie* (1983), all focus on class oppression.

In the films of Guru Dutt, intense romance and melodrama predominate while a sentimental maternalism runs alongside as a constant parallel text. Though the family is the site of action, deviant figures sometimes occupy centrestage. In his *Pyaasa* (1957) a prostitute is the central figure in a love story where no happy ending is possible – a striking contrast to conventional film endings.

The defining love story of the 1960s, however, was a historical drama, *Mughal-e-Azam* (1960), in which Prince Salim invites Akbar's wrath when he falls in love with a court dancer. She sings and dances defiantly to the unforgettable tune of "*pyar kiya to darna kya*" (nothing to fear when you're in love) in front of a furious Akbar. Such a film could only have been made at a time when the popular cinema valorised rebel lovers – once again in sharp contrast to the endless celebrations of married love or love destined to end in marriage that were characteristic of popular films in the next few decades. The box-office mega hit *Bobby* (1973), a rendering of the same theme in a modern context, showed young lovers eloping in defiance of their parents. Unlike Salim's doomed love, this ends happily in a marriage blessed by the parents. The film forms a bridge between two different moments: rebellion against, as well as accommodation with, family and society. The tragic costs of social defiance resurface in *Ek Duje Ke Liye* (For Each Other, 1981), a superhit in which the lovers kill themselves to escape implacably hostile parents.

Change was in the air by the 1990s: familial authoritarianism began to be recast as a soft, caring, and pleasurable alternative to rebelliousness. In the wildly popular *Hum Aapke Hain Kaun*

(Who Am I to You, 1994) budding romance is briefly blocked by parental interference – though the parents are unaware of the romance and relent as soon as they come to know of it. The lovers are richly rewarded for their temporary separation, and for their acquiescence, by a union that is blessed by family, temple, and ritual. The Hindu wedding itself becomes a major character, a star in itself. What stands behind it as an unstated but visually omnipresent factor – great wealth and demonstrative consumption habits. Wealth is no longer an impediment to romance, as it had been in *Bobby*, for instance; love now obligatorily blooms in same-class circles and the wedding ceremony is as safe as it is giddy and opulent.

Social anger, however, sharpened on a different register in the 1970s and 1980s, as stark representations of poverty were combined with depictions of great male violence from a vengeful underworld – *Sholay* (1975) being the supreme example. Romance survived in this genre, but in a rather muted state, and violence foreground the male stars – Dharmendra, Amitabh Bachchan, and several others – more prominently than women actors. Male and female stars as well as the unseen song writers and singers equally drive the amazing success of Bollywood.

In earlier Bollywood films the obviously erotogenous parts of the female body were less the site for visual eroticism as the woman's suggestive and expressive eyes – for instance in the iconic films of Guru Dutt. Patricia Uberoi notices an interesting departure in some other films, where the woman's naked feet signify status, but they also generate desire in a "podo erotic" shift away from the woman's eyes.

Independence split the twentieth century sharply into two clear halves. For post-colonial times, forms and genres of political activism proliferated as widely as the cultural ones. They were born out of numerous and divergent desires, of contentious moral, social, and ideological beliefs and aspirations. They displayed themselves on new expressive registers where political, social, and cultural values and practices were displayed and brought into conflict. For much of the time, the conflicts could not be resolved. Gender, therefore, remained a site of paramount – if also tension-ridden – importance in these post-Independence realities and representations. Gender relations, masculinities, and femininities are still struggling to find a stable and moral form and ideal, and the struggles too are probably destined to remain unresolved.

As the end of the twentieth century approached, the libertarian agencies and possibilities began to lose something of their strength. Right-wing conservative religious nationalism gathered greater force and authority, and this is how it remains – at least for the time being.

References and Suggested Readings for Chapter 8

Agarwal, Bina, "The Gender and Environment Debates: Lessons from India", *Feminist Studies*, Spring 1992, vol. 18, no. 1.

Agarwal, Bina, "Widows vs Daughters or Widows as Daughters? Property, Land and Economic Security in Rural India", *Modern Asian Studies*, vol. 32, no. 1, February 1998.

Agarwal, Bina, *A Field of One's Own: Gender and Land Rights in South Asia*, Cambridge: Cambridge University Press, 1998.

Agnes, Flavia, "Conjugality, Property, Morality and Maintenance", in Raka Ray, ed., *Handbook of Gender*, Delhi: Oxford University Press, 2012.

Agnes, Flavia, "Family Courts: From the Frying Pan into the Fire", in Mary E. John, ed., *Women's Studies in India: A Reader*, Delhi: Penguin, 2008.

Agnes, Flavia, *Law and Gender Inequality: The Politics of Women's Rights in India*, Delhi: Oxford University Press, 1999.

Anand, Nishant, *Women in India: The Problem of Missing Girl Child*, New Delhi: New Century Publications, 2016.

Banerjee, Nirmala, "How Real is the Bogey of Feminization", *The Indian Journal of Labour Economics*, vol. 40, no. 3, 1997.

Bardhan, Pranab, "On Life and Death Question", *Economic and Political Weekly*, Special Number, August 1974.

Basu, Amrita, *Two Faces of Protest: Contrasting Modes of Women's Activism in India*, Berkeley: University of California Press, 1992.

Basu, Tapan, *et al.*, *Khaki Shorts and Saffron Flags: A Critique of the Hindu Right*, Hyderabad: Orient Longman, 1993.

Bhatia, Bela, "Widows, Land Rights and Resettlement in the Narmada Valley", in Martha Alter Chen, ed., *Widows in India: Social Neglect and Public Action*, Delhi: Sage, 1998.

Bhatt, Chandi Prasad, *Gentle Resistance: The Autobiography of Chandi Prasad Bhatt*, Ranikhet: Permanent Black, 2024.

Biswas, Moinak, "The Couple and Their Spaces: 'Harano Sur' as Melodrama Now", in Ravi Vasudevan, ed., *Making Meaning in Indian Cinema*, Delhi: Oxford University Press, 2000.

Bosu, Bani, *Ashtam Garbha*, Kolkata, 2015.

Butalia, Urvashi, "Speaking Peace: An Introduction", in idem, ed., *Speaking Peace: Women's Voices from Kashmir*, Delhi: Kali for Women, 2002.

Chakravartty, Gargi, *Coming Out of Partition: Refugee Women of Bengal*, Delhi: Srishti, 2007.

Chatterjee, Pia, *A Time for Tea: Women, Labour and Post-Colonial Politics on Indian Plantations*, Delhi: Zubaan, 2001.

Chaudhuri, Maitreyee, *Refashioning India: Gender, Media and a Transformed Public Discourse*, Delhi: Orient BlackSwan, 2017.

Chen, Martha Alter, ed., *Widows in India: Social Neglect and Public Action*, Delhi: Sage, 1998.

Chhachhi, Amrita, "Women Workers, Liberalisation and Social Citizenship in India", in Mary E. John, ed., *Women's Studies in India: A Reader*, Delhi: Penguin, 2008.

Clark, Alice, "Social Demography of Excess Female Mortality in India: New Directions", *Economic and Political Weekly*, 25 April 1987.

Courtright, Paul B., "Sati, Sacrifice and Marriage: The Modernity of Tradition", in Lindsey Harlan and Paul B. Courtright, eds, *From the Margins of Hindu Marriage: Essays on Gender, Religion and Culture*, New York: Oxford University Press, 1995.

Custers, Peter, *Women in the Tebhaga Uprising: Rural Poor Women and Revolutionary Leadership 1946–47*, Calcutta: Naya Prakash, 1987.

Das, Veena, "Strange Response", *Illustrated Weekly of India*, 28 April, 1991.

Das Gupta, Monica, "Selective Discrimination against Female Children in Rural Punjab, India", *Population and Development Review*, vol. 13, no. 1, 1987.

Dasgupta, Rajeswari, "Towards the New Man: Revolutionary Youth and Rural Agency in the Naxalite Movement", *Economic and Political Weekly*, vol. 41, no. 19, 2006.

De, Rohit, "Mumtaz Bibi's Broken Heart", *Indian Economic and Social History Review*, vol. 46, no. 1, 2009.

Debi, Ashapurna, *Mittir Baari*, in idem, *Ashapurna Debi Rachanabali*, Calcutta: Mitra and Ghosh, 2001.

Debi, Rashsundari, *Amar Jiban*, Calcutta, 1876.

Devika, J., "Housewife, Sex Worker and Reformer: Controversies over Women Writing Their Lives in Kerala", *Economic and Political Weekly*, vol. 41, no. 17, 2006.

Devika, J., and Binitha V. Thampi, eds, *New Lamps for Old? Gender Paradoxes of Political Decentralisation in Kerala*, Delhi: Zubaan, 2012.

Engels, Dagmar, *Beyond Purdah? Women in Bengal, 1890–1930*, Delhi: Oxford University Press, 1996.

Fernandes, Leela, "The Politics of Forgetting: Class, Politics, State Power, and the Restructuring of Urban Space in India", *Urban Studies*, vol. 41, no. 12, November 2004.

Freeman, James, *Untouchable: An Indian Life History*, London: Allen and Unwin, 1980.

Ghosh, Shohini, "Forbidden Love and Passionate Denials: A Dialogue on Domesticity and Queer Intimacy", in Raka Ray, ed., *Handbook of Gender*, Delhi: Oxford University Press, 2012.

Guha, Ramachandra, *India After Gandhi: The History of the World's Largest Democracy*, Delhi: HarperCollins, 2007.

Gulati, Leela, "Female Work Participation: A Study of Interstate Differences", *Economic and Political Weekly*, vol. 10, nos 1–2, 11 January 1975.

Hardgrove, Anne, *Community and Public Culture: The Marwaris in Calcutta*, Delhi: Oxford University Press, 2004.

Harriss-White, Barbara, "Gender Cleansing: The Paradox of Development and Deteriorating Female Life Chances in Tamil Nadu", in

Rajeswari Sunder Rajan, ed., *Signposts: Gender Issues in Post Independence India*, Delhi: Kali for Women, 1999.

Hasan, Zoya, and Ritu Menon, "Creating an Enabling Environment", in Mary E. John, ed., *Women's Studies in India: A Reader*, Delhi: Penguin, 2008.

Jain, Devaki, and Nirmala Banerjee, "The Tyranny of the Household", in Mary E. John, ed., *Women's Studies in India: A Reader*, Delhi: Penguin, 2008.

Jeffrey, Robin, *Politics, Women and Well Being: How Kerala Became a Model*, London: Palgrave Macmillan, 1992.

Jhabvala, R., and R.K.A. Subramanya, eds, *The Unorganised Sector: Work Security and Social Protection*, Delhi: Sage, 2000.

John, Mary E., "Feminism, Poverty and Globalization", in idem, ed., *Women's Studies in India: A Reader*, Delhi: Penguin, 2008.

John, Mary E., and Meena Menon, "Introduction", in idem, eds, *Women in the Worlds of Labour: Interdisciplinary and Intersectional Perspectives*, Hyderabad: Orient BlackSwan, 2021.

Kabir, Nasreen Munni, *Guru Dutt: A Life in Cinema*, Delhi: Oxford University Press, 1996.

Kannabiran, Vasantha, and K. Lalita, "That Magic Time: Women in the Telangana People's Struggle", in Kumkum Sangari and Sudesh Vaid, eds, *Recasting Women: Essays in Indian Colonial History*, New Brunswick: Rutgers University Press, 1990.

Karat, Brinda, "On the Uniform Civil Code: Uniformity vs Inequality", in Raka Ray, ed., *Handbook of Gender*, Delhi: Oxford University Press, 2012.

Karlekar, Malavika, *Poverty and Women's Work: A Study of the Sweeper Community in Delhi*, Delhi: Vikas, 1982.

Katju, Manjari, *Vishwa Hindu Parishad and Indian Politics*, Hyderabad: Orient BlackSwan, 2003.

Krishnaraj, Maithreyi, "Women's Work in the Indian Census: Beginnings of Change", *Economic and Political Weekly*, 1–8 December 1990.

Kumar, Radha, *A History of Doing: An Illustrated Account of Women's Movements and Feminism in India 1800–1990*, Delhi: Kali for Women, 1993.

Lewellyn, J.E., *The Legacy of Women's Uplift in India: Contemporary Women Leaders in the Arya Samaj*, Delhi: Sage, 1998.

Majumdar, Rochona, *Marriage and Modernity: Family Values in Colonial Bengal*, Durham: Duke University Press, 2009.

Mathur, J.S., and A.S. Mathur, *Trade Union Movement in India*, Allahabad: Chaitanya Publishing House, 1957.

Mayer, Peter, "India's Falling Sex Ratios", *Population and Development Review*, June 1999.

Menon, Ritu, *India on Their Minds: 8 Women, 8 Ideas of India*, Delhi: Women Unlimited, 2023.

Mies, Maria, "Capitalist Development and Subsistence Reproduction: Rural Women in India", *Bulletin of Concerned Asian Scholars*, vol. 12, no. 1, 1980.

Murthy, Laxmi, and Mitu Varma, eds, *Garrisoned Minds: Women and Armed Conflict in South Asia*, Delhi: Speaking Tiger, 2016.

Nandwana, Shobha, and Ramesh Nandwana, "Widows and Property Rights: A Study of Two Villages in Bihar", in Martha Alter Chen, ed., *Widows in India: Social Neglect and Public Action*, Delhi: Sage, 1998.

Nandy, Ashis, "Sati in Kali Yuga: The Public Debate on Roop Kanwar's Death", in idem, *The Savage Freud and Other Essays*, Princeton: Princeton University Press, 1995.

Newbigin, Eleanor, *The Hindu Family and the Emergence of Modern India: Law, Citizenship and Community*, Cambridge: Cambridge University Press, 2013.

Nongbri, Tiplut, *Development, Ethnicity and Gender: Select Essays on Tribes in India*, Jaipur: Rawat Publications, 2003.

Omvedt, Gail, *We Will Smash This Prison*, London: Zed, 1980.

Pahuja, Nisha, *The World Before Her: Prachi's Story*, documentary film, 2012.

Palriwala, Rajni, "Economics and Patriliny: Consumption and Authority Within the Household", in Mary E. John, ed., *Women's Studies in India: A Reader*, Delhi: Penguin, 2008.

Panjabi, Kavita, *Unclaimed Harvest: An Oral History of the Tebhaga Women's Movement*, Delhi: Zubaan, 2016.

Pathak, Shekhar, *The Chipko Movement*, Ranikhet: Permanent Black, 2021.

People's Union of Democratic Rights Bulletin, May 1981.

Pillai, Meena T., "Becoming Women: Unwrapping Femininity in Malayalam Cinema", in Meena T. Pillai, ed., *Women in Malayalam Cinema: Naturalising Gender Hierarchies*, Hyderabad: Orient BlackSwan, 2010.

Randeria, Shalini, and Leela Visaria, "Sociology of Bride Price and Dowry", *Economic and Political Weekly*, 14 April 1984.

Ray, Raka, *Fields of Protest: Women's Movement in India*, Minneapolis: University of Minnesota Press, 1999.

Roy, Anuradha, "Cooking Women" (2004), https://www.outlookindia.com/magazine/story/cooking-women/223175

Reddy, M. Atchi, "Female Agricultural Labourers of Nellore, 1881–1981", in J. Krishnamurty, ed., *Women in Colonial India: Essays on Survival, Work, and the State*, Delhi: Oxford University Press, 1989.

Rege, Sharmila, *Writing Caste / Writing Gender: Dalit Women's Testimonies*, Delhi: Zubaan, 2006.

Roy, Mallarika Sinha, *Gender and Radical Politics in India: Magic Moments of Naxalbari (1967–1975)*, London and New York: Routledge, 2011.

Roy, Srila, *Remembering Revolution: Gender, Violence, and Subjectivity in India's Naxalbari Movement*, Delhi: Oxford University Press, 2012.

Sahgal, Lakshmi, *A Revolutionary Life*, Delhi: Kali for Women, 1997.

Samom, Thingnam Anjulika, "The Art of Defiance", in Laxmi Murthy and Mitu Varma, eds, *Garrisoned Minds: Women and Armed Conflict in South Asia*, Delhi: Speaking Tiger, 2016.

Sangari, Kumkum, and Sudesh Vaid, "Sati in Modern India: A Report", *Economic and Political Weekly*, 1 August 1986.

Saradamoni, K., "Women, Kerala and Some Development Issues", *Economic and Political Weekly*, vol. 29, no. 9, 26 February 1994.

Sarkar, Tanika, "Calcutta's Underbelly: Corporation 'Methars' and Their Early Strikes", in Sekhar Bandyopadhyay and Tanika Sarkar, eds, *Caste in Bengal*, Ranikhet: Permanent Black: 2022.

Sen, Amartya, "More than 100 Million Women Are Missing", *The New York Review of Books*, 20 December 1990.

Sen, Manikuntala, *In Search of Freedom*, Kolkata: Bhatkal and Sen, 2001.

Sen, Samita, "Gender and Class: Women in Indian Industry, 1890–1990", *Modern Asian Studies*, vol. 42, no. 1, 2008.

Sen, Samita, "Questions of Consent: Workers' Recruitment for Assam Tea Gardens", *Studies in History*, July–December 2002.

Sen, Samita, "Rethinking Gender and Class: Some Critical Questions for the Present", in Mary. E. John and Meena Gopal, eds, *Women in the Worlds of Labour: Interdisciplinary and Intersectional Perspectives*, Hyderabad: Orient BlackSwan, 2021.

Sen, Uditi, *Citizen-Refugee: Forging the Indian Nation after Partition*, Cambridge: Cambridge University Press, 2018.

Sengupta, Anwesha, "Moveable Migrants, Laboring Lives: Making Refugees 'Useful' in Post Colonial India", in Mahua Sarkar, ed., *Work Out of Place*, Berlin: De Gruyter Oldenbourg, 2018.

Shiva, Vandana, *Staying Alive: Women, Ecology and Survival*, London: Zed Books, 1988.

Singh, K.S., "Tribal Women: An Anthropological Perspective", in J.P. Singh, *et al.*, eds, *Tribal Women and Development*, Delhi: South Asia Books, 1988.

Som, Reba, "Jawaharlal Nehru and the Hindu Code: A Victory of Symbol over Substance?", in Sumit Sarkar and Tanika Sarkar, eds, *Women and Social Reform in Modern India*, vol. II, Ranikhet: Permanent Black, 2007.

Srivastava, Jaya, "The Widows of November 1984", in Raka Ray, ed., *Handbook of Gender*, Delhi: Oxford University Press, 2012.

Stree Shakti Sangathana, *We Were Making History: Women and the Telangana Uprising*, Delhi: Kali for Women, 1989.

Sundarayya, P., *Telangana Peoples' Struggle and Its Lessons*, Calcutta: Communist Party of India (Marxist) Publications, 1972.

Uberoi, Patricia, "Dharma and Desire, Freedom and Destiny: Rescripting the Man–Woman Relationship in Popular Hindi Cinema", in Raka Ray, ed., *Handbook of Gender*, Delhi: Oxford University Press, 2012.

Vaid, Sudesh, "Institutions, Beliefs, Ideologies: Widow Immolation in Contemporary Rajasthan", *Economic and Political Weekly*, 27 April 1991.

Vaid, Sudesh, "Politics of Widow Immolation", *Seminar*, February 1988.

Vasudevan, Ravi, *The Melodramatic Public: Film Form and Spectatorship in Indian Cinema*, Ranikhet: Permanent Black, 2010.

Xaxa, Virginius, "Women and Gender in the Study of Tribes in India", in Mary E. John, ed., *Women's Studies in India: A Reader*, Delhi: Penguin, 2008.

Yhome, Yirmiyan Arthur, "This Road I Knew", in Laxmi Murthy and Mitu Varma, eds, *Garrisoned Minds: Women and Armed Conflict in South Asia*, Delhi: Speaking Tiger, 2016.

9

The "Others": Pakistan and Bangladesh

IN THIS CONCLUDING chapter I turn the focus and look briefly at the relationship between faith and gender in Pakistan and Bangladesh.

Early Political Vicissitudes

In his address to the Constituent Assembly of Pakistan, Muhammad Ali Jinnah, founding father and first governor general of Pakistan, had announced: "You are free, you are free to go to your temples. You are free to go to your mosques . . . We are all citizens and equal citizens . . ."[1] Jinnah himself was a liberal constitutionalist, unorthodox in personal conduct, a man who never flaunted his beliefs. He had eloped with and married a Parsi woman, and his sister Fatima was his political assistant. All this, however, contrasted with his public persona: his demand for a separate state for India's Muslims, Pakistan, had ignited a mammoth communal holocaust on the eve of Partition. As in India, memories of the violence simmered for long in Pakistan, inflamed by recurrent bouts of hostility with India.

Jinnah's vision for Pakistan differed radically from that of Maulana Abul Ala Maududi, the hardcore orthodox leader who

---

[1] Cited in Sheikh, *Making Sense of Pakistan*, p. 3.

founded the Jamaat-i-Islami (JI) in 1941. Jinnah died a year after Pakistan was formed and his liberal vision found little purchase in politics thereafter; Maududi, on the other hand, had a trans-subcontinental reputation and his views on gender even influenced sections of the Egyptian clergy.

Religion became an increasingly important reference point for state decisions. But which doctrinal interpretation should prevail: a hard conservative one, or a soft liberal one? The conundrum carried the most profound implications for gender. Maududi asserted an exact congruence between divine laws and social regulations in order to redirect what he saw as wild female sexual urges into safe procreative channels. He prescribed women's dress and deportment in great detail so that no hint of female allure could escape to entrap men: "Women must not go out of homes without a genuine need," he said: they should do so only in the company of a male relative.[2]

In their Lahore Resolution of 1951, the conservative ulama suggested that the Quran and Hadith should be the basis of state laws. Maududi added that while all men should get the vote, educated women alone could be enfranchised. They had to be debarred from holding public office to avoid close contact with men. Maududi also recommended a separate women's legislature. But he confronted a formidable opponent – a women's movement that was prepared to give strong battle to orthodoxy.

Given these contrary pressures, the state played it safe. The Constitution gave the ulama an advisory status within the state apparatus. But it rejected their demands for disenfranchising women, setting up a Ministry of Religious Affairs, and separate electorates for Hindus and Muslims.

Popular discontent grew rapidly as a plutocracy of military and civil bureaucracy, large capitalists, and landlords managed to corner the bulk of the national wealth and power. In 1958 General

---

[2] Maududi, *Purdah and the Status of Women in Islam*, p. 198.

Ayub Khan seized power in a military coup. A dictator with a modern Western slant, he had first named the state the Republic of Pakistan. But in 1962 his own National Advisory Council renamed it the Islamic Republic of Pakistan. Faced with an upsurge of Bengali regional and linguistic nationalism in East Pakistan, he too began to cultivate the orthodoxy from the 1960s. Fatima Jinnah had contested the Presidential elections of 1965. Ayub condemned this as anti-Islamic and many maulvis endorsed her exclusion.

A slew of repressive laws provoked widespread popular protests. The troops failed to contain them, and in early 1969 an unnerved Ayub Khan handed over power to Commander-in-Chief General Muhammad Yahya Khan, who immediately proclaimed martial law. When the elections were called in 1970, Zulfiqar Ali Bhutto led the Pakistan Peoples' Party, the major opposition force in West Pakistan, while the Awami League (AL) was the dominant party in the East. Bhutto preferred a softer Sufi Islam, promised populist welfare measures, land redistribution, and the nationalisation of industries and democracy. Women were prominent in his campaign. He won the elections in the western parts but failed in the East which began to demand independence from Pakistan. East Pakistan's war of liberation, joined soon by India, ended in 1971 with a resounding defeat for Pakistan.

Bhutto began his rule amidst a severe national crisis and a new constitution was promulgated for a truncated Pakistan in 1973. It was democratic, secular and federal, promising gender justice and encouraging women's organisations. The right-wing opposition, consisting of religious parties, now raised the slogan of "Islam in Danger". Made president under emergency rules in 1971, Bhutto became prime minister in 1972. He set up a Women's Commission and a Women's Institute, signed the UN Resolution on Women's Rights, and often used the language of gender equality, all of which endeared him to upper- and middle-class women activists.

A nine-party conservative coalition – the Pakistan National Alliance – soon consolidated itself against Bhutto to demand an overtly Islamic state. It eventually decided that General Zia-ul-Haq, committed to the "Islamicisation" of state laws, would be a more malleable instrument in their hands. Bhutto was deposed by an army coup and the Supreme Court sentenced him to be hanged for corruption.

Scripture, Custom, Norms

Islam is often credited with a relatively high gender sensitivity. Unlike Brahmanical Hinduism, it allows remarriage for widows and divorced women, as well as inheritance entitlements for daughters. Unlike Christianity, it believes that God created man and woman from a single substance: Islamic feminists interpret this as an affirmation of gender equality. Islamic scripture allows a woman control over her own income, she can enter into a contract independently of men, she is considered a full-fledged legal person. She can acquire, dispose of, and alienate her share of property. At the same time, *muamalat* – the realm of family relationships, custody, and inheritance – allows men, designated the natural protectors of women, a far larger slice of rights.

In actual practice, women rarely have an opportunity to exercise these rights and seldom dare to assert them against family decisions. The family is their sole refuge in a world largely beyond their control. Few know the textual provisions. *Huq mehr*, or the money promised by the husband when the marriage contract is signed, is supposedly the woman's own property. But she neither has free access to it nor demands it for fear of antagonising her husband. On the other hand the restrictive parts of domestic prescriptions in Islamic law are scrupulously followed by the religious and family guardians. Purdah – as veiling and seclusion in the domestic interior – is more the preserve of conservative sections of upper-class women who can afford to be immobile. As a marker of privilege and honour, however, it has long tempted aspirational lower-middle-class women to signify their distance from labouring women. Purdah has spread among upwardly mobile subaltern women as well, who want to augment family prestige and garner admiration for their piety. They thus develop stakes of their own in patriarchal codes of honour. There is, moreover, the added advantage that purdah provides anonymity and relative safety from possible male attacks in public places.

Tribal custom has always troubled the exercise of Islamic laws. In tribal communities, once the bride price had been paid the wife was seldom allowed to return to the natal home – whether divorced, separated, or widowed. In the North West Frontier Province rural women lived under customary law – the Pukhtun *riwaj* – which encourages a marked son-preference. Woman's consent to and signature on the marriage contract are purely formal, and registration forms are seldom used. Little from the bride price is spent on her needs, the bride remaining the property of the matrimonial family even after widowhood. If she remarries she needs their consent; quite often her brother-in-law marries her to keep her labour and property share within the family. Divorce and remarriage are practically impossible since the wife symbolises the honour of the husband, which supposedly diminishes if she marries again. By and large, Islamic inheritance norms do not apply, and she is not entitled to any part of her father's land. If a man has no son, his brothers inherit his property. The agrarian areas of Sindh and Punjab, in contrast, have enjoyed relatively relaxed codes.

The 1956 Constitution had promised gender equality: its Fundamental Rights guaranteed that all positions in national life should be open to women. Gender-affirmative action remains a constitutional right, and special steps are recommended to ensure the protection of women workers, mothers, and children, as well as maternity benefits for working women. These constitutional principles, however, are not enshrined in law, and custom trumps them with impunity. Nor are the laws always observed: the Sindh Act for Prevention of Murder of Female Infants of 1970, for instance, is more often observed in the breach.

There was an interesting religious debate on contraception in 1962. The Hadith provides some indication that *coitus interruptus* (*azal*) was practised in the Prophet's time. Apparently, the Prophet once said that this amounted to child murder; yet elsewhere he also said that to see it so was a wrong-headed Jewish belief. The Jamaat-i-Islami leader Golam Azad accused the West of inventing this immoral practice and insisted that the Prophet had forbidden it. Some clerics, opposed him, with all disputing parties citing sacred texts. Golam Azad also opposed it on the grounds that it undermined the marriage tie.

The Gendering of Dress

Attired bodies are the first site of gender construction and separation, and Muslims have long debated the desired extent, rationale, and origins of purdah (literally, a curtain). The burqa has many gradations – from a cover-all garment flowing from head to toe, to a cape, to a face-covering above an upper-body drape, to a headscarf. Purdah also encompasses a larger meaning: it indicates the seclusion of women from men within domestic spaces and ensures women's distance even from her male relatives.

Pakistan's men were not stigmatised for taking to Western dress, but women were generally expected to wear the *shalwar-kameez* as the sign of their authentic Islamic womanhood. Western female attire was taken to signify Christian women while the sari was associated with Hindus. The dress code thus hemmed in the Pakistani woman's body with community markers, making her faith and faithfulness visible in dress and deportment. Every kind of dress carries its own typical mode of stride, carriage, and gait, and signifies a specific relationship with the world.

A significant change occurred under Zulfiqar Ali Bhutto. The *shalwar-kameez* was preferred as a unisex dress meant for both men and women, and redefined as *awami* – the peoples' dress. But even while this dress was universalised and invested with fresh national-populist meanings, the *dupatta*, a light scarf arranged across the chest which can also be used to cover the face, was made obligatory for women. Saris were still worn, as was the traditional *gharrara* (long skirt), but the privileged national status was restricted to the *shalwar-kameez*. Later, Zia made the heavy *chador*, an all-enveloping veil, mandatory for women in the workplace. Regardless of these male impositions on dress and deportment, Pakistani women, whether veiled or unveiled, have engaged in daring political activism, open protests, and professions involving labour. The inhibiting role of the veil appears to be highly overrated.

Women's Activism

Pakistani feminism developed vigorously in the early years, but the class and regional profiles of the activists considerably narrowed down its possibilities – a small and extremely privileged elite within the Punjab region being largely the birthplace of the leading feminists. Another restriction resulted from the general reliance on scriptures as the invariant frame of reference. With some notable exceptions, reform was accomplished without any overt questioning of the scriptural authority to define the licit parameters of gender practices and relationships. If the public activism of women pointed at secularisation, then by and large most agents of change represented themselves as upholding the sacred tradition. Conformity with Islam enabled an easy passage to change but it also obstructed certain kinds of developments since the orthodox ulama were the final arbiters of gender prescriptions.

The early years were rich in promise. Begum Ra'ana Liaquat Ali Khan – née Sheila Irene Pant, a Kumaoni Christian from Almora before her marriage – who was the widow of the first prime minister, was also the governor of Sindh; Dr Kaniz Yusuf was the first woman vice chancellor of the prestigious Quaid-e-Azam University in Islamabad; and Kaneez Fatima led the dock-workers' union, the largest in the country. They forged role models for women from the privileged classes.

The Muslim Women's League was formed in the early 1940s. Its pre-Partition support for the Pakistan movement gave its members an assured place in the new state. The first two decades of Pakistan, consequently, saw a remarkable efflorescence of women's and civil rights groups that tried to harmonise Quranic injunctions with gender justice, and with larger opportunities for women in the domestic and public arenas.

Begum Shahnawaz and Naseem Musharraf prepared a Women's Charter of Demands in 1948. They prodded the government to set up a Women's Rights Committee. The committee, in turn, demanded reserved seats for women and equal inheritance rights. Women's inheritance rights to agricultural land were, consequently, ensured in 1951. Begum Ra'ana Liaquat Ali started the Women's Voluntary Service (WVS) in 1948 to distribute material, moral, and emotional support among women refugees fleeing the Partition violence. She also introduced military training for women after the 1947–8 war with India, and in 1949 a Pakistan Women's National Guard and Pakistan Women's Naval Reserve were formed. Ironically, the state of hostilities opened up new horizons for women, combining gender empowerment with militarisation. The orthodoxy, however, disapproved of women's combat roles since they violated the traditional norms of seclusion and modesty. The WVS, in contrast, followed a welfare orientation which was more to their liking since they saw it as a legitimate extension of women's domestic roles into the national arena. Being unpaid voluntary work, as distinct from professional military service, this was also in consonance with women's unpaid work at home.

The All Pakistan Women's Association (APWA) was formed in 1949. It worked without discriminating among the country's religious communities and was even ready to demand entitlements that went beyond, or contradicted, scriptural injunctions. But being predominantly urban and middle class, its social limits acted as a counterweight to its religious inclusiveness. Unfamiliar with the lifeworlds of poor women, its members could not address subaltern problems meaningfully. It did, however, make rapid progress in the politico-legal arena with its campaigns for reserved seats for women in the national and provincial assemblies on a time-bound basis.

In 1956 the government appointed a Commission on Family Laws to review marriage, divorce, maintenance, and child-custody laws. It was meant to align colonial personal laws more firmly to Islam. Simultaneously, Islam too was aligned to modern notions of gender justice. The commission's report was put on the back burner when the orthodoxy rejected its recommendations, but Ayub Khan revived them in 1961 as the Muslim Family Laws Ordinance. This ordinance did not go as far as, for example, the Tunisian reforms of 1956 which had prohibited male polygamy, considerably eased women's access to divorce, and instituted alimony. However, Pakistan did initiate important changes, largely on the basis of suggestions made by its various women's organisations. Polygamy was restricted by several institutional impediments and the husband had to procure the first wife's consent before marrying a second time. Provisions for self-choice in marriage were strengthened for both partners, the unilateral initiation of divorce by men through their triple enunciation of "*talaaq*" was abolished, female inheritance laws were eased. Before he could divorce his wife, the husband had to seek arbitration. Marriage registration and the *nikahnama* (marriage contract) became compulsory. The minimum age for marriage for women and men had been fourteen and eighteen, respectively; now they were raised to sixteen and twenty-one.

By far the most positive legal development until that point in time, this ordinance was, predictably, much debated: secularists found it far too confined within Islamic prescriptions, while the orthodoxy alleged it actually curtailed women's rights that authentic Islam prescribed. Maududi called it anti-Islam, since Islam allowed Muslim men several wives. If polygamy was attenuated, he warned, men would be driven into obnoxious westernised practices and acquire "girl friends and mistresses" instead.

The Law Reform Commission of 1958 had cautiously warned against involving religion and religious scholars in law-making. The warning prevailed for a time. In the general elections of 1970 the Jamaat-e-Islami did not win a single seat. The Jamiat Ulema-e-Islam and Jamiat Ulema-e-Pakistan also fared badly. Failing to win power politically, they now turned to the military, creating the future nucleus of Zia-ul-Haq's military dictatorship under the banner of Islam.

The United Front for Women's Rights had been formed in 1955 to agitate for larger political rights. Women legislators led the movement for reforms in Shariat law and for economic justice for women. Pakistan signed several UN Human Rights Instruments on gender issues, including the 1953 Convention on the Political Rights of Women. But it never ratified the UN Convention on Consent to Marriage, Minimum Age of Marriage, and Registration of Marriage, claiming that its own state laws gave women much wider powers.

Women increasingly cleared a space for themselves outside the discipline of faith. The Federation of University Women and the Karachi Business and Professional Women's Club – powerful organisations of high-achieving women – affiliated themselves to the APWA. The Young Women's Christian Association opened residences and other facilities for poorer working women. In 1948 communist women organised themselves into the Anjuman Jamhooriyat Pasand Khawateen (Democratic Women's Association) in Lahore under the broader umbrella of the Women's Action Forum. This had an important presence among working-class women with their demand of equal pay for equal work. But the Pakistan government inflicted brutal repression against them; the party was banned in 1954.

Communist women in West Pakistan usually came from highly

privileged families, and some defied family discipline to engage in party work. Khadijah Omar, a highly educated woman from a rich family, used to steal away from home to attend party meetings as a young girl. In the early years of the Communist Party of Pakistan she was involved in signature campaigns, peace committees, and the Democratic Women's Association. Tahira Mazhar Khan had joined the Communist Party of India in 1943. After Partition she worked in Pakistan's refugee camps. In 1984 she joined a successful secular movement to help the persecuted Ahmadiyyas undertake Mecca pilgrimages that the Zia regime tried to prohibit.

Communist wives contributed much to their husbands' political lives. It seems that the husbands took their wives' problems rather lightly – their risks, fears, and privations, their loneliness when husbands went underground or were put in jail. This is captured in a letter that one of them wrote to her friend, the great leftist poet Faiz Ahmad Faiz:

> I sometimes feel that when future generations remember all of you, will they ever think of Alys [Faiz's wife] or me? We have always walked with you, though you were a step ahead of us. Sometimes you would look back to perhaps make sure that we were still there, following behind you. And we would reassuringly smile back although our hearts would cry out in pain . . .[3]

A crop of independent leftist women activists who began their careers in the 1970s and 1980s remain important political workers even today: Khawar Mumtaz, one of the oldest members of the WAF; Nighat Said Khan, who had to struggle against state repression without any help from the mainstream Left; Sheema Kermani, who organised political plays which were performed in working-class areas. Some formed the Tehreek-e-Niswan as a group of left-liberal cultural activists, academics, and students. Its

---

[3] Excerpt from a letter by Razia Sajjad Zaheerto Faiz, in 1951, cited in Ali, *Communism in Pakistan*, pp. 51–3.

members later organised public events and demonstrations against Zia's laws.

On the whole, secular and leftist women activists were cushioned by class privileges which distanced them from subaltern women. Most women were locked into poverty and illiteracy, and the religious orthodoxy retained its control over ordinary lives. Popular and folk traditions, as well as the new urban media and mass cultural products like television and press advertisements, promoted images of docile women as role models. So, while the work of early women's organisations was indeed remarkable and carried far-reaching consequences, its remit was critically restricted.

The Hudood Decade

Pakistan's gender relations came to be increasingly moulded by the global context from the late 1970s. In 1979 Shia-dominated Iran overthrew the millennium-old Pahlavi dynasty and established a theocracy under Ayatollah Khomeini: the Pahlavis had been traditional clients of the US. Reacting to fears that this would expand Shia and Iranian influence in the region, Sunni-dominated Saudi Arabia began to make inroads into Pakistan and Afghanistan, with an intensification of the Wahhabi orthodoxy which it exported to the Muslim-majority countries in the region. By and large, this received Western support. Wahhabism implied severe controls on women's rights and freedoms.

When General Muhammad Zia-ul-Haq reached political power through a military coup in 1977, he tapped into various conservative religious organisations, especially the Jamaat-i-Islami. When he abrogated the elections, however, the JI withdrew its support. Zia preferred the rigid Saudi Wahhabi brand of Islamic legalism, very distant from the Sufi mysticism which is also very popular in Pakistan. He developed a Council of Islamic Ideology to formulate a slew of new laws, purportedly implementing scriptural regulations.

Promulgated in 1979 and enforced from 1980, his Hudood Ordinances – supposedly derived from scripture – covered offences against property, *zina* (adultery, fornication, and rape), false accusation, and intoxicants. The battery of laws punished theft and robbery with amputation of limbs and criminalised the use of drugs and alcohol. Zia also vigorously applied the blasphemy laws. *Zina* offences were punished with lashes or stoning to death in public. In 1980 the Federal Shariat Court was made the Appellate Court. Dominated by ulama judges who had no formal training in modern law, it could declare any law to be anti-Islam – with the exception of the Constitution, Muslim personal laws, fiscal law, and standard court procedure. In 1981, however, stoning to death for adultery was challenged in the court as un-Islamic and only one judge out of five demurred. It was therefore set aside by judicial consensus. The orthodoxy staged angry rallies against the decision and the verdict was soon reversed.

Rape had earlier been attributed to men alone, conjugal rape had been criminalised, and the supposed consent of a child under fourteen to intercourse was considered immaterial: below that age, all sexual contact counted as rape. A child below seven could not be punished unless he/she proved mature enough to understand the effects of the offence. The penalty for rape was transportation for life or imprisonment, extending to ten years, plus a fine. Rape of a minor wife under twelve carried a jail sentence of two years.

Hudood changed everything. Women could now be charged with rape, conjugal rape was decriminalised, and children, regardless of age, could be punished for rape or *zina* (adultery). If consensual intercourse was proved, the offence was reclassified as adultery. Under the colonial Penal Code, women could not be sued for adultery which was a crime attributed to men alone. Women were, consequently, "secondary but protected citizens".[4] Though the colonial rulers had fully acknowledged the importance of conjugal

---

[4] Jahangir and Jilani, *The Hudood Ordinances*, p. 79.

chastity, they had nonetheless felt that child marriage and polygamy had rendered Indian women helpless and in need of special protection. Hudood removed the protection while retaining women's secondary status. Adultery became punishable by a maximum of ten years in prison plus thirty lashes of whip and a fine – for women and men alike. Adultery and fornication were now non-bailable and non-compoundable offences and the complainant could not drop the charges even if he later wanted to. Anyone could now bring charges of adultery, not necessarily the "aggrieved" party alone. The Enforcement of the Hudood Ordinance of 1979 fixed a lower age of criminal responsibility for the girl: since puberty signified her having attained majority – and apparently this then made her fit to assume responsibility for her actions – a girl of nine, if she happened to reach puberty early, became as liable to criminal responsibility as a man double her age.

Rape and adultery were taken out of criminal justice and incorporated within religious Hudood Ordinances, ensuring control by religious authorities over gender disputes which earlier used to be settled by the courts. In non-marital rape cases the male defender could claim that sex had been consensual and not forced. The woman rape victim thus easily turned into an adulterer, a criminal under the law. The raped woman could not testify on her own behalf, which made it easier to exonerate or exculpate the rapist and criminalise the victim instead, especially in cases of domestic violence.

The 8th, 9th, and 12th constitutional amendments made a narrow reading of the scriptural laws mandatory in judicial application. Federal Shariat courts introduced new laws of evidence which measured the value of evidence offered by women as half of that by men. At least four adult males, certified as satisfactory eyewitnesses by the courts, had to depose on rape in order to make the accusation stick – even though rape rarely happens in public. If the accused was a non-Muslim, eyewitnesses who were Muslim were deemed credible.

Jamaat ministers imposed confining dress codes and a separate university was formed for women. In 1980 the *chador* became mandatory for women employed in public offices – on top of a gendered segregation of the workspace. In 1982 the government initiated a campaign against what it defined as obscenity and pornography. Dr Israr Ahmad's TV programmes energetically declaimed against women's public visibility – and until a proper Islamic state was achieved, no woman must be seen in public and no rape should be punished. Women's public sports events were forbidden.

Three early trials are illuminating. In 1981 Fehmida eloped with Allah Bux, a bus driver. Before they could marry, her parents lodged a case of abduction against the bus driver. The police dragged back the pregnant daughter to her parental home and changed the charge to adultery. Allah Bux was sentenced to be stoned to death and she was to receive a hundred lashes.

In 1983 Safia Bibi, a blind girl, was raped: she became pregnant and her father filed a rape complaint. The sessions court convicted her for adultery instead, her sentence being three years of hard labour in prison, fifteen lashes, and a fine of Rs 1000. The accused rapist went free since the evidence against him was found inadequate. A huge wave of public sympathy for her, fortunately, got her acquitted. In sharp contrast, a maidservant employed by a landlord family was raped repeatedly by several men of the family. Pregnant, she gave birth to a stillborn baby and her father lodged a case of rape against her employers. The sessions judge acquitted the accused and sentenced her for adultery. These cases vividly illustrate the misogynist logic that underpinned the new laws.

The public presence of women itself was now seen to be sexually charged. The public domain, consequently, was re-masculinised; simultaneously, women's loss of the public world contracted their bargaining power at home. After the *zina* ordinances were passed, families began to hand over defiant or disobedient daughters to the police for punishment. Any man who murdered a woman could either be forgiven by her kinsmen, or else he could make reparations by paying blood money to the victim's family – his crime was now reconfigured as an offence against the family rather than against the state; by contrast, the colonial Penal Code had defined murder as an offence against the state.

As the laws shut the cage upon women, their protests managed to push it open – to an extent. A broad-based Movement for the Restoration of Democracy was born, involving the Shias, the religious minorities, political Muslims, and Muslim religious dissidents. It even included sections of the religious right wing that found the changes offensive to Islam. Angry resistance came particularly from women's organisations like the Karachi-based Shirkat Gah. They called for an all-women's protest forum, the Khawateen Mahaz-e-Amal (Women's Action Front, or WAF), which formed advocacy groups for women victims. This did achieve some measure of success against all the odds and a few proposed laws were, indeed, withheld in face of the forum's public interventions. The WAF used innovative cultural forms to mobilise protests: satire, humorous skits, and *jalsa* (dramatic performances). It attained a relatively broad mass base, drawing in even some urban working-class women. Eventually, in 2006 under the Women's Protection Act, a substantial part of the Hudood Ordinances was withdrawn or changed.

While the class status of Pakistan's modern elite feminists empowered their activism, it also curtailed their reach. With few exceptions, as noted, they had hardly any contact with rural or tribal women, or with urban women labourers. For labouring women Zia's laws did not signify too drastic an assault on their existing basket of rights since their entitlements, legal and material, hardly existed in any case. Factory work had always been gender-segregated, and the lifeworlds of rural women remained fairly untouched by the laws, old or new. Lower-middle-class urban women found it more difficult to join the protests than did their upper- and middle-class comrades who were cushioned by family wealth and support. They stood to face more social ostracism as well as loss of employment.

The WAF could neither fully bridge the class gulf by expanding its social base, nor convince women from the other social segments that the laws spelt grave danger for all of them. The focus on gender abuse alone, important though it was, excluded other vital material problems relating to everyday lives and survival which were often of greater import to subaltern women. The activists' greatest rivals were the formidable religious authorities who spoke in the name of sacred scripture or immemorial custom. Subaltern women found it especially difficult to choose between the two since their restricted lives did receive some solace – material as well as spiritual – from these orthodox custodians.

After Zia's assassination in 1988, it seemed that fresh winds were blowing across Pakistan. Benazir Bhutto won the election that year to become the first woman prime minister of Pakistan. Corruption charges dogged her rule and lost her the 1997 elections; she was assassinated in 2007. Much applauded in the West for her secular feminism, she was valued as a complete antidote to Zia-ul-Haq.

However, since Benazir's pronounced attachment to Western culture went along with a neo-liberal economic order which bore down heavily upon the poor, she strengthened the reactions against both cultural cosmopolitanism and the liberalised economy. The two now appeared complementary in popular understanding. As a backlash against her policies, honour killings spiralled in the 1990s.

Asma Jehangir – prominent feminist-activist – once said, "Islam is no more violent or fanatical than any other religion . . . There are Christian fanatics and Hindu fanatics too – put a gun in the hands of any of them and they will terrorise people."[5] She and her sister Hina Jilani started Pakistan's first female law practice. Most cases that they took on were pro bono. They became High Court advocates in the early 1980s and defended women victims in particularly notorious – hence dangerous – cases of gender abuse.

[5] Cited in Lichter, *Muslim Women Reformers*.

Asma Jahangir was a co-founder of the WAf in 1980 and went to jail after she led a public protest in 1983 against the Hudood laws. In 1986 she and Hina Jilani set up Pakistan's first free legal aid centre. She also founded the Human Rights Commission of Pakistan and became its Secretary General. Though plagued by numerous death threats, she built up an outstanding legal career, defending women as well as bonded and child labourers.

A very different form of women's welfare came to nest within conservative Islamic institutions. Many see in this a variant of Islamic feminism, as something indigenous and rooted in Muslim cultural traditions – and therefore as a contrast with the activism of rights- and equality-oriented feminists. It is necessary to recapitulate a few recent debates on this because several scholars see Islamic orthodoxy as capable of accelerating the aims of earlier women's movements, albeit on a different register. Such pietistic movements have indeed inserted large numbers of lower-middle-class women into political and economic spaces on a scale unimaginable earlier. Women wearing the headscarf have managed to infiltrate traditional male spaces by finding jobs in factories and shops, by working as immigration officers and municipal officials. The women's wing of the Jamaat-i-Islam denounces non-governmental organisations for gender justice but competes with them on the terrain of certain kinds of welfare projects. This is very similar to what has been happening in Iran.

Saba Mahmood and Humeira Iqtidar have problematised the secular feminist criticism of such tendencies. On the other hand Amina Jamal and Afiya Shehrbano Zia deny the seeming dichotomy between secular and Islamic forms of activism. Zia argues that the strategies of "Islamic feminists" who work within an exclusively religious framework tend to hide other feminist self-expressions. She points out that in the 1980s the WAF did seriously debate the place of women's religious identities within movements. There was also an acknowledgement of the empowering potential of religion which deployed progressive interpretations of Islam.

Maybe one should move away from an exclusive search for agency since, demonstrably, agency can flow from right-wing movements as well as from secular-leftist ones. Instead, we need to soberly revaluate the concepts of rights, justice, and equality on their own terms, separating them from their presumed Western origin, for these concepts always develop a life of their own in different contexts and lifeworlds. We need to imagine a world where these ideas have no meaning at all and ask ourselves if that would, indeed, make for a better place for women. On the other hand, while we certainly need to appreciate what faith does to women, we also have to make room for women who want to live lives that are not bounded by faith alone.

Bangladesh: An Outline History

Bangladesh, the third nation-state in the subcontinent, was born after a genocidal war between East and West Pakistan. The war and its aftermath significantly shaped its gender politics.

There had been considerable popular enthusiasm for Pakistan in Eastern Bengal before Partition: Muslim peasants expected a better life once Hindu landlords and moneylenders left eastern Bengal, the middle classes hoped to be rid of Hindu professional and business competition, and an Urdu-speaking elite hoped to dominate the new state. The Urdu elites were deeply contemptuous of Bengali Muslims, whereas the Bengali intelligentsia, proud of its cultural identity, resented Urdu claims to superiority – this intelligentsia included a number of women authors, social workers, and political activists. Most such people moved to East Pakistan, enabling a vibrant gender politics in the new homeland.

Soon, Pakistan instituted a variant of internal colonisation in the East. Even though East Pakistan constituted the majority population of the nation-state and earned the bulk of foreign exchange, it received only one-third of the development funds. The intelligentsia resented the dominance of the Urdu-speaking class which sought to marginalise Bengali. They resented, too, the growing numbers of Punjabis in the army and bureaucracy, and non-Bengali migrants who enjoyed preferential treatment.

A powerful Bengali sub-nationalism soon burgeoned, rapidly displacing the pre-Partition emphasis on a common religious identity. Young students, including women, protested Urdu's status as Pakistan's national language. They formed a Language Action Committee in 1948 which grew into a large movement called Bhasha Andolan (Language Agitation). The government banned the protests but the students continued to march.

On 21 February 1952 a nine-year-old boy, among several other marchers, was killed in police firing at a rally. Outrage exploded and young people – including women – gathered to build a martyr's memorial with their bare hands. Abdul Gaffar Chowdhury composed an iconic protest song: "How can I forget the 21st of February, spattered with my brother's blood?"[6]

The Pakistan government declared martial law in 1958. The East Pakistan media was brought under tight controls and contempt heaped on Bengali – to the point of attacking even Bengali-language signboards, celebrations of Rabindranath Tagore's birthday, and commemorations of the February killings. Bengali Pakistanis began to lose their sense of belonging to the nation. Islam no longer constituted their sole – or even their most significant – identity.

In 1969 the Awami League (AL) leader Sheikh Mujibur Rahman demanded full regional autonomy. Pakistan's dictator Yahya Khan promised general elections, but he faced a serious problem:

---

[6] Murshid, *The Sacred & the Secular*, p. 158.

given East Pakistan's population, the League was bound to emerge as the largest national party in Pakistan. Zulfiqar Ali Bhutto, when consulted about this, said: "We will have to kill some 20,000 people there and all will be well."[7] Tempers in the East flared further when a cyclone ravaged East Pakistan in 1970 and the government was extremely parsimonious with relief measures.

All this assured a massive AL victory in the East as well as an absolute majority of Bengal's victorious political party in Pakistan as a whole. Bhutto offered Mujib a plan for power-sharing while under cover of the negotiations West Pakistan began to secretly fly its troops into the East. Army terror was suddenly unleashed on East Pakistan from 25 March 1971, taking Mujib wholly by surprise.

Sheer horror engulfed the East as genocidal military operations targeted civilians for nine continuous months. Mujib was arrested and flown to West Pakistan. After "Operation Searchlight" finished its gruesome mission, numerous Bengali nationalists had been killed, arrested, or gone into hiding. Pockets of resistance gradually formed across the country and an independent government-in-exile was instituted in April. Defecting soldiers trained the resistance fighters of the Mukti Sena (Liberation Army) – localised and scattered but desperately courageous. Women provided indispensable logistical support. By November 1971 Mukti Sena guerrillas had liberated some areas and the Indian army began operations against Pakistan. In the last days of the war over December, Pakistan launched a final assault: its Al Badr armed gangs rounded up students, teachers, and doctors in Dhaka, blindfolded and shot them dead.

Pakistan was forced to concede defeat and sign a peace treaty with India. Mujib was released in January 1972 and he announced a parliamentary secular, democratic, multi-party government. In March 1973, in the first Bangladesh elections, the AL won

---

[7] Ibid., p. 124.

a stupendous majority, making Mujib supremely self-confident. The moment of triumph did not last long. It was marred by inter-party rivalries, the increasingly despotic conduct of the AL, and the party's failure to manage a devastating famine in 1974. Far too sure of his personal charisma, Mujib tried to outface the opposition by declaring an Emergency in December 1974, thereby suspending all civil and democratic rights. On 15 August 1975 he was assassinated in a midnight strike by the army. Bangladesh came under army rule with General Zia-ur-Rahman as head of state. He launched the Bangladesh Nationalist Party (BNP) in 1978, introduced virtual martial law, elevated Islam over Bengali identity, and amended the Constitution to drop the word "secular".

Zia-ur-Rahman was assassinated in 1981 and succeeded by Lt Gen. Hussain Mohammad Ershad in 1982; the latter declared martial law, suspended the Constitution, and dissolved parliament. Islam formally became the state religion in 1988, cancelling Bangladesh's foundational vision.

The BNP revived under Zia's widow Khaleda Zia. Married at fifteen, and altogether lacking in political experience, she exhibited surprising political acumen. Meanwhile Sheikh Hasina, Mujib's daughter, less conservative and more secular and nationalist than the BNP, rebuilt the battered AL.

Wanting to strip women of their public roles, Ershad rehabilitated fundamentalist Pakistani collaborators. Khaleda and Hasina agreed to form a common platform in 1990, eschewing their rivalries for the moment. Ershad declared an Emergency, but having lost army support he resigned in 1990 and democracy was restored to Bangladesh.

The Bengali identity proved repressive in its own way. The country withheld citizenship status from the descendants of non-Bengali Biharis who had collaborated with Pakistan. Chakma tribal demands for a separate statehood in the Chittagong Hill Tracts were repressed. Kolpona Chakma, also a defender of women's rights, led the Chakma movement.

A women's song captures their aspirations:

Some day my heartland
Will light up in the sun – the hill, the field, this forest
Will be full of light, wonderful light
. . . Mother, we have to go
. . . We have to face bullets.[8]

Gendering War

Bangladesh official figures claim that nearly a million Bengalis lost their lives, several millions their homes, and several thousand women suffered rape. The rape figures are disputed but not the brutalities inflicted on women's bodies. Women were tonsured and mutilated, their corpses were thrown into ditches, and rape survivors were pushed into sex camps to service Pakistani soldiers: East Pakistan's rape camps preceded those at Bosnia and Rwanda. Many women starved to death there and many others had to dig their own graves. Assaults on their bodies continued after the war: the government ordered compulsory abortions for pregnant women from the camps in order to cleanse the nation of "bastard Pakistanis".[9]

In 1972 Basanti Guhathakurta, a political activist whose husband had been assassinated, visited the Jagannath Hall Hostel at Dhaka University. The site had been earmarked for rapes and murders. Blood spatters and pools of dried blood were clearly visible all over the walls and desks: the "stains appearing like sparklers in the night."[10] Nightmarish memories of the war still haunt large numbers of Bangladeshis. Anger against the collaborators, who also represented the forces of "Islamicisation", imparts a strong secular aspect to it. Fundamentalism and gender orthodoxy have nonetheless made a strong comeback in more recent times.

[8] "Songs for an Endangered Motherland", trans. Meghna Guhathakurta, p. 409.
[9] Saikia, *Women, War, and the Making of Bangladesh*, p. 61.
[19] Guhathakurta, *Ekattarer Smriti*, pp. 145–6.

The new government set up rehabilitation centres for rape victims under the Nari Punorbashon (Women's Rehabilitation) programme. In an unusually sensitive move, it honoured raped women as *birangona* (heroines) to restore their dignity and replace the stigma of rape with the status of resistance fighters. It rewarded men who married raped women. But the stigma persisted: several husbands abandoned their wives after pocketing the rewards. Ironically, these awards, widely institutionalised from the 1990s, made it only too easy to identify women who had been raped – in order to ostracise and humiliate them. While some husbands did take back the wives they had abandoned, others remained hostile. They redefined rape as adultery – transferring the responsibility to the victim, and using the idiom of demasculinisation to blame the wife for a perceived offence to themselves: familial cruelty compounded enemy cruelty.

The war and its aftermath had to be countered with multiple institutional initiatives for women victims. The Bangladesh Women's Rehabilitation Organisation was set up in 1972 to attend to war widows and orphans; it became a statutory body in 1975. A National Women's Association began to co-ordinate the relief work of various government and NGO bodies. From the rehabilitation efforts grew a separate Ministry of Women's Affairs in 1978. Paradoxically, the horrors of war cleared a space for women's activism and forced gender issues on state policies.

The Integrated Rural Development Programme set up a Women's Pilot Project for family planning and rural co-operatives. Women paid small sums to become partners in co-operative banks and their savings were deposited in joint accounts. Credit schemes distributed loans to women to fund small enterprises. But the project mistakenly assumed that all rural women were on the same footing and that agrarian class differences did not matter. Women from the richer families came to dominate the schemes: they marginalised and deprived subaltern women.

Culture vs Labour

Scholars wonder if post-war economic modernisation has brought in real social change, or alternatively if conservative traditions have not in fact successfully reinvented themselves in an altered context. Women workers became a familiar sight on the urban landscape from the 1970s, when they travelled to work on rickshaws and buses or on foot. Poorer women poured into construction sites looking for jobs. The garment-manufacturing industry attracted large numbers of young women workers. Widows and abandoned women also constituted a part of the female workforce, even if their proportion was small. Many of them had a better-than-average education. Some lived with their families but a smaller number set up "messes" comprising female residential facilities.

Women workers walking to work constituted a new public visual spectacle – one, ironically, created by normative compulsions: they walked because they wanted to avoid using public transport, where they were forced into close proximity with men. Quite a few experienced violence from street *mostan*s (goons). Factory work, moreover, was gruelling, even life-threatening. Each shift stretched over eleven or twelve hours of continuous work, and whenever the demand for products peaked women had to work overnight in cramped conditions.

Social change was nonetheless visible: women were free of their absolute domestic confinement, they walked through mixed thoroughfares, they earned their own income working under non-kin male supervision. Would these changes indicate breaks with purdah rules, a confrontation between tradition and modernity? Some see the break as powered by the conventions of decorum: women workers continued to follow modest dress codes and deportment. So this variant of the modern depended on the persistence of tradition, and factory and culture shaped and reshaped each other in a symbiotic manner. Dina Siddiqi describes this as renegotiation. Women workers do not chat after their working hours, and scrupulously avoid male workers. The workplace, too, maintains a gendered division of labour. Sarah White observed a similar trend among women agricultural workers who modulated older gender practices but did not abandon them.

As elsewhere, family planning measures achieved striking success despite religious doubts, ensuring a marked decline in total fertility rates. Urban areas fared better as they enjoyed much greater access to contraceptives, and white-collar husbands were readier to use them than were sharecroppers and rural agricultural labourers. Educated wives had lower birth rates. Kabeer warns, however, that Bangladesh has been the dumping ground for several birth-control technologies which are inadequately tested or are even banned in their countries of origin. Islamic inheritance and dower rules are often ignored in practice, thus depriving subaltern women of independent resources. Though Bangladesh records less dowry deaths than India, domestic violence is just as widespread.

Gender relations, especially in rural areas, were significantly reordered from the late 1970s when the limits to government interventions became abundantly clear: they failed to resolve the problems of acute mass poverty, the devastating damages of war, and recurrent natural diasasters.

Foreign aid therefore became crucial. It was readily available, the Western powers being keen to neutralise possible Soviet inroads with their own aid agencies. Aid tripled between the 1970s and the 1990s, and the donor regime pressurised the government to allow foreign investments and privatise key economic sectors. This aggravated subaltern distress, but from the 1980s non-state actors began to exercise a profound impact on gender relations. F.H. Abed, a UK resident of Bangladeshi origin, founded the BRAC (Bangladesh Rural Advancement Committee) in Sylhet as a humanitarian relief organisation in 1972. By the 1990s it had expanded into multiple welfare sectors, from health to university education. Fundamentalists detested this, fearing the consequent rural female empowerment.

Muhammad Yunus founded the Grameen Bank in the 1970s as a research project for poverty alleviation through small credit-delivery schemes. The targets were primarily poor women without collateral; when the bank was properly set up in 1983, almost all the borrowers were women. Eventually it branched out into diverse enterprises, from mobile phones to textile mills. Yunus received the Nobel Peace Prize in 2006.

The donor- and NGO-driven economy is controversial. Some criticise its lack of public accountability, others because it relieves the government of much-needed investments in welfare. Rich peasants and village religious leaders (*matbor*s), on the other hand, loathe the potential of NGOs for loosening the rural social fabric, especially its gender and class structures. They particularly resent women's participation in the weekly Grameen meetings which disrupt their domestic responsibilities.

Political Women

Bangladesh women have a long and robust political lineage which goes back to late colonial times. A short sketch of the life of Sufiya Kamal, a noted literary and political figure, may help understand the makings of women's politics.

Sufiya (1911–2002) was a born rebel. Coming from a conservative aristocratic family where Bengali usage was avoided and women's education abhorred, she dressed like a boy to attend school. She also loved Bengali literature, which had been forbidden to women. She was married off when she was twelve, but fortunately to an enlightened husband. He died early, and she later married yet another supportive man. Her literary abilities put her in touch with towering contemporary figures like Rabindranath Tagore and Kazi Nazrul Islam. Teaching at a Calcutta Corporation school, she wrote poetry, fiction, and children's literature. Though widowed a second time with several children, she worked hard for riot relief in 1946.

She settled in Dhaka in 1948, where she worked for several women's organisations. She became a founding member of the influential Mahila Parishad in 1970. Though never a Communist Party member, she was associated with the pro-Soviet intelligentsia and always opposed dictators though they were keen to have her on board because of her great public stature. She supported Ayub Khan's family-law reforms even as she criticised his repression. She took grave risks during the war when she organised secret logistic support for freedom fighters. After Independence she remained an inspirational icon for all women's organisations, despite her differences with many. Such interweaving of literary and political activism is apparent in the careers of several other Bangladeshi activists.

Maleka Begum's autobiography reveals the variegated trajectory of women's politics. She was born to an orthodox father and a housewife mother who had borne twelve children. The mother harboured secret communist leanings and helped her communist son and daughter-in-law. Maleka studied with liberal Hindu women teachers like the anti-colonial activist Leela Nag. She participated in the Bhasha Andolon as well as in literary movements in the early years of Pakistan. Like-minded women like Noor Jehan Murshid, Badrunnissa, and Doulatennechha were elected to the provincial assembly at this time.

Women's organisations proliferated from the late 1950s: agitating for female employment rights, family law courts, special courts for juvenile offenders, and children's rights – their parallel concerns for children is an unusual feature of women's activism.

The communist movement splintered after the Sino-Soviet split and the 1965 Indo-Pakistan war, and women, too, took different sides on these issues. Though not combatants themselves during the liberation struggle, middle-class women had provided critical logistical help to freedom fighters. Village women, too, resisted the army with kitchen knives, hammers, scythes. After Independence, Basanti Guhathakurta, Nilima Ibrahim, Noorjehan Murshid, and many others threw themselves into relief work. The Mahila Parishad strengthened women like Sonabhan, impoverished mother of several infants whose husband was killed by the Pakistan army. Orthodox village bosses objected when she took up a job; she retorted that they should then feed her family for the rest of their lives. The Parishad also demanded reserved constituencies for women candidates.

The Parishad presented Mujib with a Sixteen-Point programme for women's education and vocational training, anti-dowry measures, and equal inheritance rights. Registrations of marriage and divorce were made legally compulsory in 1974.

Atrocities against women began to mount under the orthodox backlash that followed Mujib's death: Saleha, for instance, was killed in 1978 over dowry issues. The AL and the BNP together set up an anti-dowry committee. The Parishad formed a special Nari Niryatan Protirodh Committee to protest the horrendous rape of infants. A new wave, however, unsettled its unity as its younger members became self-aware feminists who objected to persistent mansplaining by their male leaders. Their concept of patriarchy surprised the Parishad. "That was the first time I heard of words like struggle against patriarchal controls," recalled Maleka.[11]

Several feminist organisations had emerged by the late 1980s, led by Shirin Huq, Nasreen Huq, Meghna Guhathakurta, Shamim Akhtar, and others. They formed groups like Sanhati, Rupantar, and Naripakkha to agitate for women's control over their own bodies, their right to sexual desire. They expressed solidarity with sex-workers' struggles against pimps and agents. When some men demanded that mosques replace brothels and offered sex workers alternative employment, the latter refused: the work

---

[11] Begum, *Nari Andolaner*, p. 142.

offered was nowhere as well paid as sex work. Feminists also mobilised the media to report on the abuse of women domestic workers. Older activists often found their campaigns and their political vocabulary difficult to digest and a generation gap sometimes divided the women's movement.

Political crises nonetheless smoothened internal differences from time to time, and an unusual broad front was formed in 1974. This was the Aikyabaddha Nari Samaj (United Front of Women), with nineteen member organisations comprising disparate elements: business groups, professional bodies, the Lions Club, and left-wing women's organisations. It opposed the new Islamic designation instituted for Bangladesh. But older women often proved more cautious. When Naripakkha brought a suit against the nomenclature of Islamic Bangladesh, a more moderate Parishad desisted, being wary of a possible offence to faith. When the feminist writer Taslima Nasrin was threatened with a fatwa in 1993, the Parishad again stood aside: "We could not accept her judgements, we thought she pushed back the movement."[12] Taslima Nasrin, outspoken about the religious roots of patriarchy, had written a book about the anti-Hindu conflagration in Bangladesh.

The Mahila Parishad was the largest women's organisation in Bangladesh, with a membership of 30,000 in 1980. Closely associated with the AL, it professed secular values and gender equity. It remained restricted, however, to the urban middle classes and failed to adequately address the livelihood issues of subaltern women. Its relative political moderation also limited its reach among younger and militant feminists.

Gender and Faith

The 1972 Constitution had defined Bangladesh as a secular state committed to gender equity. It banned the Jamaat and Muslim

[12] Ibid., p. 180.

League for collaborating with Pakistan's forces. Fatwas issued by religious establishments no longer carried legal or constitutional force, though they continued to influence popular conduct.

Zia-ur-Rahman (r. 1977–81) replaced the word "secularism" in the Constitution with " absolute faith in Allah". Simultaneously, he rehabilitated the banned organisations, which were now free to mobilise supporters.

Around 1988 there began a systematic Islamicisation of the state. Unlike Pakistan's Hudood era, however, this did not see substantive legal changes and the civil, criminal, and penal codes remained fairly intact. Personal and family laws, too, continued much as before. Nor were the verdicts of the *quadi*s or *mufti*s (consultants and adjudicators of Islamic laws) made legally binding.

Some laws even contradicted the scriptures: though the Quran prescribes physical punishment for adultery, this found no place in the criminal laws. Yet a strong social conviction assumed that the wife is the husband's personal property, and adultery charges were therefore frequent. The definition of adultery proved highly elastic and cruel physical punishment – branding or even death – made a sickening return from the 1990s, especially in the rural areas. The social underbelly of the legal-constitutional regime continued to be largely moulded by orthodox morality.

The state's response was Janus-faced: it did not overtly challenge the religious opposition but nor did it change the laws or curtail the NGOs. Zia-ur-Rahman, in fact, tried to promote a sort of "progressive" Islam. In the wake of the International Women's Year he formed the Bangladesh Jatiya Mahila Sangstha (Nationalist Women's Organisation), reserved seats for women in parliament and government jobs, and promoted subsidiary occupations to help poor rural women: cattle-rearing, home-based sewing, and kitchen gardens.

An interesting split therefore marked the gender domain: the woman's place in the household went unchallenged but she did acquire an enlarged public and economic role. Religious parties reacted strongly against emancipatory progress and the Jamaat began to insist on total female seclusion and strict domesticity.

The state diverged from rural development and poverty alleviation schemes when Western NGOs pressurised the government to remove its rural subsidies and focus on industries. Jamaat and other conservative agencies stepped into the breach. The privatisation of national resources sometimes made them the sole support structure for the rural poor and Jamaat combined rural welfare with proselytising for a return to pristine Islam. This was strengthend by Saudi inputs into scholarships, vocational training, and employment channels. While these excluded women, they nonetheless skilfully mobilised young, educated women as recruiters for their fronts: their religious messages had penetrated the universities. Ershad, who was president until 1990, also imposed severe dress codes on elite women, and gave mosques and religious schools tax benefits and exemptions. He refused to ratify several clauses in the UN charter on inheritance, divorce, marriage, and child custody.

The consequences were abysmal. In January 1993, in Sylhet District, 22-year-old Nurjehan was dragged out of her home. She had married a second time, years after her divorce from her first husband, and the local imam had duly solemnised the second marriage. But the villagers insisted that the divorce was not formalised and that the new marriage was adulterous. Under *salish* (a local council of village notables) recommendations, husband and wife were stood up in a waist-deep pit and pelted with stones 101 times; her elderly parents were also stoned. Nurjehan committed suicide.

How did the orthodox backlash gain traction – especially as Jamaat and similar groups had invited enormous popular revulsion after the war? State rehabilitation certainly aided their power, but deeper social convictions also helped and some scholars find in this the perennial tradition *vs* modernity confrontation. S.M. Shamsul Alam, however, disputes the reality of either a pristine tradition or an essential modernity, arguing that both may assume diverse forms, depending on the context. Since the Iranian revolution of 1979, conservative Islamic Shia movements pitted a fundamentalist form of Islam against Western modernity in their respective countries. Wahhabism, on the other hand, also became a formidable force in the Muslim world. Diasporic Bengali Muslims from the Middle East channellised these influences back home.

On the ground, however, local conditions have proven decisive: the stances of local elites, the extent of poverty, and varied community customs offering multiple options. Subaltern women may choose orthodox values, believing that resistance does not stand a chance. Orthodoxy, on the other hand, may provide them with the resources that the neo-liberal state has withheld.

Maimuna Huq underlines the failures of the secular state. The privatisation of education and the retraction of rural welfare blocked alternative sources of succour for the poor and created a space for orthodox religious initiatives. Nor have all conservatives been entirely fundamentalist. Some do address women's insecurities in public places, though always on their own terms. They underline the media stereotyping of modern women which emphasises their physical attractions, thereby enhancing their insecurity outside their homes. They offer instead their own version of gender justice, advising women that obedience to conservative mores helps women navigate everyday problems and movements better. Paradoxically, women themselves invest in conservatism to win male respect. Women pilgrims to Mecca – *hajji*s – enjoy considerable domestic status. Pietistic orthodoxy, therefore, becomes hegemonic rather than merely coercive, making women complicit with their own docility and subordination.

Muslim laws are often qualified by local practices. The *mehr* entitlement remains largely on paper and divorce is a protracted business, the woman being eligible for alimony only for three successive menstrual periods after her divorce. Post-divorce, the mother has custody over a son until he is seven, and over a daughter up to her puberty. The man is allowed a maximum of four wives at a time: an Act of 1961, however, made the formal consent of the first wife and of the union chairman mandatory for a second marriage. The daughter receives only half of her brother's share of inheritance. Bangladeshi feminists agitated for a gender-just Uniform Civil Code in the 1980s and the early 1990s. When the communalised forces of the religious right became stronger, they began to fear that the beleaguered religious minorities might see the Uniform Civil Code as a majoritarian imposition – gender equality could degrade their religious freedom. The demand for uniform gender just laws was thus shelved.

Hindu women could not initiate divorce; their marriage did not require civil registration, and polygamy was allowed. Dayabhaga laws were cited to deprive daughters of inheritance and wives of absolute rights to the husband's property. Archaic religious norms, long overhauled in India, remained in place, revealing a compact between majority and minority patriarchies.

Christian and Buddhist laws suffered the same fate. Matrilineal tribals are under pressure to conform to patriliny. All women, however, share the provisions of the Dowry Prohibition Act of 1980; the Cruelty to Women (Deterrent Punishment) Ordinance of 1983; and the 2000 law to prevent the oppression of women and children.

Political correctness, even if notional, has entered political discourses. Both the AL and the BNP talk of *narir khamotayan* (women's empowerment), while the Jamaat, interestingly, uses the term *adhikar* (rights), even if defined in terms of the sharia. Mainstream parties accept the UN conventions on gender, though the Jamaat acknowledges the UN Convention on Child Rights alone. It refuses to criticise or recognise gender inequality.

Military rule clearly colluded with conservative, even fundamentalist, forces, and neo-liberal privatisation drives – undertaken by relatively secular governments – have pushed subaltern women to shelter under pietism, which offers them at least a few opportunities.

References and Suggested Readings for Chapter 9

Abdullah, Abu, "Social Change and Modernization", in Rounaq Jahan, ed., *Bangladesh: Promise and Performance*, Dhaka: The University Press, 2000.

Afshar, Haleh, *Islam and Feminisms: An Iranian Case Study*, London: Macmillan, 1998.

Ali, Kamran Asdar, *Communism in Pakistan: Political and Class Activism, 1947–1972*, London: I.B. Tauris & Co., 2015.

Ali, Shaheen Sardar, "Women of the North Western Frontier Provinces", in Mian N. Nazir and Saiyeda Zia Jalaly, eds, *Participation of Women in Rural Economic Activities in North Western Frontier Provinces*, Islamabad: Ministry of Women Development, Government of Pakistan, 1987.

Amin, Sonia Nishat, *Ekattarer Smriti*, ed. Basanti Guhathakurta, Dhaka: The University Press, 1991.

Barton, Mukti, *Scripture and Empowerment for Liberty and Justice: The Experience of Christian and Muslim Women in Bangladesh*, Bristol: University of Bristol, Centre for Comparative Studies in Religion and Gender, 1999.

Begum, Maleka, *Nari Andoloner Paanch Dashak*, Dhaka: Anya Prakashak, 2002.

Begum, Maleka, ed., *Rajpathe Janapathe Sufiya Kamal*, Dhaka: Osmani Ghani Agami Prakashani, 1997.

Bose, Sharmila, "Anatomy of Violence: Analysis of Civil War in East Pakistan in 1971", *Economic and Political Weekly*, 8 October 2005.

Bose, Sharmila, "Losing the Victims: Problems of Using Women as Weapons in Recounting the Bangladesh War", *Economic and Political Weekly*, 22 September 2007.

Carroll, Lucy, "The Pakistan Federal Shariat Court, Section 4 of the Family Laws Ordinance and the Orphaned Grandchild", *Islamic Law and Society*, vol. 9, issue 1, 2002.

Cleland, John, et al., *The Determinants of Reproductive Change in Bangladesh: Success in a Challenging Environment*, Washington, DC: The World Bank, 1994.

Feldman, Shelley, "(Re)Presenting Islam: Manipulating Gender, Shifting State Practices, and Class Frustration in Bangladesh", in Patricia Jefferson and Amrita Basu, eds, *Appropriating Gender: Women's*

Activism and Politicised Religion in South Asia, New York and London: Routledge, 1998.

Guhathakurta, Meghna, and Willem van Schendel, eds, *The Bangladesh Reader: History, Culture, Politics*, Durham: Duke University Press, 2013.

Guneratne, Arjun, and Anita M. Weiss, eds, *Pathways to Power: The Domestic Politics of South Asia*, Maryland: Rowman and Littlefield, 2014.

Hartmann, Betsy, and James Boyce, *A Quiet Violence: View from a Bangladesh Village*, London: Zed, 1983.

Iqtidar, Humeira, *Secularizing Islam? Jamaat e Islami and Jamaat Dawa in Urban Pakistan*, Chicago: University of Chicago Press, 2011.

Jahan, Rounaq, *Bangladesh Politics: Problems and Issues*, Dhaka: The University Press, 1980.

Jahan, Rounaq, ed., *Bangladesh: Promise and Performance*, Dhaka: The University Press, 2000.

Jahangir, Asma, and Hina Jilani, *The Hudood Ordinances: A Divine Sanction?* Lahore: Rohtas Books, 1990.

Jamal, Amina, *Jamaat e Islami: Women in Pakistan – Vanguard of a New Modernity?*, New York: Syracuse University Press, 2013.

Jeffrey, Patricia, *Frogs in a Well: Indian Women in Purdah*, Delhi: Vikas Publishing House, 1979.

Kabeer, Naila, "Minus Lives: Women of Bangladesh", in *Change: International Reports – Women and Society*, London: British Library (undated, c. 1983).

Kabeer, Naila, "The Quest for National Identity: Women, Islam and the State in Bangladesh", in Deniz Kandiyoti, ed., *Women, Islam and the State*, London: Macmillan, 1991.

Lichter, Ida, *Muslim Women Reformers: Inspiring Voices Against Oppression*, New York: Prometheus Books, 2009.

Mahmood, Saba, *Politics of Piety: The Islamic Revival and the Feminist Subject*, Princeton: Princeton University Press, 2005.

Maududi, S. Abul Ala, *Purdah and the Status of Women in Islam*, Lahore, 1962.

Mookerjee, Nayanika, *The Spectral Wound: Sexual Violence, Public Memories and the Bangladesh War of 1971*, New Delhi: Zubaan, 2015.

Murshid, Tazeen M., *The Sacred & the Secular: Bengali Muslim Discourses, 1871–1977*, Calcutta: Oxford University Press, 1995.

Naher, Ainoon, "Rich Peasant Resistance to Development Organisations", in Meghna Guhathakurta and Willem van Schendel, *The Bangladesh Reader: History, Culture, Politics*, Durham: Duke University Press, 2013.

Nazneen, Sohela, "Men Aboard? Movement for a Uniform Family Code in Bangladesh", in Mulki Al-Sharmani, ed., *Feminist Activism, Women's Rights and Legal Reform*, London: Zed Books, 2012.

Rouse, Shahnaz, *Shifting Body Politics: Gender, Nation, State in Pakistan*, Delhi: Women Unlimited, 2006.

Rozario, Santi, "Gender Dimensions of Rural Change", in Kazi Ali Toufique and Cate Turton, eds, *Hands Not Land: How Livelihoods are Changing in Rural Bangladesh*, Dhaka: BIDS, 2002.

Saikia, Yasmin, *Women, War and the Making of Bangladesh: Remembering 1971*, Delhi: Women Unlimited, 2011.

Shehabuddin, Elora, "Contesting the Illicit: Gender and the Politics of Fatwas in Bangladesh", in Therese Saliba, Carolyn Allen, and Judith A. Howard, eds, *Gender, Politics and Islam*, Chicago: University of Chicago Press, 2002.

Sheikh, Farzana, *Making Sense of Pakistan*, London: Hurst, 2018.

Siddiqi, Dina, "Discipline and Protect: Women Factory Workers in Bangladesh", *Grassroots*, vol. 1, no. 2.

Talukdar, Maniruzzaman, *The Bangladesh Revolution and Its Aftermath*, Dhaka: The University Press, 1980.

Toor, Sadia, *The State of Islam: Culture and Cold War in Pakistan*, London: Pluto Press, 2011.

van Schendel, Willem, *A History of Bangladesh*, Cambridge: Cambridge University Press, 2009.

White, Sarah, *Arguing with the Crocodile: Gender and Class in Bangladesh*, Dhaka: The University Press, 1992.

Zia, Afiya Shehrbano, "Feminist Slogans: Men, Money, Mullahs and the Military", *Feminist Review*, issue 91, 2009.

Index

Abdullah, Sheikh 120, 294
Abed, F.H. 338
abortion 92, 123, 188, 248, 335; compulsory 335; risky 92; sex-selective 248
Abul Fazl 14; *Akbarnama* of 14
Acharya, Pandit Sudarshan 234
Act: III of 1870 58; of 1872 61; of 1836 19; of 1891 61, 67, 69; of 1923 69, 208; of 1930 72, 208; Act XV, July 1856 (to Remove all Legal Obstacles to Marriage of Hindoo Widows) 53
activism 90, 99, 102, 113, 119, 144, 158, 169–70, 184, 188, 256, 265, 280, 283, 285, 290, 293, 305, 319, 328, 330, 336, 340; constructive 265, 293; Gandhian 169–70; political 184, 283, 305, 319, 340; public 99, 319
activists: political 121, 156, 189, 331, 335; women 72, 100, 106, 156, 160, 179, 246, 284, 315, 323–4
actors/actresses 8, 61, 148, 236–7, 302, 305, 338
Ad Dharam 202
Adi Brahmos 60
Adi Hindu 202, 291

Adi Samaj 59
Adivasi 28, 30–1, 140, 244, 267–8; gender relations 267, 268; quotas for 244; women 267
adoption 26, 275; Bill 277
adult franchise 159, 187
adultery 20, 33, 42, 91, 124, 214–15, 277, 325–7, 336, 343
Afghanistan 115, 324
Afiya Shehrbano 330
Africa 107, 169, 247
Agarkar, Gopal Ganesh 87, 90
Agarwal, Bina 259; *Field of One's Own* 259
Age of Consent Act of 1891 61, 69
age: of cohabitation 66; of consent within marriage 64–5, 67, 72–3, 95, 282; of conjugal cohabitation 63; of marriage 63, 72–3, 95
Agnes, Flavia 279
agrarian: depression 68; movements 257; sector 245
agricultural sector 252, 253, 256
Ahmad, Nazir 111; *Mir'at al Arus* of 111
Ahmadiyyas 323
Ahmedabad 136–7
Aikyabaddha Nari Samaj 342

INDEX

Akbar, Mughal emperor 13–14
akhlaq (conduct) 13–14
alcohol/alcoholism 199, 288, 289, 293, 325
Ali, Ameer (Bengali Muslim judge) 115, 323
Ali, Mumtaz 5, 37, 110, 114
Ali, Sharifa Hamid 39, 117
Ali, Syed Mumtaz 113
Aligarh 110, 113, 120; Women's College 120; Zenana Madrasa 120
All India Democratic Women's Association (AIDWA) 286–7
All India Muslim Education Conference 120
All India Muslim Ladies' Conference 117
All India Trade Union Congress 252
All India Women's Association 117
All India Women's Conference (AIWC) 73, 144, 156, 160, 209, 284, 286
All India Women's Education and Social Conference 72
All Pakistan Women's Association (APWA) 320, 322
All-India Shia Personal Law Board 278
Ambedkar, B.R. 74, 107, 160, 244, 275–6, 291–2, 299; convert to Buddhism 292; *Riddles in Hinduism* 107
Amended Special Marriages Act 71
American Baptist missionaries 83
American women 100, 195–6, 257
Ammaiyar, Narayani 107
Ammaiyar, Ramamirtham 107
Ammaiyar, Thamaraikanni 107

Ammini, E.J. 42
Anandamoyee Ma 198
Andaman: Cellular Jail 173; Islands 184, 204, 215, 253
Anderson, Benedict 220
Andhra: Communist Party 285; Mahila Sabha 284; Mahila Sangham 285; Pradesh 252, 282
Anglo-Indians 145, 186
Anjuman-e-Khawatin (Islamic Women's Association), Calcutta 121
Anthropological Survey of India 31
anti-alcohol agitations 289
anti-Brahman politics 96
"anti-buggery" laws 20
anti-caste discourses 70
anti-colonial: struggles 95, 168, 242; movements 72, 149, 155–6, 160–2, 171, 181; political rhetoric 66; turbulence 73; upsurges 121, 153, 160
anti-dowry: activism 280; committee 341
anti-Hindi campaigns 107
antisemitism 208
Anumarana 46
apostasy 38–9
armed forces 32, 285, 293–4
Armed Forces Special Powers Act (AFSPA) 293, 295
art 64, 68, 121, 137, 166, 220–1, 289, 301, 303; local forms of 221
artisans 17, 166
artistes 134, 148
Arunachal Pradesh 32, 292
Arunima, G. 68
Arya Mahila Sabha, Poona 99, 234

Arya Samaj 56, 65, 104, 196, 266
Asaf Ali, Aruna 155, 167–8
asceticism/ascetics 12, 100, 223
Ashapurna Debi 162, 297–8;
    Pratham Pratishruti 298;
    Subarnalata 162
Asiatic Society 221
Assam 31, 89, 111, 138, 148, 172, 254, 292, 294, 296
assembly elections of 1937 168
associations 45, 59, 63, 69, 70, 84–5, 87, 90, 94–5, 97, 102, 107, 117, 121, 126, 156, 158, 175, 198, 265, 284, 290
asylums 215–17
Athavale, Parvatibai 102, 226;
    Majhi Kahani 226; travels to Western lands 102
Atmiya Sabha 59
Aurangzeb, Mughal emperor 12
author/s 71, 114, 147, 213, 223–5, 231–2, 298–9, 299–300, 331
autobiography(ies) 55, 114, 147, 213, 223–6, 230–1, 299–300, 340; Bengali 224–5; left-wing 232, 299; Malayalam 231; Marathi 225; study of 230
autonomy 121, 181, 205, 246, 255, 260, 267, 332; day-to-day 181; lack of 260; sexual 246
Awami League (AL) 315, 332–4, 341–2, 346
Azad, Chandra Shekhar 174, 230
Azhagiyar, Munnagara 107

Babri Mosque 247, 279

Bachchan: Amitabh 305; Harivansh Rai 230
Balasaraswati 17
Balfour, Margaret 144
Balmiki caste 258
Bande Mataram 162
Bangladesh 1, 32, 202, 244, 313, 331, 333–6, 338–9, 342–3; anti-Hindu conflagration in 342; Bangladesh Nationalist Party (BNP) 334, 341, 346; Bangladesh Women's Rehabilitation Organisation 336; Constitution 334, 342–3; creation of 244; Emergency in December 1974 334; Islam and 334; women in 339
Baptist missionaries 47, 48, 83, 103
Basanti Devi 161, 174
Bauls 202, 203
Begum Hazrat Mahal 155–6
Begum Rokeya Sakhawat Hossain 119–21, 126, 232; "Amader Abanati" (Our Decline) 119; critique of religion 119; "Nurse Nellie" 126; *Sultana's Dream* 232
Begum Sultan Jahan of Bhopal 126; *Al Hijab or Why Purdah is Necessary* 126
beliefs 19, 29, 49–51, 98, 102, 122–3, 202, 268, 271, 306, 313, 318
Bengal 9, 15, 25–6, 32, 40, 44–50, 53, 55, 58, 61–4, 85, 88–9, 95, 104, 118, 121, 132, 135–7, 139, 141–5, 148–9, 161, 164–5, 167, 173–6, 180, 183–5, 198, 202, 211, 216,

222, 236, 246, 251–4, 258, 261, 265, 267, 273, 284, 286–8, 331, 333; caste genealogies in 15; census of 1931 135; Bengal Corporation Scavengers' Union 144; famine of 1943 180, 184; Presidency 45, 47, 95; theatre 148, 236
Bengali: Hindus 64; Hindu widows 91; Muslims 66, 115, 118, 331, 345; school of Hindu law 46; Shudra castes 62; upper-castes 102; women 19, 96–7, 145, 290
Bentinck, Governor General 49–50
Bethune, J.F. Drinkwater 103
Bhagat, Anandibai 109
Bhagat, Manjul 299
Bhagavad Gita 9
Bhandarkar, Ramakrishna Gopal 87, 94, 100–1
Bharatiya Janata Party (BJP) 246–7
Bhasha Andolan (Language Agitation) 332, 340
Bhatia, Bela 273
Bhatt, Chandi Prasad 256, 289
Bhatt, Ela 265
Bhattacharya, Malini 287
Bhil women 81
Bhopal 115–16, 126
Bhore, Parvati 179
Bhutto, Benazir 329
Bhutto, Zulfiqar Ali 315–16, 318, 333
Bi Amman 161
bi-gender 203
Bible 83, 108–9
bigamy 42, 60, 277
Bihar 47, 50, 141, 166, 168, 178, 180, 207, 259, 267, 288
Bihishti Zewar (Heavenly Treasure) 111
Binodini Dasi 237
biographies 213, 234
Birla, G.D. 95, 167
birth control 122–4, 264–65, 338
boldness 121, 224–5, 299, 302
Bollywood 15, 301, 303, 305
Bombay 36, 44, 48, 56, 65, 69, 86–90, 92–3, 95, 97, 101, 108, 116, 124, 136–8, 141–2, 148, 155, 167, 178–9, 185, 207–8, 248, 281, 287, 301, 303–4; Act 207; cotton mills 136–8, 142; film industry 304; High Court 56; Legislative Council 87; mercantile associations 69; municipality 207; Presidency 36, 44, 48, 86–7, 95; textile workers 179; University 148
Borade, Savitribai 292
Bose, Kadambini 145
Bose, Nandalal 238
Bose, Subhas Chandra 155, 160, 211, 300
Bosu, Bani 262
Brahmanical: dietary inhibitions 102; order 199
Brahmans 15, 26–7, 46–7, 52, 54–5, 62, 67–8, 86, 88, 90–1, 96, 98, 102, 108, 124, 179, 194, 198–200, 215, 243, 270, 273, 297; Bengali 215; Chitpavan 98; Maharashtrian 179, 243; orthodox 90; pandits 15, 26, 47; priests 194; widows 46, 91, 96, 102

Brahmo/s 55, 59–60, 64, 87, 145, 167
bride/s 32–3, 54, 62, 83, 111, 249, 267–8, 317; price 32–3, 83, 267–8, 317
Britain 18–19, 21, 24, 158, 210–11; homosexual practices in 211; legal-judicial habits 24
British: army 49, 154; rule 55, 211, 242; women 19, 107, 144, 148, 187, 210–11; Crown 29; government 49, 116, 201; India 4, 31, 201; Indian Association 63–4, 156
brothels 185, 206–8, 341
Broughton, G.M. 139, 144
Buddhism/Buddhist 26, 60, 70–1, 291, 292; nuns 11, 17
Burma 184, 186
burqa 318
Butler, Judith 235
behaviour 10, 12–13, 16, 29, 165, 185, 194, 201, 212; female 12–13; ideal 10, 12; sexual 16, 201

Calcutta 26, 40, 54–6, 63–4, 69, 82, 85, 88, 95, 99, 103–4, 120–1, 126, 141–7, 155, 157, 164–5, 170, 176, 178, 184, 195, 198, 210, 222–3, 228, 236, 254, 261–2, 269, 271–2, 287, 302, 339; Calcutta Corporation 126, 143, 339; Calcutta Female Juvenile Society 103; Calcutta High Court 40, 56, 271; Calcutta Marwari Association 95; Calcutta Medical College 145–6

Cama, Madame Bhikaji 158
capitalism 6, 25, 86, 220
Carpenter, Mary 63, 94, 144
caste(s) 2, 8–12, 14–18, 25–6, 28, 33, 37, 41, 44–7, 50, 54–7, 59, 61–2, 65, 67–71, 74–5, 81, 83–6, 88, 92–3, 97, 99, 101–3, 105, 107–9, 121–2, 124, 126, 132–5, 139–40, 143–5, 147, 149, 156, 160–1, 166, 168, 177–9, 181–2, 201–2, 205, 211, 213–14, 216–17, 220, 230–1, 235–7, 243–4, 253–4, 257–8, 261–2, 264, 267, 270–1, 273, 275, 279, 283–4, 289, 291–2, 299–300, 303; critiques of 182; differences 54; divisions 201–2, 300; high 10, 12, 15, 56, 83–6, 92, 99, 108, 134, 145, 147, 156, 166, 237; low 9, 12, 14–15, 17–18, 56, 74, 99, 103, 108–9, 122, 132, 139–40, 182, 201, 214, 216, 231, 253–4; lower 12, 15, 92–3, 109, 133, 161, 178; Mahar 291–3, 299; practices 109, 202, 235; scavenger 126, 144; Shudra 15, 46–7, 62, 86, 92, 99, 166; status 16, 44; untouchable 14, 41, 93, 105, 143; upper 9, 12, 14, 33, 50, 54–5, 61–2, 67, 84, 86, 92, 102–3, 105, 107, 133–4, 143–4, 149, 156, 166, 181, 202, 213, 236, 253, 261–2, 270, 273, 284, 299
celibacy 168, 173–4, 176
Cellular Jail, Andaman Islands 173, 215
censuses: 1871–2 33, 247; 1901 147; 1911 135; 1921 122;

1931 145; 1991 248, 250, 272; 2001 250
Central India 81, 135, 153–4, 186
chador 319, 327
Chandal 134, 217
chastity 15, 54, 62, 106, 169, 171, 173, 231, 234–5, 280, 326
Chattopadhyay, Bankimchandra 228; *Anandamath* 228
Chattopadhyay, Saratchandra 230; *Pather Dabi* 230
Chauhan, Subhadra Kumari 155
Chhatra-Mazdoor-Yuva Sangharsh Vahini 259
Chhattisgarh 16, 135
child: childbearing 66, 264; childbirth 91, 125–6, 133, 140–1, 146, 205, 233; childcare 139, 234, 255, 265; custody 344; childhood 9, 44, 87, 113–14, 134, 222, 261; labour 136, 254, 297, 330; marriage 12, 33, 44, 62–3, 65, 71–3, 84, 89, 98, 104, 122, 149, 156–7, 169, 197, 268, 292, 326; mothers 66; rearing 89; widows 47, 93, 170, 179; wives 63–4, 197
Chipko Movement 256, 289
Chittagong 173, 175–6, 334
Christianity 40–4, 81, 95, 100–1, 103, 107, 171, 195–7, 316; conversions to 40, 43, 44, 81, 195
Christian/s 26, 33, 40, 41, 42, 43, 44, 49, 60, 64, 70, 82, 94, 98, 103, 105, 107, 108, 109, 111, 126, 145, 148, 156, 186, 222, 228, 231, 277, 288, 302, 318, 319, 322, 329, 346; laws 41, 42; marriage rules 42; missionaries 33, 105, 111, 222; Personal Laws 43; reforms 107; women 42–3, 108, 156, 318
Chughtai, Ismat 214, 233; "Lihaf" 233
cinema 15, 82, 123, 148, 185–6, 220, 236, 248, 301–5; *Alam Ara* 148; anti-prostitution propaganda 185; *Aparajito* 301; *Apur Sansar* 301; art 301; Bengali 302; *Bobby* 304–5; Bombay 301; *Charulata* 301; *Coolie* 304; *Debi* 301; *Do Beegha Zameen* 304; documentary 82, 248; *Ek Duje Ke Liye* 304; *Garam Hava* 301; "high art" 303; *Hum Aapke Hain Kaun* 304; *Kisan Kanya* 304; *Kismet* 185; Malayalam 302; *Mother India* 71, 304; *Mughal-e-Azam* 304; "new wave" 303; *Padmavat* 15; *Pather Panchali* 301; *Pyaasa* 304; *Sholay* 305; Urdu-language 301; *World Before Her* 248
citizenship 271, 301, 334
civil: disobedience movements 95, 163, 165–6, 171, 183; law 40, 68; marriage 55, 58–60, 70, 99, 275, 277; rights 282, 291; war 183, 243
class 1–2, 6–7, 18, 45–6, 52, 74, 81, 84–6, 94, 97, 99–100, 116, 118, 122–4, 126, 134–5, 137–8, 142–5, 149, 156–7, 162, 164–5, 168, 176–9, 181, 186, 195, 198, 202, 208–9, 214, 220, 222–3, 231–3, 235–6, 238, 243, 246, 248–51,

254–5, 257, 263, 265, 267, 279, 283–4, 287, 289–91, 297, 300, 302–4, 315–17, 319–20, 322–4, 328–9, 331–2, 336, 339–40, 342; lower 116, 165; privileges 176, 324; upper 126, 214, 235, 316; working 1, 122–3, 137–8, 144, 179, 208, 251, 257, 265, 283, 322–3, 328
clothes/clothing 48, 83, 95, 102, 117, 217, 225
coal mines 140, 186
Cochin 43, 259, 264
cohabitation 63–4, 66
Colebrooke, H.T. 27, 47
colonial/colonialism 8, 25, 85, 107, 132; government 7, 75, 172, 274; India 21, 201, 242–3, 250, 284; laws 24, 153, 163; misrule 65, 215; modernity 8, 221; Penal Code 21, 325, 328; personal laws 25; rule 6, 21, 242; rulers 25, 35, 70, 325; states 24, 32, 135, 159
Committee on the Status of Indian Women 6, 279
communal/communalism 266, 289, 296; anxieties 123; civil war 183; divisiveness 183; Hindus 188; holocaust 313; politics 183; property 34; tension 39
communist: movements 179, 340; Communist Party of India (CPI) 179, 245, 252, 264, 286–8, 323; Communist Party of India (CPI)(Marxist) 245–6, 286; Communist Party of Pakistan 323; women's brigades 284
concubines 41, 45, 47, 134–5, 205, 209
conduct 4, 9, 13, 26, 28, 31, 35, 52, 58, 91, 93, 114, 156, 165, 195, 199, 313, 334, 343; manuals 4, 13
conflicts 38, 56, 104, 181, 306
conjugal: cohabitation 63, 66; conjugality 11, 16, 80, 85, 203, 226; duty 51, 182; life 19, 86; love 68, 226
consent 33, 47–50, 59–60, 64–7, 72–3, 75, 95, 114, 166, 188, 276, 282, 317, 321, 325, 346; first wife's 33, 321
conservatism 75, 85, 94, 98, 158, 268, 345
Constitution of India 187, 244, 278, 295; Article 25 278; Article 370 295; Constitution of Pakistan 314, 317, 325; 8th, 9th, and 12th constitutional amendments 326
Contagious Diseases Act 20, 207
contraception 123, 318
contraceptives 123–5, 248, 264, 338; female 124–5
controversy(ies) 39, 44–5, 66, 68–9, 117, 278; anti-Bill 66; conversion 68; widow remarriage 68
Convention on the Political Rights of Women 1953 322
conversions 40–4, 68, 81–3, 101, 103, 105, 109; instruments for 103; large-scale 83
converts 40–2, 44, 107–8

convictions 2, 25, 73, 210, 343; convicts 176, 215
cooking 115, 118, 134, 142, 169, 232, 234, 251, 261, 288
corruption 88, 104, 245, 316, 329
cotton mills 136–7, 142
court cases 26, 28, 41, 97–8, 147, 245, 294
Courtright, Paul 271–2
courts 4, 14, 18–19, 25–9, 31, 33–5, 38–44, 47–9, 54, 56–7, 64, 74, 96–8, 109, 115, 147–9, 165, 185, 209–10, 212, 245, 264, 271, 278–9, 281, 294, 304, 316, 325–7, 329, 340; colonial 31, 35; verdicts 26, 34
crime/criminality 18, 203, 205, 254, 280, 325, 328; criminal cases 208, 215; Criminal Investigation Department 167; criminalisation 206, 211, 271; criminal justice 326; Criminal Law Amendment Act of 1885 20; criminal laws 26, 113, 211, 279, 343; Criminal Law (Second Amendment) Act 280; Criminal Procedure Act 280; Criminal Procedure Code 277; Criminal Tribes Act, 1871 203
cruelty 39, 90, 96, 98, 115, 187, 195, 210, 215, 222, 225, 233, 280, 283, 296, 299, 302, 336; domestic 98, 195, 225; familial 90, 96, 302, 336; Cruelty to Women (Deterrent Punishment) Ordinance of 1983 346
culture/cultural 13, 18, 27, 81–2, 110, 117, 120, 156, 213, 220, 222–3, 238, 250, 271–2, 302, 329, 337; activities 16, 133; genres 220, 238; hub 115–16; nationalism 94–5, 108, 235; norms 2, 26; performers 134, 147, 236; practices 8, 57; production 221, 223; religious differences 102; traditions 42, 221, 330
customary: law 28, 35, 56, 317; practice 36, 50, 85
customs 5, 24, 26, 28–37, 54, 56–7, 74, 83, 93, 101, 107, 110, 112–13, 179, 266, 268, 273, 275, 277, 296, 316–17, 329, 345; community 36, 273; domestic 110, 112; Hindu 5, 28, 113, 277; local 28, 31

Dada Lekhraj 199–201
Dalits 14, 46, 73–4, 86, 93, 105–7, 109, 125, 133–4, 160, 162, 244, 257, 262, 273, 277, 287–9, 291–2, 299; quotas for 244; social reforms 105; women 74, 109, 160, 257, 291–2
dances/dancers 16, 17, 20, 106, 133, 147, 186, 201–2, 209, 210, 297, 304
Das Gupta, Monica 248–9
Das, Bina 176–8
Das, Chittaranjan 165, 174
Das, Kalyani 177, 178
Das, Kamala 300
Datta, Sukumari 61; *Apurba Sati* 61
daughters 6, 12–13, 15, 32–4, 36, 38, 42–3, 58, 61–3, 67, 69, 81, 83, 87, 92, 97–9, 102–4, 108, 111, 115, 120–1, 142, 177, 187, 206, 232, 237, 244,

248–50, 255, 261, 264, 267, 276, 298, 301–2, 316, 327, 334, 340, 345–6; inheritance rights of 36, 43, 320, 341
Dayabhaga 9, 27, 46, 91, 346
Dayanand Anglo-Vedic (DAV) schools and colleges 105
Deb, Radhakanta 85, 88
Defence of India Rules 167
deities 11, 201
delegated divorce (*talaq i tafwid*) 39, 117
Delhi 246, 249, 252, 258, 272, 280, 283, 296, 301
Democratic Women's Association 286, 322–3
Deoband seminary 2, 35, 38, 72, 110, 194
Deorala sati episode 266, 270–1
Derozio, Henry Louis Vivian 88–90
Deshmukh, Gopal Hari 90
desire 6, 16, 25, 41, 51, 59, 67, 71, 80, 91, 93, 198, 212–14, 226–31, 236–7, 289–91, 302, 305, 341
Devadasis 16–17, 106–7, 201, 209
devotees 74, 194–201, 269; Western 196
Dhaka 302, 333, 335, 340
*dharmasabha*s (religious assemblies) 15
Dharmashastras 3, 27, 99
disease(s) 124, 126, 185, 205–8, 214, 216, 233; anaemia 126; cholera 115; eclampsia 126; osteomalcia 126; sexual 214; tuberculosis 126; venereal 185, 205, 206, 208, 233

displacement 31, 236, 293, 295–6
disputes and conflicts 25–6, 35, 40–1, 44, 122, 154, 231, 279, 306, 326, 344
Dissolution of Muslim Marriages Act, 1939 118, 278
divine incarnation 198–9
divorce 10, 19–20, 26, 30–1, 36–9, 42–4, 82, 84, 115, 117, 268, 275–6, 278–9, 284, 317, 321, 341, 344–6; rules 19, 43, 84; divorced women 10, 19, 83, 278–9, 287, 316
docility 119, 345
domestic: abuse 279, 284, 289, 293; chores 104, 186, 250; confinement 113, 337; consumption 169, 186; cruelty 98, 195, 225; duties 132, 298; labour 46, 134; practices 72, 98; responsibilities 118, 132, 146, 195, 257, 339; service 134–5, 254; workers 18, 342
domesticity 5, 7, 10–11, 80, 85, 110, 112, 166, 168, 179, 181–2, 228, 234, 238, 255, 267, 272, 288, 344
double standards 51, 96, 237
dowers 19, 26, 39, 117, 185, 278, 338
dowry 32, 58, 122, 249, 267, 279–80, 338, 341
Dowry Prohibition Act of 1980 276, 279, 346
dress 82, 178, 203–4, 314, 318–19, 327, 337, 344; code 82, 203, 318, 327, 337, 344; ethnic 82; European 82; peoples' 319; sari 82, 92, 178, 257, 287, 292,

318; sex-differentiated 82;
unisex 318; Western 318
Dufferin Fund 101, 146
Duncan, Jonathan, Resident at
Benares 58
Dundee Courier 144
Dutt, Guru 304–5
Dutt, Kalpana 175, 176
Dutt, Michael Madhusudan 223;
Buro Shaliker Ghare Ron 223;
Ekei ii Boley Sabhyata 223
Dutta, Sukumari 173, 237; *Apurba Sati Natak* 237; *Chittagong Armoury Raiders* 173
dynasty 10, 15, 17, 45, 172, 201, 324

East Bengal 165, 180, 198, 331
East District Women's Association 293
East India Company (EIC) 4, 25–7, 35, 205
East Pakistan 180, 244, 253, 284, 315, 331–3, 335; February killings 332; genocidal military 333; prison 180; rape camps 335
east/eastern India 9, 27, 31, 91, 132, 140, 186, 201, 207, 222, 246
economy 18, 243, 250, 329, 339
education 5, 82–5, 87–9, 95, 97, 100–3, 105–6, 110, 112–14, 116–18, 120–1, 124, 156–7, 159, 167, 178, 182, 198, 225, 244, 248, 252, 254, 258, 263–4, 266–7, 297, 337, 339, 341, 345; girls' 84, 85; higher 157, 178; institutions 20, 163, 196, 244, 266; modern 83,

118; qualifications 158, 266; quotas 244; religious 105, 113, 198; women 147, 149, 187, 314, 344
employment 20, 84, 102, 106, 136, 141, 148, 179–80, 251–2, 264, 288, 328, 340–1, 344; loss of 136, 328
empowerment 101, 320, 339, 346
endogamy 59, 67, 292
England 4, 19, 21, 48, 63–4, 73, 94, 100, 103, 107, 116, 132, 158, 177, 209, 211
Englishwomen 20, 107, 115
entitlements 10, 19, 34, 36–7, 42–3, 46, 53, 56, 92, 258, 261, 277, 287, 316, 320, 328, 345; inheritance 10, 316; legal 19; remarriage 56; scriptural 36–7; usufruct 34, 46
equality 39, 42–3, 74, 80, 106, 113, 116, 157, 164, 168, 170, 176, 199, 244, 295, 315–17, 330–1, 346; electoral 168; gender 39, 42–3, 74, 116, 157, 199, 315–17, 346; political 168, 170
erotic/eroticism 226, 300, 305
Ershad, Lt Gen. Hussain Mohammad 334, 344; declares Emergency 334; martial law 334; resigns in 1990 334
ethnography 51, 261
Europe/Europeans 30, 41, 43, 88, 116, 144, 187, 208–11
exogamy 33, 267
exploitation 91, 138–9, 231
extra-marital 199, 214

factory 84, 132–3, 135–42, 144,

149, 157, 250–5, 297, 330, 337; Act of 1881 136; Act of 1911 137; Factory Commission 136; work 132, 135, 138–9, 253; workers 135–6, 141, 157
faith 13, 25–6, 28–9, 39–42, 54, 58–60, 70–1, 74–5, 104, 106, 110, 194, 196–7, 199, 201–2, 212, 225, 233, 243, 255, 271, 277–8, 313, 318, 322, 331, 342–3; Islamic 41–2; Zoroastrian 29
fakir 202, 231; family: conservative 179–80; controls 178, 279; elite 103, 116; family planning 106, 248, 336, 338; honour 82; joint 89, 277; landlord 166, 225, 272, 327; liberal 102, 157; matrimonial 32, 261, 279, 317; middle-class 186; natal 261, 279; nationalist 161, 177, 234; orthodox 182, 196; Parsi 148; property 34, 70, 277; ties 40, 89, 101, 173, 176, 201; upper-caste 55, 103, 213
famine 180, 183–5, 253, 334; devastating 180, 334; of 1974 334; relief 180; survivors 185; victims 180, 183
father/s 9, 13, 15, 33, 41–2, 52, 59, 67–8, 92, 96, 98, 148, 166, 209, 211, 248, 277, 297, 302, 313, 317, 327, 340; biological 42; consent to marriage 59; patriarchal 68
fatwa 35, 38, 159, 194, 342–3
Federal Shariat Court 325–6
female: behaviour 12–13; bodies 82, 195; infanticide 57, 83; inheritance 32, 36, 276, 321; labour 140, 144; seclusion 11, 133, 344; sexuality 62, 122; work participation 249, 253
femininity 7, 83, 119, 231, 302, 306
feminism 81, 157, 252, 283, 292, 300, 319, 329–30; groups 246, 280, 282, 287; Islamic 330; Pakistani 319; secular 329
feminists 1–2, 6–7, 20–1, 37, 39, 43, 49, 51, 73, 80, 97–8, 100, 119, 156, 158, 179, 187, 224, 232, 244, 246–7, 259, 265, 270–2, 279–83, 287, 289, 292, 298, 300, 303, 316, 319, 328–30, 341–2, 346; Bangladeshi 346; Bengali 119; British 73, 158; English 98; independent 246; Indian 97, 279; Islamic 316, 330; Maharashtrian 224; Marxist 6–7; militant 342; post-colonial 7; scholars 6, 7, 259; secular 100; studies 1, 179; Victorian 20
fertility 123, 144, 338
festivals 82–3, 202, 269–71
fiction 110–11, 149, 213–14, 221, 223–4, 227–8, 232–3, 297–8, 300, 340
Five Year Plans 245, 248, 258; First Plan of 1951–6 248; Second Plan 245; Seventh Plan 258; Sixth Plan of 1980–5 258
foeticide 66, 93
folk: culture 222; religious cults

201; spiritual leaders 202; tales 221; traditions 202
food 52, 88, 91, 117, 125, 184–5, 258, 260–2, 298–9; leftover 298, 299; "polluted" 88; stimulating 91
foreign: garments 162; goods 161, 163–5, 169
forests 31, 34, 84, 96, 165, 176, 251, 253–6, 335
fornication 325–6
Fort William College, Calcutta 26, 47
Forum Against Oppression of Women 281
Forum Against Rape 281
franchise 158–9, 168, 187; female 158–9, 168; male 158; rules 159; universal adult 159
freedom 4–5, 11–12, 17, 57, 59, 74, 81–2, 97, 100, 104, 117, 140, 173, 177, 180, 188, 208, 242, 244, 246, 265, 271, 278, 293, 324, 340–1, 346; individual 59; political 177; relative 81, 180; religious 278, 346
Fyzee, Atiya 116–17, 182

Gandhi, Indira 244–6, 296, 301
Gandhi, Mahatma 72–4, 95, 123, 159, 162–3, 166–71, 209, 242–3, 247; ideology 170–1; murder of 243, 247; political action 169
Gandhian: movements 169; non-violence 174; struggle 167; women 170
Ganguly, Dwarakanath 89, 145
Garhwal 171, 273, 289

Garo hill tribe 31–2, 256–7, 267–8
gay/gay-lesbian 7, 212, 214, 283; agitations 284; marriages 284; rights organisations 283
gender 1–9, 13, 15, 17–19, 21, 24–7, 29, 31, 33, 36–9, 42–3, 51, 74, 80–1, 84, 86–7, 95–8, 100, 105, 107, 116, 118–19, 122, 132, 146, 148, 153, 156–7, 160, 164, 167, 169, 171, 176, 178–9, 181, 183, 189, 194, 197, 199, 201, 203–4, 220, 223–4, 226–7, 233–5, 238, 243–5, 248–9, 251, 259, 263, 265, 267–8, 272, 275, 283, 288–90, 292, 297–8, 300–1, 303, 306, 313–22, 324, 326, 328–31, 335–6, 338–9, 342–3, 345–6; asymmetry 51, 272; Brahmanical 100, 105, 292; concerns 3–4; differences 13; discrimination 37; equality 39, 42–3, 74, 116, 157, 199, 315–17, 346; equity 183, 342; gap 223; injustice 119; issues 29, 74, 97, 179, 181, 189, 220, 288, 322, 336; justice 38, 275, 315, 320–1, 330, 345, 346; laws and norms 6, 15, 27, 29, 118, 157, 167; practices 3, 31, 33, 74, 84, 292, 319, 338; problems 183, 292, 303; reform 86–7, 197, 263; relations 5, 7, 17, 81, 132, 153, 164, 189, 238, 265, 267–8, 324, 338; roles 1, 146, 176; studies 1–3, 6
gendering: conventional 232; dress

318; labour 250; pogroms 295; property 258; state repression 292; war 335
Ghadar Party 173
Ghatak, Ritwik 302; *Meghe Dhaka Tara* 302; *Titash Ekti Nodir Naam* 302
Gidumal, Dayaram 63, 65
girls 16, 20, 32, 41, 48, 58, 61–4, 66, 71, 73, 82, 84–6, 89, 91, 95, 103–8, 116, 120–1, 147–8, 166, 178, 183–4, 186, 210–11, 229, 233, 235, 248, 266, 269, 281–2, 302, 322–3, 326–7; age of consent for 64, 73; below ten 91; dancing 16, 210; education 84, 85; Indian 211; marriages below fourteen 73; sale of 184; school-going 120; schooling for 20, 116; schools 86, 95, 104, 147–8, 235; servant 233; slave 210; subaltern 108; working 186; young 71, 106, 178, 229, 235, 323
Goddess Kali 88, 227
Gopalakrishnan, Adoor 303
Government of India 5, 25, 54, 62, 94, 136, 159
Government of India Act of 1935 159
Guardian and Wards Act 42
guardians 102–3, 119, 161, 167, 176, 179, 207, 316; family 316; male 103, 161, 207; natal 102; religious 316
Guha, Ranajit 92; "Chandra's Death" 92
Guhathakurta, Meghna 335, 341; *Ekattarer Smriti* 335

Gujarat 45, 75, 92, 95, 148, 163, 249, 265, 273–4, 288
gurus 100, 104, 194, 196–7, 199–200, 205, 223; male 197

hadith 35, 314, 318
Hamilton, Charles 28, 35; *Hedaya* 28, 35
Hanafi: jurisprudence 28; laws 28, 36, 39; handicrafts 116, 121, 132, 253
harems 11, 14
Haryana 249, 253, 282
hatred 181, 243, 247
health 14, 74, 116, 125–7, 146, 185, 205, 234, 254, 258, 264, 339; healthcare 101, 248, 264; maternal 125, 234, 254; moral 205; physical 205; reproductive 125; sexual 185; visitors 126
heroines 233, 238, 336
hetero-normativity 211, 283
hijras (eunuchs) 14, 203–4
Hindoo Law of Inheritance 54
Hindu Adoption and Maintenance Act 276
Hindu Succession Act of 1956 258, 276–7
Hindu Undivided Family (HUF) 69–70, 95, 275
Hindu women 4–5, 10–11, 45, 109, 112, 170–1, 182, 187, 200, 235, 266, 340, 346; abductions of 266; conditions of 109; lives and deaths of 45; Muslim outrage against 266; peripatetic 11; upper-caste 12, 14
Hindu: Child Marriage Bill, 1927 73; Code Committee 275;

devotional practices 122; Dharma Vyavasthapak Sabha 93; gender differences 13; Marriage Act 276; marriages 43–4, 57, 64–5, 67, 69–70, 96, 274–5; Muslim conflagrations 279; religious cultures 13; wars 270

Hinduism 16, 59, 63, 94, 100, 107, 196, 316

Hindus 4–5, 9–17, 25–8, 31–2, 36–8, 40–6, 49–52, 54–7, 59–60, 62–7, 69–74, 83–8, 90–1, 93–6, 98–104, 106, 108–13, 115–16, 121–4, 147, 156, 160, 163, 170–1, 181–2, 184, 187–8, 195–202, 204, 215–16, 228–9, 235, 242–3, 247, 258, 266, 270, 273–9, 287, 290–2, 295–6, 301–2, 305, 314, 318, 329, 331, 340, 342, 346; besieged 104; communal anxieties 123; conservative 104; domestic practices 98; educated 108; families 40, 42, 147, 182; gender practices 31; high-caste 10, 83–4; infuriated 74; landholding 36; landlords 50, 331; landowning 32; laws 26–7, 41, 44; legal reform 274; liberal 66, 85; life-cycle rites 66, 196; monarchs 43; monastic order 196; Muslims and 13, 163, 242–3, 314; opprobrium 94; orthodox 85; orthodoxy 70, 90; personal laws 122, 187; religion 60; religious affairs 65; religious nationalism 63; ritualistic symbols 156; revivalism 90, 95; scriptural rules 28; society 98–9, 106; texts 9, 52; traditional 104; unreformed 88; upper-caste 50, 84

Hindustan Socialist Republican Association (HSRA) 174

Hindustan Socialist Revolutionary Association 230

history 1, 4–5, 28–9, 45, 52, 75, 99, 116, 153, 216, 227, 235, 242, 286, 291; acrimonious 45; colonial 29; domestic 227; gender 5; Indian 7, 45; life 216; modern Indian 7; multi-dimensional 8; writing 5

Ho 33–4, 267–8; custom 34; women 34, 268

Holocaust 187–8

home: marital 229; matrimonial 34, 44, 277, 280; patriarchal control of 182; rural 133

homelands 188, 242

homophobia 211

homosexuality 14, 20–1, 88, 212–14, 283

honour 9, 82, 142, 204, 235, 317, 329; killings 329

Hosain, Attia 121, 300; *Sunlight on a Broken Column* 121, 300

Hossain, Begum Rokeya Sakhawat 119; "Alankar Na Badge of Slavery?" 119; "Amader Abanati" 119

House of Commons 45, 48, 158, 186

households 1, 11–14, 17, 67–8, 96, 109, 111–15, 125, 132–5, 140, 194, 205, 209–11, 214,

228–9, 231, 234–5, 247, 258–62, 274, 277, 299–300, 343; Bengali 140; British 209; colonial 211; elite 17, 134; European 210; Hindu 96; imperial 11; Indian 210; landed 67; landowning 67; management 14, 112, 114–15, 234; patriarchal 229; peasant 133; royal 13, 134; urban 125, 262; worship 194
housewives 104, 111–12, 147, 179, 216, 225, 236, 260, 340; homebound 147; pious 225
Hudood Ordinance of 1979 324–6, 328, 330, 343
Human Rights Commission of Pakistan 330
humiliation 177, 245; sexual 245
Hunter Commission of 1882 101, 188
hunting 31–2, 83, 267
husbands 9–13, 19, 32, 39–47, 50–4, 56–7, 62, 64, 66–8, 72–3, 81, 83–4, 86, 89–91, 97–9, 102, 109, 112–13, 115–18, 120, 124, 142, 145, 159, 167–9, 175, 179, 185, 188, 198–200, 207, 210, 215, 222, 225–6, 228–9, 231–5, 260–1, 268, 272, 274, 276–7, 279, 281–2, 285, 288, 295, 299, 316–17, 321, 323, 335–6, 338–9, 341, 343–4, 346; conservative 159; converted 109; cruelty of 115; divorced 276; drunk 169; first 53, 56–7, 97, 344; funeral pyre of 45; Hindu 44; insensitive 299; jobless 142; political

lives of 323; polygamous 276; property and 46, 53, 56–7, 215, 272, 346; rights over children 68; self-reflexive 229; worship of 10, 99
Hyderabad 39, 280–1, 285, 290

iddat 279
identity 2, 7, 38, 40, 59, 103, 118, 137, 153, 157, 176, 203–4, 229–30, 251, 270, 292, 330–2, 334; anti-caste 230; Bengali 334; Bengali Muslim 118; extrafamilial 103; female working class 137; gendered 176; individual 103; legal 38; moral 229; political 230; religious 59, 330, 332; sectarian 157; sexual 203, 204; working-class 137, 251
ideology 4, 106, 170–1, 179, 181–2, 220, 261, 266, 270, 283; communal 220; communist 179; domestic 266; Hindu nationalist 4; patriarchal 261, 283; socialist 106
idolatry 87–8, 121; abolition of 88
illiteracy 98, 244, 324
immolation 4, 13, 18, 45–51, 54, 73, 83, 85, 177, 238, 260, 266, 269–72, 292; criminalisation of 271; disapproval of 51; inappropriate 47; kinds of 46
immorality 103, 223, 251, 277
impotence 39, 203–4
impunity 277, 283, 296, 318
income: family 132, 261; landowning 86; personal 90;

self-earned 19, 43, 277; tax 69
India and Pakistan 187, 242–4, 315, 320, 333, 340; borders 242; peace treaty of 1971 333; war of 1947–8 320; war of 1965 340; war of 1971 244, 315
Indian Christians 26, 40–2, 60, 186
Indian Contagious Diseases Act of 1868 207
Indian Divorce Act of 1869 42
Indian Ladies' Magazine 231
Indian Muslims 5, 10, 19, 28, 37, 110, 313; nineteenth-century 5; women 10, 19, 110
Indian National Army 155, 211
Indian National Congress (Congress Party) 37, 39, 65, 72, 106, 158–64, 166–8, 170–1, 174–7, 185, 188, 209, 211, 234, 244–5, 252, 258, 263–4, 275–6, 284–8, 295–6
Indian Penal Code, 1860 63–4, 113, 203, 207, 212, 214, 280; provisions 64, 203
Indian People's Theatre Association (IPTA) 180, 233, 304
Indian Succession Act 42–3, 277; Act of 1865 43; Act of 1925 43, 277
Indian Union 43, 106, 285, 292–3
Indian women 4, 6, 10, 20, 65, 72, 98, 101, 107, 121, 126, 145, 148, 153, 158, 186–7, 210, 245, 326; ancient 10; healthcare for 101; Muslim 10, 19, 110; voices and activism 158

Indian: army 205, 333; beliefs 29, 49; civilisation 4; classical languages 26; communities 29, 194; conservatism 75, 158; criminal laws 211; customary practices 57; cultural nationalism 108; education 101; feminism 81; fiction writers 221; gender issues 7, 29; 283; government 63, 278; history 45; intermediaries 25; labourers 89; legislators 70–2; literary past 222; political fiction 228; public opinion 63; religions 114; religious authorities 26; ritual regimes 18; sacred traditions 28; sepoys 49, 154; social perceptions 173; society 8, 204; widows 56, 272
industrialists 29, 167, 270
industry(ies) 84, 245, 315, 344
inequality 262, 346
infant 53, 62, 64–6, 73–4, 90–1, 125, 134, 138, 141, 184, 203, 207, 222, 225, 234, 237, 264, 269, 285, 341; marriage 62, 65–6, 73; mortality 66, 264; kidnapping 203; widows 91
infanticide 53, 57–8, 83, 93, 96, 248
inheritance 4, 10, 19, 25–6, 31–8, 40–1, 43, 51, 53, 56–7, 67–71, 259, 268, 273, 275–7, 316–17, 320–1, 338, 341, 344, 346; access to 71; claims 56; entitlements 10, 316; female 32, 36, 276, 321; formal 10; laws of 4; natal 34; patterns 31; rights 38, 43, 51, 53, 57, 69–70, 268, 320, 341; scriptural 38

insurrectionary groups 268, 293–4
intellectual(s) 25, 29, 85, 87, 117, 195; cosmopolitan 29; exchanges 197; Hindu 85; modern 25, 195; traditions 7, 87
Intelligence Bureau 164, 178
intelligentsia 85–6, 109, 331–2, 340; Bengali 331; modern 85, 109; pro-Soviet 340
intercourse 64, 66, 209, 212, 282, 325
International Labour Organisation 140–1
International Women's Day 281
International Women's Year in 1974 5, 343
intimacy 16, 33, 82, 173, 178, 213; homosocial 173; non-heterosexual 16; premarital 33, 82
Iran 324, 330
Islam 5, 10, 35–6, 38–9, 41–2, 61, 66, 105, 110–15, 117, 197, 278, 314–16, 319, 321–2, 325, 328–32, 334, 339, 343–5; conversions to 41, 105, 117; interpretations of 331; pristine 110, 344; Shia 278, 324, 345
Islamic: criminal laws 113; faith 41–2; jurisprudence 27; laws 5, 114, 316–17, 343; legalism 324; legal traditions 28, 37; norms 5; practices 36; protofeminism 113; religious discourses 109; theology 5

Jahan, Rashid 232, 233
Jains 17, 60, 70–1
Jamaat-i-Islami (JI) 112, 314, 318, 322, 324

Jamiat Ulema-e-Islam 322
Janaki Devi 166–7
jatis 46, 96, 262
jauhar (collective female suicide) 15, 266
Jehangir, Asma 329–30
Jehangir, Mughal emperor 11, 329
Jew/jewish 43, 98, 117, 208, 318
Jhansi 153, 154, 155, 171, 300
Jharkhand 267–8
Jinnah, Fatima 183, 313, 315, 319
Jinnah, Muhammad Ali 37–9, 72, 117, 183, 188, 243, 313–15
jobs 184, 186, 188, 195, 244, 251–2, 254–5, 257–8, 262, 266–7, 330, 337, 341, 343; factory 251–2; government 267, 343; quotas 244; responsibilities 195
joint family 89–90, 277
Judicial Plan of 15 August 1772 27–8
justice 14, 38, 40, 210, 221, 294, 296, 315, 320–2, 326, 330–1, 345
jute mills 136–7, 139, 142, 144, 251–2

Kailashbashini Debi 89, 96
Kali, Hindu goddess 88, 198, 227
Kanitkar, Kashibai 97, 226
Kanwar, Roop 270
Kanya gurukul 105
Kanya Manoranjan 235
Kapur, Anuradha 237, 238
Kapur, Prakasvati 230; *Lahore Se Lucknow Tak* 230
Kar, Ajoy 302; *Saptapadi* 302
Karachi 183, 185–6, 322, 328
Karve, Dhondo Keshav 93–4, 101

Kerala 42–3, 67–8, 74, 224, 230, 245–6, 249, 252–3, 258, 263–4, 288, 300, 302–3; Agrarian Relations Bill 258; Congress government 258; female sex ratio 264; gender model 288; Left government 263; Synod for Syrian Christians 43
Kesavan, C. 231; *Jeevitasamaram* 231
Khadi programmes 95, 166–7
Khairunnissa Khatun 118, 121
Khan, Ayub 315, 321, 340
Khan, General Muhammad Yahya 315, 332
Khan, Syed Ahmad 110, 113–14, 204
Khan, Yasmin 186; *Raj at War* 186
Khasi 31, 267, 268
Khatun 120, 121, 235
Khilafat movement 161, 182, 235
killings 58, 66, 96, 175–6, 187, 208, 210, 248, 267, 279–80, 283–4, 329, 332
kinship 31, 134, 161, 175, 268
Kolkata 143, 262
Kosambi, Meera 226; *Crossing Thresholds* 226
Kripalani, J.B. 275
Kripalani, Sucheta 167, 169
Krishnan, Rajam 297; *Verruku Nir* 297
Kulin Brahmans 62
Kumaon 289
Kumar, Radha 138
Kumar, Udaya 230
Kumar, Uttam 302
Kumari, Surya 266

labour/labourer 6, 8, 13, 18, 21, 28, 31–2, 46, 73, 84, 89, 92, 133–4, 136–45, 157, 164, 172, 176, 179, 184, 186, 215, 245, 249–50, 252–5, 257, 262–3, 268, 290, 297, 317, 319, 327–8, 330, 337–8; agricultural 18, 157, 253, 338; cheap 84, 252; child 136, 297, 330; domestic 46, 134; farm 253; female 140, 144; forced 172; gendered division of 338; hard 21, 215, 327; indentured 133, 184; landless 179; laws 133, 140, 263; migrant 140; patriarchal control over 28; patterns 268; processes 6; production of 13, 92; rural 252, 253; sexual division of 31, 290; tribal 140, 179; unionism 144–5; unpaid 179; waged 255
Lady Dufferin Fund 101, 146
Lahiri-Dutt, Kuntala 141
Lahore 39, 110, 114, 117, 157, 175, 183, 230, 235, 314, 322
Lahore Resolution of 1951 314
Lal Nishan Party 289
Lalan Fakir 202
landlord/landowner 46, 50, 55, 86, 122, 166, 225, 231, 233, 261, 270, 274, 281, 284, 288, 290, 314, 327, 331; feudal 290; peasant struggles against 122; rich 233, 261; upper-caste 55, 86
landownership 249, 258
Language Action Committee 332
language and literature: Arabic 85, 110–11, 115, 118; Bengali 82,

111, 118–19, 147, 224–5, 228, 339; Bhojpuri 222; children's 340; classical 4, 26, 85, 221; court 115, 226; descriptive 228; English 19–20, 25–7, 30, 42, 63, 98, 111, 115–16, 186, 214, 231, 237, 254, 300; foreign 82; Garhwali 256; Gujarati 229; Hindi 106–7, 111, 115, 197, 206, 214, 226, 233–4, 298, 301; historical 2; Malayalam 214, 231, 303; Marathi 92, 224–5; monastic 17; mystical 202; Oriya 231; patriotic 229; Persian 85; political 161; Punjabi 231; regional 301; sacred 107, 112, 221; Sanskrit 13, 16, 27, 85, 98–9, 105–6, 197, 221; spoken 222; Tamil 5, 11, 17, 105–6, 124, 228, 248–9, 252–3, 286, 297, 301; vernacular 222

Law Commission 42, 53–4, 135, 282

Law Reform Commission of 1958 322

laws and norms: ameliorative 139; ancient 4; Brahmanical 88; British 5, 41; child-custody 321; colonial 24, 153, 163; conservative 96; conventional 201; criminal 26, 113, 211, 279, 343; cultural 2, 26; customary 28, 35, 56, 84, 273, 275, 317; desirable 10; disciplinary 9; divine 314; enforcement 208, 212; English 30; established 35; family 343; female chastity 106; gender 6, 15, 27, 29, 118, 157, 167, 201; histories of 8; Islamic 5, 317, 343; lax 83; moral 297; non-Muslim 35; orthodox 199, 205; patrilocal 34; permissive 60; personal 25–6, 35, 40–2, 45, 60, 68–9, 122, 187, 321, 325; progressive 4; protective 136; punishments and 15; purity–pollution 15; Quranic 66; rape 280; religious 8, 26–7, 29, 41, 60, 346; remarriage 94, 229; repressive 315; scriptural 13, 56–7, 114, 326; sexual 83, 124; social 44, 58, 88, 90, 105, 170, 291; statutory 28, 56; two-child 248; unjust 163; widowhood 170; written 28

leader/leadership 14, 33, 72, 74, 89, 107, 115, 118, 122, 154, 156–7, 160–1, 163, 167–8, 171, 179, 181, 183, 189, 200–2, 242, 244, 271, 284–6, 339, 341; folk spiritual 202; male 163, 181, 189, 284–5, 341; spiritual 202

Left Front 246, 254, 258

legal: authorities 24; change 37, 63, 98; discrimination 160; intervention 37, 49; issues 269; orders 24; pluralism 24; traditions 9, 28, 37

legislation 28, 56, 136–7; state 28; women workers and 136

lesbian/lesbianism 14, 21, 125, 212, 283

liaisons 15, 68, 93, 224; cross-caste 15; inter-caste 68; inter-community 15; secret 93

Libertarianism 33, 203
literacy 19, 100, 225, 244, 263–4; female 19, 225, 263; genres 220, 223; inclinations 223
literary: movements 340; representations 16
livelihood 34, 84, 133, 141, 223, 246, 253, 259, 283, 287, 296, 342; issues 246, 342; tribal 34
London Missionary Society 108
Lord Ayyappan's temple, Sabarimala 74
love 10, 12, 15–16, 33, 59, 61, 68, 71, 75, 80, 85, 88, 119, 173, 176, 179–80, 185, 195, 200, 202, 205, 211–14, 226–30, 234, 237–8, 302, 304–5; affairs 185, 213; chaste 200; conjugal 68, 226; constrained 228; cross-caste 15; familial 173; forbidden 227, 229; forms of 226; gay 214; heterosexual 226; homosexual 214; illicit 213, 227; inter-community 228; marital 237; married 173, 304; mercenary 205; non-marital 226; patriotic 230; premarital 226; same-sex 213–14; stirring tales of 16; thwarted 229; tragic 227
low-caste movements 122
Lucknow 16–17, 120, 156–7, 188, 205, 230
Ludhiana 248–9
lyrics 226–7

Ma Sarada, Ramakrishna's wife 198
Maclean, Kama 173; *Revolutionary History of Interwar India* 173

Madhavikutty 224, 300; *Ente Katha* 300
Madhya Pradesh 248, 249, 252, 254
Madras 27, 41, 43–4, 48, 54–5, 68, 90, 103–5, 136, 145, 156–7, 201, 228, 253, 264, 293; High Court 43; Hindu Social Reform Association 90; Legislative Council 90; Marumakkayathayam Act 68; Medical College 145; Presidency 44, 48, 55, 90, 103, 105, 136, 201, 264
Mahabharata 10
Mahalanobis, Gurucharan 55–6; *Atmakatha* 55
Mahar satyagraha 291
Maharaja libel case of 1861–2 89
Maharaja of Darbhanga 166, 178
Maharani of Cooch Behar 147
Maharashtra 12, 45, 148, 161, 179, 252, 257, 281, 287–90
Maharshi Karve's Widows' Home 101
Mahasweta Devi 290, 299; *Aranyer Adhikar* 299; *Hajaar Churashir Ma* 290
Mahila: Atmaraksha Samiti (MARS) 180; Dakshata Samiti 280; Navjivan Mandal 284; Parishad 157, 340–2; Samakhya Samiti 265; Samta Sainik Dal 289; Sansads 292
Maine, Henry 28, 59–61; *Ancient Law* 28; *Village Communities in the East and West* 28
Majumdar, Dakshinaranjan Mitra 222; *Thakumar Jhuli* 222

Malabar 68, 259, 264
Malabari, Behramji 62–3, 94; *Appeal on Behalf of the Daughters of India* 63; *Note on Infant Marriages* 62; *Notes on Enforced Widowhood* 94
Malaviya, Pandit Madan Mohan 72
male and female 13, 82, 156, 170, 194, 208, 215, 231–2, 258, 260, 305; bodies 82; capabilities 232; holiness 194; ideal behaviour 13
Malthusianism 122
Manipur 171–2, 292–3
Manu 9, 51, 171
manufacture: cashew and coir 253; commodities 250; handloom 253; market-oriented 250; piecemeal 250
Manusmriti 9–10
Mao Zedong 289
Maratha 96, 115, 134
marital: discord 185; limits 125; partners 60
markets 18, 104, 123, 125, 132, 134, 138, 140, 172, 186, 220, 224, 250, 252, 265, 274, 301; boycott of 172; conditions 140; Indian 186, 252; open 134; world 132; women and 172
marriage(s): adult 30, 87; *agnisakshi* 274; arranged 10, 33; bigamous 61; Brahmanical practices 62; by capture 10, 33; caste-defined rules 9; civil 19, 55, 60, 70, 275; companionate 80; compulsory 62, 277; consensual 59, 114; contracts 39, 117, 185, 316–17, 321; dissolution of 13, 84; early 81, 104; endogamous 10; forced 268; forms 67, 84; fraudulent 61; high-caste 12; hypergamous 67; hypogamous 99; indissoluble 12; inferior version of 92; inter-caste 59, 61, 75, 139, 211, 275; inter-community 30, 59, 247, 277; interfaith 75; interracial 209, 211; intra-lineage 275; kinds of 10; laws 44, 59, 274; levirate 32, 272; love 10, 33, 59, 61, 75, 80, 88; market 104; minimum age for 321; monogamous 33; multiple 13; Muslim 38, 39; Nara 92; parallel practice of 33; post-pubertal 62; practices 33, 62, 67, 83; real 66; reforms 114; registrations of 341; religious provisions 60; renunciation of 173; rules 9, 19, 42, 65, 95; sacramental 12; safety of 75; same-sex 214; saptapadi 274; second 41, 57, 94, 276, 344, 346; sexless 169; tie 83, 89–90, 185, 209, 318; tribal group 83; unorthodox 99
married: women 20, 266, 276, 282; Women's Property Act of 1874 42; Women's Properties Act of 1882 19
Marwaris 69–70, 95, 164, 172, 254, 269–72; opinion 69; traders 69, 172, 254
masculinity 3, 7, 14, 71, 80, 82–4, 89, 153, 173, 196, 204, 229, 231, 306; conventional notions

of 84; conventions of 204; Indian 71; martial 14; Mizo notions of 82; notions of 82, 84; political 173; warlike 83
mass movements 161, 164, 284
maternal: care 182, 265; child welfare 140; health 74
maternalism 157, 197, 229, 300, 304; possessive 229; sacred 197; sentimental 304
maternity: Benefit Act 138; Benefit Bill 141; facilities 143; homes 126; leave 139, 142, 186; paid 142
matrilineal/matriliny 32, 67, 68, 231, 257, 258, 264, 267–8
Maududi, Maulana Abul Ala 112–13, 313–14, 321; *Purdah and the Status of Women in Islam* 112, 314
maulvis 26–7, 29, 315
Mayo, Katherine 71, 73, 149
Mecca pilgrimages 116, 323, 345
medical training 89, 101, 146
Meghalaya 32, 82, 256, 268, 292
mehr (dower) 13, 19, 26, 39, 117, 278, 316, 338, 345
Meira Paibi 293
Meitei 293
Menon, O. Chandu 230; *Indulekha* 230
middle class 6, 74, 84–5, 118, 124, 133–4, 142–5, 149, 156, 162, 165, 177–8, 181, 186, 195, 198, 202, 209, 222–3, 231, 233, 236, 238, 248–50, 254–5, 263, 265, 267, 284, 290–1, 297, 300, 315, 317, 320, 328, 330–1, 340, 342; liberal 84; lower 195, 248, 254, 317; modern 198; opinion 85; upbringing 198
midwife 125–6, 133, 146, 206
migrants: non-Bengali 332; Punjabi 173
migration 242, 253, 295
militancy 142, 162, 164, 179, 251, 295
Mill, James 4; *History of British India* 4
Mill, John Stuart 19, 97; *On the Subjection of Women* 97
mines 31, 84, 133, 135–6, 140–1, 149, 186, 254
mining 84, 136, 141, 255, 274
minority(ies) 61, 244, 247, 275, 295, 328, 346; religious 244, 247, 295, 328, 346
miscegenation 46
missionary(ies) 33, 42, 45, 47–8, 82–3, 86, 100, 102–3, 105, 107–9, 111, 114, 123, 125–6, 146–8, 222, 228; agencies 108; British Protestant 107; creation and 42; European 108; female 103; medical 125–6; missions 126; schools 82, 263; twentieth-century 82
Mitakshara 9, 27
Mitra, Ila 180, 284
Mizo: church services 82; insurrectionary groups 268
Mizoram 82, 292
modernity 7–8, 87, 110, 146, 194, 200, 221, 223, 225, 234, 238, 271, 337, 344–5; colonial 8; Indian 87, 221; Western 110, 345
modesty 225, 235, 320; womanly 225, 235

Mohanty, Gopinath 18; *Paraja* 18
monarchs 43, 112; women 112
monks and saints 11–12, 170, 194–5, 197–200; contemporary 199; Hindu 11, 200; male 197; modern 200; women 197–9
Montagu–Chelmsford reforms 70
morality 4, 40, 51, 60, 93, 147, 177, 205, 224, 231, 235, 260, 277, 343; conventional 231; orthodox 93, 343; patriotic 235; religious 40; sexual 277; social 4; westernised 205
mortality rates 6, 123, 144
mosques 194, 313, 341, 344
Mother India 304
motherhood 33, 146, 161, 179, 224, 234; patriotic 234; virtual 161
motherland 162, 174, 229, 238, 335
mothers 34, 58, 66–7, 108, 118, 125, 181–2, 255, 260–2, 264, 279, 290, 317; lactating 261
Mughal: court 14, 25; rule 14
Muhammadi Begum, Mumtaz Ali's wife 113–14, 147, 235
Mukherjee, Rudrangshu 155; *Begum and a Rani* 155
Mukherjee, Syama Prasad 275
Mulji, Karsandas 88–9
Mullens, Hana Catherine 228; *Phulmani o Karunar Bibaran* 228
Munda 33–4
Murshid, Noorjehan 332, 340–1; *Sacred & the Secular* 332
music 20, 50, 117, 236
Muslim League 37, 38, 117, 160, 183, 184, 188, 315, 320, 332, 333, 343; Central Committee 183; flag 183, 184
Muslim men 13, 118, 124, 182, 194, 266, 322; ceiling of four wives 13
Muslim women 5, 10, 19, 36–7, 72, 109–10, 112–18, 121, 147, 157, 178, 182–3, 200, 285; economic security of 36; elite 35; formal inheritance entitlements 10; ideal 111; modern 112, 116; nineteenth-century 115; North Indian 110; scriptural inheritance rights for 38; secluded 35
Muslim Women's League 320
Muslim: Dissolution of Marriage Act of 1939 39; Family Laws Ordinance 321; Girls' Students' Federation 183; "Muslim Ladies Defend the Sarda Act" 72; Personal Law 38, 118, 278
Muslims 5, 10–11, 13, 15–16, 19, 26, 28, 32, 35–42, 47–9, 60–1, 64, 66, 70, 72, 87–8, 109–18, 120–4, 126, 144, 147, 156–60, 162–3, 166–7, 174, 178, 182–4, 187–8, 194, 197, 200, 202, 205, 210, 216, 227–8, 231, 235, 242–4, 247, 266, 270, 274–5, 277–9, 285, 295–7, 300–1, 313–14, 318, 320–2, 324–6, 328–31, 342, 345; custom 36; divorce and maintenance rules 278; draft marriage contract 39; female political activism 184; feminist movement 39; landowning 32; liberal 278; marriages 205;

non-Indian 10; orthodox 278; political 328; religious 60; rioters 187; rule 5; sacred law 72; scriptural rules 28; social contact 36; society 112; widows 47; wives 39, 278–9
Muthulakshmi Reddy *see under* Reddy
mythology 199, 237

Nachole movement 284
Nagaland 83, 171, 292
Nagas 82–3, 171, 268, 293–4; femininity 83; head-hunting practices 83; vernacular script for 82
Namboothiri Brahman 67–8
Nandy, Ashis 7, 271
Nari: Bahini 284; Dharma 270; Niryatan Protirodh Committee 341; Naripakkha 341–2; Nari Punorbashon (Women's Rehabilitation) programme 336; Narishilpa Bidyalay 121
National Council of Women in India 209
National Federation of Dalit Women 292
National Federation of Indian Women (NFIW) 281, 286–7
National Women's Association 336
nationalism 63–4, 74, 94–6, 108, 163, 165–6, 170, 177, 221, 229, 234–5, 238, 306, 315, 332; anti-colonial 96, 235; cultural 94–5, 108, 229, 235; liberal 74; linguistic 315; political 64, 229; regional 315; religious 63, 306

nationalist 4, 7, 64–6, 71–3, 95, 106, 142, 155–6, 158, 160–2, 165–9, 171, 175, 177, 208, 211, 234, 238, 300, 333–4; ardour 169; campaigns 166; cultural 64, 66; movements 160–1, 168; Hindu 72; Indian 7, 158; legislators 71; passion 162; tribal 155
Nationalist Women's Organisation 343
Native Christian Marriage Act 42
Nautanki songs 222
Naxals/Naxalites 246, 290–1, 299
Nayar 67–8, 258, 263–4
Nayar Service Society 263–64
Nazil, Begum of Janjira 117
Nazrul Islam, Kazi 227, 339
Nehru, Jawaharlal 155, 157, 159–60, 171, 188, 198, 242–5, 263, 275–6, 301
Nehru, Rameshwari 157, 234–5
Nellie massacre 296
New Woman 74, 178
newspapers and journals 30, 49–50, 63, 65, 85, 89, 92, 94, 112–13, 115, 117–18, 147, 221, 231, 234–5, 246, 266, 289; Bengali 147; Bengali Muslim 118; Hindi 234; liberal 118; modern 234; Urdu 112–13, 115
NGOs 296, 336, 339, 343–4
Nikahnama 114, 321
Nizam of Hyderabad 284–5
Noakhali 165, 171
Non-Cooperation–Khilafat movements 160, 163, 209
North West Frontier Province 183, 203–4, 317

novels 68, 85, 109–11, 121, 162, 182, 214, 221, 227–31, 234, 262, 290, 294, 297–300; Bengali 228; controversial 162; didactic 228; educational 111; Gujarati 229; historical 221; Malayalam 214; Oriya 231; Punjabi 231
Numani, Maulana Shibli 117
nurses 97, 125, 186, 264; European 186; nursing 82, 232
nutrition 248–9

O'Hanlon, Rosalind 13, 96, 205; *Comparison Between Women and Men* 96
obedience 14, 189, 260, 345
obscenity 224, 327
offence 53, 60, 207, 214–15, 279–80, 325–6, 328, 336, 342; cognisable 279–80; non-bailable 280; positive 53; suspected 53
Offences Against the Person Act of 1828 20
old women 14, 104, 342
Oldenburg, Veena Talwar 17, 205
Omvedt, Gail 257; *We Will Smash This Prison* 257
Operation Bluebird 294
oppression 86, 90, 119, 139, 231, 246, 288, 299, 303–4, 346; landlord 288; patriarchal 246; rural 303; sexual 139
oral: compositions 222; traditions 222, 234
Oraons 33, 267
organisations: communal 124, 279; leftist 287, 289; political 37–8, 145, 294; religious 234, 324; women's 71, 74, 144, 157, 159–60, 181, 278, 283, 287, 315, 321, 324, 328, 340, 342
Orissa 17–18, 50, 141, 201, 249, 254
orthodoxy 29, 50, 52, 57, 70, 80–1, 84, 88, 90, 93–5, 98, 196, 220, 234, 266, 278, 314–15, 320–1, 324–5, 330, 335, 345; gender 335; hard 234; opposing 88; pietistic 345; religious 81, 324
ostracism 12, 89, 94–5, 213, 260, 328; family 89
Oudh (Awadh) 116, 155, 203
outcastes 40, 44, 57, 61, 89, 108
outrages 55, 60, 65, 71, 117, 177, 232, 266, 332

Pakistan 1, 117, 180, 182–4, 187–8, 242–4, 253, 284, 295–6, 313–16, 318, 320–4, 328–35, 340–1, 343; Constitution of 317; 1970 elections 322; 1997 elections 329; army 341; creation of 183, 295; demand for 182; female support for 183; gender relations 324; government 322, 332; martial law 315, 332, 334; presidential elections of 1965 315; refugee camps 323; Zia regime in 323
Pakistan National Alliance 316
Pakistan Peoples' Party 315
Palriwala, Rajni 260–1
panchayat/Panchayati Raj 245, 248 265, 267, 297; Acts 248; Bill 245

Pande, Mrinal 298; "Hum Safar" 298
Pandit, Vishnushastri 87, 93, 97
pandits 15, 26–7, 29, 46–7, 85, 295
Parsis 26, 29–30, 42–3, 60, 62, 70, 85, 94, 108, 148, 156, 237–8, 277–8, 304, 313
Partition 117, 149, 180, 183–4, 244, 253, 262, 274, 290, 295–6, 301, 313, 320, 323, 331–2; demand for 183; violence of 320
Partition of Bengal 64
Patel, Sardar 275, 285
Pathak, Shekhar 256, 289; *Chipko Movement* 256
pativrata (the chaste wife) 9, 96
patriarchy 6, 201, 257, 290, 341–2
patriliny 34, 67, 346
patrilocality 67–8
peasants 55, 86, 161, 165, 178–9, 185, 216, 246, 284–5, 290–1, 331, 339; women 166, 258–9, 261, 285
Periyar 74, 105–7
Persia/Persian 4, 13, 26–7, 29–30, 85, 115; conduct manuals 4, 13
personal laws 25–6, 28–9, 35, 40–2, 44–5, 57–8, 60, 68–9, 122, 187, 321, 325; Christian 40–2, 44; colonial 321; Hindu 44–52, 71; Muslim 35–40, 325; Parsi 29–30; tribal 30–5
Peshwas 45, 91–2
Phule, Jotirao 74, 86, 96, 102; *Gulamgiri* 86
Phule, Savitribai 86, 105

piety 82, 87, 111, 121, 195, 200, 223, 317; domestic 195; filial 82; legendary 200; Muslim female 111; orthodox 223
pilgrimage 74, 104, 115, 215, 269
Pillai, Padmanabha 124–5; *Ideal Sex* 124
*pir*s 194–5
plantations 31–2, 133, 138–9, 149, 254, 263
plays and stories 61, 232, 237, 280; autobiographical 61, 237; mythological 237; *Om Swaha* 280; social 237; street 280
pleasure 91, 124, 231, 283, 289; sexual 91, 283, 289
poem/poetry 16, 86, 118, 212–13, 223, 226–7, 234, 256, 340; Hindi-Urdu 212, 226; modern 223
politicians 84, 117, 245
politics 7, 59, 72, 74, 87, 96, 100, 153, 156, 159, 161–2, 164, 167–71, 176, 178, 181–3, 189, 211, 246, 266, 283, 288, 291, 299–300, 302–3, 314, 331, 339–40; agitational 182; American 100; anti-Brahman 96; communalisation of 159; emancipatory 181; factional 87; feminist 283; Gandhian 167; insurrectionary 246; Left 178, 300; legislative 72; mass 169; modern 153; parliamentary 246; public 162; revolutionary 176, 299
polygamy 30, 33, 39, 46, 92, 115, 117, 275–6, 321–2, 326, 346
polygyny 268

polytheism 59, 121, 196
Poona 92–3, 99, 101, 108, 148
Poona Widow Remarriage Association 93
poor 17, 46, 52, 86, 121–3, 164, 168, 180, 182, 198–9, 216, 231, 233, 245, 249–50, 258, 261, 296, 298, 321, 329, 339, 343–5; culpability of the 122; idealisations of the 233; rural 344
pornography 303, 327
poverty 17, 98–9, 149, 205, 249, 263, 266, 299, 305, 324, 338–9, 344–5; alleviation 339, 344
Prarthana Samaj 87
Pratiloma 15, 99
preachers 82, 99, 181, 266–7
pregnancy 53, 91, 106, 125, 126, 147, 180, 265, 335; illicit 53; pre-marital 147; unwanted 106
Premchand 226
prescriptions 2, 26, 29, 49, 157, 316, 319, 321; domestic 316; Islamic 321; sacred 157
press 45, 55, 63, 117, 142; Indian 63; Muslim 38, 117; nationalist 142; orthodox 103
princely states 43–4, 153, 172, 201, 264, 285
print 27, 45, 85–6, 110, 194, 214, 220, 222, 227; capitalism 86, 220; culture 27, 110
prison 21, 94, 98, 167–8, 170, 176–7, 180, 214, 215, 230, 246, 280, 288, 326, 327
prisoners 155, 167, 215, 246; of war 155; political 246; women 167

Progressive Writers' Association (PWA) 232–3
prohibitions 53, 55, 74, 92–3, 96, 122, 209, 271
property 5–6, 8, 13, 16, 19, 28, 30–2, 34–6, 38, 41–3, 45–6, 51, 53, 56–7, 67–8, 70, 92, 97, 115, 148–9, 157–9, 164, 208, 215–16, 229, 258–9, 267–8, 272, 274–5, 277, 284, 287, 316–17, 325, 343, 346; access to 31; acquired before marriage 43; arrangements 8; bourgeois relations 6; communal 34; division of 187; family 34, 70, 277; fathers' 36, 38; individual 34; inheritance 31, 68, 97; landed 32, 68; laws 68; loss of 216; management 32; matrimonial 19; moveable 249; natal 19, 272; ownership 19, 32, 67; patriarchal control over 28; rights 5, 34, 51, 115, 215, 272, 274–5, 284; share 32, 34, 36, 53, 56–7, 267, 272, 317; titles 259
Prophet 12, 37, 61, 112, 114, 318
prostitutes 14, 16, 30, 61, 89, 101, 136, 148, 170, 185, 197, 206–8, 216, 236–7, 268, 304
puberty 62, 66, 74, 210, 326, 346
Punjab 28, 32, 37–8, 104–5, 109, 121, 141, 161, 163, 174–5, 183, 196, 202–3, 248–9, 253, 266, 298, 317, 319
Puranas, the 45, 99
purdah 112, 114, 126, 166, 169, 266, 314, 316–18, 337
purity–pollution 15, 18, 201, 262;

Brahmanical 201; taboos 201, 262

Qudsia Begum 115
Queen Victoria 29, 65, 156
Quit India movement of 1942 155, 167, 176
Quran, the 35, 110, 112, 118, 126, 212, 314, 343

Raghunandan 62, 91
Rahman, Sheikh Mujibur 332–4, 341
Rai, Lajpat 174–5
Rajasthan 95, 199, 221, 249, 260–1, 269–70
Rajputs 14–15, 45, 58, 83, 115, 134, 266, 270, 273
Rakhmabai 97–8, 146, 224
Ramakrishna Paramahansa 195–8
Ranade, Justice Madhav Govind 65, 87, 89–90, 97, 100–1, 157, 226
Ranade, Ramabai, India's first woman doctor 87, 89, 97–102, 108–9, 149, 157, 226; *Amchya Ayushyatil Kahi Athavani* 226; approach to widowhood reforms 101; *High Caste Hindu Woman* 101; *India Calling: The Memoirs of Cornelia Sorabji* 149; interpretation of Christianity 100; prostitutes' home 101; *Testimony of Our Inexhaustible Treasure* 98, 99
Rani Gaidinliu 154–5, 171
Rani Jhansi Brigade 155, 300
Rani Lakshmibai of Jhansi 153–5, 171
rape 18, 42, 63–4, 66, 147, 171, 187, 210, 279–83, 285, 293–4, 297, 325–7, 335–7, 341; custodial 281–2; gang 281–3; law 279; marital 63, 147, 282, 326; non-marital 326; police 281; revenge 297; survivors 171, 335
Rashsundari Debi 147, 224–5; *Amar Jiban* (My Life) 225
Rashtrasevika Samiti 181, 247
Rashtriya Swayamsevak Sangh (RSS) 181–2, 243, 247, 275, 284
Ravi Varma, Raja 68, 238; "There Comes Papa" 68
Reddy, Muthulakshmi 157, 159–60, 201
reformers 6, 17, 29–30, 36–7, 39, 51–6, 62, 65, 80–1, 84–7, 89–90, 92–4, 96–7, 101, 107, 109–12, 115, 117, 123–5, 138–9, 144–5, 201, 223–4, 236, 291, 329; Andhra 55; Bengali 53, 89, 125; conservative 37, 39, 110; Hindu 37, 86; labour 139; male 96, 101; Muslim 36, 109, 111, 117; poet 90, 94; social 55, 86, 201
reforms 7, 30, 51, 59, 63–5, 68–71, 74, 80–1, 84–90, 93–6, 101, 105–7, 110, 114–15, 121–2, 144, 156–7, 159–60, 166, 197–8, 220, 229, 234, 245, 258, 263, 265–6, 274, 282, 319, 321–2, 340; constitutional 71, 159, 263; educational 85; gender 86–7, 197; legal 69, 74, 115, 160, 274, 282; liberal 198; movement 88, 156; social 59, 65,

70, 80, 85, 95, 105–6, 156, 160, 166, 197, 220, 229, 234; widowhood 101
refugees 188, 242–3, 253–4, 290, 320, 323; camps 253, 323; women 188
relationships 2–6, 8, 14–16, 21, 67, 93, 140, 153, 173, 189, 209, 213, 224, 226–7, 230, 235, 284, 296, 316, 319; extra-marital 140, 224; familial 6, 316; hetero-sexual 6, 21, 173, 224; sexual 209, 224
religion 10, 35, 41, 49, 57, 60–1, 66, 70, 112, 114, 118–19, 121, 170, 177, 188, 202, 275, 289, 314, 322, 329, 331, 334; bonds of 119; monolithic 35
religious: affiliation 70, 277; authorities 26, 111, 326, 329; communities 26, 30, 38, 58, 118, 157, 320; education 105, 113, 198; establishments 202, 343; gurus 104, 200; identity 59, 332; injunctions 40, 275; institutions 25, 266; laws 27, 41, 60; leaders 115, 118, 200, 339; life 10, 110, 114, 195; norms 8, 26, 29, 346; prescriptions 2, 29, 157; reform 51, 87, 90; scholars 115, 322; schools 194, 344; texts 3, 74, 196; traditions 11, 85, 87; trust 36, 71; vocation 11, 170
remarriage 12–13, 19, 32, 51, 53–7, 68, 81, 85, 87–90, 92–7, 101, 104, 106, 122, 124, 197, 229, 234, 273, 284, 316–17; authoritarian form of 56; Bengali tract on 92; campaign for 53, 89, 92, 101; forms of 56, 92; law 94, 229; prohibition against 53; social acceptance 53; utilitarian form of 56
repression 31, 160, 165, 168, 181, 246, 285, 287, 292–5, 322–3, 340
revolution 179, 230, 290, 345
revolutionaries 80, 162, 166, 172–77, 229–30, 291, 299; armed 172, 291; Left 291
rights 5, 8, 34, 36, 38, 43, 51, 53, 57, 67–70, 97, 109, 113–15, 119, 157, 215, 234, 243, 245, 256–9, 263, 267–9, 271–5, 279, 283–5, 288, 291, 295, 299–300, 316, 320–2, 324, 328, 330–1, 334, 340–1, 346; citizenship 271; civil 245, 334; conjugal 97; custodial 53, 279; democratic 245, 334; inheritance 38, 43, 51, 53, 57, 69–70, 268, 320, 341; political 322; property 5, 34, 51, 115, 215, 272, 274–5, 284; scriptural 36; tenancy 259; women's 36, 114, 157, 269, 321, 324, 334
riots 171, 246, 253, 340
rites 13, 15, 27, 50, 57, 59, 66, 82, 94, 106, 196–7, 203, 285, 317, 327, 337, 343–4; conscience 59; funeral pyre 45, 48; funerary 57; Hindu 44, 46, 66, 196; idolatrous 59; life-cycle 66, 195–6; mourning 104, 197; practices 4, 26; pyre 12, 45–6, 48, 51; sati 51;

widow immolations 4, 13, 54, 83, 238, 292
romance 33, 68, 89, 111, 176, 178, 230, 237, 303–5
Roy, Rammohun 4, 19, 46, 49–52, 59, 85, 87, 260, 262

sacred: texts 9, 27–8, 37, 39, 47, 62, 91, 104, 106, 196, 318; thread 88, 199
Sahamarana 46
sainthood 197, 198, 200
Sanger, Margaret 123, 264
sanitation 83, 143, 263
Sanskrit 13, 16, 27, 85, 98–9, 105–6, 197, 221
Santhal 32–4, 85, 140; custom 34; marriages 33; rebellion 85
Sarala Devi 156–7
Sarda Act 72, 74
Sarda, Har Bilas 72–3
Sarkar, Sumit 118–19, 137, 142, 221–2, 273
Sarojini Naidu 157–8, 161, 163
sati 45–6, 49, 51, 177, 266, 269–72; arguments against 49; cancellation of 45; commemorations 269; practice of 45; worship 269, 271
Satthianadhan, Krupabai 108, 228; *Kamala* 228; *Saguna* 228
Satthianadhan, Samuel 228, 231
Satyashodhak Samaj 86
schooling 20, 30, 102–3, 105, 116
schools 4, 27, 28, 36, 39, 46, 82–3, 86, 89, 95, 103–5, 107–9, 111, 116, 120–1, 124, 147–8, 155, 166, 177, 198, 211, 213, 235–6, 247, 254–5, 263–4, 266, 269, 339, 344; boarding 103, 120; enrolment 266; girls' 120, 166; government 82, 147, 264; mission 82–3, 103, 107–8; science 111–13, 125, 235
Scotland 21, 108; gender laws 19
scripture 5, 9, 13, 25, 27–9, 35, 37, 46, 50, 54, 71–4, 90, 96, 99, 107, 109, 114, 316, 319, 325, 329, 343; holy 35, 50; Islamic 9, 13, 109, 316; reinterpretations of 114; written 28
seclusion 11, 95, 110, 112–14, 116, 119, 126, 133, 147, 159, 162, 166, 316, 318, 320, 344; domestic 126; female 11, 133, 344
secularism 188, 343
Self-Employed Women's Association (SEWA) 265
Sen, Amartya 247; "More than 100 Million Women Are Missing" 247
Sen, Keshub Chandra 59, 87, 99, 104
Sen, Surya 173, 176
Senapati, Fakir Mohan 231; *Chamana Atha Guntha* 231
servants 14, 17, 26, 117, 134–5, 188, 201, 209–11, 216, 233, 253, 260, 262, 300; domestic 210, 216; female 135, 201, 210; Indian 135, 209; male 134–5, 253
sex 6, 30, 64, 67, 82, 123–5, 147, 185, 197, 199–201, 203, 205–9, 212–14, 233, 236, 247–9, 263–4, 289, 326, 335,

341–2; lesbian 212, 233; ratio 6, 247, 249, 263
sex workers 205–9, 233, 236, 341; compulsory medical examination of 206; criminalisation of 206; existence of 205; run-of-the-mill 205; struggles 341
Shah Bano, Begum 278
Shankaracharya 87, 93
Sharada Sadan 93, 101
sharecroppers 180, 258, 284, 338
sharia/shariat 37, 38, 118, 322, 325–6, 346
shastras (Sanskrit sacred texts) 27
Shetkari Sangathana 289
Shillong 82, 171, 268
Shiva, Vandana 255–6; *Staying Alive* 256
Shudra (menial workers) 15, 46–7, 62, 86, 92, 99, 166
Sikhs 26, 32, 36, 38, 45, 60, 70, 121–2, 174, 197, 231, 245–6, 296; guru 197; landholding 32, 36; victims of 1984 riots 246, 296
Sindh 317–19
singers 133, 147–8, 202, 205, 236, 305; women 202, 236
Singh, Bhagat 174–5, 230
skills 104, 107, 114–15, 121, 137, 177–8, 186, 201, 210, 265, 274, 296; cultural 201; development programmes 263; diplomatic 210; English-speaking 186; feminine 115; homemaking 104; income-generating 121, 296; military 210; political 107; riding and military 115

slaves/slavery 1, 14, 19, 48, 52, 86, 109, 119, 134, 177, 201, 210, 233, 289; sexual 201, 233; upper-caste 134
slums 121, 126, 133, 144, 170, 178
Sobti, Krishna 298; *Mitro Marajani* 298
sodomy 42, 203–4, 206, 212
soldiers 14, 184–7, 204–7, 333, 335; American 184–5; British 184, 204; European 187, 205–6; foreign 185; Indian 184–6, 204–6
songs 11, 16, 109, 143, 155, 162, 183, 186, 202, 221–2, 226–7, 256, 259, 302, 305, 332, 335; devotional 109, 227
Sorabji, Cornelia 148–9, 158
South India 14, 17–18, 108, 246, 272
Special Marriage Act 61, 69–70, 237, 277; Act of 1872 70, 237; Act of 1923 69; Act of 1954 61
spinning and weaving 132, 136, 166, 169, 243
Stephens, Julia 24, 28, 39
Stree Shakti Sangathana 281, 284, 286
stridhanam 43
subordination 2, 6, 10, 99, 106, 113, 158, 183, 189, 272, 283, 345
suffrage 20, 157–8, 160; campaign 20, 158
Sufi 115, 194, 201, 315, 324
suicide 15, 109, 171, 229, 275, 280, 293, 344; racial 275
Sundarayya, P. 286; *Telangana*

Peoples' Struggle and Its Lessons 286
Supreme Court of India 27, 42–3, 74, 278, 281
Supreme Court of Pakistan 316
surveillance 14–15, 109, 207, 293
Swadeshi: movement 64; upsurge 162
Swami Acchhutanand 202
Swami Dayanand 56, 65, 104, 196–7
Swami Vivekananda 100, 195–7

Tagore, Abanindranath 238; "Bharatmata" 238
Tagore, Rabindranath 125, 162, 202, 222, 229–30, 332, 339; *Chaar Adhyay* 230; *Chokher Bali* 229; *Ghare Baire* (Home and the World) 162, 229; *Gora* 229; "Streer Patra" 125, 229
Tahzib un Niswan (Women's Culture) 113, 117, 235
tahzib-al-akhlaq manuals 14
talaaq, triple enunciation of 321
talaq i tafwid 39, 117
Tambe, Ashwini 206, 208
Tamil Nadu 11, 248–9, 252–3, 286
Tamil Sangam literature 5
Tangkhul Shanao Long (TSL) 293–4
*taravad*s 67, 68, 259
Taslima Nasrin 342
Tata, Herabai 158
*tawaif*s 16–17, 133, 147, 205, 236
Tebhaga sharecroppers' movement 180, 284
temple(s) 14, 16–17, 74–5, 106, 194, 201, 209, 223, 247, 269–71, 291, 297, 305, 313; dancers 17, 106, 209, 297; priests 17, 106, 201
Thanawi, Maulana Ashraf Ali 5, 38–9, 110–11, 113
theatres 85, 148, 180, 220, 223, 233, 236–8, 301, 304; Bengali 237; male personnel 236; Parsi 148, 237, 304
Therigatha 11
Tilak, Bal Gangadhar 65, 94, 98
Tod, James 221; *Annals and Antiquities of Rajasthan* 221
traditions 7, 9, 11, 14, 21, 28–9, 33–5, 37, 42, 80, 82, 85, 87, 91, 105–6, 110, 144, 148, 174, 177, 196, 201–2, 212–14, 221–2, 229, 234, 236, 238, 257, 271, 300, 319, 324, 330, 337, 344–5; cultural 42, 221, 330; intellectual 7, 87; invention of 33; literary 213–14; religious 11, 85, 229; sacred 28, 201, 319
Traimbakayavajivan 9; *Streedharmapaddhati* 9–10, 13
transgender 7, 214
Travancore 43, 259, 264, 288
tribal/tribe 18, 28, 30–4, 57, 62, 81, 83–4, 94, 140, 155, 164, 171, 179–80, 203, 246, 256, 267–9, 273, 277, 281, 289–90, 293, 297, 299, 317, 328, 334, 346; groups 62, 293; personal laws 34–5; widows 31, 273
Tripathi, Govardhanram 229; *Saraswatichandra* 229
Tripura 45, 246, 292
Tulsidas 227; *Ramayana*, the 227

ulama 38, 109–10, 117, 314, 319, 325
UN: charter on inheritance 344; Convention on Child Rights 346; Convention on Consent to Marriage 322; conventions on gender 346; Human Rights Instruments on gender issues 322; Resolution on Women's Rights 315
Uniform Civil Code 273, 278, 346
United Provinces 104, 120, 123, 196, 202, 214, 232
United States (US) 86, 100, 102, 173, 196, 257, 324
untouchability 4, 262–3, 285
Untouchables 14, 41, 62, 92–3, 105, 140, 143, 146, 166, 205, 217, 285, 299
Urdu 110–13, 115–16, 118, 194, 212–14, 226, 232–3, 235, 299, 301, 331–2; didactic fiction 111; pedagogical fiction 110; romances 111; schools 111
Uttar Pradesh (UP) 105, 249, 252, 266, 279, 300

Vanita, Ruth 7, 246
Varkey, Akkamma Cheriyan 288
Vedas 45, 99, 104, 157, 196
vegetarianism 91, 199
veil 9, 114–16, 161, 316, 319
victims 30, 67, 180, 183, 200, 246, 280, 296, 328–9, 336; rape 336; women 328–9, 336
Vidyalankar, Mrityunjoy 47
Vidyasagar, Ishwar Chandra 54–5, 57, 62–3, 85–6, 89, 92–3, 103–4; *Balyabibaher Dosh*

(Problems with Child Marriage) 62; Bengali tract on remarriage 92; *Bidhababibaha* 93; campaign for widow remarriage 85; efforts 92
violence 32, 50, 167–9, 174, 176, 187, 215, 242–3, 246, 255, 283, 287, 290–1, 293, 295–7, 305, 313, 320, 326, 337–8; communal 242, 295, 296; domestic 169, 287, 293, 326, 338; sexual 287, 290, 297; state 246, 287
Viresalingam 55, 90
virgin/virginity 54, 62, 200, 210
Vishwa Hindu Parishad (VHP) 247

Waddedar, Pritilata 175–6
Wahhabism 324, 345
waqf 36–7
weddings 55, 83
welfare measures 116, 144, 164, 180, 245, 315
West Bengal 202, 246, 251–4, 258, 265, 267, 273, 286
West Pakistan 244, 315, 322, 331, 333
Western India 12, 15, 29, 53, 85–6, 91, 96, 256, 291, 299
Western: culture 82, 329; women 126, 215, 234
widow immolation 4, 13, 18, 45–9, 51, 54, 73, 83, 85, 238, 260, 266, 269–72, 292; abolition of 54, 73, 83
widow marriage/remarriage 12–13, 32, 51, 53–6, 59, 68, 81, 85, 87–90, 94–7, 104, 106, 122, 197, 284; campaign for 89, 95;

prohibition of 81, 96; Widow Remarriage Act of 1856 56; Widow Remarriage Association 87, 93
widowers 56, 119
widowhood 18, 53, 90, 93–4, 98, 101, 124, 170, 229, 272–3, 317; Brahmanical 170, 272; Hindu 124, 229
widows 4, 12, 13, 16, 19, 31, 32, 41, 43, 44, 45, 46, 47, 48, 50, 51, 52, 53, 54, 55, 56, 57, 59, 68, 73, 80, 81, 83, 85, 87, 88, 89, 90, 91, 92, 93, 94, 95, 96, 97, 99, 100, 101, 102, 104, 106, 115, 122, 123, 124, 134, 153, 169, 170, 173, 179, 197, 198, 213, 216, 224, 228, 229, 234, 238, 253, 261, 269, 270, 272, 273, 274, 277, 284, 292, 295, 296, 316, 319, 334, 336, 337; Brahman 46, 91, 102; childless 56, 272–3; elderly 46, 229; tribal 31, 273; young 124, 173, 224, 229, 269, 273
wife/wives: abused 19, 279; child 61, 63–4, 197; educated 80, 266, 338; Muslim 39, 278–9; second 39, 41, 155, 276, 278
Wise, James 125, 216
witches 31–2, 179, 267; hunting 31–2, 267; killing 267; trials 179
Women Writing in India 233
Women's Action Front (WAF) 322–3, 328–30
Women's Auxiliary Corps 186
Women's Charter of Demands, 1948 320

Women's Civil Disobedience Committee 165
Women's Indian Association (WIA) 72, 156, 158, 209
Women's Liberation Organisation 281
Women's National Guard 183, 320
Women's Protection Act, 2006 328
women's: education 87, 88, 100, 102, 105, 110, 113, 116, 118, 156, 182, 225, 263, 339, 341; rights 36, 42, 114, 157, 269, 321, 324, 334; work 132, 149, 169, 252, 257; writers 117, 224, 226, 271, 297
workers 18, 47, 84, 108, 132–3, 135–9, 141–5, 149, 157, 174, 179, 181, 188, 205–9, 233, 236, 250–3, 263, 265, 274, 290, 296–7, 317, 319, 323, 331, 337–8, 341–2; agricultural 252, 338; male 136, 138, 149, 251, 338; productive 250, 253; sanitation 143, 263
World War, First 172–3, 184
World War, Second 149, 184
worship 10, 812, 88, 99, 104, 121, 170, 194, 196, 270–1
writers 117, 221, 224–6, 232–3, 297, 299, 305

Yashpal 230; *Dada Kamred* 230; *Sinhavalokan* 230
Young Women's Christian Association 322
Yunus, Muhammad 339

Zaif 109
Zamana i Tahsil (A Time for Education) 117

Zia-ul-Haq, General 316, 319, 322–5, 328–30; assassination in 1988 329; laws 324, 328
Zia-ur-Rahman, General 334, 343; assassinated in 1981 334; virtual martial law 334
Zina ordinances 325, 327
Zutshi, Ladorani 157, 161

www.ingramcontent.com/pod-product-compliance
Lightning Source LLC
Chambersburg PA
CBHW051555230426
43668CB00013B/1857